IT TAKES COURAGE!

by Marcia L. Ball, Ed.D. and Jennie A. Cerullo, Ph.D.

Kerus Global Publishing
1866-C East Market St. #300
Harrisonburg, VA 22801
www.kerusglobal.org

Edited by Lynn Copeland

Design by Lauri Martino Worthington

Page layout by Genesis Group

Illustrations by Rhet Miles and courtesy of Shellbook Publishing Systems

Printed in the United States of America

ISBN 0-9752917-0-X

It is with great affection and admiration that
we dedicate this book to our parents:

Rudy and Edith Cerullo

&

Marvin and Irene Ball

They taught us to love God, care for others, work hard, and make family a priority. Through the years their lives have modeled what it means to be persons of character and to courageously go out into the world and make a difference. Their steadfast love and encouragement have taught us to "see" with our hearts, find joy and laughter in every situation, and love extravagantly.

Contents

Preface 9
Acknowledgments 11
Reviewers 13
Using This Manual 15

Introduction 29
Character Development 32
It Takes Courage! 34
Health and Wellness 35
Life Skills 37

Creating a Vision for Life 41
Two Critical Questions 44
A Vision for Character: "Who Do I Want to Become?" 45
A Vision for My Calling and Purpose: "What Am I Here to Do, and Why?" 51
Character Connection: Primary and Secondary Greatness 53
A Personal Mission Statement 54
It Takes Courage! 55
Activities 1–13 57

Communicating Effectively 103
What Is Communication? 106
Verbal and Nonverbal Communication 107
Communication Styles 112
Character Connection: The Golden Rule 115
Conflict Resolution 116
It Takes Courage! 120
Activities 14–28 121

Building Healthy Relationships **177**
The Search for Intimacy 180
Understanding Healthy Relationships 182
Personal Boundaries 183
Evaluating Relationships 185
Types of Relationships 187
Character Connection: Forgiveness 193
It Takes Courage! 195
Activities 29–43 .... **197**

Making Wise Decisions **241**
The Decision to Grow 246
Managing Negative Emotions 247
Handling Conflict with Others 249
Choosing Wisely Under Pressure 250
Avoiding Risky Behavior 252
Character Connection: Rationalizing Behavior 259
It Takes Courage! 260
Activities 44–62 .... **261**

Preventing HIV/AIDS **333**
HIV/AIDS Overview 338
Associated Symptoms 339
Voluntary HIV Counseling and Testing 340
Ways HIV is Spread 342
Discussing HIV Transmission 346
Preventing the Spread of HIV 347
Universal Precautions 354
Living Longer with HIV 358
HIV Infection and Sexual Relations 361
Treatments and Cures 361
Character Connection: Empathy and Compassion 363
Community Involvement in HIV/AIDS 365
It Takes Courage! 367
Activities 63–77 .... **369**

Contents

Teaching Through Storytelling 433
A Father's Love 437
A Glass of Milk 440
All God's Creatures Have Work to Do 441
Are You Going to Help Me? 444
Appointment with Love 446
Father Kolbe 449
Gather Your Gossip 451
Nails in a Tree 452
Mandela: The Long Walk to Forgiveness 455
One at a Time 458
Puppies for Sale 459
Racheltjie De Beer 461
Sacrifice of a Champion 463
S. T. 466
The Ambulance in the Valley 468
The Little Girl Who Waited 470
The Man, the Boy, and the Donkey 472
The Man Who Would Not Drink Alone 474
The Merchant and the Builder 475
The Oxpecker and the Giraffe 478
The Purse of Gold 480
The Two Gifts 481
Three Fish 483
Activities 78–84 485

Resources 507
End Notes 509
Bibliography 513
About Kerus Global Education 517
About the Authors 519

Preface

We are excited to put *It Takes Courage!* in your hands. There is power in this guide—information, interactive learning strategies, and stories that you can use to inspire youth and help them to reach their goals. Consider this your tool kit—all that is needed is your desire, concern, and enthusiasm to bring the content to life.

You may be familiar with the story of a man who was walking along a river on a beautiful day when he suddenly heard panicked cries for help. He looked upriver and saw a young girl struggling to stay afloat in the current, screaming with every ounce of her energy. Immediately, the man took off his coat and shoes, jumped into the river, and rescued the girl. Everyone called him a courageous hero. A few days later he was walking along the same river and saw two new people caught in the current that was rushing by. He called to a friend and they both performed another courageous rescue. A week later numerous others were spotted in the river and it took many more courageous souls to pull them out. The rescuers decided to take turns watching along the river so they could quickly spot those who were in trouble and save them. While thrilled at their excellent success rate in saving people, they were growing quite overwhelmed by the problem. This went on for some time until finally someone suggested that perhaps going upriver to find the source of the problem would be a good idea.

As educators and youth workers, we often find ourselves "in the river" pulling young people to safety. There are many who are willing to help rescue, but often we get so bogged down in a rescue mentality that we forget to go upriver to try to intervene at the source of the problems that young people are facing today.

It Takes Courage! is a resource guide that will assist you in your efforts to teach youth to stay far from the river's edge, and will give you more tools to help you rescue those who venture into the turbulent waters of alcohol and drug use, violence, and early sexual involvement. But more important, the activities in *It Takes Courage!* can serve as a catalyst for youth to focus their lives toward their dreams and become men and women of character.

We want each and every adolescent and young adult around the world to learn how to be healthy and experience happiness and hope for their future. That's why we have used a unique design that is easily adaptable to any setting and is thorough enough to be an effective tool to help bolster current prevention outreaches, especially the prevention of HIV/AIDS. Whether you are working in a classroom, an orphanage, a faith community setting, or in your home with your own children or grandchildren, you were in mind when we created this guide.

It is our sincere desire that the material and teaching strategies we have chosen will help to bring about the following:

- Strong relationships between young people and their parents
- Healthy adult role models reaching out and mentoring children who need extra guidance
- Youth development strategies that focus on the entire person: physically, mentally, socially, emotionally, spiritually, and occupationally
- Youth who are full of hope and optimism and able to create a vision for their lives, identify and avoid dangerous people and situations, and establish meaningful relationships and healthy families of their own

We have spent the past decade traveling the world meeting with educators, physicians, faith workers, and other health and human service professionals who work tirelessly each day to improve the lives of adolescents and young adults—often in very difficult places with little or no assistance. They have sat in our seminars and conferences and we have visited in many of their homes and schools. They are our heroes and heroines—people who love extravagantly and refuse to give up on our youth. This resource guide is designed to assist them, and you, by offering a fresh perspective and new ideas to emotionally connect with youth and create opportunities to communicate essential life truths and skills.

Acknowledgments

No one ever achieved much without the contributions of others, and this book is no exception. It is a collective representation of the professional training and experience of our colleagues working in universities, clinics, hospitals, faith communities, orphanages, and classrooms in both small villages and large cities around the world. Who we are and what we do is always seasoned by what we have learned from them and we are immensely grateful. From the time we first decided to write *It Takes Courage!* we have been blessed by the encouragement and assistance of the many wonderful and talented people listed below.

Deborah M. Garrick, M.A., worked with us steadily and sacrificially over the two years it took to complete this project. Debbie's training as a teacher and counselor was particularly helpful. Her creative mind and diligent spirit put many of our collaborative ideas for activities into written form. She also wrote and rewrote many of the stories found in this text.

Diana Langerock, R.N., edited and scrutinized each word of this text time and again. Her 25 years of service in Africa provided invaluable insight for cross-cultural considerations. Diana's cheerful attitude, determined spirit, friendship, and personal sacrifice carried us through many difficult days.

Sue Heneberger, B.S., is our faithful assistant. Her family generously provided a beautiful beach condo in which we could write the majority of this book. We do what we do largely because Sue makes it possible.

Ellen Campbell, B.S., spent long hours collecting and organizing the stories and writing insightful discussion questions. Ellen's life exemplifies service to others and we benefited from her loving care day after day.

Steve Cannizzaro, B.S., helped us create the framework for this text. His attention to detail, inspiration, and encouragement were necessary components to moving our mission forward. We especially want to thank Steve for the stories he composed.

James Judge, M.D., gave invaluable tips from his own experience as a physician who has worked abroad and as an author—storyboarding on the floor, editing, writing, and making sensitive suggestions for improvement and bringing life and humor to the manuscript.

Rich Lane, M.D., M.P.H., is someone we can always count on to help us with a writing project. Rich has extensive international experience as a physician and educator. We particularly appreciated his help with writing activities and his insight about teaching the concept of forgiveness.

Persida Himmele, Ph.D., has enthusiastically supported our work for many years. Persida provided many creative ideas on teaching literature interactively. Her background in language acquisition and cross-cultural communication was invaluable to this project.

Marilyn Hale, M.S., provided ideas for several activities. Her extensive training in promoting character education in a school environment and her work with at-risk youth helped us to choose and present activities in effective ways. Marilyn's consistent friendship, encouragement, and support helped to make this project possible.

Katie McConnel, B.A., edited sections of the text and provided valuable input in the design and marketing of this product. She walked beside us every step of the way through this long process.

Caroline Campbell, M.P.H., helped us to develop a practical framework for this book and contributed fun and creative ideas for many activities.

Barb Lester, M.A., reviewed and edited several activities and provided encouraging words when we really needed them.

Jessie Hanebury, **Rachael Pierson**, **Jennifer Valle**, and **Ashley Walkley** created several fun-filled activities and rewrote some of the stories. Their energy and enthusiasm were infectious.

Lynn Copeland of the Genesis Group spent many hours laboring over the text and helping us to get the content in an easy-to-read and grammatically correct format. We are especially grateful to Lynn for the long hours, humor, and the patience she demonstrated under the pressure of a short timeline.

The Staff of Shellbook Publishing: Mike Trainum donated the time and talent of many of his staff to make this book a reality. Joanne Nobile and Dave Nealon gave valuable input on the manuscript, and Zeke Trainum and Rhet Miles provided the creative illustrations.

We would like to express our heartfelt thanks to our CrossRoads team in Orlando and to our other colleagues around the world from whom we have had the privilege of learning so much over the years. Several stories in this book were translated and sent to us from our friends in various countries.

This project would not have been possible without the love, prayers, and financial support of our Kerus Partners, who are too many to mention by name. We love you and appreciate all that you do. A special thanks is extended to our 94-year-old dear friend Bill Brown, whose prayers, encouragement, and financial support have been a vital part of our work since its beginning.

Reviewers

We are especially grateful to the following friends and colleagues who served as reviewers for this text.

Nurleign Gashu Abebe, M.D.
Assistant Professor of Internal Medicine
Gondar University College
Gondar, Ethiopia

Glory Alexander, M.D.
Founder and Director, ASHA Foundation
Bangalore, India

Jonathan Beesigomwe, B.S.
CrossRoads Coordinator
Gaborone, Botswana

Steve Cannizzaro, B.S.
Founder, The North Star Company
Norfolk, VA, USA

Muno Chirovamavi, M.Th.
Pastor and Theological Educator
Baptist Theological Seminary of Zimbabwe
Harare, Zimbabwe

Harvey Elder, M.D.
School of Public Health
Loma Linda University
Loma Linda, CA, USA

Deborah M. Garrick, M.S.
Garrick Graphics
Norfolk, VA, USA

Marilyn Hale, M.S.
School of Education and Behavioral Studies
Azusa Pacific University
Irvine Unified School District
Irvine, CA, USA

Kate Hendricks, M.D.
Medical Institute for Sexual Health
Austin, TX, USA

Persida Himmele, Ph.D.
Assistant Professor of Elementary and Early Childhood Education
Millersville University
Lancaster, PA, USA

Novikova Nina Ivanivna, Ph.D.
Director of Natural and Mathematics Education
L'viv Region of the Postgraduate Pedagogical Institute
L'viv, Ukraine

James Judge, M.D.
Assistant Professor of Family Practice
Loyola University
Wheaton, IL, USA

Rich Lane, M.D.
Light Medical Center
Lynchburg, VA, USA

Diana Langerock, R.N., M.A.
Africa Strategy Coordinator, CrossRoads
Orlando, FL, USA

Betty-Mae Lawrence, B.S.
Founder/Director, Youth Enhancement Service (YES)
Montego Bay, Jamaica W.I.

Bailey Marks, M.B.A., and Denise Marks, M.S.
Director, CrossRoads
Orlando, FL, USA

Olinick Valentina Mekolaivna, Ph.D.
Assistant Director, L'viv City Methodological Center
L'viv, Ukraine

Ozerny Vitalli Mikilovna, B.S.
CrossRoads Education Department
L'viv, Ukraine

Susanne B. Montgomery, Ph.D.
Director, Center for Health Research
Loma Linda University
Loma Linda, CA, USA

Dave Nealon, M.S.
Director of Educational Projects, Shellbook Publishing Systems
Harrisonburg, VA, USA

Mayeya Ngalande, M.A.
CrossRoads Coordinator
Lusaka, Zambia

Joy Obwoya, B.S.
Southern & Eastern Africa Director, CrossRoads
Harare, Zimbabwe

Valentina Mickolaivna Olinik, Ph.D.
Methodologist, Ministry of Education
L'viv, Ukraine

Godfrey W. Onyango, B.D.S
Principal Dental Officer and Lecturer
School of Public Health Officers and Kampala International University
Kampala, Uganda

Ingrid Taljard, B.A.
Co-Founder, Christian Youth and Beyond
Machadodorp, South Africa

Mihret Alem Zewdu, B.S.
CrossRoads Coordinator
Addis Ababa, Ethiopia

Using This Manual

Over the last decade we have had the pleasure of working with thousands of educators and other youth service providers around the world, and we have designed this guide with their needs—and yours—in mind. Many of these dear friends and colleagues have asked for such a resource—a "cookbook" of information and activities that will help youth to build core character traits, develop essential life skills, and have the motivation and courage to put it all into practice when they are under pressure. There are many curricula on the market, but few are designed with the flexibility to accommodate both the caring adult who is making an occasional presentation and the teacher or youth worker who needs some new activity ideas. This is not a curriculum to be taught lesson by lesson—it is a collection of information and stories, designed to be mixed and matched to meet your needs. Just look up a topic of interest and you are ready to go!

The information and activities in this guide are designed to entertain, promote discussion, and help build relationships within the group. Use them to add interactive learning strategies to an existing curriculum; to plan special talks in faith group settings, in discussions with athletic teams, and at youth camps and other meetings; to integrate activities into weekend retreats; or to create fun teaching opportunities for your own children. Our desire is that you are well-equipped to engage young people in discussions about their lives, build mentoring relationships, and create opportunities for them to act with courage and character.

This is truly an international resource guide. Because we did not write to any one particular culture group, it is neutral in its cultural orientation and cross-culturally versatile. The activities are kept simple so that they require minimal preparation, are inexpensive, can be used in both traditional and non-traditional educational settings, and can be easily translated. Feel free to modify these activities to meet your needs. Be creative and celebrate the needs and uniqueness of your culture! Relevant and fun discussions will keep your students' attention.

Adolescents and young adults are our target audience, yet as an experienced educator or youth service provider, you will find that each activity can be easily modified for older or younger audiences. We've used many of these activities in our university classes, with adult groups around the world, and in our work with children. The content applies to youth and adults and the methodologies can be easily changed to meet the developmental needs of your learning environment.

Section Overviews

It Takes Courage! is divided into the six sections listed below. We strongly encourage you to take the time to read the content overview of each section, particularly the section "Creating a Vision for Life," before you begin teaching any activities. Each overview will give a comprehensive explanation of the topic, and is the primary content that will be taught through the related activities and stories. Knowing this information will assist you when processing any of the activities. Following is a description of each section.

1) Creating a Vision for Life. Those who aim at nothing are likely to hit the target. Many young people go through life aimlessly, without an idea of where they want to end up. We believe that many young people engage in risky behaviors out of a sense of hopelessness and an inability to see that they are unique, exceptional, precious, significant, and free to make their own choices in life. This section will help youth to identify who they want to become as individuals and to begin to discover how their unique giftedness can be used in their future.

2) Communicating Effectively. The ability to communicate effectively is the key to meaningful relationships and greatly impacts our success in life. Good communication skills are essential to getting our ideas, needs, and interests across to others and to understanding what others are saying. Teaching young people to communicate well can positively influence almost every area of their lives. This section focuses on the different forms of communication and the verbal, nonverbal, and listening skills that will help youth to become good communicators.

3) Building Healthy Relationships. The desire for community is something we all have in common. Relationships are what make our lives meaningful. They are also the cause of our greatest challenges in life as we struggle to understand and get along with others. Our relationships with ourselves, our families, and our community require commitment on our part if they are to be strong and long-lasting. This section will help young people to discern the difference between healthy and unhealthy relationships and will describe practical steps anyone can take to build and maintain a healthy approach to all of their interactions with others.

4) Making Wise Decisions. Our lives are shaped by the decisions we make. We carve a path for ourselves one choice at a time, and few of us are aware of our direction until experiences in life make that path obvious. The goal of this section is to enable young people to live a purposeful life—to see the effect their current choices are having on their lives and to recognize that unhealthy choices, such as drug use and early sexual involvement, will quickly sabotage their dreams. It will help them to focus their decisions toward realizing their dreams and becoming people of character.

5) Preventing HIV/AIDS. Implementation of an "ABC" approach to preventing AIDS—Abstinence until marriage, Being faithful in marriage, and Condom use for the highest risk groups—has resulted in a dramatic decrease in the spread of HIV/AIDS in Uganda and in other parts of the world. This section will focus on the practical information everyone should know about HIV/AIDS and prevention. Topics include HIV transmission, infection with HIV, living with someone who is infected, and avoiding infection through abstinence until marriage and faithfulness in marriage.

6) Teaching Through Storytelling. We believe the telling of stories is one of the most effective ways to communicate moral messages; they help to clarify abstract concepts and make them easier to understand. A good story presents a non-threatening way for young people to identify with common life events and the impact of one's choices. This section contains favorite stories from around the world, organized by specific character traits or topics related to human interactions. It also includes teaching strategies to help you maximize the effectiveness of any good story. These stories are one more vehicle you can use to communicate the concepts in the other sections.

Two common threads run throughout this guide: character and courage—essentials for any good decision-maker. In addition to the character concepts sprinkled throughout the text, each section includes a Character Connection, which will explore a character trait that is essential to the concepts in that section. Each section also includes a box labeled It Takes Courage! Until young people have the courage to make wise choices, they will falter. They need to know the price they may pay for character and they need the motivation and assurance that the price to obtain character is affordable—if they have the courage to endure. The It Takes Courage! paragraphs will explore how courage relates to the section topic.

Activities

Following each section overview are numerous activities, which use a variety of interactive learning methods to help convey the points related to that topic. Each activity begins with a purpose and an overview statement so you can quickly determine if the activity fits your instructional need. Each activity also identifies two core character traits and a corresponding life skill that are taught in the activity. All the details you need are included: the estimated time, appropriate group size, preparation, instructions, and applications. There is even a section called "Going Deeper" for those who would like to explore the concepts more fully. Quotes and a statement of courage have been added to increase motivation. Where necessary, handout masters have been supplied.

The charts on the following pages will help you quickly find an activity you are searching for or locate an activity to teach one of the 15 character traits identified in this text.

Activities to Teach Specific Character Traits

Creating a Vision for Life	Empathy	Excellence	Fairness	Forgiveness	Gratitude	Honesty	Humility	Kindness	Loyalty	Patience	Perseverance	Respect	Responsibility	Self-control	Service	Page
1. Paper Puzzle	◆											◆				58
2. The Winner Box												◆	◆			60
3. Spending Your Life Game						◆							◆			62
4. Hit the Mark										◆	◆					66
5. Dream Makers and Breakers										◆	◆					72
6. The Flower Pot						◆								◆		76
7. Character Match	◆	◆	◆	◆	◆	◆	◆	◆	◆	◆	◆	◆	◆	◆	◆	80
8. Snack Time										◆	◆					86
9. The Award Speech						◆						◆				88
10. Take a Seat		◆					◆									90
11. Head, Heart, and Feet								◆							◆	92
12. Making My Mark on the World		◆											◆			96
13. My Brochure		◆									◆					100

Activities to Teach Specific Character Traits

Communicating Effectively	Empathy	Excellence	Fairness	Forgiveness	Gratitude	Honesty	Humility	Kindness	Loyalty	Patience	Perseverance	Respect	Responsibility	Self-control	Service	Page
14. Paper Doll	◆							◆								**122**
15. Guess the Message	◆													◆		**124**
16. Do You Hear What I'm Not Saying?												◆	◆			**128**
17. A Nonverbal Chat										◆		◆				**132**
18. Silent Movie										◆	◆					**134**
19. One-Way Communication							◆					◆				**138**
20. More Than Ears										◆				◆		**142**
21. Are You Listening to Me?	◆						◆									**146**
22. Assertiveness Role-Playing													◆	◆		**150**
23. Guess the Emotion						◆								◆		**154**
24. Behind the Scenes				◆				◆								**158**
25. People's Court			◆			◆										**162**
26. Flip Book Journals		◆											◆			**168**
27. The Golden Rule			◆				◆									**172**
28. How Do You Rate?						◆						◆				**174**

Activities to Teach Specific Character Traits

Building Healthy Relationships	Empathy	Excellence	Fairness	Forgiveness	Gratitude	Honesty	Humility	Kindness	Loyalty	Patience	Perseverance	Respect	Responsibility	Self-control	Service	Page
29. Candle Burning								◆				◆				198
30. Community Circle of Trust								◆	◆							200
31. Opposite Poems	◆					◆										202
32. Putting It Into Practice													◆	◆		204
33. Web of Encouragement					◆			◆								206
34. Listen to Your Feelings								◆				◆				208
35. Boundaries												◆		◆		212
36. Parent Preferences						◆						◆				214
37. Family Bank Account									◆						◆	218
38. Genuine and Counterfeit Friends							◆		◆							222
39. The Giving Tree								◆							◆	224
40. The Comparison Game	◆	◆	◆	◆	◆	◆	◆	◆	◆	◆	◆	◆	◆	◆	◆	226
41. Stereotypes	◆		◆													228
42. The Cold Within	◆			◆												232
43. What's Your Style?						◆						◆				236

Activities to Teach Specific Character Traits

Making Wise Decisions	Empathy	Excellence	Fairness	Forgiveness	Gratitude	Honesty	Humility	Kindness	Loyalty	Patience	Perseverance	Respect	Responsibility	Self-control	Service	Page
44. The Choices We Make											◆		◆			262
45. Processionary Caterpillars													◆	◆		264
46. Rescue Mission											◆	◆				268
47. The Cake										◆	◆					272
48. Hidden Squares		◆												◆		274
49. The Problem Box		◆								◆						278
50. Red Light, Yellow Light, Green Light	◆													◆		282
51. What's Your Opinion?						◆							◆			286
52. Drama-in-a-Bag						◆								◆		290
53. Step by Step										◆			◆			294
54. A Crowded Bed						◆								◆		298
55. Sex in the Media						◆							◆			302
56. Pressure Points						◆					◆					306
57. Sex Pros and Cons	◆													◆		310
58. My Most Courageous Moments										◆	◆					314
59. When Is It Okay to Lie?						◆								◆		318
60. Nine Dots										◆	◆					320
61. Appointments								◆				◆				324
62. In the Court Today						◆							◆			328

Activities to Teach Specific Character Traits

Preventing HIV/AIDS	Empathy	Excellence	Fairness	Forgiveness	Gratitude	Honesty	Humility	Kindness	Loyalty	Patience	Perseverance	Respect	Responsibility	Self-control	Service	Page
63. Fast Facts		◆											◆			370
64. Dr. Truth												◆			◆	372
65. Know the Risk	◆												◆			378
66. What Do You Know?						◆						◆				382
67. Story Problems						◆							◆			384
68. Looks Can Be Deceiving						◆							◆			392
69. Reach and Teach		◆	◆													394
70. Forbidden Fruit													◆	◆		398
71. How Can We Help?	◆														◆	400
72. That's Not True						◆							◆			404
73. Spread the Word													◆		◆	412
74. Make a Statement T-Shirts						◆						◆				416
75. Safety First							◆						◆			420
76. Where's the Risk?													◆	◆		426
77. A Quick Check						◆	◆									430

Stories to Teach Specific Character Traits

Stories	Empathy	Excellence	Fairness	Forgiveness	Gratitude	Honesty	Humility	Kindness	Loyalty	Patience	Perseverance	Respect	Responsibility	Self-control	Service	Page
1. A Father's Love				◆			◆									437
2. A Glass of Milk					◆			◆								440
3. All God's Creatures Have Work to Do		◆											◆			441
4. Are You Going to Help Me?									◆		◆					444
5. Appointment with Love									◆			◆				446
6. Father Kolbe	◆						◆							◆		449
7. Gather Your Gossip							◆							◆		451
8. Nails in a Tree				◆						◆						452
9. Mandela: The Long Walk to Forgiveness				◆										◆		455
10. One at a Time	◆										◆					458
11. Puppies for Sale	◆							◆								459
12. Racheltjie De Beer									◆				◆			461
13. Sacrifice of a Champion		◆									◆					463
14. S.T.							◆						◆			466

(continued)

Stories to Teach Specific Character Traits

Stories (continued)	Empathy	Excellence	Fairness	Forgiveness	Gratitude	Honesty	Humility	Kindness	Loyalty	Patience	Perseverance	Respect	Responsibility	Self-control	Service	Page
15. The Ambulance in the Valley											◆				◆	**468**
16. The Little Girl Who Waited						◆				◆						**470**
17. The Man, the Boy, and the Donkey							◆							◆		**472**
18. The Man Who Would Not Drink Alone			◆									◆				**474**
19. The Merchant and the Builder						◆							◆			**475**
20. The Oxpecker and the Giraffe					◆								◆			**478**
21. The Purse of Gold			◆		◆											**480**
22. The Two Gifts	◆														◆	**481**
23. Three Fish													◆	◆		**483**

Activities to Teach Specific Character Traits

Teaching Through Storytelling	Empathy	Excellence	Fairness	Forgiveness	Gratitude	Honesty	Humility	Kindness	Loyalty	Patience	Perseverance	Respect	Responsibility	Self-control	Service	Page
78. Character Card Banners	◆	◆	◆	◆	◆	◆	◆	◆	◆	◆	◆	◆	◆	◆	◆	486
79. Story Connections	◆	◆	◆	◆	◆	◆	◆	◆	◆	◆	◆	◆	◆	◆	◆	488
80. Literature Circles	◆	◆	◆	◆	◆	◆	◆	◆	◆	◆	◆	◆	◆	◆	◆	492
81. Character Quilts	◆	◆	◆	◆	◆	◆	◆	◆	◆	◆	◆	◆	◆	◆	◆	496
82. Venn Diagrams	◆	◆	◆	◆	◆	◆	◆	◆	◆	◆	◆	◆	◆	◆	◆	498
83. Hot Seat Interviews	◆	◆	◆	◆	◆	◆	◆	◆	◆	◆	◆	◆	◆	◆	◆	502
84. Character Trait Interviews	◆	◆	◆	◆	◆	◆	◆	◆	◆	◆	◆	◆	◆	◆	◆	504

Suggestions As You Begin

Capturing the attention of young people and motivating them to look at the serious issues presented in this book can be quite a challenge. As we have observed professionals around the world working with a variety of youth development programs, we have identified five elements that are necessary to maintain the attention and respect of the youth. Whether you are a teacher or youth service provider in Asia, Europe, Latin America, Africa, the United States, or the Middle East, these elements, listed below, will help you to influence youth toward positive lifestyles.

Live the Message

An African proverb states, "I can't hear your words because of the thunder of your actions." We can't fool young people—we must live our message if it is to have power. When our lives don't match our rhetoric, adolescents will see the hypocrisy, quickly discount the message, and develop an attitude that there is a double standard for adults and adolescents. Be a positive role model for your youth; share your life and experiences; be human. You don't have to be perfect, just possess a passionate desire to live life as a person of good character.

Adopt a "Team" Mentality

Caring enough to get involved in the lives of youth is essential, but more is required. If we are leading and teaching groups, it is also essential that we communicate in relational ways, use accurate information, and be relevant to the realities of their world. Take advantage of training seminars in your area and adopt a "team" mentality. Make it a point to learn from others. For example, most physicians need help with teaching skills, and most teachers need help communicating medical facts. Network with others and grow from their knowledge and experiences.

Create a Positive Learning Environment

A positive and safe environment is the foundation for building trusting relationships. When learning about character and making wise choices in life, young people must feel a certain amount of trust to be open and honest about their struggles. They need to feel free to talk about issues without worrying that someone will ridicule or discount their feelings or give them a long lecture. Here are a few thoughts to keep in mind about creating an environment conducive to learning:

- Be enthusiastic.
- Learn and use the names of students, and refer to past comments they have made.
- Arrange the room in an interesting way.

- Laugh often.
- Use personal examples of strengths and weaknesses.
- Establish ground rules, such as prohibiting condescending or disrespectful comments, maintaining confidentiality, and following directions.
- Vary teaching strategies, teaching to different learning styles.

Connect with Youth Emotionally

For true learning to take place, it must involve the emotions. The key is to use interactive learning to engage adolescents with materials relevant to their daily lives. Ask open-ended questions and be ready to listen. Create real-life problems to solve and allow them to communicate in creative ways. When we show interest in their personal lives and demonstrate that we genuinely care, youth will respond with surprising sincerity. It is vital that young people establish an emotional connection to the communicator or to the content in order to develop good character and learn wise decision making.

Partner with Parents

Parents are the primary teachers of their children. Through their words and actions they influence and teach their children values and beliefs every day. Research clearly shows that youth who feel connected to their parents are less likely to venture into trouble, so anything we can do to strengthen parent-child relationships will be beneficial. Offering parent meetings may allow you to share your dreams for their children.

Involving parents in the educational process will enable you to build trust with them, and most parents are very enthusiastic about being included. They are a vital part of the educational team! Working together, reinforcing the same values, will provide wonderful opportunities for young people to grow.

In summary, a relaxed, interesting environment where relevant information is presented in a kind and compassionate way, and conducted by people whose lives model these concepts, becomes a powerful means to reach and teach youth. This book will help you to challenge young people and encourage them to make wise choices and courageously pursue a healthy vision for their lives.

A Prayer for Children

Ina J. Hughs

We pray for children
who put chocolate fingers everywhere,
who like to be tickled,
who stomp in puddles and ruin their new pants,
who sneak candy before supper,
who erase holes in math workbooks,
who can never find their shoes.

And we pray for those
who stare at photographers from behind barbed wire,
can't bound down the street in a new pair of sneakers,
who never "counted potatoes,"
who are born in places we can't even imagine,
who never go to the circus,
who live in an X-rated world.

We pray for children
who bring us sticky kisses and fistfuls of flowers,
who sleep with the dog and bury goldfish,
who hug us in a hurry and forget their lunch money
who cover themselves with Band-Aids and sing
off-key,
who squeeze toothpaste all over the sink,
who slurp their soup.

And, we pray for those
who never get dessert,
who watch their parents watch them die,
who have no safe blanket to drag behind,
who can't find any bread to steal,
who don't have any rooms to clean up,
whose pictures aren't on anybody's dresser,
whose monsters are real.

And we pray for children
who spend all their allowances before
Tuesday,
who throw tantrums in the grocery store,
and pick at their food,
who like scary stories,
who shove dirty clothes under the bed
and never rinse the tub,
who don't like to be kissed in front of their friends,
who squirm in church and scream in the phone,
whose tears we sometimes laugh at
and whose smiles can make us cry.

And we pray for those
whose nightmares come in the daytime,
who will eat anything,
who have never seen a dentist,
who aren't spoiled by anybody,
who go to bed hungry and cry themselves to sleep,
who live and move, but have no being.

We pray for children
who want to be carried,
and for those who must.
For those we never give up on,
and for those who don't get a second chance.
For those we smother,
and for those who will grab the hand of
anybody kind enough to offer it.[1]

Introduction

Character Development 32
It Takes Courage! 34
Health and Wellness 35
Life Skills 37

Introduction

Whether you are new to working with youth, or you are a seasoned educator or youth service provider, *It Takes Courage!* can make your work easier. These pages are full of information and teaching strategies that can make preparing and delivering your programs more efficient and effective. Although the activities are fun and the literature is engaging, the guide is not designed to entertain youth; it is about purpose-driven education delivered in a captivating and relevant way. Any concerned adult around the world who desires to come alongside youth and help them to become happy and mature adults will find this guide helpful. This Introduction will give you an overview of the framework and fundamental principles presented in this guide.

Imagine that you were given the joy of providing the youth in your community with some special gifts that would almost guarantee them healthy, meaningful, productive lives. What would you give? Most people would answer that question with some or all of the following in mind:

- **A Sense of Belonging:** Being part of a community and having relationships with caring adults
- **A Sense of Purpose:** Finding meaning in life
- **A Sense of Competence:** Being able to do something well
- **A Sense of Faith:** Having spiritual identity and direction
- **A Sense of Service:** Being a contributor to the lives of others
- **A Sense of Autonomy:** Having control over daily life and the future
- **A Sense of Morality:** Having concern for what is good and right

Giving these gifts to youth would transform our communities! Oh, how amazingly different so many of their lives would be! Adolescents would be equipped to face life's challenges, enjoy meaningful relationships, and have a chance to thrive. Joys would multiply, and many troubles would cease. We believe these gifts can be given to our youth. But what will it take to make these gifts a reality? The answers are numerous; some are the responsibility of us, as adults, to provide, and others are the responsibility of each adolescent to choose and work toward. At the core, we believe that young people must learn to see themselves as precious human beings who embody a courageous spirit—willing to take risks to grow as individuals in each area of their lives and willing to stand up for what is right.

We passionately believe that there are four absolute essentials which youth need in order to achieve lifelong success. The following core essentials will help young people to achieve healthy, meaningful, and productive lives:

1. Character development
2. Courage to make difficult decisions

3. A vision for life that includes a proper understanding of health and wellness
4. The ability to execute core life skills

When parents, schools, and communities focus on these four essentials by building strong emotional ties with youth, serving as role models, and providing opportunities for growth, we believe youth will be well on their way to becoming mature adults. We will briefly explore each of these four essentials in the following pages.

Character Development

Haim Ginott, in *Between Teacher and Child,* tells of an interesting letter that a high school headmaster sent to his teachers at the beginning of each school year. The headmaster had survived Hitler's concentration camps of World War II.

Dear Teacher:
My eyes saw what no man should ever witness: gas chambers built by learned engineers, children poisoned by learned physicians, infants killed by trained nurses, women and babies shot and burned by high school and college graduates. So, I am suspicious of education . . .

My request is: Help your students become human. Your efforts must never produce learned monsters, skilled psychopaths, educated Eichmanns. Reading, writing, arithmetic are important only if they serve to make our children more human.[1]

To train a person in mind and not morals is to train a menace to society.
–Theodore Roosevelt, former U.S. President

Education involves more than learning to read and write and preparing for a profession. And as this letter indicates, without an appreciation for other human beings and a commitment to doing what is right, learned men and women become skilled menaces in society. Character development is therefore a crucial aspect of education. To have good character, one must possess values that lead to positive actions. In 1992, The Josephson Institute for Ethics convened a panel of 29 ethicists, educators, and youth service professionals representing various cultural groups and religions in order to study the issue of values and character. Members of the panel were asked to identify core ethical values represented in their faiths and cultures. Although the panel members had areas of disagreement, they all agreed that trustworthiness, respect, responsibility, fairness and justice, kindness and caring, and good citizenship were values supported by their cultures.[2] These six categories became known as the Six Pillars of Character and form the foundation for the highly successful international character education

program, *Character Counts!*[3] Expression of these values varies from culture to culture, but the underlying principles are quite similar. Each value serves as an umbrella covering many different character traits. For example, the value of trustworthiness encompasses the character traits of honesty, integrity, and loyalty.

15 Core Character Traits

1. *Empathy*
2. *Excellence*
3. *Fairness*
4. *Forgiveness*
5. *Gratitude*
6. *Honesty*
7. *Humility*
8. *Kindness*
9. *Loyalty*
10. *Patience*
11. *Perseverance*
12. *Respect*
13. *Responsibility*
14. *Self-control*
15. *Service*

We have chosen 15 character traits for you to teach through the activities, stories, and illustrations in this resource guide. These character traits (some of which were also identified as core ethical values) are essential to making wise choices. If youth can understand and be motivated to develop these traits, they will be well equipped to chart a healthy course for their lives.

Being a person of character involves conscience and heart. Our conscience is like a compass that points us toward goodness, and if we follow it we typically feel good about ourselves. If we don't, we tend to experience feelings of shame and guilt. Each of us has a conscience, and we can learn to listen to it or ignore it. Some Native American tribes describe the conscience as a triangular stone inside our bodies. Every time we choose not to listen to it, the stone turns and cuts, but as it cuts its edges are worn down a bit. If we choose time and again to ignore our conscience, it becomes increasingly dull until the triangular stone becomes a circle. At that point, our conscience can no longer cause us any pangs of guilt—and it ceases to serve its purpose. As we teach about character and focus on core character traits, we help to reinforce the work of the conscience.

Choosing to be a person of character is also about heart. Our hearts are strong motivators for doing what is right, because we tend to protect what we love and cherish. If our affections are self-centered, that will be reflected in our behavior —selfishness. If our affections are cultivated to care about others, our actions toward others will reflect our concern for them.

Our goal, as overwhelming as it may seem, is to help youth shape and nurture a positive view of the world that will teach them the importance of being a person of good character. Their character will influence the big and small decisions of their lives. Good character is not something that can be casually acquired; it must be intentionally developed over time, with hard work. When young people live in an environment where good decision making is modeled, they will be more likely to value and make good decisions themselves. We can be instrumental in shaping their young lives as we work with parents, caregivers, faith communities, and schools to provide opportunities for young people to grow in character. In doing so, we will help to create productive members of society—people who take care of themselves and contribute to the lives of others.

As adolescents work to become persons of character, we must remember that character is dynamic—it changes for better or for worse throughout our lives as we make difficult decisions. It is important for youth to understand that good character does not mean perfection. Everyone makes poor decisions and is selfish from time to time. We must view character development as a process of "becoming." Although none of us will "arrive," we can improve day by day. Each wise decision strengthens our character.

It's never too late to be who you might have been.

–George Eliot, English novelist

Many of the youth with whom you are working have made numerous poor decisions and tremendous mistakes in their young lives. They have not cultivated good character, and they know it. Some are living with lifelong consequences of their choices. Many have assumed negative labels for themselves and have created an identity steeped in hopelessness. They need to hear that their lives can be different and that, by acknowledging and taking responsibility for their unwise decisions and humbly asking for assistance, they can do better in the future. That is why it is so important for us to develop relationships with them, offering our guidance and encouragement. Many will respond when they experience our care and see us modeling good character. We can offer hope by teaching them that they have the ability to choose differently.

In today's world we are almost surprised when we meet individuals who possess true depth of character. We don't expect people to make ethical decisions; it seems that few are willing to pay the high price of being a person of character. Many succumb to personal or family pressure, fear public ridicule, or just desire an easy life. Typically, young people are hesitant to take a stand and do what is right. Their underlying reasons are much the same; fear of mockery by their friends is almost crippling. Good character can be achieved only if we possess one very important virtue—courage. This courage is not the courage of heroic rescues, but rather the courage to do what is right, even at the risk of being misunderstood or ridiculed by friends.

It Takes Courage!

We view courage as the coal which powers the engine that pulls the character train forward. It enables individuals to stand alone, when necessary, in order to make uncompromising choices that will build maturity, integrity, and character.

Introduction

Courage has been described as a settled disposition that allows us to stand our ground. In a world where the moral high ground is challenged every day from so many directions, we believe that courage is absolutely essential.

> *Courage is not simply one of the virtues, but the form of every virtue at the testing point.*
>
> –C. S. Lewis, English author

We see courage as foundational because it allows character to manifest itself in difficult situations. Courage provides the motivation and drive to make the sacrifices needed for the growth of the whole person. Moral fiber, like muscle fiber, grows as it daily works against resistance. It is while consistently making small choices to do the right thing—despite fear, pain, fatigue, and misunderstanding—that our character muscles will gain strength. It takes courage for a young person to risk being different as the result of a right choice. It takes courage to stand up against the relentless surge of peer pressure that drives so much risky behavior, be it substance abuse, violence, or sexual involvement. Courage enables young people to tolerate being set apart, alienated, or even ostracized. It empowers them to persevere, and in the fires of perseverance, their character will be forged.

As we work to develop character in the next generation, we believe we must first ensure that the virtue of courage is firmly established. We must come alongside youth and help to create an environment of safety where courageous decisions are both recognized and rewarded. Only then will the right choices—the building blocks of character—be carved out and laid atop one another to create a fortress strong and secure, able to withstand any challenge.

Health and Wellness

Character and courage are necessary to be truly healthy, because health is often determined by the ability to make wise decisions. But what does it really mean to be healthy? The World Health Organization has defined health as "a state of complete physical, mental and social well-being and not merely the absence of disease or infirmity." True health involves optimal well-being or wholeness in each of the following dimensions:

- **Physical:** This dimension includes the functions and activities of one's body such as muscular strength, endurance, flexibility, and body composition. It is the dimension where we can experience physical pain and disease or energy and optimal physical functioning.

- **Emotional:** This dimension includes the ability to experience a wide range of situations and feelings. It is where one learns to give and receive love, to cope with the spectrum of emotions, and to enjoy life.

- **Social:** This includes one's ability to interact in relationships with others. It involves the ability to demonstrate empathy, showing respect for others in conversation and through one's actions. It also involves one's ability to set relational boundaries—emotionally and physically—and to create positive social support systems.
- **Mental:** This includes one's ability to think logically and creatively. It involves mental alertness and one's ability to understand life.
- **Spiritual:** This dimension is most often misunderstood; it is not one's religious affiliation. It encompasses one's beliefs, values, and ethics, and enables one to find meaning and purpose in life. It involves a pursuit of the meaning of relationships with others and answering questions about God. For many, it includes issues of faith and hope.
- **Occupational:** This dimension involves one's ability to earn a living and enjoy it.[4]

Most young people do not consider all of these dimensions when they think of health. Like many people, they assume that they are healthy unless they are sick. Broadening their understanding of health will enable young people to begin to pay attention to the various areas of their lives. Simply understanding these dimensions, however, is not enough. Good health is usually a by-product of having the courage to make good choices.

All the dimensions of a person are interrelated. If youth make positive choices in one area of their lives, they are likely to experience positive benefits in that area as well as in the others. Conversely, poor choices in one area can negatively impact the other dimensions. For example, a choice to engage in sexual activity involves much more than physical consequences; this choice can bring with it emotional, social, spiritual, occupational, and mental consequences as well. These results are often issues that young people overlook until it is too late. Reorienting their thinking in terms of "investing" in each of the dimensions can greatly improve their overall health and well-being.

Our health and wellness is largely determined by daily choices such as: wearing seat belts, choosing nutritious foods, avoiding drugs and alcohol, choosing good friends, taking time to relax, washing our hands, accessing good medical services, etc. Each positive choice is an investment toward a healthy life. This guide is designed to lead youth to consider their overall well-being as they make daily choices.

Life Skills

Soccer is a game loved around the world. Imagine that a young teacher at a school has just been asked to coach the school soccer team. There are a couple of twists: it is a co-ed team (boys and girls playing together), and few of the students have ever played the game of soccer. In fact, some have never even seen a game. The coach arrives at the first meeting and discovers that the youth are not as enthusiastic as he is; they seem confused, unimpressed, and quite disinterested. Some don't even like soccer, most don't know the rules, and a few of the boys don't want girls on their team.

The coach devises a plan. First, he tells them the history of soccer and explains all the rules of the game. Some of the students are now interested, but others still don't want to play. Next, he decides that what the students are lacking is motivation—so he gives his best motivational speeches, introduces them to great soccer players in the community, and asks their parents to encourage them at home.

At each practice the coach talks to the players in detail about what they need to know and what they need to do. But something isn't right—after three or four games the players seem discouraged. Their attitudes begin to sour, and many of them quit. The coach gets discouraged too and decides that maybe coaching isn't for him.

What went wrong? The coach provided knowledge, he worked on attitudes, he made winning the game seem of value, and he talked at length about how to play the game. At first glance, it would seem to be a good combination. Yet there was one thing he didn't take into account: the feelings of his players. Even though they knew the rules and wanted to play, the students knew that they weren't very good. Most of their practice time was spent talking. They still didn't understand how to execute the skills properly, and the coach constantly corrected everything they did. They were embarrassed. Their lack of skill negatively influenced their attitudes, leading them to think, *Why should we try? We'll never be able to do this!* In the end, they decided that soccer wasn't worth the risk of being embarrassed in front of their families and friends. Besides, it wasn't fun.

So often we think that knowledge alone will change behavior. But until people *want* to change, and *believe* they can execute the necessary skills to change, they probably won't. The soccer coach needed to allow more time for the players to practice the skills.

In *It Takes Courage!* we use the term "life skills" to describe a core set of skills associated with building and maintaining healthy lifestyles. The term "life skills" has been defined by UNICEF in the following way:

> This term refers to a large group of psycho-social and interpersonal skills which can help people make informed decisions, communicate effectively, and develop coping and self-management skills that may help them lead a healthy and productive life. Life skills may be directed toward personal actions and actions toward others, as well as actions to change the surrounding environment to make it conducive to health.[5]

These skills help children learn how to maintain their bodies, grow as individuals, work well with others, make logical decisions, protect themselves when they have to, and achieve their goals in life. The chart "Sample Life Skills" represents a few of the life skills we highlight in the activities.

Sample Life Skills

Creating a Vision for Life
- Planning for the future
- Setting personal goals
- Coping positively with personal and life stressors
- Distinguishing between right and wrong
- Seeking out advisors of good character
- Periodically assessing personal strengths and weaknesses in character
- Identifying and developing gifts and talents

Communicating Effectively
- Speaking positively about others
- Interpreting nonverbal cues in communication
- Recognizing strong emotions in others
- Exercising active listening
- Identifying the communication strategies of others
- Owning and expressing one's feelings without blaming others
- Choosing to face and resolve conflicts responsibly

Building Healthy Relationships
- Sharing honestly and protecting the confidences of others
- Noticing the difference between a person's words and actions
- Contributing to family in meaningful ways
- Recognizing real and counterfeit friendships
- Analyzing the healthiness of a relationship
- Setting and maintaining personal boundaries
- Recognizing the need for forgiveness and reconciliation

Making Wise Decisions
- Expressing thoughts and opinions appropriately
- Avoiding unhealthy behaviors
- Recognizing negative influences
- Coping positively with life's challenges
- Socializing in healthy ways
- Anticipating and avoiding negative consequences
- Building strong support systems
- Managing anger in constructive ways

Preventing HIV/AIDS
- Accessing accurate information concerning health issues
- Transferring basic facts to real-life situations
- Discerning truthful statements over false ones
- Influencing a community with healthy life messages
- Analyzing risk factors
- Practicing sexual self-control
- Implementing universal precautions when necessary
- Speaking out against stigmatization and discrimination toward persons with HIV/AIDS

If we want young people to develop character and make healthy choices, we must do the following:

1. Provide *knowledge* about what it means to have character and lead a healthy lifestyle.
2. Help them to develop the right *attitudes* about being a person of character and living a healthy lifestyle.
3. Encourage them to practice life *skills* so they can execute them when needed.

If any of these three components is missing, the desired behavior will not be present. When youth know what they need to do, when they believe it is important, and when they feel that they can execute the desired behavior, they are most likely to change.

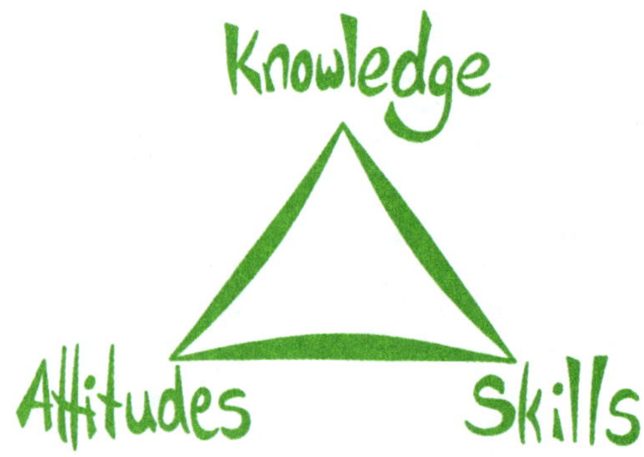

Our essentials of (1) character development, (2) courage to make difficult decisions, (3) a vision for a healthy lifestyle, and (4) the ability to execute core life skills are interwoven throughout this guidebook. Each activity identifies two character traits and a core life skill to emphasize. There is also a text box describing how courage applies to the topic. We have designed these activities to maximize discussions around the central themes of character and courage. You will find that the section on "Going Deeper" will give you the opportunity to explore these four essentials in more detail.

Creating a Vision for Life

Two Critical Questions 44

A Vision for Character: "Who Do I Want to Become?" 45

A Vision for My Calling and Purpose: "What Am I Here to Do, and Why?" 51

Character Connection: Primary and Secondary Greatness 53

A Personal Mission Statement 54

It Takes Courage! 55

Creating a Vision for Life

...unique...exceptional...precious...significant...and free to choose.
—Os Guinness[1]

In our world today, success is often defined by material possessions, power, or position—the external things of life. We admire famous athletes, politicians, and business leaders who "make it to the top" and who do just about anything it takes to stay there. Yet, despite their achievements, they are seldom happy with what they have. Rarely do we celebrate people for the internal aspect of their lives—their character. Persons of good character are those who would trade nothing for their reputation, who would rather fail or be poor than to lie, cheat, or steal. These are the people who can look themselves in the mirror and like what they see. And typically these are the persons who enjoy healthy relationships and are content with what they have while working hard to achieve more. As youth choose a vision for their lives, they will do so largely based on what they see others choose to value. When they observe adults committed to living a life of character, they will learn to understand the satisfaction that comes from having character. Character-based living helps people to achieve their individual goals, enjoy their families, create and maintain special relationships, and positively shape the communities in which they live.

A personal vision is much like a dream—a dream that we have chosen with the intent to make it happen. It is a mental picture of where we want our lives to end up, a powerful guiding image that provides us with a compass for every decision we make. When we begin with the desired result in mind and work backward from that point, we are able to figure out how to get to our destination. Once a vision is in place, all decisions can be measured against that end to determine whether they move us toward our destination or create a detour that may prevent us from getting there at all. If personal vision is missing, we may never get to where we want to go.

> *Vision looks inward and becomes duty. Vision looks outward and becomes aspiration. Vision looks upward and becomes faith.*
>
> –Rabbi Stephen S. Wise

Although the importance of choosing a vision for our lives seems obvious, it's surprising to discover that many people never consciously do so. Some young people experience such strong feelings of hopelessness that dreaming about where they want their lives to end up seems like a waste of time at best, and almost cruel at worst. But the truth is that if young people don't choose a vision for their lives, someone else will—society, the media, or friends. If they simply follow the crowd, they will end up wherever the crowd is going, relinquishing control over their own lives and letting someone else sit in the driver's seat. This pattern is almost never healthy. The choices young people make, whether actively or passively, produce either positive or negative consequences for themselves, their futures, and their families. Thus, it is important for young people to realize that they are free to choose, to be in charge of their own lives, and to ultimately determine their own destiny. Discovering a healthy personal vision empowers and motivates adolescents to choose well.

In the Introduction, we discussed the different dimensions of who we are as human beings—physical, mental, social, emotional, occupational, and spiritual. Each of these dimensions is interrelated and is an integral component of our health and well-being. Numerous research studies have documented the value of spiritual identity and practice to healthy decision making. The spiritual dimension anchors the other dimensions. It encompasses beliefs, values, and faith, and involves questions related to hope, meaning, and purpose in life, such as: "Why am I here?" and "Is there a God and, if so, what does that mean?" The spiritual dimension is the very core of what we think, believe to be true, and value, and it is expressed by how we treat others and the world around us. In his best-selling book *The Purpose-Driven Life*, Rick Warren writes that God is not just the starting point of our lives, but is the source of our lives. He suggests that a true vision for one's life must begin with an understanding of its source and that when we achieve this understanding, our talents and dreams find focus and purpose.[2] A personal vision will involve goals and decisions in each dimension, but it will be driven by our spiritual core.

Two Critical Questions

Creating a vision for life involves taking the time to seriously explore two critical questions:

- Who do I want to become?
- What am I here to do, and why?

The first question involves who we are internally, and relates to our character; the second involves who we are externally, and relates to our calling and purpose. Discovering the answers to these questions will enable young people to discern the things in life that are most important and to see how they can individually contribute to the world. As they define a personal vision, youth begin to realize that they have the power to structure many of the components of their own lives. They become more motivated to take control of their attitudes and choices and channel them toward their goals. Over time, as they gain confidence in making goal-driven, character-based decisions, they will build self-esteem, confidence, and personal satisfaction.

As youth work to develop a personal vision, they will need your guidance in understanding that life is about much more than they might initially perceive. Walking young people through this process helps them to realize the importance of vision in defining who they want to be, and contributes to their ability to lead themselves successfully. The activities and discussions in this section will help youth to answer the two critical questions mentioned earlier. These are not easy questions to answer, even for adults, but it is through the process of struggling with these questions that a personal vision can be born.

Which of the following statements is most true about your youth?

- Young people today are most concerned with what they want.
- Young people today are most concerned with what they want to be.

The first statement focuses on external desires—acquiring possessions, reputation, and power. The second statement focuses on an internal desire to protect and strengthen the inner person—to acquire attitudes, qualities, and skills that can help in building a good, successful life.

Our challenge is to help young people understand the substantial difference between these two orientations and to help them to prioritize the second statement—the one that turns them inward and addresses the heart's desire to be a person of character.

A Vision for Character: "Who Do I Want to Become?"

"Who do I want to become?" is a question of internal vision. As such, its answer is not dependent on money, talent, or professional aspirations. Our answer will guide us toward or away from being a person of character, and will ultimately become our reputation.

There was once a very rich man whose lifelong friend was a builder. The builder had worked for the rich man for many years. One day the rich man went to the builder's home and asked the builder if he would help him with a project. The project was to build the rich man a special house. He would be traveling for six months and needed the project completed by his return. The builder agreed and so the rich man gave his friend a large sum of money for the project.

If one advances confidently in the direction of his dreams, and endeavors to live the life which he has imagined, he will meet with a success unexpected in common hours.

–Henry David Thoreau, English poet

The builder thought carefully about the new house. He could use all the money to purchase the best building materials available or he could buy cheap materials and keep the rest of the money as additional profit. He chose to go the cheaper route, except for the paint. He would make the outside look beautiful and impress his friend. The rest of the money would be spent on a vacation with his family.

Six months later the rich man returned. The builder gave the rich man the keys, and together they drove to the rich man's new residence. Sure enough, the house looked great. The rich man was very pleased and unusually excited. Before getting out of the car, he turned to his friend and said, "We have been friends for many years. I have always wanted to give you a special gift. You did not build this house for me, you built it for yourself." He handed the keys back to the builder and said, "This is now your house."

To create a vision for character, we must begin with a firm understanding of what character is. Our character is our true self, and it is revealed by what we do when no one is looking. The builder had obviously fooled his friend who considered him trustworthy; his true character was revealed when the rich man was away.

The word "character" derives from the Greek word *kharassein*, which means to inscribe or deeply engrave, just as an engraver uses a chisel to make a mark. It implies building, creating, or sculpting. Our character is chiseled into our being one decision at a time. Each action makes a mark on our lives as our character is engraved, as the essence or core of who we are is being sculpted. Typically, when someone is said to possess character, it is implied that it is good character, unless otherwise stated. Aristotle described character as "the life of right conduct."

Core Character Traits

Possessing certain core character traits will protect young people from serious dangers and enable them to succeed in life. We have identified 15 core traits that we believe will help adolescents to relate well to others, find meaning in life, and realize their dreams. These traits are empathy, excellence, fairness, forgiveness, gratitude, honesty, humility, kindness, loyalty, patience, perseverance, respect, responsibility, self-control, and service. We suggest that you reinforce these traits as you teach the material and activities throughout this resource guide.

It is not the brains that matter most, but that which guides them—the character, the heart, generous qualities, progressive ideas.

–Fydor Dostoyevsky, Russian author

15 Core Character Traits

empathy

Being able to feel what someone else is feeling and to understand what that person is experiencing
People show empathy by putting themselves in another person's shoes and imagining what that individual is feeling in a given situation.

excellence

Doing something to the best of one's ability
People show excellence by consistently putting forth their best effort in carrying out their responsibilities, never settling for "good enough."

fairness

Being consistent and impartial in the way one deals with others
People show fairness by considering both sides of a conflict equally, making sure that each person has what is needed in a given situation, and not making decisions based on a preference for one person over another.

forgiveness

Letting go of the desire to hold someone responsible for an offense
People show forgiveness by relinquishing the urge to retaliate, by recognizing that all people (including themselves) make mistakes, and by releasing their anger toward the offender.

gratitude

Being appreciative of what one has been given
People show gratitude by being quick to genuinely thank those who have given to them and by enjoying what they have, rather than desiring or expecting more.

honesty

Being truthful and open
People show honesty by telling the whole truth rather than altering it to benefit themselves, doing their own work rather than using someone else's, and working for what they need rather than taking it.

humility

Being realistic about one's own strengths and weaknesses and not considering oneself better than others
People show humility by refraining from boasting or being overly self-critical, by showing genuine interest in others' lives, and by putting others' needs before their own.

kindness

Acting out of concern and thoughtfulness for others
People show kindness by treating others with consideration, by saying and doing things that will make others feel good, and by willingly offering help to others.

15 Core Character Traits *(continued)*

loyalty

Remaining faithful to the commitments and relationships one has made
People show loyalty by supporting friends and family members during difficult times, by defending them to others, by believing in them when others don't, and by telling them the truth.

patience

Handling delay or delayed gratification calmly
People show patience by waiting calmly, without anger or frustration, for a delayed outcome, by waiting for others with a positive attitude, and by not complaining in the midst of difficult situations.

perseverance

Continuing on a course of action in the face of difficulties and obstacles
People show perseverance by persisting in a situation despite difficulties, by seeking help to solve problems rather than giving up, and by trying new ways of doing something when other ways don't work.

respect

Treating oneself and others with high regard
People show respect for others by listening to them, by talking courteously to them and about them, by taking care of their belongings, and by acknowledging their opinions and desires. People show respect for themselves by making healthy choices for their lives and by refraining from negative self-talk or excessive self-criticism.

responsibility

Fulfilling one's obligations and commitments
People show responsibility by doing what they say they will do, by dependably executing all duties, by looking for things that need to be done and doing them, by being on time, and by following rules.

self-control

Being in charge of one's actions and reactions
People show self-control by saying no to wrong behaviors, by not losing their tempers, by doing what they should even when they don't feel like it, and by not doing what they shouldn't even when the temptation is great.

service

Making positive contributions to others' lives
People show service by helping others, even those they don't know, and by sacrificing in order to make others' lives better.

To help instill character in their children, parents all over the world teach what is called the Golden Rule:

Do to others as you would have them do to you

The Golden Rule asserts that we should consider others' feelings and welfare as being as important as our own. A person of good character will live out this rule by displaying core character traits that demonstrate respect and responsibility, affirming the rights and dignity of others. The Golden Rule is an excellent tool for teaching young people about character development. It is simple, easy to remember, and it enhances what parents and most faith groups teach as the appropriate way to live. Although the forms may vary, all societies honor those with good character traits, and pass these values from generation to generation through stories, poems, and parables. Character is not simply a list of do's and don'ts for us to follow; it is foundational to the long-term success and health of both the individual and the community. We must help young people see that being a person of character not only enhances society, it enhances their lives as well.

You can tell a lot about a man by the way he treats those who can do nothing for him.

-Unknown

Dr. Tom Lickona, a longtime leader in the character education movement, identifies three important areas that we should address when teaching about character:

1. *Moral knowing:* Understanding the difference between right and wrong
2. *Moral feeling*: Having a heart that wants to do what is right
3. *Moral action:* Having the opportunity to practice doing what is right[3]

The process of character development requires cultivating, not just telling. Dr. Lickona suggests that families, communities, and schools need to work together to help young people understand, care about, and act with good character. These three concepts can be illustrated by referring to different parts of the human body: head (moral knowing), heart (moral feeling), and feet (moral action).

Moral Knowing (Head)

Moral knowing focuses on the intellect. Essentially, it is one's ability to discern right and wrong. Moral knowing involves listening to one's conscience—the internal judge of right and wrong—as it prompts us to do the right thing. If we listen and respond accordingly, we feel good about ourselves. If we choose to ignore our conscience and make a wrong choice, feelings of guilt and shame frequently result.

Although each of us has a conscience—our own internal moral compass—the many competing messages from the media, friends, and even some adults can often make simple choices of right and wrong seem confusing. Moral knowing involves the ability to be discerning and to apply wisdom in difficult circumstances. In order to learn the difference between right and wrong decisions, adolescents must have adults in their lives who specifically teach core character traits and who model healthy moral decision making.

Moral Feeling (Heart)

Our hearts, often described as the center of our passions and feelings, strongly influence our character. The things and people we love often drive our choices. At the core of moral feeling is empathy—the ability to see the world from the perspective of others, identify with their feelings, and care about their welfare. Empathy is critical to character development, bringing out such traits as compassion, kindness, and courage.

Moral feeling also involves a positive regard for goodness—caring about what is good and right. People of character learn to love things that are good and right because these things are essential to the health and well-being of themselves, their families, and their communities. We can help young people build a love for what is good by enabling them to see how they and others benefit when people act with good character.

Moral Action (Feet)

Moral action involves one's determination to do what is right. It is a function of the will. Determination and the courage to act are essential to good character. It is not enough to know what is right and to love what is right—one must also find the courage to practice being a person of good character, whether that involves personal discipline, service, self-control, or standing up for others.

> *We must teach youth to know the good, love the good, and do the good.*
>
> -Kevin Ryan, professor of ethics

One day a soap maker came to a rabbi and said, "Rabbi, what good is religion? Religion teaches honesty. But just look at all the dishonest people in the world. And religion promises peace, but just look at all the wars. What good is religion?"

The rabbi answered him, "My dear soap maker, we both know that there are many different wonderful soaps in the world. And just look at how many dirty people there are."

Religion and other moral teachings—just like soap—work only when we use them.[4]

Character does not come cheaply. As we work with young people, we need to be honest about the costs of good character. The price of living wisely will involve forgoing some pleasures. It may also mean being misunderstood by friends and family or losing the relationships of those who do not understand or like what we are doing. Being people of character involves making hard decisions to keep going in the positive direction we have chosen, regardless of the consequences. To encourage character growth, we must teach adolescents to seek environments where good character is encouraged, to follow the Golden Rule, to practice the teachings of their faith community, to seek relationships with adults and friends who have good character, and to cultivate the courage to put it all into practice.

Building character is a lifelong challenge. The result, however, is a life full of meaning and purpose—a life that is worth living. The rewards of developing character are worth the costs.

Ways to Develop Character

1. Seek an environment of good character where there are others like you who want to live a character-based life.
2. Try to live by the Golden Rule.
3. Follow the core teachings of your faith community.
4. Seek relationships with adults of good character.
5. Find friends of good character.
6. Draw on your courage to make the right choices in difficult situations.

A Vision for My Calling + Purpose: "What Am I Here to Do, + Why?"

In addition to giving young people an internal vision for character, we also want them to develop an external vision for their calling and purpose in this world. Deep in their hearts, all young people long to find and fulfill a purpose bigger than themselves, and to do so in their own unique ways. Whether as an aerospace engineer, a teacher, or a rock star, youth today are searching for something in this world that will capture their hearts, give them a reason for being, and inspire them to heights they could never reach on their own. Theirs is a search for confirmation of the hope that burns inside them, the hope that they are indeed "unique, exceptional, precious, significant, and free to choose." These qualities, identified by author Os Guinness, aptly define the desire of all young people.

Unique

Many young people dress alike, wear their hair alike, and use the same expressions, mannerisms, and products. Yet under it all is a small but inextinguishable voice saying, "You are the only you there is; there is no one else in the world exactly like you." A firm belief in this truth about themselves will bring adolescents freedom—freedom to make the right choices in difficult situations, and freedom to choose a path that is uniquely suited to them.

Exceptional

Understanding that we are all gifted is integral to developing a personal vision for the future. Young people too often look in the mirror and see only flaws, not beauty. Each person stands out from the crowd in some special area. Whether it be a talent for singing or playing an instrument, or an ability to listen, to make people laugh, or to be a good friend, each individual has some quality that is exceptional, something worth celebrating and developing.

Precious

Surrounded as they are with negative messages, repeatedly reminded of all the ways in which they fall short, it's easy for young people to lose their sense of value. How many of today's successful leaders can point back along the path of their lives to that one person who believed in them, esteemed them highly, and sent an unequivocal message that they were precious? Knowing for certain that there are others who value them greatly can make the critical difference in the lives of young people and provide the courage for them to imagine and achieve bold dreams.

Significant

We are all on a search for significance, pushed forward by an innate desire to make a difference, to leave a legacy. It is one of the essential, compelling forces that makes for progress, both personally and as a community. Young people feel the pressure of this force deeply and have a strong desire to make their mark. It is our job as adults to help them to appreciate what a difference they can make and to know what differences are most worth making.

Free to Choose

We have the freedom to choose the kind of person we are going to be. Who we are going to be is determined by the daily choices we make. Our job is to help adolescents realize that they have the freedom to choose, to encourage them to make good choices, and to hold them responsible for those choices.

Fame is a vapor, popularity an accident, riches take wing, and only character endures.

–Horace Greeley, U.S. author

External vision is good, healthy, and essential, but it needs to be secondary to one's internal vision of becoming someone who possesses character. Character should never be compromised in the pursuit of one's calling or purpose in the world.

Character Connection: Primary and Secondary Greatness

We all admire people who are great—great athletes, great businesspeople, great leaders, great musicians. We may envy them for their accomplishments, or we may make it our life's dream to be great too. As we encourage young people to look inward and develop a vision for their lives, it is helpful to consider greatness as a goal. Is greatness obtainable by the average person?

Stephen Covey, author of numerous books on character and leadership, suggests that character is essential to greatness and divides greatness into two categories: primary and secondary.[5] Secondary greatness, says Covey, consists of positive personality traits, talents, and skills. This external kind of greatness is the form recognized by the world. It can lead to social status, position, fame, power, and wealth. Many people work the majority of their lives to achieve these things, then spend the remainder of their lives worrying about losing them. They may be willing to do just about anything—lie, cheat, steal, take advantage of others—to hold on to their greatness.

Primary greatness, on the other hand, is inner greatness. It is character—who and what a person is—and it is courage—courage to put character into action, even if that means losing the power, fame, fortune, and reputation of secondary greatness. Primary greatness, according to Covey, is the basis for all long-term success, and without it, secondary greatness is superficial and unsustainable. Secondary greatness is easy to see—it's external. Primary greatness, which is internal, is most easily seen in a person's integrity and maturity.

Our goal as teachers and youth service providers is to help young people wrestle with and process these issues of character. Secondary greatness can be positive, but only if it has primary greatness as its foundation and it is used for good. We certainly want young people to develop their talents and positive personality traits so they can be productive and successful. Yet secondary greatness alone will not bring true happiness. True happiness and greatness spring from our inner persons—from our ability to develop a sense of purpose, cultivate core character traits, and find the courage to act accordingly.

A Personal Mission Statement

As young people begin to arrive at answers to the two critical questions—"Who do I want to become?" and "What am I here to do, and why?"—their personal mission starts to come into focus. They begin to see how their character traits, interests, and talents can work together to help them to make a difference in the world. As they begin to make good choices, they grow in self-esteem and motivation to succeed. Helping youth to capture and articulate this sense of mission can be accomplished by the creation of a personal mission statement.

A personal mission statement is a statement of purpose, a personal credo or motto that says what our lives are all about. It is something easy to remember and is meaningful, serving as reminder of who and what we want to be. Mission statements can be either created or discovered. Some people discover a song, a poem, or even a quote that serves as a good mission statement. Others make up their own statements.

Activities in this section are designed to help youth discover the core components of who they are and give them a chance to express their unique identity and purpose in life. As they discover their mission, it's a good idea to write it down in whatever form suits them. The advantage of putting a mission statement in writing is that it passes from something vague to something definitive, it becomes easy to share with others, and it serves as a benchmark for personal progress. A good mission statement is like a tree with roots running deep into the earth—it is firm and secure, yet growing at the same time.

Here are some examples of personal mission statements written by teens:

- Others first
- Love my family
- Fight for my beliefs
- Nothing less![6]
- Before you change others, you must change yourself

Mission statements serve as a daily touchstone or reminder for young people, encouraging them to carefully think through their daily decisions in order to reach their goals. Your guidance will be essential as they hammer out these statements, helping them to see the big picture of their lives, process their individual strengths and weaknesses, and identify the things in life that they consider most important. They are free to choose, but they need you to teach them to choose wisely.

Each of us will one day be judged by our standard of life—not by our standard of living; by our measure of giving—not by our measure of wealth; by our single goodness—not by our seeming greatness.

-William Arthur Ward, university administrator

By helping youth to create a vision for their lives, you can give them a sense of direction and hope. A life vision enhances their motivation to work hard in school and to avoid peer pressure. Vision also provides a foundation for career and personal decision making. The earlier that young people formulate a personal vision for their lives—to become a person of character and to pursue a purpose and calling in life—the sooner they will feel anchored, be able to avoid danger, and begin to achieve true success.

Ordinary people, even weak people, can do extraordinary things through temporary courage generated by a situation. But the person of character does not need the situation to generate his courage. It is a part of his being and a standard approach to all life's challenges.

–Michael S. Josephson, Josephson Institute of Ethics

It Takes Courage!

There is one final element that cannot be overlooked: creating a vision for one's life requires courage. It's important for young people to know that courage is not the absence of fear; courage is action in spite of fear.

It can be scary for young people to dream about the future, to envision all that they wish to do and be. Answering the questions "Who do I want to become?" and "What am I here to do, and why?" is not easy. Identifying and then owning a vision may make young people feel like they're setting themselves up for failure. But, as the old adage states, "those who aim at nothing are likely to hit the target." If young people do not learn to identify their goals, they will never attain them. To be happy, productive, and healthy, young people must dare to identify a dream for their lives.

Being a person of character requires vision, tenacity, courage, and lots of practice. We must create opportunities for young people to practice good character traits and to gain confidence as they make difficult decisions. Without a doubt, they will encounter obstacles. The world and its values will inevitably stand in their way. We need to be there to encourage young people both when they fail and when they succeed.

Young people must believe that character is worth fighting for—that it really will give them a life of meaning and purpose. It is our job to help them make the vision connection—to help them see that establishing a vision for their lives gives them the direction, stability, and hope they will need to successfully weather life's challenges. They can live life successfully, but first they must dream the dream.

Creating a Vision for Life - Activities

1. Paper Puzzle 58
2. The Winner Box 60
3. Spending Your Life Game 62
4. Hit the Mark 66
5. Dream Makers and Breakers 72
6. The Flower Pot 76
7. Character Match 80
8. Snack Time 86
9. The Award Speech 88
10. Take a Seat 90
11. Head, Heart, and Feet 92
12. Making My Mark on the World 96
13. My Brochure 100

Activity #1 Paper Puzzle

45-60 Minutes

Character Connection
Empathy & Respect

Purpose To demonstrate that each individual is unique and special and emphasize the importance of possessing a vision for one's life

Overview Participants will make a large puzzle representing the entire group. All group members will be given a puzzle piece on which to explain their lives in pictures. They will each have the opportunity to explain their puzzle piece to the group and then fit their puzzle piece into the group puzzle.

Life Skill Planning for the future

Group Size Any

Cultural and Age Considerations None

Materials Large pieces of paper, such as chart paper; scissors; one set of colored pencils or crayons per small group (any writing tool that will not soak through the paper)

Preparation Using one large section of paper per small group, cut the paper into sections so that each group member will have one piece. These pieces should be large, irregular, puzzle-type shapes similar to the example below. Use a paper clip to keep all the pieces of each section together.

Instructions

1. Divide participants into groups of four or five individuals.
2. Give each group a set of pieces and have each participant take one piece. Instruct them to draw a picture of their lives on their pieces of paper. To encourage their creativity, avoid giving any further explanation or direction.
3. When everyone in the group is finished drawing, instruct participants to take turns briefly explaining their pictures to the entire group. Encourage the group to ask questions to learn more about each person.

4. Instruct the participants to turn the paper over. On the back, ask them to draw a picture of their lives in 5 to 10 years.
5. When the participants are finished drawing, instruct them to briefly explain their picture to the group and invite the group to ask questions.
6. Once the discussion is completed, instruct the participants to assemble all of their pieces into a complete puzzle. Tape the puzzle together.
7. Hang each puzzle on the wall if possible.

Application and Insight

Every person is unique and special.

Being able to envision a future is an essential component for fulfilling personal dreams.

Having a vision or dream for one's life helps a person to grow in positive ways.

It is important to value and respect the commonality as well as diversity of relationships.

Going Deeper

What do you think about your life as it is now?

What is the importance of envisioning your future?

What do you have in common with those in your group?

If you were to change the shape of your puzzle piece, how would that affect the entire puzzle?

What can we learn from this activity about valuing and respecting others who are different?

If you want to know how to live your life, think about what you want people to say about you after you are gone, and live your life backwards. —Unknown

It Takes Courage!

to share your vision with others

The Winner Box

30–45 Minutes

Character Connection
Respect & Responsibility

Purpose To encourage participants to understand that they are precious and competent individuals with the ability to be "winners" in life

Overview The Winner Box provides participants with a place to treasure important pledges they make to themselves to lead healthy lives. This box also provides a place to keep the positive input and encouragement they receive from others.

Life Skill Building self-esteem

Group Size Individual activity with any size group

Cultural and Age Considerations You may need to supply boxes or some other container for participants who may not be able to provide for themselves.

Materials Markers, crayons, colored paper, boxes to be decorated, glue, scissors

Preparation Each participant should make or find a special box, about the size of a shoebox or smaller, and bring it to class for this activity.

Instructions

1. Give participants time to personalize their boxes (color, carve, decorate).
2. Once they are finished, say something like this to them:

   You are all special and winners, even though you may not feel that way. This special box is for you to keep throughout the years ahead, to hold precious notes, letters, and small items that family, friends, or others may give you. Let's start with writing a note to yourself and then placing it in the box. On this note, write a commitment or pledge to remind you that you are special and a winner. An individual pledge to invest in your future is a powerful thing, so I encourage you to consider writing something that will make a big difference in your life, such as:

The Winner Box

I pledge to stay away from alcohol, tobacco, and other drugs because I'm a beautiful person with a good mind and I don't want to hurt myself or jeopardize my future.

3. Ask participants to place their note in their box and take the box home. The box serves as a reminder of the fact that they are precious and special.

Application and Insight

Making commitments and pledges serves as an important practice for building self-esteem.

Self-esteem is built over time and needs reinforcement.

In order to be successful in life, it is important to view ourselves as winners.

Going Deeper

Because self-esteem is built over time, it is important to do this activity as an ongoing practice. Take time in later sessions to have participants write other notes at appropriate occasions.

Write a personal note to each participant expressing something positive that you appreciate about that individual. Ask participants to place the note in their box.

Request that parents or other family members write notes that can also be added to the box.

Our life is what our thoughts make it. —Marcus Aurelius, Roman emperor

Author's Note: *This activity is a particularly special one for me. When I was a teenager, a dear friend and mentor, Tania Omalev McKinney, gave me an antique cigar box with the brand name "The Winner" printed on it. She told me, as she did on many occasions, that I was special, precious, and a sure "winner." She encouraged me to write down promises to myself and to put them, along with notes and letters from people who loved me, in my "Winner Box." Sadly, Tania died of cancer several years later, but what she instilled in my life has been invaluable to this day. I still have that box, and it's filled with notes from my parents and others who have encouraged me along my life journey. Just a glance at that old box is a precious reminder that I am loved and a winner! —Jennie Cerullo*

It Takes Courage!
to believe we are lovable and capable

Activity #3 Spending Your Life Game

30–45 Minutes

Character Connection
Honesty & Responsibility

Purpose To help participants identify and better understand their personal values

Overview Participants will play a game with 10 circles representing various aspects of their lives: their time, their talent, and their resources. During the game, they will be given several pairs of options and will have to choose how to "spend" their circles on those options. As participants play the game, they will discover many of their beliefs, attitudes, and values, and will do so in a fun, nonthreatening way.

Life Skill Investing to achieve a meaningful life

Group Size Individual activity with any size group

Cultural and Age Considerations You may want to change some of the options listed in the Spending Your Life Guide to more realistically match the choices your participants face. By offering appropriate choices, this activity can be adapted for any age group or cultural setting.

Materials Spending Your Life Game Handout; Spending Your Life Guide (Facilitator Notes); pens or pencils; pictures, cards with words, or paper cutouts of the various items offered for sale (optional)

Preparation Carefully read the Spending Your Life Guide (Facilitator Notes). Optional: Prepare a visual representation of the game options using pictures, cards, or paper cutouts.

Instructions

1. Distribute the Spending Your Life Game Handout and make sure all participants have a pen or pencil.
2. Explain the rules of the game to participants and lead the game by following the script in the Spending Your Life Guide (Facilitator Notes).

Spending Your Life Game

3. After completing the game, divide participants into groups of three to five individuals and ask them to discuss their purchases by answering the following questions:
   - Do you have any regrets concerning what you might have purchased?
   - What aspects of the game frustrated you?
   - What elements of the game would you like to change? Why?
4. Ask a few volunteers to share their answers with the large group.

Application and Insight

Although participants may offer suggestions to make the game seem easier and "more fair" to everyone, real life doesn't work that way. In real life:

- *A person cannot undo a past decision.*
- *A person cannot predict which options will be available in the future.*
- *No one can take advantage of every opportunity, because there will always be limited time, talent, and resources.*
- *Every choice has a cost, and this cost is often more than originally anticipated (as was the case with the five years of doing whatever you wanted).*
- *When people do not invest their lives wisely, they may leave this world falling short of their potential.*

Going Deeper

Based on the choices you made during the game, what values did you identify as being important to you?

Which value would you identify as most important to you? Why?

What actions or attitudes do you want to change to better reflect the things that are most important to you?

Adapted and used with permission from Dr. Gary Stanley.

We are shaped and fashioned by what we love. —Johann Wolfgang von Goethe, German statesman and poet

It Takes Courage!
to invest wisely in life

Spending Your Life Game

Each circle represents your time, talent, and resources. You will be presented with a series of two options. You may "purchase" either option or pass. You may not choose both options at one time. Write in it the name of the item you purchase as you spend each circle.

Spending Your Life Guide

Explain to participants the following rules of the game, then use this script as you lead the game.

In this game, each circle represents who you are and all the various aspects of your life—time, talent, and resources. Several pairs of choices will be offered to you during the game. With each pair of choices, you can decide to "spend" or "save" your circles. As you do so, you will be either spending or saving a part of yourself.

When each pair of choices is offered, you can buy one item or the other, but not both items. You may also choose to buy neither one of those items. If all of your circles are spent, you can't purchase anything else. No questions will be allowed during the game. As you make a purchase, write the item in the correct number of circles and then place an X through those circles.

Are you ready? Here are the first two items up for sale:

Option A	***Option B***
A nice apartment or house (one circle)	*A new car (one circle)*

Who would like to purchase one of the first two items? If you would like to purchase either item, write the item you purchased in one circle, and then mark an X through that circle.

Next:

Option A	***Option B***
An all-expenses-paid, one-month holiday to any place in the world for you and a friend (two circles)	*The guarantee that the person you would most like to marry right now will definitely marry you in the near future (two circles)*

Write the item you purchased in the two circles it cost you, and then mark an X through those circles.

Spending Your Life Guide *(continued)*

Next:

Option A	Option B
To be the most popular person in your circle of friends for two years (one circle)	*To find one true friend (two circles)*

Write your choice in the circle or circles it cost you, and then mark an X through any used circles.

Next:

Option A	Option B
A good education (two circles)	*A profitable business (two circles)*

Write your choice in the circles it cost you, and then mark an X through those circles.

Next:

Option A	Option B
A healthy family (three circles)	*World fame (three circles)*

Did you make your choice? If you chose to purchase the healthy family, you get two circles back as a bonus. Just draw two additional circles on your paper.

Let's continue. Next:

Option A	Option B
The ability to change any one thing about your physical appearance (one circle)	*Life-long personal satisfaction (two circles)*

Write your choice in the circle or circles it cost you, and then mark an X through them.

Spending Your Life Guide *(continued)*

Next:

Option A	Option B
Five years of doing anything you want to do when you want to do it (two circles)	*The respect and love of those you care about the most (two circles)*

Has everyone made a choice? Well, guess what? Anyone who purchased 5 years of doing only what they want must now pay an additional circle, if you have one, because some things just cost more than we expect them to. Write your choice in the circles it cost you and then mark an X through those circles.

Next:

Option A	Option B
A clear conscience (two circles)	*The ability to succeed at doing any one thing you desire (two circles)*

Write your choice in the circles it cost you and then mark an X through those circles. Next:

Option A	Option B
A miracle for someone you love (three circles)	*The chance to relive or repeat any one event in your past (two circles)*

Write your choice in the circles it cost you and then mark an X through those circles. Next:

Option A	Option B
Seven additional years of life (three circles)	*When the time comes, a painless death (three circles)*

Write your choice in the circles it cost you and then mark an X through those circles.

How many of you have circles left? How many of you spent all your circles? No further purchases can be made. Any circles you have left over are now worthless. Please put an X through them.

Hit the Mark

30–45 Minutes

Character Connection
Patience & Perseverance

Purpose To help participants understand the importance of developing a vision for their lives

Overview This simple, fun activity uses the analogy of a soccer goal to explore essential questions in developing a vision for a healthy, meaningful, and productive life.

Life Skill Setting personal goals

Group Size Any

Cultural and Age Considerations You may want to describe the game as a more popular or culturally appropriate one, such as baseball or basketball. The Striker Questions may need to be adapted so they are culturally relevant to your audience.

Materials Striker Questions (Facilitator Notes); two small foam or other types of soft balls suitable for indoor use; chalkboard, chart, or wall on which to draw the goal; chalk or marker; paper and pencil for the scorekeeper

Preparation On the board or wall, draw a "goal" (about 2 feet square). On a corner of the board, draw a box with two columns labeled "Hits" and "Misses."

Instructions

1. Inform participants that this activity will help them understand the importance of a personal vision. They will be asked to consider questions like, "Who do you want to be?" "What do you want to do?" and "What will your life look like in the future?"
2. Choose three participants and assign each a role as striker, goalie, or scorekeeper.
3. Instruct the striker to stand far away enough from the "goal" that hitting it will be a challenge. The goalie should stand near the striker to retrieve the ball as needed and should also be given the second ball. The goalie should try to obstruct the striker's throws occasionally (every third throw or so). Have the scorekeeper record the striker's "Hits" and "Misses" throughout the activity.
4. Ask the striker how old he or she will be in 10 years. Then ask the first question on the Striker Questions list. Have the striker answer before throwing the ball at the

Hit the Mark

goal. The goalie should retrieve the ball as needed, and the scorekeeper should put a mark under the appropriate column on the board.

5. Ask the second question on the Striker Questions list. If the answer is positive, redraw the goal to be a little smaller; if it is negative, leave the goal the same size. If the participant gives an extreme response such as, "I'll be making a million dollars," redraw the goal significantly smaller to reflect the increased difficulty of reaching this extremely high goal. Ask the striker to throw the ball at the goal again.
6. Continue this process until the striker has answered all the questions and the final pitch has been thrown.
7. Ask the scorekeeper to total the "Hits" to find the striker's final score.
8. Use the Discussion Questions to lead the group in a discussion of the importance of vision in our lives and what we can learn about vision from this activity.

Application and Insight

A personal vision is important to leading a healthy, productive, and rewarding life. If you aim at nothing, you are sure to hit it!

Aiming for something—a personal vision or a life goal—requires concentration, commitment, determination, discipline, patience, perseverance, and practice. Fulfilling a personal vision or a life goal requires a person to consider the answers to the two critical life questions: Who do I want to become? What am I here to do, and why?

The greater the goal, the more effort it takes to attain it.

Going Deeper

Provide participants with the Striker Questions, and ask them to write their answers. Challenge them to keep their answers as a reference as their personal vision unfolds.

Challenge participants to write their answers to the two essential life questions. Ask them to be prepared to share one answer to each question with the group.

Adapted and used with permission from The North Star Company.

To accomplish great things we must not only act but also dream, not only plan but also believe. —Anatok France, French novelist

It Takes Courage!
to develop a personal vision for life

Striker Questions

1. Will you have graduated from college?
2. Will you own a car?
3. Will you have a job?
4. Will you have a job you love to do? What will you be doing?
5. What kind of person will you be? Name at least three adjectives to describe the kind of person you would like to be.
6. How much money will you be making?
7. Will you be buying a house?
8. Will you be married?
9. Will you have children?
10. What other things will have happened that are important to you?

Discussion Questions

1. What is the purpose of this activity? What am I trying to illustrate?

   Developing a personal life vision is important to leading a healthy, productive, and rewarding life. If you aim at nothing, you're sure to hit it.

2. By drawing the goal, what did I provide for you?

   Something to aim for.

3. What does the goal represent for you?

   A vision for your life.

4. What does it take to score a "Hit"?

   Concentration, aim, skill, determination, discipline, and practice.

5. What happened as the goal got smaller? What will it take for you to fulfill your personal life vision?

   The goal became harder to hit and more effort was required. One needs concentration, commitment, determination, discipline, patience, perseverance, and practice. Developing life skills and making wise decisions will help you fulfill your personal life vision.

6. Would you be able to hit the target as easily using either hand? How does that relate to fulfilling your personal vision?

   It is important to use your strengths.

7. How did the goalie's efforts affect you? What obstacles get in our way in fulfilling our life vision?

   Obstacles that keep us from fulfilling our vision include drugs, alcohol, crime, abusive behavior, abusive relationships, and so on.

Notes

Live your life each day as you would climb a mountain. An occasional glance toward the summit keeps the goal in mind, but many beautiful scenes are to be observed from each new vantage point. Climb slowly, steadily, enjoying each passing moment; and the view from the summit will serve as a fitting climax for the journey.

–Harold B. Melchart, poet

Dream Makers and Breakers

45–60 Minutes

Character Connection
Patience & Perseverance

Purpose To help participants consider the ways they enhance or decrease their chances of reaching their dreams

Overview This activity utilizes the imagination to help participants understand and be prepared to deal with the obstacles that could stand in the way of achieving their dreams in life.

Life Skill Coping positively with personal stressors

Group Size Individual activity with any size group

Cultural and Age Considerations Use a children's story that will be appropriate for your age group and cultural setting.

Materials My Story Handout, story, paper, pens or pencils

Preparation Choose a children's story with which your group would be familiar. Make one copy of the My Story Handout for each participant.

Instructions

1. Read the children's story you have brought.
2. Discuss with the group the following questions based on the story you have chosen:
   - What is the treasure or goal sought in the story?
   - What obstacles stand in the way of the main character reaching the treasure?
   - What evil characters opposed him or her?
   - What personal characteristics hindered the main character in his or her pursuit?
   - How were these obstacles overcome?
   - What outside help did he or she have?
   - What personal character traits helped the main character to succeed?
   - What personal decisions did he or she make that made a difference?

Dream Makers and Breakers

3. Distribute the My Story Handout. Tell the group that each member will now be creating a story. They will each be on a journey to claim a treasure. The journey will be filled with characters, events, successes, and failures from their own experience. Give the group 15 to 20 minutes for each person to complete the handout, which allows them to incorporate events and factors from their own real-life adventure.
4. Once the pages are completed, allow various group members to share their stories. Discuss personal dreams and what kinds of things make or break those dreams in real life.

Application and Insight

We all have dreams; dreams are needed to give us motivation in life.

There are many obstacles in life that can prevent us from seeing our dreams come true.

Our character and decisions can make or break our ability to pursue dreams.

Going Deeper

Are all dreams possible to achieve? How do you handle a dream that seems impossible to reach, such as becoming an astronaut or a millionaire?

Why are dreams important? What purpose do they serve?

What are some practical steps you can take now toward fulfilling your dreams?

What is hanging up cannot be reached sitting down. —Amhara proverb, Ethiopia

My Story

Consider each of the following questions about your own life story and write your answers in the boxes.

What is the name of your world?	
What is your treasure?	
Who or what are your enemies along the way?	
What obstacles stand in your way?	
What personal character traits make it difficult for you to reach the treasure?	
What are or will be some of the important stops on your road to success?	
What character traits do you have that will help you overcome obstacles?	
What character traits do you need to develop to help overcome obstacles?	
What outside help is needed in your journey?	
What kinds of decisions will make a difference to the success of your journey?	
How does your story end?	

Notes

Hold fast to dreams for if dreams die,
life is a broken-winged bird that cannot fly.
Hold fast to dreams for when dreams go,
life is a barren field frozen with snow.

—Langston Hughes, American poet and author

Activity #6 The Flower Pot

15–30 Minutes

Character Connection
Honesty & Self-control

Purpose To help participants define character, determine character's relationship to behavior, and distinguish the difference between character and behavior

Overview This simple activity uses a flowering plant to raise questions and generate discussion about character.

Life Skill Maintaining a lifestyle consistent with good character

Group Size Any

Cultural and Age Considerations None

Materials Flower Questions (Facilitator Notes), flowering plant, watering can, plant food, artificial flower, twist tie or string

Preparation Display the plant, watering can, and plant food so they are visible to the participants.

Instructions

1. Ask the group to define character and behavior, and discuss how they are different.
2. Begin the discussion of character by asking participants the Real Flower Questions (Facilitator Notes).
3. Attach the artificial flower to the plant with the twist tie or string. Ask the Artificial Flower Questions (Facilitator Notes).

Application and Insight

Our character is the unseen dimension that reveals itself in our behavior.

Our behavior demonstrates our true character.

The most effective way to change behavior is to develop good character from within.

The Flower Pot

Going Deeper

What is one way you can develop your character over the next 30 days?

Write a one-page summary of what you've learned at the conclusion of the 30 days.

Adapted and used with permission from The North Star Company.

Find the seed at the bottom of your heart and bring forth a flower. —Shigenori Kameoka, Asian poet

It Takes Courage!

to admit the need to grow

Flower Questions

Real Flower Questions

1. What kind of plant is this? How do you know?

   By its shape, color, texture, fragrance, etc.

2. What are the characteristics of this plant?

   Where it can be found, what it smells like, the care it requires, how often it flowers, etc.

3. How would you define character?

   Consistently choosing to do what is right.

4. What part of this plant represents character, and why?

   The roots. Out of the roots grow the stem, branches, leaves, and flowers. The roots are the unseen support of the plant. They ground it, holding it firmly in the soil. From the roots the plant obtains nutrients and moisture from the soil that enable it to grow and blossom.

5. What is the relationship of character to behavior?

   Our character determines our behavior.

6. What part of this plant represents behavior?

   The flowers.

7. What is the relationship of roots to the flower of this plant?

   The roots provide the nutrients and moisture so the flower can blossom.

8. How do you cultivate the growth of this healthy plant?

   Care for the soil. Feed it nutrients. Water it. Provide it with sunlight. Prune it.

9. How do you cultivate the growth of a healthy character?

   Become friends with people who encourage you to become a person of good character. Spend time with an older person you admire and learn how they live.

   Be accountable to others for the decisions you make. Set aside regular time to reflect on the direction your life is taking.

Artificial Flower Questions

1. Even though I tied this flower onto the plant, can you tell it is artificial? How?

   Yes. It does not appear to be genuine or match the other blossoms. The texture is different and it does not have a fragrance.

2. How does tying this artificial flower onto a real plant illustrate the way we behave?

   We may try to appear like someone we are not or may show behavior that does not reflect our true character.

3. What typically results?

   Trying to be something we're not does not impress people. They soon discover what is false and not genuine. In time our true character becomes apparent.

Notes

Character is the foundation stone upon which one must build to win respect. Just as no worthy building can be erected on a weak foundation, so no lasting reputation worthy of respect can be built on a weak character. Without character, all effort to attain dignity is superficial and the results are sure to be disappointing.

–R.C. Samsel, author and business executive

Character Match

15–30 Minutes

Character Connection
All Traits

Purpose To introduce essential character traits

Overview This simple matching game provides a fun way to quickly introduce or review character traits and definitions. It can be used as a catalyst for any type of discussion on character or to highlight specific character traits.

Life Skill Recognizing good character traits

Group Size Any

Cultural and Age Considerations None

Materials Character Trait Cards and Character Definition Cards (Activity Materials); Character Trait Definitions (Facilitator Notes)

Preparation Copy and cut out one complete set of the Character Trait Cards and Character Definition Cards for each group. The Trait and Definition Cards may be printed on two different colors of paper if desired. Keep the two types separate, and place each type in a separate envelope or bind them with a rubber band.

Instructions

1. Divide participants into groups of three to four individuals.
2. Give each group a set of Character Cards (Trait Cards and Definition Cards).
3. Allow the groups to work for 5 minutes to match each trait with its proper definition.
4. Read the correct answers from the Character Trait Definitions (Facilitator Notes). Discuss whether the participants agree or disagree with the definitions and what changes they would suggest to more accurately reflect each character trait.
5. Choose one or more character traits, and ask participants to list various ways each quality might be seen in a person's life (for example, kindness is shown when you offer to help a friend who has too many books to carry; responsibility is shown when you finish your homework even though it's late and you don't feel like doing it, etc.).

Character Match

6. Make a large poster listing these character traits and their definitions, and hang it on the wall of the classroom for continued reference.

Application and Insight

Character is the foundation of a purposeful and healthy life.

There are essential character traits everyone should seek to develop in their lives.

Going Deeper

Why is it important to be a person of good character?

How does one become a person of good character?

Do any traits seem to be more important than others?

What happens if individuals are weak in specific character traits? How will those deficiencies affect or change their lives? Their relationships?

Sow a thought, reap an act;
Sow an act, reap a habit;
Sow a habit, reap a character;
Sow a character, reap a destiny.
—Anonymous

It Takes Courage!
to be a person of good character

Character Trait Cards

Copy and cut out each of these cards. Make two piles: one for the name of the trait, and another for the definitions. Be sure to mix up (shuffle) both sets of cards—they should not be in order!

Empathy	***Excellence***	***Fairness***
Forgiveness	***Gratitude***	***Honesty***
Humility	***Kindness***	***Loyalty***
Patience	***Perseverance***	***Respect***
Responsibility	***Self-control***	***Service***

Character Definition Cards

Copy and cut out each of these cards.

Fulfilling one's obligations and commitments	Being in charge of one's actions and reactions	Making positive contributions to others' lives
Being able to feel what someone else is feeling and to understand what that person is experiencing	Doing something to the best of one's ability	Being consistent and impartial in the way one deals with others
Letting go of the desire to hold someone responsible for an offense	Being appreciative of what one has been given	Being truthful and open
Being realistic about one's own strengths and weaknesses and not considering oneself better than others	Acting out of concern and thoughtfulness for others	Remaining faithful to the commitments and relationships one has made
Handling delay or delayed gratification calmly	Continuing on a course of action in the face of difficulties and obstacles	Treating oneself and others with high regard

Character Trait Definitions

empathy	Being able to feel what someone else is feeling and to understand what that person is experiencing
excellence	Doing something to the best of one's ability
fairness	Being consistent and impartial in the way one deals with others
forgiveness	Letting go of the desire to hold someone responsible for an offense
gratitude	Being appreciative of what one has been given
honesty	Being truthful and open
humility	Being realistic about one's own strengths and weaknesses and not considering oneself better than others
kindness	Acting out of concern and thoughtfulness for others
loyalty	Remaining faithful to the commitments and relationships one has made
patience	Handling delay or delayed gratification calmly
perseverance	Continuing on a course of action in the face of difficulties and obstacles
respect	Treating oneself and others with high regard
responsibility	Fulfilling one's obligations and commitments
self-control	Being in charge of one's actions and reactions
service	Making positive contributions to others' lives

I Am a Winner

. . . because I think like a winner, prepare like a winner, and perform like a winner.

. . . because I set high but attainable goals, work toward those goals with determination and persistence, and never stop until I reach them.

. . . because I am strong enough to say "NO!" to those things that would make me less than my best, and to say "YES!" to the challenges and opportunities that will make me grow and improve my life.

. . . because total commitment is my constant companion, and personal integrity is my life-time mentor.

. . . because I am learning to avoid the tempting shortcuts that can lead to disappointment and the unhealthy habits that could result in defeat.

. . . because I have well-learned confidence in myself, a high regard for my teammates and co-workers, and a healthy respect for those in authority over me.

. . . because I have learned to accept criticism, not as a threat but as an opportunity to examine my attitudes and to improve my skills.

. . . because I persevere in the midst of obstacles and fight on in the face of defeat.

. . . because I am made in the image and likeness of my Creator, who gave me a burning desire, a measure of talent, and a strong faith to attempt the difficult and to overcome the seemingly impossible.

. . . because of my enthusiasm for life, my enjoyment of the present, and my trust in the future.

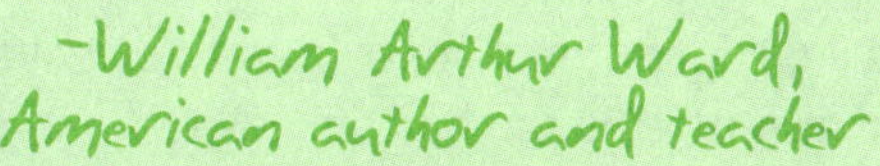

Snack Time

15–30 Minutes

Character Connection
Patience & Perseverance

Purpose To help participants understand how to develop good character in their lives

Overview This activity uses seeds to make a comparison between physical nutrition and the nourishing of our inner character.

Life Skill Developing relationships with people of good character

Group Size Any

Cultural and Age Considerations Use seeds or other items that represent the typical foods of your area.

Materials A variety of seeds of common food items (such as apple seeds or beans); small bags or envelopes (one per participant) to hold a few seeds; one basket or other container big enough to hold all the individual bags; chalkboard and chalk

Preparation Fill each bag with a few seeds or beans (one type per bag) and label bags with the name or a picture of the item inside. Place all the small bags in the basket.

Instructions

1. Inform participants that you've brought a snack for them to eat, then pass the basket around and have each person take one of the "snack" bags.
2. Ask them if they would like to eat what they have chosen. When they answer "No," ask them, "Why not?"
3. Talk about what would be necessary to turn each item into something edible. Ask participants to list the steps and materials necessary for the growth of a plant (good soil, water, sunlight, time, weeding). Record this list on the chalkboard.
4. Discuss how the various food items contribute to our overall physical health (each one provides different nutrients the body needs to function, the body needs them all to be balanced and healthy, etc.).
5. Ask participants to think of each type of seed as a positive character trait in their lives (such as respect or honesty). Each trait is one element of a healthy life, and

Snack Time

true health requires a balance of character traits. Point out that each participant possesses the seeds of positive character, but those seeds need to be nurtured. Ask the group to compare the growth and nurturing of plants to the growth and nurturing of one's character for a healthy life. They may give direct correlations for the elements of plant growth (good soil = good education and relationships; water = trials and challenges; etc.).

Application and Insight

Good character does not just happen. Good character must be developed, which takes time and hard work.

It is important to develop a network of friends and mentors who will provide necessary nourishment to help cultivate positive character qualities.

Going Deeper

What strengths do you see in your character? What weaknesses?

What are some practical ways you can begin to nurture and strengthen your character, especially your areas of weakness?

What difference does it make to have a balance of character traits rather than just a few strong areas?

Character is like a tree and reputation is like its shadow. The shadow is what we think of it; the tree is the real thing.
—Abraham Lincoln, 16th U.S. President

It Takes Courage!
to choose friends who will help us grow

The Award Speech

15–30 Minutes

Character Connection
Honesty & Respect

Purpose To enable participants to evaluate their present character and consider opportunities to develop their future character

Overview This activity provides an opportunity for participants to look at themselves through others' eyes by writing their own congratulatory speech.

Life Skill Periodically assessing personal strengths and weaknesses in character

Group Size Individual activity with any size group

Cultural and Age Considerations This activity is best used with ages 10 to adult. Various cultures view "talking about oneself" differently; therefore, adapt this activity to your cultural setting.

Materials Paper; pens or pencils; chalkboard and chalk

Preparation Write a sample speech as an example to share with the group.

Instructions

1. Explain to participants that they will write a speech about their own lives that will be read as if they were receiving an award. They will create the name of the award and include the things that might be said about who they are as a person, their character qualities, the names of people who have helped them, and how they have helped.
2. Read the sample speech about your life, then ask the group to create their own.
3. Ask several volunteers to read their speeches.
4. After these presentations, ask participants to identify the kinds of things they would like people to say about them. List these items on the chalkboard.

The Award Speech

Application and Insight

True character is always evident to others over a period of time.

Personal greatness is a result of cultivating core character traits.

The benefits of good character will remain long after a person is gone.

Going Deeper

What are the things people say about you now?

How do you feel about who you are right now?

What would you like people to say about you in the future?

How can you begin to move in that direction?

The unexamined life is not worth living. —Socrates, third-century Greek philosopher

It Takes Courage!

to honestly assess our character and be challenged to grow

Activity #10 Take a Seat

15–30 Minutes

Character Connection
Excellence & Humility

Purpose To help participants understand the difference between secondary and primary greatness

Overview In this activity, two boxes labeled with various examples of greatness are presented to the group. Although the boxes appear to be similar, the participants learn after sitting on them that the structure of the boxes is very important to their stability. As a result, they discover that true greatness lies below the surface and provides a firm foundation in life.

Life Skill Recognizing the importance of greatness

Group Size Any

Cultural and Age Considerations Choose volunteers who will be comfortable with the activity and will not be easily embarrassed. Use examples of secondary greatness that are appropriate for your group.

Materials One sturdy wooden or plastic box that can hold the weight of one person; one flimsy cardboard box that cannot hold the weight of one person (both boxes should be approximately the same size and large enough for a person to sit on); two cloth or plastic sheets large enough to completely cover the boxes; paper; marker; pins or tape

Preparation *Refer to page 53 for an explanation of primary and secondary greatness.* On the paper, write several words or phrases that are examples of secondary greatness (president, mother, doctor, prizewinner, popular athlete, movie star, scientist who discovers a cure, etc.), and cut them out. Pin or tape them on the sheets. On the wooden or plastic box, write character traits that are examples of primary greatness (excellence, honesty, integrity, etc.). Cover the boxes with the sheets and place them in the front of the room.

Instructions

1. Ask for two volunteers to help with a special task. Invite each volunteer to stand next to one of the boxes.

Take a Seat

2. Explain to the group that the boxes are covered with common examples of greatness, and that many individuals aspire to be these types of people.
3. Casually ask the two volunteers to sit on their boxes so you can begin the activity.
4. After the one volunteer has realized that the cardboard box is too weak to support his or her weight, remove the sheets from both boxes.
5. Point out that the wooden box has many examples of primary greatness and thus provided a firm foundation of good character. Although both boxes have secondary greatness, it is the box with primary greatness that stays intact.

Application and Insight

True greatness means having good character inside.

Secondary greatness impresses the world; primary greatness changes the world.

Secondary greatness comes from what we do; primary greatness comes from who we are as individuals.

Going Deeper

How does your life reflect each type of greatness? Which one is more evident?

Who are the people you most admire? Which type of greatness do you admire most in them?

If who I am is what I have and what I have is lost, then who am I? —Anonymous

It Takes Courage!
to cultivate good character

Activity #11 Head, Heart, and Feet

15–30 Minutes

Character Connection
Kindness & Service

Purpose To help participants understand and identify moral knowing, moral feeling, and moral action

Overview Participants are given three brief scenarios from everyday life to consider. They must decide whether moral knowing, moral feeling, and moral action are displayed in each situation.

Life Skill Developing character in mind, heart, and action

Group Size Any

Cultural and Age Considerations None

Materials Head, Heart, Feet (Facilitator Notes); Head, Heart, Feet Scenario Cards (Activity Materials); chalkboard and chalk

Preparation Write the Moral Knowing, Moral Feeling, and Moral Action descriptions from Head, Heart, Feet (Facilitator Notes) on the chalkboard. Copy and cut out the Head, Heart, Feet Scenario Cards. *Refer to pages 49–50 for an explanation of these three concepts.*

Instructions

1. Referring to the descriptions on the chalkboard, discuss the concepts of moral knowing, moral feeling, and moral action. Invite participants to suggest additional words to describe each concept.
2. Divide participants into three groups, and give each group a different Scenario Card.
3. Ask each group to read its Scenario Card aloud, and decide which Head, Heart, Feet aspects (moral knowing, moral feeling, or moral action) are displayed in that scenario.

Head, Heart, and Feet

4. Repeat this process with the other two scenarios:
   - Scenario 1: Moral knowing present, but not moral feeling or moral action.
   - Scenario 2: Moral knowing and moral action present; moral feeling is not present.
   - Scenario 3: All three aspects are evident.
5. Ask participants to think of evidence they see of each HHF aspect in their own lives or in the lives of others.

Application and Insight

It is not enough to know what is right—knowledge and feeling must be followed by action.

Going Deeper

How would you rate yourself on each HHF aspect? Which is your strongest category?

What changes are needed in your life in your weak areas?

What difference does it make if any HHF aspects are missing in a person's life?

We must teach youth to know the good, love the good, and do the good. —Kevin Ryan, professor of ethics

It Takes Courage!

to do what is right

Head, Heart, Feet

Write the description of each category on the chalkboard.

Moral Knowing

Intellect
Understanding
Conscience
Discernment
Respect
Fairness

Moral Feeling

Empathy
Passion
Caring
Goodness
Compassion
Kindness

Moral Action

Doing
Determination
Deciding
Discipline
Will
Practice

Head, Heart, Feet Scenario Cards

Copy and cut out the Scenario Cards and give one to each group of participants.

Scenario 1

Michael's mother sent him to the store to buy some bread for dinner. While he was waiting in line to pay for the food, some money fell out of the pocket of the person in front of him. The person didn't notice so Michael reached down to pick it up. He looked around and saw that no one had seen what he did, so he put the money in his pocket.

Scenario 2

Esperanza and Lee were classmates. Lee's family didn't have much money, and Esperanza often made fun of Lee's second-hand clothing and worn shoes. One day, Lee saw Esperanza trip and fall in the hallway, sending her books flying all over the floor. Instead of feeling sorry for Esperanza, Lee felt happy about her embarrassing situation because of the way she treated her. However, although Lee wanted to walk on by, she still stopped and helped Esperanza collect her books even though she didn't want to do it.

Scenario 3

As a top student in school, Jamal had no problems completing his schoolwork each day. However, his little sister Esther struggled, especially with math. Numbers just didn't make sense to her. Jamal loved his little sister and hated to see her hurting, so he decided to set aside time each night to sit down with Esther and help her get her work done.

Activity #12 Making My Mark on the World

45–60 Minutes

Character Connection
Excellence & Responsibility

Purpose To encourage participants to develop an individual mission statement

Overview Participants will use this easy, step-by-step guide to create a personal mission statement for their lives.

Life Skill Mapping a direction for life

Group Size Individual activity with any size group

Cultural and Age Considerations None

Materials Personal Reflections and My Mission Statement Handouts; large pieces of paper; pens, colored pencils, markers, or crayons

Preparation Make one copy of both handouts for each participant. *Refer to page 54 for information on creating a personal mission statement.*

Instructions

1. Discuss the importance of creating a personal mission statement. Give a couple of examples of mission statements that others have created.
2. Distribute the Personal Reflections and My Mission Statement Handouts, and allow participants time to complete them.
3. When participants are finished, ask a few volunteers to share their mission statements.
4. Give each person a large piece of paper. Ask participants to write their mission statement on the paper and to creatively illustrate it by drawing a picture or decorating it. They may also want to frame it.
5. Encourage the participants to display their mission statements in a prominent place to serve as a reminder of their commitments.

Making My Mark on the World

Application and Insight

Expressing thoughts on paper clarifies and strengthens commitments.

People make better decisions when they know their direction in life.

Going Deeper

Why does it make a difference to write down your desired direction in life instead of just thinking it?

How will having a personal mission statement change what you do today and tomorrow?

The end depends on the beginning. —Latin proverb

It Takes Courage!
to plan our tomorrows

Personal Reflections

Briefly answer each of the following questions in the space provided.

Who do I want to be like? List two or three people you look up to as examples and what you like about them. Why do you want to be like them?

Who am I now? What five words would best describe you now? What words would you like to add to the list that you don't think are true of you now?

What do I think makes a difference? What jobs or roles in the community do you think are the most important? Which ones would you most like to do? Why?

Where do I want to be in 20 years? If you read an article about your life in 20 years, what do you hope it will say about you? What will you be doing? What relationships will be in your life (family, friends, etc.)? What kind of person will you be?

What will people remember about me? If you were to read your epitaph after your death, what would you hope people would say? What do you want to be most remembered for?

My Mission Statement

Say It All. Based on what you've written on the Personal Reflections Handout, take 10 minutes to write anything that comes to mind about who you are, what you want to accomplish in life, and what is important to you. Don't worry about wording or order—just write! You can sort it out later.

Say It Short. Now try to condense everything you just wrote into one or two short statements.

Say It Out Loud. Put your statements into a final form, such as a poem or a slogan like you would see on an advertisement—anything that communicates what your life is all about. This is your mission statement. Write it in the box.

My Brochure

45–60 Minutes

Character Connection
Excellence & Perseverance

Purpose To help participants to think about their lives at present and where they hope to be in the future

Overview This activity guides participants to develop a vision for their lives by creating a brochure that explains who they are—their history, talents, and dreams to come. *This activity will need to be done over two sessions. Explain the brochure activity to participants, describing the topics to be included, and encourage them to bring any desired photos to the next session.*

Life Skill Identifying and developing gifts and talents

Group Size Individual activity with any size group

Cultural and Age Considerations The topics of the brochure may be changed to be more relevant for your group. If photographs are difficult for participants to bring for this activity, drawings can be used instead.

Materials Brochure Topics Handout; blank sheets of paper that can be folded into thirds (one per participant); photos (if available); pens, colored pencils, markers, or crayons

Preparation Make a copy of the Brochure Topics Handout for each participant. Ask participants to bring any photos of themselves, their family, home, pet, or anything they wish to include in their brochure.

Instructions

1. Discuss the importance of knowing who we are—how unique and special we are as individuals—and where we are heading in the future. You may want to point out some of the various talents of the participants.
2. Give each participant a Brochure Topics Handout and a sheet of paper.
3. Introduce the brochure activity and clearly explain each section.
4. Encourage participants to be creative with their format and design, but to be sure to include all the topics listed on the Brochure Topics Handout.

5. Instruct participants to fold their paper into thirds so there are six panels, and to begin creating their brochures.

Application and Insight

Each person is unique and special and possesses a variety of talents and abilities.

Understanding one's unique qualities, important values, and desired direction for the future enables a person to stay focused in life.

Going Deeper

Do people see the same person on the "cover" of your life as they do when they open the brochure and get to know you better?

How well does your present life match your brochure? What positive steps can you take to reflect your vision more accurately?

—Native American proverb

It Takes Courage!

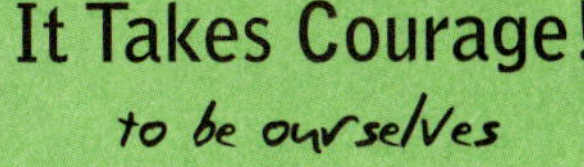

Brochure Topics

Front Cover

Create a symbol or crest that represents you. Draw original artwork, use photos, or create a collage of magazine pictures that represent you. Write a few sentences to introduce yourself.

Include the following topics in your brochure:

Family Tree

- Who are the members in your family?

Heroes or Heroines

- Who do you admire? Explain why you admire them and how they influence you or others.

What I Believe In

- What beliefs are important to you?

My Talents and Hobbies

- What do you do well? What do you enjoy doing?

What I'm Proud Of

- What accomplishments are you proud of?

My Dreams for the Future

- Who do you want to be in 10 years? What do you want to be doing?

Communicating Effectively

What Is Communication? 106

Verbal and Nonverbal Communication 107

Communication Styles 112

Character Connection: The Golden Rule 115

Conflict Resolution 116

It Takes Courage! 120

Communicating Effectively

It is with the heart that one sees rightly; what is essential is invisible to the eye.

—Antoine de Saint-Exupéry, The Little Prince

Communication is vital not only to our happiness, but to our survival. A newborn baby boy quickly learns that a cry brings forth action on his behalf. It is a natural response: no one taught the infant to do this, but he learns that crying works. The baby is connecting to the humans around him—he is communicating. But as that baby grows, our expectations for his behavior change. The growing child is expected to communicate his needs in more socially appropriate ways. A hungry adult who wails at a restaurant would get a different response than a wailing infant. Becoming mature means that we learn to communicate our thoughts and feelings appropriately.

Communicating well involves having a command of both verbal and nonverbal language skills and listening skills. It also requires many of the core character traits, such as respect, responsibility, kindness, honesty, patience, self-control, and humility. And without practicing the Golden Rule, one cannot be a good communicator, especially when conflict arises. At those times, the character of those involved will determine the outcome—whether they view it as an argument to be won to preserve their pride, or choose to respectfully disagree, even at the risk of looking weak and unintelligent. Although each situation is different, the underlying principles, such as kindness and respect, are universally nonnegotiable. When people feel respected, they give others a lot of leeway for communication blunders.

As we have traveled the world, we have certainly learned the power of nonverbal communication, which often is the only way we can communicate our care and concern for those in our conferences. At times our facial muscles just ache, but we keep smiling because we know a smile may be the only way to communicate our heart's attitude. Of course, there are also occasions when we communicate what we *don't* want to. For example, one of us had been given a beautiful gold ankle bracelet just before one of our first conferences in Africa. As we began a four-day teacher training conference on character development and HIV/AIDS prevention, we worked hard to build relationships and to communicate the need for teaching abstinence education and for adults to be good character role models for youth. At the end of our first day, a sweet elderly lady approached us and ever so gently offered a suggestion—to remove the ankle bracelet, which in their culture indicated that someone was a prostitute!

In today's media-centered world, many youth tend to mirror the way people communicate and relate on television, in movies, and on the radio. Without input from healthy adults, their communication teachers may be soap opera and sitcom characters and other media personalities who typically do not portray the character qualities presented in this resource guide. Learning the art of communication can be quite discouraging for adolescents. Extreme emotional swings, insensitivity on the part of peers, and the desire to "fit in" make it hard for youth to perceive and respond well to situations. They are constantly adapting to the world around them—our encouragement is vital. It is important for us to commend them for areas of growth, and gently offer correction when they make mistakes. As young people watch us communicate well, especially through disappointment and conflict, we can help them to see that learning the art of communication is worth the effort.

We dedicated an entire section of this book to communication because it is foundational to young people "living out" the topic in each section: *articulating* a vision for their lives, *connecting* in their relationships, *conveying* clearly their decisions, and *understanding* HIV/AIDS. The ability to communicate appropriately is a wonderful personal asset and usually produces more harmony in relationships. Poor communication typically results in unnecessary pain and heartache and can lead to the loss of meaningful relationships, family ties, or even one's employment. Our ability to communicate our needs and desires in positive ways can also help us to stand firm against pressure to engage in unhealthy behaviors.

Communication styles and gestures differ from culture to culture. Please fill in the concepts in this section with specific examples from your culture.

What Is Communication?

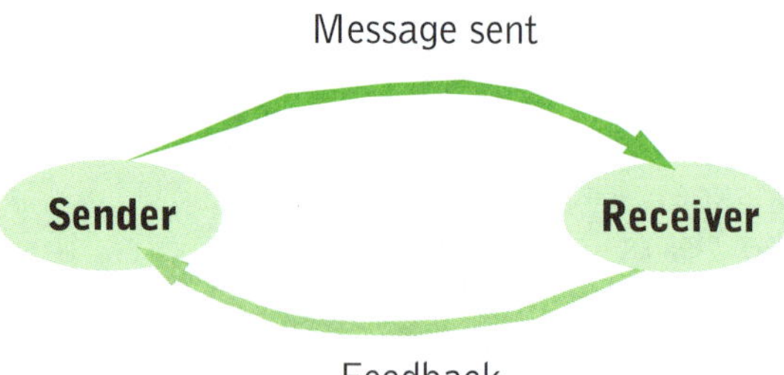

In communication, information is given to or exchanged with others. Spoken words, written words, body posture, and gestures are all forms of communication. It is simply a process of sending messages between two or more people; words may or may not be used. Communication involves the following.

Sender: The sender desires to send a message to another person, the receiver. The sender must create a message by selecting verbal and nonverbal strategies to communicate the thought or feeling to the receiver.

Receiver: The receiver begins to decipher the sender's message by looking for a number of verbal and nonverbal clues. The more clues there are to work with, the more likely the incoming message can be understood. The receiver then sends some type of feedback to let the sender know the message was received and understood. Again, this can be done in verbal and nonverbal ways.

This process of creating and deciphering messages continues throughout a conversation. For effective communication to take place, the sender will need to quickly determine the characteristics and mood of the receiver and the situation surrounding the conversation in order to construct effective messages. The receiver must be able to "read" the incoming message and must possess the skills to provide the right feedback so that the sender knows the intended message was received. Both persons must do their jobs well; failure on either person's part will likely result in miscommunication that leads to confusion, hurt feelings, or conflict. Learning the skills associated with sending and receiving clear messages is a valuable asset that will strengthen our professional and personal relationships.

Verbal and Nonverbal Communication

We use verbal and nonverbal strategies to both send our messages and provide feedback about what we have interpreted. While choosing kind, respectful words is essential to good communication, words are only a part of what we communicate. Our nonverbal communication is equally important. What we say needs to match how we say it.

Most of what we "say" about our feelings, character, and personality is accomplished without ever uttering a word. We communicate an image, planned or unplanned, through our appearance. We also communicate our feelings and inner character through facial expressions and other forms of body language and even through the tone of the words we select. Various researchers have concluded that we communicate almost 90 percent of the emotion of any message by our nonverbal communication, which is why most people prefer to have serious discussions face to face.

As you teach nonverbal communication skills, it is important to remind youth that the world is getting smaller. Travel and immigration have increased the need to be aware of cross-cultural differences in communication. What is acceptable in one culture may be disrespectful in another. For example, one U.S. president visiting another country gave an enthusiastic crowd of well-wishers a thumbs-up gesture—a gesture meaning "good job" in America, but meaning something nasty where he was at the time! Whenever possible, we want to teach youth to have an appreciation for their own culture while increasing their ability to connect cross-culturally.

Although we use thousands of words each day, it is the nonverbal cues we use to communicate them that determine how our messages are received. Communication skills, especially those involving nonverbal communication, are fun for youth to learn and practice. Let's look at the various aspects of nonverbal communication.

Paralanguage

Why is it that we can hear the words "I'm sorry" from a person but not believe them? It is because of the "paralanguage" that is being used—language that is louder than the actual words. Although the words say one thing, we know that the apology is insincere. Paralanguage is not the words we choose, or the quality or richness of our voice; it is the tone, pitch, stress, and speed we use when expressing our message. It can provide relational and emotional cues that indicate sincerity or deception. For example, an air of superiority can be communicated through sarcasm, expressed through our tone of voice. Paralanguage can also be used to clarify a message and make it easier to understand and remember.

Suggestions for Teaching Young People About Paralanguage

Tone:
- Speak confidently and sincerely
- Use a respectable rather than condescending voice

Pitch:
- Avoid fading at the end of a sentence
- Raise and lower your voice to clarify the message

Stress:
- Emphasize key words
- Enunciate to be heard clearly

Speed:
- Vary the rhythm
- Pause for emphasis

Body Language

Body language encompasses everything about the appearance and positioning of our bodies when we communicate with others. Body language usually communicates our emotions, such as fear, joy, tension, indecision, or love. It can demonstrate our inner character and can reveal states of our heart, like pride, selfishness, meanness, or disrespect for others. Certain body

movements can be expected when we do something wrong, such as telling a lie (blinking a lot, looking away, or acting nervous). Body language also demonstrates our good character qualities, such as humility and respect for others (bowing, standing as someone enters the room, letting others go first). Our gestures, facial expressions, posture, and appearance communicate a great deal about what we are thinking and feeling about ourselves and others.

When a person's words disagree with what is conveyed via his tone of voice, gesture, or other non-verbal channel, the emotional truth is in how he says something rather than what he says.

—Daniel Goleman, Emotional Intelligence

Gestures

Gestures refer to how we use our hands as we talk. Gesturing helps us bring our message to life and deliver it in an interesting, animated way. We can use our hands effectively to emphasize an important point that we want people to remember. Failure to use our hands can communicate as well. Typically, hiding our hands by crossing our arms or sitting on them may send a message that we are defensive, emotionally withdrawn, or uncomfortable. Although gestures vary greatly from culture to culture, pointing is one gesture that is considered rude and condescending in many cultures, particularly when we point at a person.

Facial Expressions

Have you ever seen yourself on video or in a photo and thought that you had an odd expression on your face? We can be unaware of our facial expressions while we are talking, and yet our facial expressions convey so much of our message. Smiling when we speak shows enthusiasm or friendliness; wrinkling the forehead shows concern, doubt, or maybe even gives our listener a clue that we have a headache. Often our gestures will mimic our facial expressions. Our expressions can put others at ease or make them feel uncomfortable just by a certain look. Probably the most important lesson to teach young people is that our facial expressions should match our words.

Posture

Posture often reveals what people think of themselves; for example, it can communicate confidence, timidity, arrogance, humility, respect, or insecurity. Sitting up straight rather than slouching is a more confident, assertive way to communicate. The way people carry and position themselves varies greatly among cultures, especially when showing respect to others. Be sure to consider your own cultural norms when discussing this topic.

Appearance

It is important to help youth understand that their appearance does leave others with impressions of them, whether positive or negative. Hairstyle, clothing, and personal grooming can communicate many things—degree of wealth, religion, sense of style, self-respect. Although the Golden Rule tells us to treat others as we want to be treated, we do make judgments based on appearance. We form initial conclusions about people that begin to paint a picture of what we believe to be true about them. However, until we take the time to get to know people, we will have only a partial picture of who they are. We need to spend time with others in order to determine their values, interests, and character. If we judged every book by its cover, we would miss out on some wonderful literature!

Eye Language

It has been said that the eyes are the windows to the soul. We communicate a lot with our eyes. Eyes can convey a threat, like our mother's look when we misbehaved; an interest in others, like flirting; or an emotion such as true concern and empathy. How we use our eyes in conversation provides meaning and understanding. Eye language also affects how others interpret our messages and whether they believe us and trust what we are saying.

The appropriate eye contact in conversation can also vary greatly among cultures. In Western societies, looking someone directly in the eye and maintaining eye contact throughout a conversation is considered respectful and shows interest and active listening. However, in many parts of the world, the opposite is the case. Lowering of the eyes is a sign of respect, and maintaining direct eye contact with someone who is older or in a higher position would be seen as disrespectful or challenging. This is another area where you are the cultural expert and will need to provide specific instruction about appropriate eye language.

Space Language

By using "space language," setting a nonverbal boundary, we can make someone feel comfortable or uncomfortable. We can vary the feeling of a setting from formal, to informal, to intimate just by the distance we have between ourselves and the person with whom we are speaking. For example, sitting behind a desk in a room with the door closed creates a more formal environment, whereas sitting side by side at a table with an open door sets a relaxed tone.

The appropriate space between two people in discussion varies from culture to culture. Standing too close to someone can be seen as aggressive or confrontational. In most countries, the comfortable distance between people when talking is the length from the elbow to the shoulder. In many Western countries it is double that distance—from the hand to the shoulder. As we talk with people from other cultures, being aware of the appropriate distance will help us communicate effectively and not cause offense.

It can be overwhelming to think of all that we need to do while communicating! We will need to (1) think about the topic at hand; (2) read the nonverbal cues of others; (3) use nonverbal communication that is consistent with our message; and (4) at all times treat the other person in a respectful way, despite our emotions. This is difficult even for adults! Adolescents who are dealing with negative emotions, are worried about peer pressure, or feel insecure about themselves have an especially difficult challenge.

Considerations for Nonverbal Communication

- If you are sitting down while having a conversation, lean forward.
- Face the person.
- Maintain eye contact as culturally appropriate.
- Nod your head to show understanding or agreement.
- Use facial expressions to show interest.
- Be aware of doing things that may be distracting such as tapping, fidgeting, or looking away.
- Be aware of postures-such as crossing your arms-that may make you appear defensive or uninterested.

Learning the art of sending and deciphering nonverbal cues is only one tool for good communication. Another vital tool is the art of active listening—not just hearing words, but using a process to ensure that what is being said verbally is interpreted accurately.

Active Listening

We enjoy being with people who listen to us. It makes us feel that we are respected and valued as individuals, that they really care about us, and that our feelings, thoughts, and opinions are valid. We often find that simply being heard is enough to satisfy our problem or need. Being a good listener is just as powerful as being a good speaker. The key to good communication is for both people to feel that they are heard and validated.

Drs. Tony Alessandra and Phil Hunsaker, in their book *Communicating at Work*, suggest there are three attitudes present in a good listener:

1. What others say to you is just as important to you as what you say to them.
2. Listening saves time—there is usually less need to revisit a discussion or clarify hurt feelings because something was misrepresented or misunderstood.
3. It is important and worthwhile to listen to everyone. Humility—having the attitude that you can learn from others—is essential.[1]

Active listening is a technique we can use to affirm that the speaker is being heard and understood. Generally this is done in four ways, using a combination of verbal and nonverbal communication strategies:

1. **Eye Contact:** Focusing on the person, not on other things in the room, and using culturally appropriate eye contact to show respect
2. **Body Language:** Smiling, leaning forward, nodding the head, and other gestures that show connection to what the speaker is saying

3. **Verbal Affirmations:** Words and sounds to communicate that you are listening and following the discussion: "Oh," "Hmmm," "Really?" "Tell me more," and so on
4. **Clarifying:** Using questions or rephrasing what was said in order to ensure that it was understood

Considerations for Active Listening

- Create an environment with few distractions.
- Use the person's name occasionally during the conversation.
- Don't interrupt.
- Acknowledge the person's feelings.
- Ask questions to clarify what is being said.
- Repeat back and summarize your understanding of the core message.

Communication Styles

Each of us has learned a style of communication that we use to express our thoughts and feelings to others. This style, adopted through trial and error and composed of verbal, nonverbal, and listening patterns, is our way of interacting with others to get our needs met. Our style of communication comes naturally to us, and depends on our personality and our environment. It consists of habits that we have learned to protect ourselves emotionally, to get others to do what we want, or to control a situation. The style we adopt is largely influenced by cultural expectations and the culture of our families. For example, the "acceptable" way for a woman to address a man, or for a child to address an elder, is determined by cultural norms.

There are four distinct communication styles: aggressive, passive, passive-aggressive, and assertive. Which style we choose will greatly influence how stressful and challenging our relationships and interactions with others will be. As we work with young people, it is important to discuss these styles in the context of being a person of good character. In good verbal communication, both the speaker and the listener must effectively convey their messages while maintaining a respectful and caring attitude, having as much concern for the thoughts and feelings of the other person as for their own. It is essential that we challenge youth to learn how to skillfully communicate their way out of difficult situations and to clearly express their desire to avoid risk-taking behavior. As they gain a better understanding of communication styles, they will begin to recognize healthy and abusive relationship patterns in themselves and in others. The four communication styles are explained below.

Aggressive

Someone with an aggressive communication style comes across as very controlling and domineering. Blame, intimidation, demands, harsh language, and verbal put-downs—often stated in a loud, forceful voice with strong body language—are common tactics of an aggressive communicator. Someone who speaks aggressively may sound like this:

"You never . . ."
"Just do it."
"You always do that."
"You made me mess up . . ."

Passive

People who are passive in their communication appear weak and unsure. They rarely state their opinion, and when they do, it is with soft, apologetic words and tone. Passive communicators will let others dominate the conversation. It is hard for them to get to the point, and they may sound very uncertain and helpless. Someone who speaks passively may sound like this:

"Well, I guess that will be okay."
"I'm really not sure . . ."
"Whatever you want."
"I'm so sorry to bother you."

Passive-Aggressive

People who are passive-aggressive appear to be subtle or indirect in their conversation. Many times their actions do not match their words. They may appear to agree, but how they really feel isn't stated. They lack verbal hostility and intimidation in their speech, yet their manner of communication is hurtful and manipulative and may include sarcasm or indirect cutting remarks. Someone who speaks passive-aggressively may sound like this:

"I could have told you that."
"I didn't think that would work."
"Oh well, you did it your way."
"Don't worry about me; go ahead and do what you have to do."

Assertive

Assertive communicators are able to express their thoughts in a positive and honest way. They are able to clearly and kindly communicate what they believe and what they want, and they are able to express themselves without belittling or manipulating others in the process. Their body language and voice exude confidence, but not arrogance, and they communicate with respect for the other person. Conflict is viewed as something to be worked through, not won. Assertive communicators are quick to take responsibility for their part in a conflict and will not focus on blaming others. They will respectfully listen to the other person's opinion and feelings and will stand up for what they believe, even when it feels uncomfortable. They are good listeners and problem-solvers and are solution-focused. Someone who speaks assertively may sound like this:

"I see your point, and I agree."
"We may view the solution differently, but let's find the common ground."
"Please give me the opportunity to explain."
"Let's explore other options."

As you read through the definitions of these four styles, it's easy to see that we probably communicate with some aspects of each style. We believe that youth need to learn the skills to be assertive communicators, even if it is not the primary communication style of their culture. Given the temptations and pressures of their world, especially in the area of sexual involvement, any communication style other than assertive can get youth into trouble. This is especially true for young girls, who often believe they can't say "no" to the males around them. Teaching youth to be assertive will help them to avoid unwise decisions or behaviors without appearing angry or judgmental to their peers. The way young people conduct themselves, especially in difficult situations, may save them from trouble and allow them to take control of the situation.

Assertive Communicators:

1. *Are active listeners*
2. *Apply the Golden Rule*
3. *Do not blame others*
4. *Take responsibility for their wrongs*
5. *Assume the best of others*
6. *Are sincere and honest*
7. *Avoid stereotypes*
8. *Do not interrupt others*
9. *Seek a win-win solution*
10. *Are courageous*

Communicating assertively, however, requires a lot more discipline and is a much greater challenge than using the other approaches to communicate our thoughts and feelings. Assertive communicators are able to demonstrate many positive character traits in their communications, such as honesty, respect, kindness, and self-control. The other approaches to communication lack many of these traits and are self-focused rather than relationship-focused. A true person of character wants to *be heard*, but genuinely desires to *hear* as well. It takes a lot of practice, perseverance, and courage to communicate kindly, respectfully, and sincerely—in other words, assertively. These traits are essential to the most challenging task: communicating through conflict.

Character Connection: The Golden Rule

The Golden Rule—"Do to others as you would have them do to you"—is one of the best reminders for teaching about character and communication. The Golden Rule states that the feelings of others are important and that we should always consider the welfare of others, not only of ourselves. Often when we communicate, especially when we are stressed, we tend to forget this rule. We become so focused on our own need to be heard and understood that we forget about the feelings and needs of the other person. Our desire should be a balanced conversation where both persons are heard and understood.

One of the most difficult concepts to teach young people is how damaging their words can be to others. Name-calling and gossip can cause deep hurts that sometimes last a lifetime. Talk with them about these issues and do not hesitate to stop an activity in defense of individuals who are on the receiving end of unkind communication. We must create an environment in the school and in youth groups where put-downs are not allowed. You may want to post the Golden Rule in your meeting room to emphasize its importance. Learning skills such as active listening and using "I" messages will help to provide an excellent framework for conversation consistent with the Golden Rule. Youth need to be reminded that people make judgments about us based on our choices; by observing whether we are kind to others, show patience in a difficult situation, take dangerous risks, or break rules, people determine what they believe our character to be. When they see us consistently following the Golden Rule, we are communicating that doing what is right is important to us. Words aren't even needed; others understand just by watching us make right choices.

The Golden Rule should be applied to the messages we send ourselves, too. Many people are their own worst critic; they are far more harsh and critical of themselves than others ever are: "I am stupid." "I'm never going to be able to do that." "I hate myself." "I can't read." How would we feel if a teacher or a close friend said those same words to us? They would be extremely hurtful and demoralizing. As we work to help youth understand the Golden Rule, we must help them to see the importance of treating themselves with respect and being responsible to themselves as well as to others. Encourage them to learn an internal language that is positive and respectful.

Conflict Resolution

Disagreements can often occur over differences in goals, values, perceptions, styles, or ideas. Conflicts can be particularly difficult when we perceive we have been purposely mistreated in some way. Because we are each unique, conflict is inevitable, but whether that conflict ends in a healthy disagreement or spirals into a heated, disturbing clash depends on when and how we handle the delicate situation.

Many conflicts are simply the result of poor communication. Using poor communication in a conflict is like pouring gasoline on a fire. Such conflicts are sure to escalate and could even lead to violence. Teaching young people to understand their common reactions to conflict and helping them learn how they can manage those reactions are essential to putting out the fires of conflict. We have three choices in a conflict: (1) fight to be understood and to get our own way (aggression); (2) act like the conflict never happened (avoidance); or (3) talk it through and agree on a solution (negotiation). The three types of responses, and their typical attributes, are as follows:

1. Fighting (Aggression): Dominates; blames; is loud and abusive; interrupts constantly; is a poor listener; has intimidating, glaring eyes; uses strong, hurtful words; has arrogant nonverbal language: pointing in face, invading space, intimidating posture, heavy breathing, disgusted tone of voice.

2. Hiding (Avoidance): Will not speak up—allows the other to dominate the conversation; leaves and pretends nothing is wrong; withholds opinions and feelings; is agreeable while not really agreeing; is a poor listener; uses soft, apologetic words; has passive nonverbal language: poor posture, arms crossed, looks at the floor or away from the person, uncertain tone of voice.

Rules for Good Communication

1. *Practice the Golden Rule at all times.*
2. *Assume the best of others.*
3. *Develop good listening skills.*
4. *Learn to read the body language of others.*
5. *Use humor wisely.*
6. *Apologize when you are wrong, and be quick to forgive.*
7. *Use "I" messages.*
8. *Try to be calm in conflict; walk away before you are rude.*
9. *Focus on fixing, not blaming.*
10. *Practice, practice, and practice some more.*

Steps to Resolving Conflicts

Resolving conflicts can be quite challenging for youth. As you help them to improve their verbal, nonverbal, and active listening skills, they will have a strong foundation from which to work through issues. In addition to the basic communication skills, it is important to teach youth to keep in mind the following points when trying to solve interpersonal problems:

1. *Get your emotions under control.* This may mean that you need to walk away from the situation and choose to discuss it at a later time.
2. *Try to understand both sides of the situation.* Use active listening skills and verbal communication to clarify the situation. If you need help in understanding, don't hesitate to ask an objective person for assistance.
3. *Apologize for any offenses you have caused.* It will take courage to do this, especially if you believe the other person's offenses are greater than yours. However, it is always important to take responsibility for any wrong actions and admit your mistakes, regardless of whether the other person apologizes for any perceived offenses.
4. *Find out what both persons need in the situation.* Once both persons understand the situation, make a list of what each person feels is needed to resolve it.
5. *Consider ideas that would meet the needs of both persons.* Collaborate and make a list of ideas that may help solve the problem.
6. *Select an option both persons can agree on.* To complete this step, both persons need to honestly agree that the idea chosen will work toward a positive solution. Again, if you need help, don't hesitate to ask an adult or an objective friend for assistance.
7. *Make a plan.* Decide when and how you intend to implement your ideas.

3. Problem Solving (Negotiation): Discusses opinions and feelings openly; relates feelings, needs, and wants honestly and directly; has confident eye contact; is an active listener; uses direct, kind words; has assertive nonverbal language: straight posture, open and confident body language, kind but direct facial expressions, clear tone of voice.

Young people will typically choose to respond to conflict using the same style that is modeled at home. Even though we may know how we should communicate, when we are under stress or feel challenged we often gravitate back into a less productive pattern of expressing ourselves (aggressive, passive, or passive-aggressive). It's vital that we help youth see that good communicators are able to control their initial reactions to conflict, manage their emotions, and work toward a healthy solution. Learning to use the following concept can help them to resolve conflicts.

"I" Messages

Conflict can often escalate out of control just by our choice of words. It's an all-too-common human response to blame the other person when we disagree. However, if we resort to using blame and inflammatory words, the other person will certainly become defensive, and the listening will end. Conflicts typically center around the word "you," as in statements such as: "You are so . . ." "You make me . . ." "You don't think . . ." "You knew I was . . ." "You don't care . . ." These types of messages almost always trigger a negative, hurtful conflict.

Teaching youth how to use "I" statements to express their feelings when they are angry or frustrated will help them to effectively resolve conflicts. "I" statements provide a positive, respectful way to express a viewpoint without placing blame or criticizing. More importantly, they keep the focus on the specific behavior rather than on the person as a whole. Learning how to replace the "you" blaming messages with these types of feeling statements is not easy—it requires a lot of practice and self-control. In fact, using "I" statements may even seem artificial at first. Role-playing the use of "I" statements is a fun teaching tool that gives youth the opportunity to practice. With just a little practice, healthy disagreements will begin to replace hostile, aggressive conflicts. Following are examples of contrasting "I" messages and "you" messages in conversation.

"I" Messages	"You" Messages
I am angry.	You make me angry.
When you won't answer my questions, I feel like you don't care about what I have to say.	You never listen to me! You don't care about what I say.
I don't like to be the one who usually cleans the kitchen.	You never clean the kitchen.
I would like to choose what we do sometimes.	We always do what you want to do.
I feel very alone and frustrated when you get mad and slam the door.	You always walk away when you get angry.
I need time so that I know I am making a good decision.	You always push me to make a quick decision.

The general idea in using "I" messages is to avoid blaming or attacking someone and to keep the focus on your own feelings. Blaming and attacking involve words like "always," "never," "can't," "don't," and "make me"—put the word "you" in front, and it sounds like you are on the offensive. The word "you" should be used only to describe a behavior in a neutral tone. The following is an example of how to construct "I" statements.

I ____

(insert feeling)

when you ____

(insert specific behavior)

because ____.

(insert how it affects you)

or

When you ____

(insert specific behavior)

it's a problem because ____.

(insert how it affects you)

Learning to use "I" statements effectively requires self-discipline, especially when someone is attacking us. People are going to hurt our feelings, disappoint us, frustrate us, and sometimes just be plain mean to us. A good communicator must not only practice good communication skills, but also be a person of good character.

It Takes Courage!

Peer pressure is a very powerful force when it comes to communication. When someone has offended us, others may be quick to encourage a negative response: "Let her have it!" "Just give him a piece of your mind!" "Set her straight!" The world encourages us to attack—either to the person's face or behind his or her back. When all the world is pushing for a response that is inconsistent with the Golden Rule, a person of character will have to find the courage to do what is right.

Good communicators can experience failure and take responsibility for their poor communication. They have the courage to admit their personal weaknesses and work hard, even though they may fail often, in order to grow in their ability to communicate respectfully. When they make mistakes by hurting someone's feelings, they are able to apologize and ask for forgiveness, even if others think they look weak. Learning to be a good communicator requires almost all the character traits we have identified in this guide. It is easy to know what we should do to communicate in a kind and respectful way, but it takes an immense amount of courage to put it into action.

Communicating Effectively – Activities

14. Paper Doll 122
15. Guess the Message 124
16. Do You Hear What I'm Not Saying? 128
17. A Nonverbal Chat 132
18. Silent Movie 134
19. One-Way Communication 138
20. More Than Ears 142
21. Are You Listening to Me? 146
22. Assertiveness Role-Playing 150
23. Guess the Emotion 154
24. Behind the Scenes 158
25. People's Court 162
26. Flip Book Journals 168
27. The Golden Rule 172
28. How Do You Rate? 174

Paper Doll

15–30 Minutes

Character Connection
Empathy & Kindness

Purpose To help participants realize the effect of negative words on others

Overview A simple paper doll helps participants understand the impact of negative words on other people.

Life Skill Speaking positively about others

Group Size Any

Cultural and Age Considerations None

Materials Large sheet of plain paper, scissors, tape

Preparation Cut the paper into the shape of a person (as large as possible).

Instructions

1. Pass the doll around the group, asking each person to say something mean or hurtful about the doll and to rip off a small piece of the doll. Instruct participants to keep the pieces they've torn off.
2. After the doll has circulated around the group, pass the doll back around the same way it came.
3. Ask participants to now say two good things about the doll and to tape their pieces back onto the doll.
4. Discuss the following questions:
   - What have you learned from this activity?
   - How did you feel when you tore a piece off the doll? How does that relate to how you treat your friends?
   - How do you feel when people say mean or unkind things to or about you?

Paper Doll

- How well did the positive statements at the end of the activity repair the damage done by the negative comments? How does that work in relationships?

Application and Insight

Negative comments are hurtful and difficult to repair.

Choosing uplifting and encouraging language is important for building relationships.

Going Deeper

What are the long-term effects of negative language on relationships?

What does it take to truly repair a relationship once it is damaged?

If you judge people, you have no time to love them. —Mother Teresa, Yugoslavian missionary to Calcutta, India

It Takes Courage!

to refuse to speak unkindly about others

Guess the Message

30 Minutes

Character Connection
Empathy & Self-control

Purpose To help participants identify the components of nonverbal communication

Overview This fast-paced activity uses the setting of a relay race to teach the group how to effectively convey messages. As a fun variation of charades, participants use nonverbal methods to communicate a specific attitude to one another.

Life Skill Interpreting the nonverbal cues of others

Group Size Large (10 or more)

Cultural and Age Considerations None

Materials Attitudes Sheet (Facilitator Notes), Attitude Cards (Activity Materials), masking tape or string, chalkboard and chalk

Preparation Clear a space in the room large enough to create several lanes for a relay race. This activity can also be conducted outside. Using masking tape or string, mark out lanes for participants to run in. Create one lane per group, each about 10 feet long. Copy and cut out one set of Attitude Cards for each group. Place a set of Attitude Cards at the far end of each lane. Write the information from the Attitudes Sheet (Facilitator Notes) on the chalkboard.

Instructions

1. Ask participants to suggest common phrases or words that they use every day, such as: Yes. What? Excuse me. I don't know. See you later. Thank you. I'm sorry.
2. Write these suggestions on the chalkboard.
3. Explain that participants will be running a relay race. Divide participants into groups of four to six individuals, and assign each group to a different lane.
4. Ask one participant from each group to stand at the end of the lane by the Attitude Cards, and the remaining participants to stand at the opposite end.
5. To start the first round, call out one of the suggested phrases and then shout "Go!"
6. Instruct the first person in each line to run down to the Attitude Cards and pick up one card. He or she must say the designated phrase using a tone of voice and body

Guess the Message

language to indicate the attitude that is written on the card. The participant already standing there must guess which of the six attitudes the person is trying to convey.

7. If the answer is correct, the participant who guessed should run back to the group with the card and place it on the floor or some other designated spot. If the answer is wrong, the card is placed back in the deck, and the participant who guessed runs back to the group empty-handed.
8. The first runner stays at the end of the lane to guess the card of the next runner.
9. As soon as the first person reaches the group, the next runner runs down the lane and repeats the procedure.
10. The relay continues until one group correctly guesses all the cards and brings the last card back to the starting point.
11. To play another round, have the groups reset the cards, and send a different participant to stand at the other end of the lane. Call out another phrase and shout "Go!"
12. Once the game is over, introduce the four types of nonverbal communication: Paralanguage, Body, Eye, and Space language. Ask the group to identify the factors that made each attitude obvious (fearful = tone of voice, sad = facial expression, etc.).
13. Discuss how we use nonverbal communication in daily life. Ask participants to give some examples from their own lives.

Application and Insight

There is much more to communication than just words.

Understanding nonverbal messages is essential for good communication.

Going Deeper

Why is it important to understand nonverbal communication?

What are some examples of times when you or someone you were speaking to missed those messages? What happened as a result?

Our actions speak louder than our words. —Unknown

It Takes Courage!

to take time to understand what a person is really saying

Attitudes

Write the following words on the chalkboard.

Judgmental

Encouraging

Sad

Confident

Enthusiastic

Fearful

Attitude Cards

Copy and cut out one set of cards for each group.

Activity #16 Do, You Hear What I'm Not Saying?

15–30 Minutes

Character Connection
Respect & Responsibility

Purpose To help participants recognize the importance of both verbal and nonverbal communication

Overview This role-play will help participants see just how much is communicated without using words. It will highlight the fact that clear messages are sent when our nonverbal actions are consistent with our words.

Life Skill Communicating the same message both verbally and nonverbally

Group Size Any

Cultural and Age Considerations This activity is more appropriate for ages 12 and older. Choose a situation such as taking illegal drugs, using alcohol, stealing, or gossiping. Consider language and behavior that is culturally acceptable to your audience.

Materials Nonverbal Role-Play Summary (Activity Materials), Nonverbal "No" Handout

Preparation Copy the Nonverbal "No" Handout for each participant. Make two copies of the Nonverbal Role-Play Summary for the actors.

Instructions

Part 1

1. Choose two participants, a male and a female, to role-play a scenario that will be repeated four times using different body language each time.
2. Give a copy of the Nonverbal Role-Play Summary to the two actors. Take a few minutes to go over the instructions with them, and have them practice briefly.
3. Distribute the Nonverbal "No" Handout to the rest of the group. As the scenarios are performed, participants should evaluate the behaviors in each situation, writing down the meaning and examples of what they see happening in each scenario.

Do You Hear What I'm Not Saying?

4. Once the scenarios are completed, discuss the handout with the group, emphasizing the need to have our words match our messages. Also emphasize that when people say the word "no," our respectful response is to always assume that they mean it. We should stop the situation and ask for clarification before proceeding.

Part 2

5. Instruct all participants to stand and choose a partner.
6. Ask pairs to practice sending nonverbal gestures that would communicate positive messages in a conversation. No words can be used—only gestures. After a few moments, have the pairs share with the group the types of things they did.
7. Next, ask participants to send nonverbal messages that would destroy communication. Be sure to tell them that nasty gestures are not appropriate. Again, ask them to report the types of gestures they used.
8. Summarize the activity by reinforcing the power of our nonverbal communications and how they can make us look strong and confident, or weak and vulnerable.

Application and Insight

Effective communication is based on consistent verbal and nonverbal messages.

If verbal and nonverbal messages don't match, the nonverbal message is typically the one that is received.

Respecting others, even those who may not communicate consistently, is a habit that should be cultivated.

Going Deeper

What can you do to be aware of your verbal and nonverbal communication style?

Ask a close friend to help you improve your communication by pointing out things you do that may not be consistent with what you say.

Fortitude is the capacity to say "no" when the world wants to hear "yes." —Erich Fromm, philosopher and psychologist

It Takes Courage!

to communicate clearly and respectfully in difficult situations

Nonverbal Role-Play Summary

The two participants are at a party, and the male wants the female to have sex with him. He is trying to get her to drink alcohol so she will be more easily persuaded.

His line is always, "Come on, it will be fun."

Her line is always, "I don't want to." With each account of the situation, she uses the same line, but varies her message to him by changing her nonverbal communication. She will communicate each of the following messages while still saying, "I don't want to."

Scenario	Meaning	Examples of Nonverbal Cues
Scenario 1	Yes	She may stay close to him, hold the bottle, put her head on his shoulder, use a tender and sweet voice, etc.
Scenario 2	Maybe	She moves in, then moves back, has a puzzled look on her face, holds the bottle, then sets it down and picks it up again, looks around to see if anyone else can see her, uses a tentative voice, etc.
Scenario 3	No and means it	Her body language matches her words, yet is not aggressive; she steps back, puts her hand up in refusal, uses a clear voice, etc.
Scenario 4	No and leaves the situation	She says "no" forcefully and walks away.

Nonverbal "No"

Two people will act out a scenario four times. Watch them closely. They will say the exact same words each time. The only change you will observe is their body language and paralanguage. Fill in the meaning of the message and the specific examples of nonverbal cues used in each scenario.

Scenario	Meaning	Examples of Nonverbal Cues
Scenario 1		
Scenario 2		
Scenario 3		
Scenario 4		

SLAM

Activity #17 A Nonverbal Chat

30–45 Minutes

Character Connection
Patience & Respect

Purpose To demonstrate the power of nonverbal communication

Overview Participants are involved in a silent word game that helps them to become more aware of how to use nonverbal cues in communication.

Life Skill Utilizing nonverbal signals in communication

Group Size Large (10 or more)

Cultural and Age Considerations None

Materials Blank unlined paper, marking pens of different colors, basket, bell or whistle

Preparation From the list of character qualities, choose one or more words so that the number of letters matches the expected number of participants. Count the number of letters in each word and add them up. Cut the same number of small paper squares, so there is one square per letter. Write the character qualities that you chose on the squares, one letter per square, using a different colored marker for each word (for example, "kindness" would use eight squares, all written in blue, and "honesty" would use seven squares, all written in red). Place the letters for all the words in a basket, making sure they are thoroughly mixed together.

Instructions

1. Explain that this is a silent activity and there should be no talking or verbal clues given.
2. Give each participant one letter. Give any leftover letters to individuals with the same color letter. Participants should place letters face down so that no one else can see them.
3. Explain that participants will be unscrambling words that are character traits. They will have five minutes to unscramble the words and define them. When the bell or whistle sounds, they must stop the process wherever they are in the game.

A Nonverbal Chat

4. When you say "Go," participants should:
   - Turn their letters over and display them for everyone to see.
   - Gather in groups according to the color of their letters (all reds together, etc.).
   - Unscramble the letters to form a word using all the letters.
   - Define the given character trait using only nonverbal clues (written information is not allowed).
5. When all groups are finished, have them demonstrate their nonverbal definitions to the other groups until the character trait is guessed or several minutes have passed. At the end of each demonstration, ask each group to hold up the letters to display its character trait, whether or not the trait was guessed by the other groups.
6. After all the groups have had an opportunity to share their traits, ask them to discuss the following questions:
   - Was it an easy or a difficult task? Why?
   - Would talking have made the process easier or more efficient?
   - What nonverbal clues helped form the group and the word?
   - What did you learn from this activity?

Application and Insight

To effectively communicate and fully understand others, one must be aware of what is being said nonverbally.

Styles of communication vary greatly; it takes a lot of patience to "hear" what others are trying to communicate through nonverbal cues.

Going Deeper

Ask the group to discuss examples of how they have been hurt or offended by someone through nonverbal communication, for example, by facial expressions, body language, or tone of voice.

He speaketh not and yet there lies a conversation in his eyes.
—Henry Wadsworth Longfellow, poet

It Takes Courage!
to communicate with character

Activity #18 Silent Movie

45–60 Minutes

Character Connection
Patience & Perseverance

Purpose To help young people interpret nonverbal communication

Overview This activity seeks to help participants learn to recognize the nonverbal aspects of communication in the absence of verbal cues. The nonverbal aspect is especially important in communicating emotions. Participants will work in small groups to silently act out an emotion to the rest of the group.

Life Skill Recognizing strong emotions in others

Group Size Large (10 or more)

Cultural and Age Considerations None

Materials Emotion Cards (Activity Materials), paper bag

Preparation Copy and cut out at least one Emotion Card per participant. Place the cards in a paper bag.

Instructions

1. Ask each person to select one Emotion Card from the paper bag.
2. Divide participants into groups of three to five individuals. Ask each group to design a three-minute *silent* drama that demonstrates all the emotions selected by their group members.
3. As each small group performs their drama before the whole group, instruct other participants to guess the emotions being demonstrated.
4. When all dramas are finished, have the group discuss the various emotions and how they were displayed.

Silent Movie

Application and Insight

Communication involves more than words.

Feelings are often better communicated through nonverbal means.

It is important to be sensitive to nonverbal messages, because these cues offer increased insight and better understanding of another person.

Going Deeper

Do verbal and nonverbal messages always agree?

What can you do to develop more consistency between your verbal and nonverbal messages?

How can nonverbal cues help you better understand another person?

How can you show respect for others in nonverbal ways?

A smile is the light in the window that lets people know you are home. —Anonymous

It Takes Courage!

to communicate our true emotions

Emotion Cards

Copy and cut out cards.

Sadness	Happiness	Disappointment
Anger	Amazement	Frustration
Fear	Bitterness	Embarrassment
Shyness	Boldness	Pride
Cautiousness	Love	Hatred
Respect	Sincerity	Nervousness

Notes

When it comes to body language, there are some that have better vocabularies than others.

—Doug Larsen, author and women's advocate

Activity #19

One-Way Communication

15–30 Minutes

Character Connection
Humility & Respect

Purpose To help participants understand the importance of two-way communication in developing healthy relationships

Overview This activity allows participants to see the effect of one-way communication as one member of the group instructs another member in a simple drawing task. The participant drawing the picture cannot ask any questions.

Life Skill Pursuing two-way communication with others

Group Size Any

Cultural and Age Considerations None

Materials One-Way Communication Diagrams (Activity Materials), paper and pencil

Preparation Choose one of the One-Way Communication Diagrams and make two copies of it.

Instructions

1. Choose two volunteers from the group. Give one volunteer a copy of the diagram, and the other volunteer the paper and pencil. Ask them to sit back to back, so that the person who will be drawing cannot see the diagram and is facing away from the group.
2. Ask the volunteer who has the diagram to carefully describe it verbally. No hand signals or gestures may be used.
3. Instruct the second volunteer to draw the diagram as it is being described. This person is not allowed to ask questions during this process, and comments from the group are not allowed.
4. Once the drawing is completed, display the other copy of the diagram so everyone can compare the two versions.

One-Way Communication

5. If time allows, repeat the activity and allow two-way communication between the two volunteers using a different diagram.

Application and Insight

The most effective communication is two-way.

Asking questions can help prevent misunderstandings.

Going Deeper

How well did the one-way communication method work? What were some of the difficulties?

What difference would two-way communication make?

How do you see these issues reflected in relationships?

How can we make our communication with each other more effective?

We don't see things as they are; we see them as we are.
—Anaïs Nin, French-American author

It Takes Courage!
to ask questions when we don't understand

One-Way Communication Diagrams

Choose one of the diagrams and make two copies of it.

Diagram 1

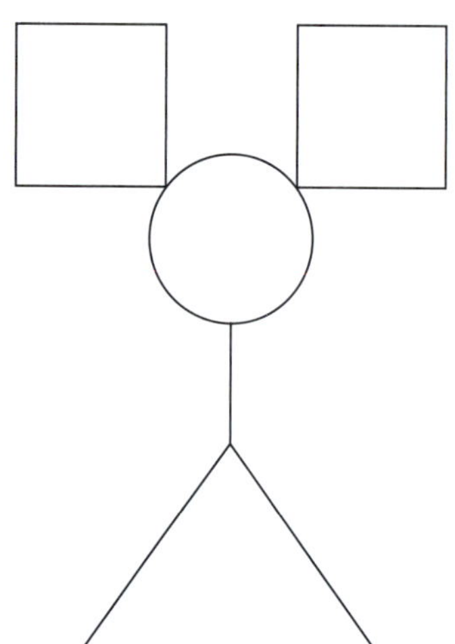

Diagram 2

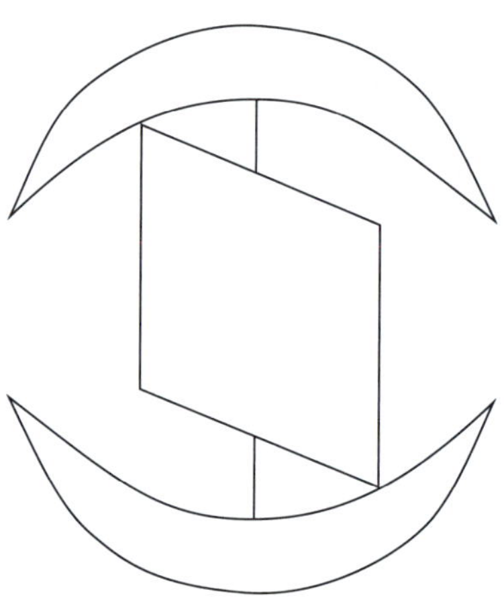

Diagram 3

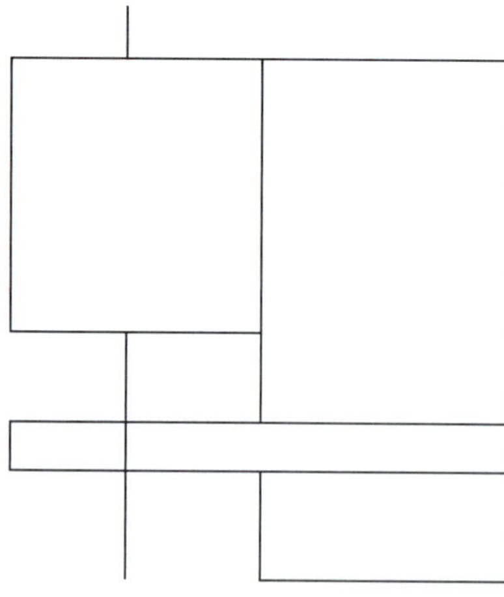

Diagram 4

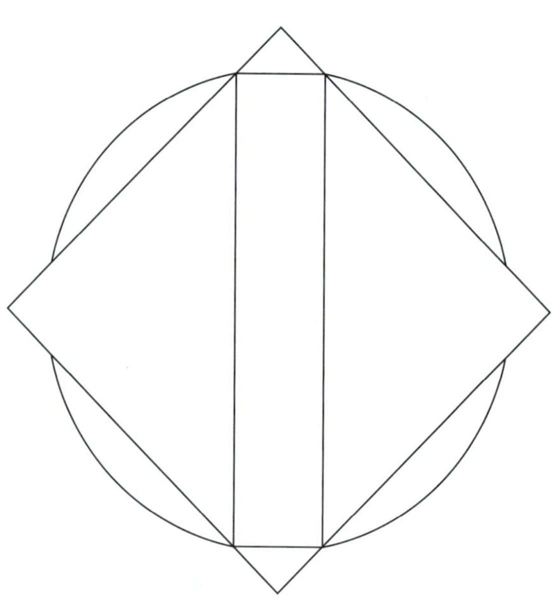

Notes

There may be no single thing more important in our efforts to achieve meaningful work and fulfilling relationships than to learn to practice the art of communication.

—Max De Pree, author and business executive

Activity #20 More Than Ears

15–30 Minutes

Character Connection
Patience & Self-control

Purpose To help participants evaluate their own ability to listen and encourage them to develop better listening skills

Overview Listening is vital to developing and maintaining relationships. This activity provides a self-assessment of listening skills and seeks to motivate participants to learn to be better listeners.

Life Skill Listening patiently to others

Group Size Individual activity with any size group

Cultural and Age Considerations Participants need to be able to honestly evaluate and rate themselves. They will also need basic addition and multiplication skills to calculate their individual scores.

Materials Listening Skills Handout, pens or pencils

Preparation Make one copy of the Listening Skills Handout for each participant.

Instructions

1. Give a copy of the Listening Skills Handout to each participant.
2. Explain that all participants will rate their own listening skills by responding to the seven statements.
3. Ask participants to add up their scores and identify the type of listener that describes them according to the scale located at the bottom of the handout.

Application and Insight

Listening demonstrates respect for others.

When people perceive that they are being understood, they are more likely to try to understand another point of view.

More Than Ears

Learning to listen helps a person to develop better relationships with others.

Going Deeper

What types of things distract you from listening?

What makes you the most angry when you are speaking?

How can you appear more interested?

How can you communicate understanding when listening to someone else?

Why is it that in a world of sophisticated communication we often suffer from a shortage of listeners? —Erma Bombeck, humorist and author

It Takes Courage!

to ask others to help us learn to listen

Listening Skills

Use the scale below to answer each of the following statements.

5 = Always 4 = Most of the time 3 = Some of the time 2 = Seldom 1 = Never

______ I am careful not to interrupt when someone else is speaking.

______ I make every effort to try to understand what a speaker is feeling.

______ I write down notes of important phrases and facts when a teacher is speaking.

______ When I do not understand what a speaker means, I tend to ask questions or request a further explanation.

______ I do not allow myself to become angry or upset when I disagree with a speaker.

______ I tune out distractions when I am listening to others.

______ I try to listen carefully even when I am not interested in the subject being discussed.

______ **Total Points**

Evaluating Your Listening Skills

Add the numbers in your responses to determine your score.

- 30–35 *Excellent:* You are a great listener.
- 25–29 *Good:* You have better than average listening skills.
- 21–24 *Okay:* You should spend time becoming a better listener.
- 20 or less *Need Help:* You should work extra hard to improve your listening skills.

I am a(n) ______________________________ listener.

Notes

To love you as I love myself is to seek to hear you as I want to be heard and understand as I long to be understood.

—David Augsburger, professor and author

Activity #27

Are You Listening to Me?

15–30 Minutes

Character Connection
Empathy & Humility

Purpose To teach participants active listening skills

Overview This activity clearly illustrates both good and poor listening skills. One participant will role-play a conversation with the facilitator as the facilitator demonstrates both types of listening skills.

Life Skills Exercising active listening with others

Group Size Any

Cultural and Age Considerations None

Materials Communication Skills List (Facilitator Notes), chart paper, marker

Preparation None

Instructions

1. Ask several participants to suggest a fictitious problem or important topic they need to discuss with someone, such as "My boyfriend broke up with me" or "I failed a math exam."
2. Select one topic and choose one participant to come to the front of the room and discuss it with you in a role-play.
3. As the participant begins the role-play, demonstrate poor verbal and nonverbal listening skills (see the Communication Skills List). Several minutes into the discussion, change your approach and start using good communication skills.
4. After the role-play, ask participants to discuss the following:
   - What examples of poor and good listening skills did you see?

Are You Listening to Me?

- Where did you see a change in my listening skills?
- What differences did you see in the other person when my communication skills changed?

5. Give the participant who is doing the role-play an opportunity to share his or her observations as well.
6. Ask the group to compile a list of active listening skills. Write their ideas on a chart.
7. Display the chart listing good and poor listening skills in a visible place for future reference.

Application and Insight

Practicing active listening skills is essential in helping a person to better understand the feelings and attitudes of others.

Demonstrating active listening skills is one of the simplest, most effective ways to communicate compassion.

Going Deeper

Why is it important to demonstrate active listening skills?

Is it possible to have positive relationships without demonstrating active listening skills? Give a few examples.

Listen, or thy tongue will make thee deaf. —Native American proverb

It Takes Courage!
to listen patiently and intently

Communication Skills

Poor Verbal Skills

- Interrupt the participant
- Fail to demonstrate a clear understanding of the problem
- Dismiss the topic as unimportant
- Change the subject

Good Verbal Skills

- Listen patiently
- Repeat the topic to the participant to clarify understanding
- Stay focused on the subject
- Use comments and questions to demonstrate your concern and caring, such as: "I see. I am sorry. I certainly understand why this is so difficult for you. What can I do to help?"

Poor Nonverbal Skills

- Slouch
- Look away distractedly
- Make poor eye contact
- Move restlessly
- Roll your eyes
- Sigh heavily
- Yawn

Good Nonverbal Skills

- Lean forward
- Make eye contact where appropriate
- Avoid distracting behavior
- Show empathy, concern, or caring with your facial expressions

Notes

There are two types of people— those who come into a room and say, "Well, here I am!" and those who come in and say, "Ah, there you are."

–Frederick L. Collins, politician

Activity #22 Assertiveness Role-Playing

45–60 Minutes

Character Connection
Responsibility & Self-control

Purpose To help participants understand passive, passive-aggressive, aggressive, and assertive communication styles

Overview Participants will act out a variety of scenarios so the group can experience these communication styles and learn to recognize both healthy and unhealthy behaviors.

Life Skill Identifying the communication strategies of others

Group Size Large (10 or more)

Cultural and Age Considerations None

Materials Behavior Cards and Scenario Cards (Activity Materials)

Preparation *Refer to pages 112–114 to review the communication styles.* Copy and cut out Behavior Cards (one card for every two participants). Copy and cut out one Scenario Card for each group.

Instructions

1. Divide participants into two to four groups and give each group a different Scenario Card.
2. Within each group, have participants form pairs (three members is acceptable).
3. Ask each pair to choose a Behavior Card from the stack and practice acting out a scenario using the communication style that is listed on their card.
4. Ask all the pairs in one group to act out their scenarios first, and then the next group. At the end of each pair's demonstration, ask the other small group to try to guess which communication style was being demonstrated.
5. When all the pairs have finished, have the entire group discuss the characteristics of the various styles and the behaviors typically associated with them.

Assertiveness Role-Playing

Application and Insight

It is easier to be passive or aggressive, but these are unhealthy responses to conflict. Assertive behavior is the best choice for resolving conflicts with others.

Going Deeper

What is the goal of conflict resolution? How well do the various responses accomplish this goal?

What is your typical response in these situations? What changes will you make in your own way of handling conflicts?

I cannot hear what you say because of the thunder of your actions. —Cameroonian proverb

It Takes Courage!
to stand up for ourselves

Behavior Cards

Copy and cut out one card for every two participants.

passive	*passive-aggressive*	*aggressive*	*assertive*
passive	*passive-aggressive*	*aggressive*	*assertive*
passive	*passive-aggressive*	*aggressive*	*assertive*
passive	*passive-aggressive*	*aggressive*	*assertive*
passive	*passive-aggressive*	*aggressive*	*assertive*

Scenario Cards

Copy and cut out one card for each group.

Scenario #1

Someone is cheating on a test by looking at your paper.

Scenario #2

Some boys are teasing your sister.

Scenario #3

Your younger sibling borrowed your favorite shirt without asking and badly stained it.

Scenario #4

You are waiting in a long line for a bus and someone cuts in front of you.

Activity #23

Guess the Emotion

15–30 Minutes

Character Connection
Honesty & Self-control

Purpose To give participants an opportunity to express a variety of emotions

Overview A deck of Emotion Cards is used in different ways to help participants learn to recognize and express a variety of emotions.

Life Skill Comprehending the emotions of others

Group Size Large (10 or more)

Cultural and Age Considerations You may want to modify the cards to make them more appropriate for your group.

Materials Emotion Cards (Activity Materials), chalkboard and chalk, tape

Preparation Copy and cut out the Emotion Cards (see each game for the number required).

Instructions

The following games are played with the same deck of Emotion Cards. Choose one or more games as time allows.

Game #1: Emotional Charades

Write the emotions listed on the Emotion Cards on the chalkboard. Ask each participant to take an Emotion Card and act out that emotion without using any words. The rest of the group should guess which of the listed emotions is being portrayed.

Game #2: Emotional Mirror

Tape an Emotion Card to each participant's back. Instruct the group to move around and "mirror" to each person they meet the emotion written on the other person's back. After both participants have identified the emotions that are listed on their backs, they can move on to other participants.

Guess the Emotion

Game #3: What's My Mood?
(Note: This game requires multiple copies of four Emotion Cards.)
Choose four participants and give each a different Emotion Card. Ask them to go to different locations in the room. Give each of the other participants an Emotion Card. Instruct the people at the four locations to demonstrate their assigned emotion without using words. Have the rest of the participants go stand near the person displaying the emotion shown on their Emotion Card. Ask each group to discuss what it was about the person's actions or expressions that communicated their assigned emotion.

Game #4: Emotion Party
Choose one participant to be the "host" of a party. Choose three other participants to be "guests" at the party. Give each "guest" a different Emotion Card. As the guests enter the party one at a time, have them greet the host and act out their assigned emotion through words and actions. They should never directly say what the emotion is (for example, they should not say, "I feel angry!"). The emotion should only be implied by tone, inflection, and so on. The host and the group should try to guess the emotion each guest is trying to display.

Application and Insight

Body language communicates as much as words.

During interactions with others, it is important to recognize our own emotions as well as the emotions of others.

Going Deeper

What difference does it make to know what emotion you are feeling in a given situation?

How can identifying the emotions of others help us to understand and communicate more effectively?

What happens when you don't know how you're feeling? How does that affect your decision making?

Preach . . . and when necessary use words. —St. Francis of Assisi, founder of the Franciscan Order (1182–1226)

It Takes Courage!
to be honest about our own emotions and attitudes

Emotion Cards

Copy and cut out the number of cards needed for each game.

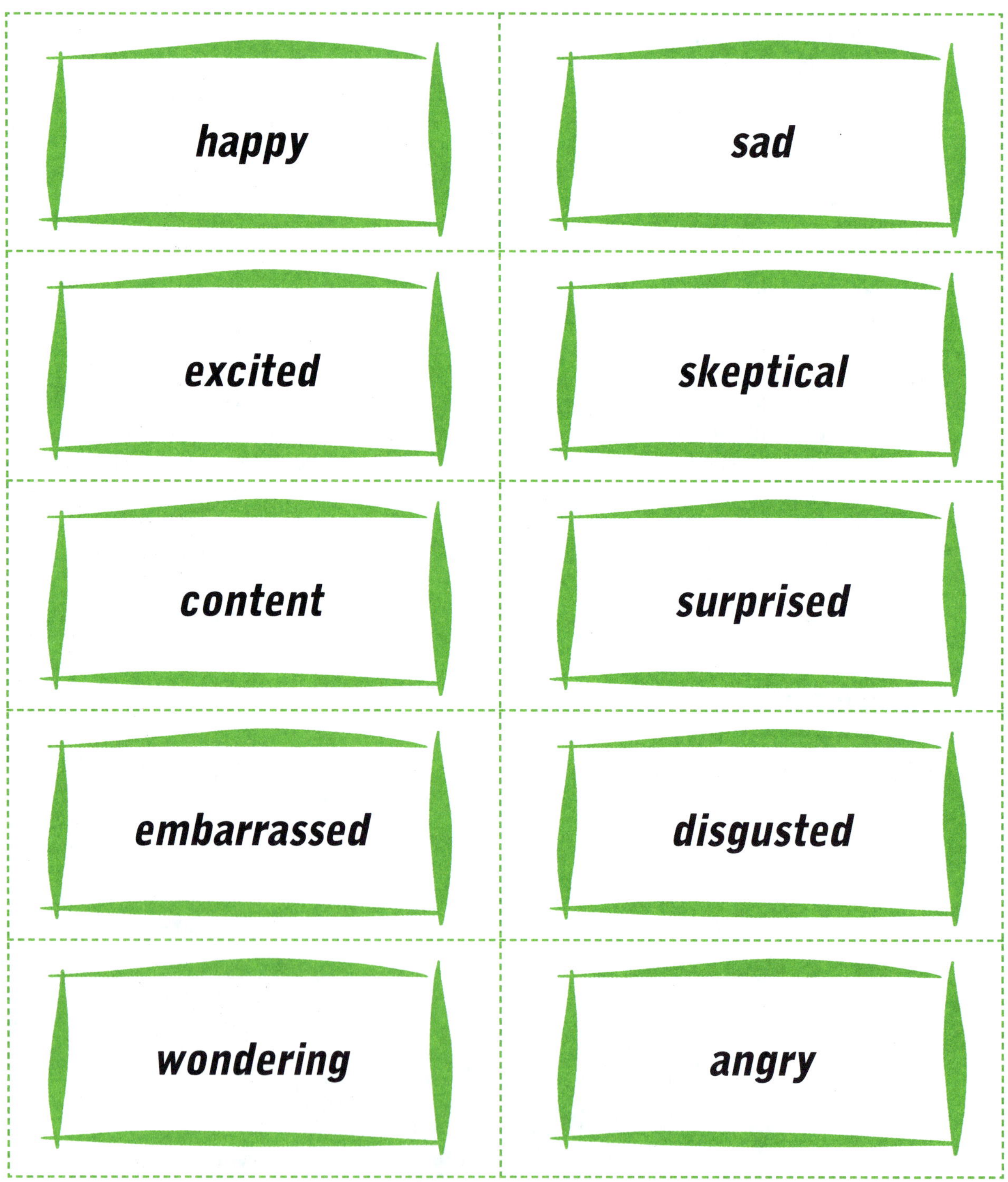

Emotion Cards *(continued)*

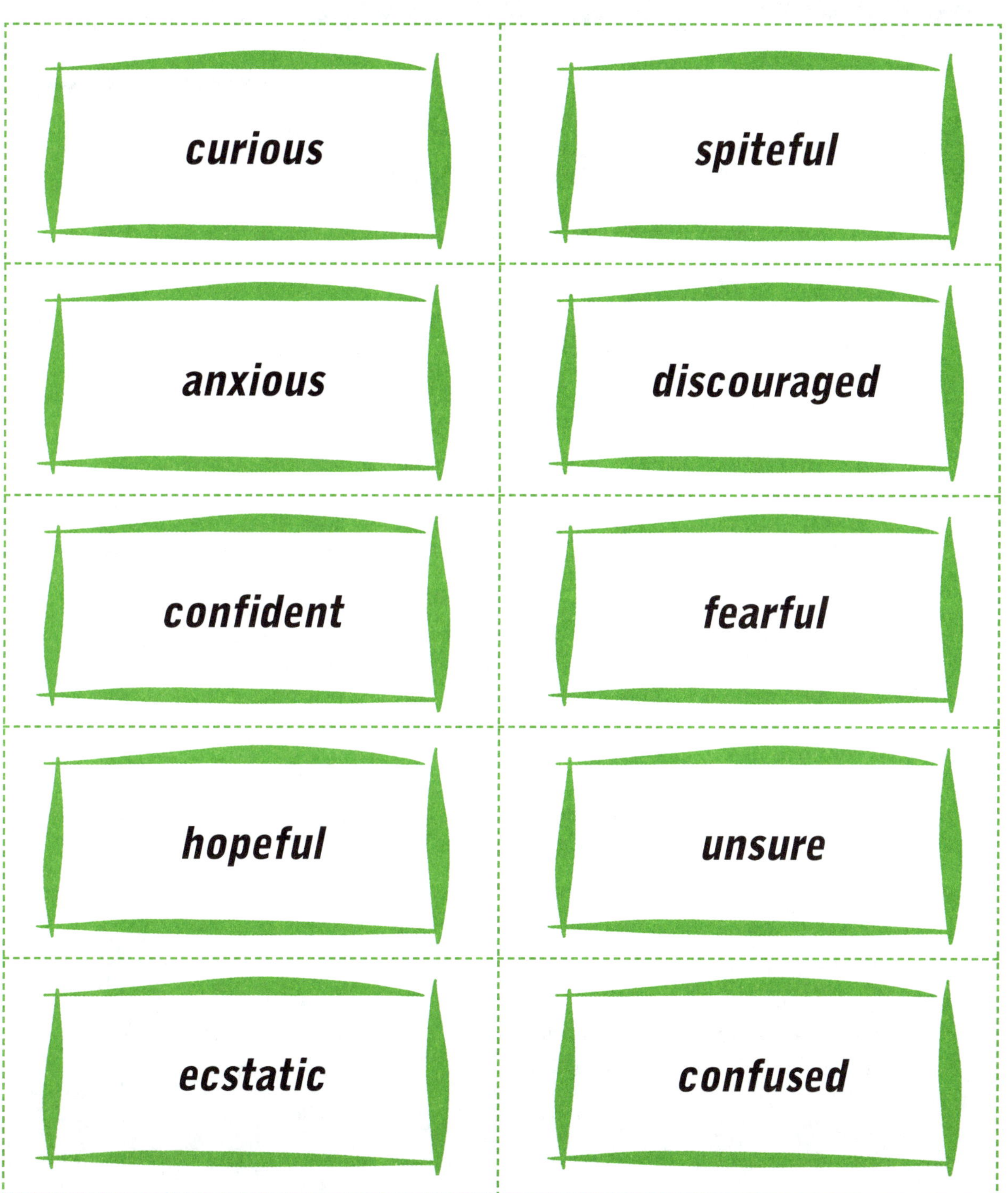

Behind the Scenes

15–30 Minutes

Character Connection
Forgiveness & Kindness

Purpose To help participants learn how to productively communicate negative thoughts and emotions in a conflict by taking responsibility with "I" statements

Overview This role-play demonstrates two different methods of communicating negative feelings in a conflict. Participants are given an opportunity to evaluate how they can better approach conflicts on their own.

Life Skill Owning and expressing one's feelings without blaming others

Group Size Any

Cultural and Age Considerations The scenario may be changed to a more appropriate situation for the age and culture of the group.

Materials Scenario Card and My Side Cards (Activity Materials), What Message Are You Sending? Handout, chalkboard and chalk

Preparation *Refer to pages 118–119 to review "I" and "you" messages.* Copy and cut out the Scenario and My Side Cards. Make one copy of the What Message Are You Sending? Handout for each participant.

Instructions

1. Choose two volunteers to come to the front of the room. Explain that these two people are involved in a conflict with each other and have agreed to meet to work it out.
2. Read the Scenario Card to the group.
3. Give each volunteer a different My Side Card, and allow them a minute to read it silently.
4. Instruct Volunteer 1 and Volunteer 2 to discuss this problem using the "You" Message paragraphs on their My Side Cards as the dialogue.

Behind the Scenes

5. Ask the group to make some observations of this interaction: its effectiveness, problems they saw in the way things were handled, and so on. Write their observations on the chalkboard.
6. Instruct the volunteers to repeat the conversation, using the "I" Message paragraphs instead.
7. Lead the group in a discussion of the two interactions, comparing the effect of each one on the listener.
8. Discuss the importance of "I" messages versus "you" messages in resolving conflicts.
9. Distribute the What Message Are You Sending? Handout and ask participants to complete it.

Application and Insight

Negative feelings and reactions are most effectively expressed without placing blame on the other person.

It is important to define and take responsibility for one's own reactions and feelings.

A person cannot make someone else do or say anything. These reactions are a choice.

Going Deeper

Do you take responsibility for your own reactions and feelings?

What is your usual style of communication? How could it be improved?

How do you react when someone approaches you with "you" messages instead of "I" messages?

The tongue kills quicker than the sword. —Turkish proverb

It Takes Courage!
to communicate negative feelings without blaming and judging

SCENARIO CARD

Volunteer 1 (V1) and Volunteer 2 (V2) are best friends. They usually do everything together. Two weeks ago, a new family moved in next door to V1 with a son/daughter of the same age. V1 and V2 have befriended him/her, inviting him/her to walk with them to school every day. Yesterday morning, V2 waited at the usual corner for the other two, but they never came. V2 finally went to school, slipping into class late, and found them already there. At the first break, V1 and V2 meet each other on the playground.

MY SIDE (Volunteer 1)

"You" Message (read angrily)

Where in the world were you guys? **You** didn't tell me you weren't coming. **You** made me late to school. It's **your** fault I got a detention. Besides, it's obvious I'm no longer your best friend. **You're** a terrible friend, and I'm never going to speak to you again.

"I" Message

Where in the world were you guys? I was worried about you at first, then I started to feel deserted. Then, when I got to school and saw you were already there, I felt mad, partly because I got in trouble, but more because I felt betrayed as a friend. I feel like I'm being replaced, and that hurts, especially since you're my best friend.

MY SIDE (Volunteer 2)

"You" Message (read angrily)

What's **your** problem? **You** don't own me. Besides, **you** don't even want to know what happened, do **you**? **You'd** rather just blame me. Forget you! I don't need that kind of a friend. I'd rather hang out with (the new friend) anyway.

"I" Message

I'm so sorry you didn't know what was going on. (The new friend) told me last night that he had to go to school early and didn't want to go alone because it was dark and he still didn't know his way that well. I couldn't get a hold of you to tell you. You're my best friend, and I wouldn't leave you out like that on purpose.

What Message Are You Sending?

Step 1: Think of a conflict you've had recently or one you've seen between other people. Explain it briefly.

Step 2: Write out a possible "you" message that might be said in this situation.

Step 3: Write out a possible "I" message that might be said in this situation.

Activity #25 People's Court

45–60 Minutes

Character Connection
Fairness & Honesty

Purpose To equip participants with a strategy for resolving conflicts

Overview This courtroom role-play takes participants step by step through a real-life conflict and its resolution.

Life Skill Choosing to face and resolve conflicts responsibly

Group Size Large (10 or more)

Cultural and Age Considerations This activity works best for ages 10 and older.

Materials Conflict Resolution Handout, Conflict Resolution Agreement Form Handout, paper, pens or pencils

Preparation *Refer to page 117 to review conflict resolution strategies.* Make one copy of the Conflict Resolution Handout for each participant and one copy of the Conflict Resolution Agreement Form Handout (optional: make one copy per participant).

Instructions

During this role-play, you will serve as the judge who is helping two individuals to work through a conflict resolution process.

1. Ask for volunteers to play each of the following roles: Ben, Ben's representative, Larry, Larry's representative, court reporter.
2. Read the following scenario to the group:

   Ben and Larry are in court to resolve the following conflict: Ben and Larry became friends just this year in school. Larry needed some money for an emergency, and Ben gave it to him, not making it clear whether it was a gift or a loan. Weeks went by, and Larry didn't repay the money. Ben became concerned about Larry's failure to repay him, and that concern soon escalated into irritation and eventually anger. What should Ben do?
3. Give the remaining participants a copy of the Conflict Resolution Handout to fill out as the role-play is performed.

People's Court

4. Give each side a few minutes to generate their client's view of the conflict: why he is reacting the way he is and what assumptions he is making about the other person:
   - Larry: why he hasn't paid Ben and why he thinks Ben is upset
   - Ben: why he thinks Larry isn't repaying him and why he's so upset about it

   Encourage the volunteers to be creative as they make up their scenarios. Neither side should know what the other side is going to say.
5. Once their stories are ready, begin the following process:

   Step 1: Get emotions under control.
   - Each representative should give his opening argument in which he tells only the assumptions his client has made about the other (blaming).
   - After the arguments are finished, the judge should instruct each side to present only what they know to be fact, which is their client's side of the story. They cannot deal with this case in anger or assumption.

   Step 2: Try to understand both sides of the situation.
   - Each side should restate their arguments using only the facts they know about their client with no comments about the opposition (using active listening skills to listen and to clarify the situation).

   Step 3: Apologize for any offenses caused.
   - Once both cases have been stated, instruct each side to identify and acknowledge the mistakes that its client made in the conflict. Give each side time to discuss what it wants to say and then have the representatives present the conclusions.

   Step 4: Find out what both persons need in the situation.
   - Instruct each side to decide what its client needs from the other in order to resolve the situation (for example, Ben may need money or some other type of compensation depending on his situation; Larry may need time or some alternative for repaying Ben). Let them discuss, then have the representatives present conclusions.

   Step 5: Consider ideas that would meet the needs of both persons.
   - Instruct each side to decide how these needs can be met, then have representatives present ideas.

People's Court

Step 6: Select an option that both persons can agree on.

- Representatives can propose an alternative if the wishes seem unreasonable or unmanageable.
- Ask both sides to discuss together the options for resolution until an agreement is reached that will satisfy both clients.

Step 7: Make a plan.

- Each side should decide on a specific plan of action to resolve the current problem, as well as a plan for avoiding this type of problem in the future. The court reporter should record this information on the Conflict Resolution Agreement Form. Ask each client to sign the document.

6. Once the case is closed, ask the group to discuss the conflict resolution process they just saw demonstrated. The group should then discuss how effective the process was and how this process could be applied to real-life situations.

Application and Insight

It is important to learn how to resolve conflicts well.

Resolving conflicts takes skill and effort.

Resolving conflicts requires the participation of both parties.

Going Deeper

How good are your skills in resolving conflicts?

What is your normal approach when you have a problem with another person?

Why is conflict resolution important? What happens in a group when conflicts are not resolved well?

Seek first to understand...then to be understood.

—Stephen R. Covey, author

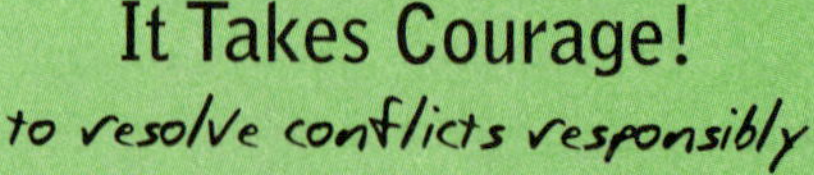

Conflict Resolution

Note how you see each step accomplished as you watch the courtroom proceedings.

Step 1: Get emotions under control.

Step 2: Try to understand both sides of the situation (using active listening skills to listen and to clarify the situation).

Step 3: Apologize for any offenses made.

Step 4: Find out what both persons need in the situation.

Step 5: Consider ideas that would meet the needs of both persons.

Step 6: Select an option that both persons can agree on.

Step 7: Make a plan.

Conflict Resolution Agreement Form

I ______________________________ and I ______________________________ ,
(list names of those involved)

have had a disagreement about ______________________________
______________________________ .

We have chosen to solve the problem by:

____
____
____
____
____

We agree that in the future we will:

____
____
____
____

Signed ______________________________

Signed ______________________________

Date ______________________________

Witnessed by ______________________________
(Signature of facilitator)

Notes

Three things in human life are important: The first is to be kind. The second is to be kind. And the third is to be kind.

—Henry James, novelist

Activity #26 Flip Book Journals

30–45 Minutes

Character Connection
Excellence & Responsibility

Purpose To encourage participants to reflect on their own character development as they learn the topics discussed in this guide

Overview Participants create their own Rules of Good Communication journals in which they record thoughts and reflections on the Ten Rules of Good Communication throughout the various lessons presented.

Life Skill Analyzing and modifying communication weaknesses

Group Size Individual activity with any size group

Cultural and Age Considerations None

Materials Ten Rules of Good Communication (Facilitator Notes); Creating a Flip Book (Facilitator Notes); chalkboard, chart paper, or overhead transparency; chalk or marker; 5 pieces of paper for each participant; pens or pencils; staplers

Preparation Write the Ten Rules of Good Communication on the chalkboard, chart paper, or an overhead transparency. As an option, you may want to copy the page to give as a handout, as well as the Creating a Flip Book instructions.

Instructions

1. Give each participant five pieces of paper to make a flip book journal.
2. Demonstrate how a flip book is created. Allow 5 minutes for participants to create their flip books.
3. Instruct participants to title each page of their flip book journal with one of the Ten Rules of Good Communication, using the abbreviated version listed on Creating a Flip Book (Facilitator Notes).

Flip Book Journals

4. Explain that the journal is to be used to record quotes, notes, and reflections they have concerning their use of the communication rules and their own personal development as good communicators.
5. As an optional activity, the Ten Rules of Good Communication can be made into a class book by having one or more participants illustrate each of the rules.

Application and Insight

Good communication skills are developed over time.

Keeping a record of one's progress is encouraging.

Being accountable for one's communication style helps to develop positive communication skills.

Good communication is a key to developing close relationships.

Going Deeper

Do you consistently communicate in kind and effective ways?

Do you change your communication style with your family, friends, and others? In what ways?

What are some practical ways you can improve in one area of communication?

Good communication is as stimulating as black coffee and just as hard to sleep after. —Anne Morrow Lindberg, poet

It Takes Courage!

to take responsibility for your progress

Ten Rules of Good Communication

1. Practice the Golden Rule at all times.
2. Assume the best of others.
3. Develop good listening skills.
4. Learn to read the body language of others.
5. Use humor wisely.
6. Apologize when you are wrong, and be quick to forgive.
7. Use "I" messages.
8. Try to be calm in conflict; walk away before you are rude.
9. Focus on fixing, not blaming.
10. Practice, practice, and practice some more.

Creating a Flip Book

1. You will need 5 pieces of paper.
2. Lay the first piece of paper on the table. Lay the next piece of paper on top of the first one leaving ½ inch of the first paper exposed at the bottom. Lay the third piece on top, leaving ½ inch of the second paper exposed at the bottom. Repeat with each additional page. The papers should look like ½ inch steps (layers).
3. Carefully grab the top edge of the papers and pull them down to meet the steps (layers). All the papers should line up in equal proportions.
4. Place two or three staples at the top (where the papers are folded).
5. Label each exposed edge with one of the Ten Rules of Good Communication, using the abbreviated versions below:

Ten Rules of Good Communication

1. Golden Rule
2. Assume the best
3. Good listening
4. Read body language
5. Humor
6. Apologize and forgive
7. "I" messages
8. Be calm
9. Focus on fixing
10. Practice

Activity #27 The Golden Rule

15 Minutes

Character Connection
Fairness & Humility

Purpose To help participants understand the Golden Rule

Overview This quick, lighthearted game helps to illustrate the true meaning of the Golden Rule.

Life Skill Choosing to consider the thoughts and feelings of others

Group Size Large (10 or more)

Cultural and Age Considerations None

Materials None

Preparation None

Instructions

1. Invite six volunteers to come to the front of the room.
2. Instruct them to stand in two rows of three, with the rows facing each other.
3. Ask the individuals in one row to think of something they would like the person they are facing to do for them in front of the class (such as sing, run to the back of the room, spin around, touch their toes, etc.—the funnier the better). They should each then tell the person standing across from them what they want them to do, but the people should not do it yet.
4. Ask the group to state the Golden Rule: "Do to others as you would have them do to you." Ask how the rule would apply to this situation. They should soon realize that the person giving the command is the one who will need to do that command if the Golden Rule is to be followed.
5. Once the group has realized this application, ask the individuals in

Do unto others...

The Golden Rule

the first row, one at a time, to do exactly what they had requested the other people to do.

Application and Insight

It is important to consider other people first.

A person should never ask someone else to do what he or she is not willing to do.

Going Deeper

Why is the Golden Rule important?

In what ways would applying the Golden Rule change your daily behavior?

How do you want others to treat you?

Authors' Note: *This is an activity we learned from a high school teacher in Tegucigalpa, Honduras.*

Do to others as you would have them do to you. —The Golden Rule

It Takes Courage!

to put others first

Activity #28 How Do You Rate?

15–30 Minutes

Character Connection
Honesty & Respect

Purpose To help participants recognize the strengths and weaknesses of their personal communication patterns

Overview In this activity, participants are given a list of various everyday scenarios. For each scenario, they use a communication rating scale to rate how they would react in that situation.

Life Skill Improving personal interactions with others

Group Size Individual activity with any size group

Cultural and Age Considerations You may need to change the examples on the How Do You Rate? Handout to make them more culturally and age appropriate.

Materials How Do You Rate? Handout, pens or pencils

Preparation Make one copy of the How Do You Rate? Handout for each participant.

Instructions

1. Give each participant a copy of the How Do You Rate? Handout.
2. Ask participants to complete the handout by honestly analyzing how they interact with others.
3. When the group has finished, ask each participant to identify an area of improvement.
4. Ask them to identify at least three ways they can work to improve, and to record their ideas at the bottom of the handout.
5. Discuss the participants' ratings and the various ideas they suggested to improve their communication patterns.

How Do You Rate?

Application and Insight

It takes commitment to change one's communication style.

Learning to communicate well is a lifelong process.

Evaluating one's communication style can help to determine strengths and identify areas needing improvement.

Going Deeper

What kinds of outside factors affect the way you communicate?

Why is it difficult to communicate effectively at all times?

Ask participants to complete the handout again after several months have passed and compare the results to help them evaluate growth in their personal communication.

I am still learning. —Michelangelo, Italian sculptor and painter (1475–1564)

It Takes Courage!

to admit our faults

How Do You Rate?

Rate yourself by circling the number that represents your likely response to each scenario.

1. Your best friend confides in you that he or she may have a sexually transmitted infection.

Nurturing ⟷ Judgmental

0 1 2 3 4 5 6 7 8 9 10

2. Your sibling borrows your cell phone and breaks it, then comes to you to apologize.

Embracing ⟷ Angry

0 1 2 3 4 5 6 7 8 9 10

3. You find out your friend has just applied for a job that you have also applied for. Your friend doesn't know that you have applied.

Open ⟷ Secretive

0 1 2 3 4 5 6 7 8 9 10

4. Working on a group project, one of your peers suggests an idea that you think wouldn't work as well as the idea you have.

Cooperative ⟷ Ridiculing

0 1 2 3 4 5 6 7 8 9 10

5. Your classmate asks for your help with a very simple math question.

Respectful ⟷ Condescending

0 1 2 3 4 5 6 7 8 9 10

6. You are waiting in line at a store. The person behind you keeps bumping into you.

Polite ⟷ Disrespectful

0 1 2 3 4 5 6 7 8 9 10

7. A new student enrolls in your school. He is from another country, has an accent, and dresses differently.

Accepting ⟷ Rejecting

0 1 2 3 4 5 6 7 8 9 10

8. Your friend gets a better grade on a test for which you studied very hard.

Supportive ⟷ Spiteful

0 1 2 3 4 5 6 7 8 9 10

9. The neighbor's dog chewed up your laundry that was hanging on the clothesline.

Composed ⟷ Threatening

0 1 2 3 4 5 6 7 8 9 10

10. In a large group, your friend mistakenly says something out loud that you told her in private. You want to confront her about this.

Patient ⟷ Impulsive

0 1 2 3 4 5 6 7 8 9 10

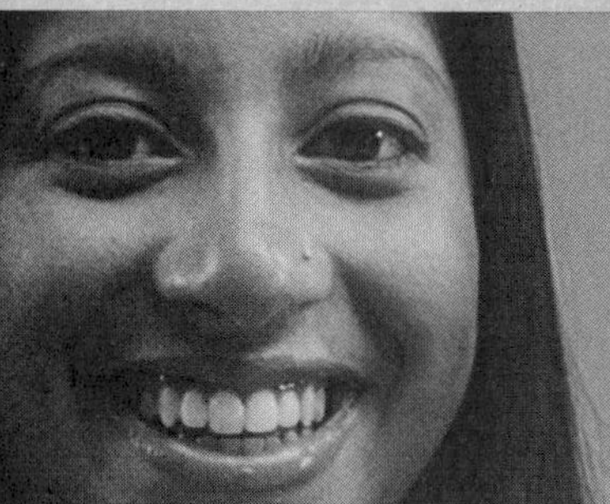

Building Healthy Relationships

The Search for Intimacy 180
Understanding Healthy Relationships 182
Personal Boundaries 183
Evaluating Relationships 185
Types of Relationships 187
Character Connection: Forgiveness 193
It Takes Courage! 195

Building Healthy Relationships

It's in the shelter of each other that people live.

—Irish proverb

Our travels have taken us to the amazing continent of Africa many times over the years. We marvel at the vastness, majesty, and beauty of the open savanna where animals roam freely. On several visits we have had the opportunity to go on safari. What an awesome adventure—driving past a herd of zebra running through the bush, observing baby hippos at play in a lake, spotting a lioness and her cubs resting under the shade of an acacia tree, watching a group of enormous elephants plod across the dirt road right in front of our jeep. It is always a breathtaking experience, as well as educational.

We love talking with the local guides and learning about the habits of the animals. Elephants absolutely amaze us! They express a broad range of emotions: they cry and grieve, express joy and anger—they even laugh! The typical elephant family unit consists of 12 to 20 members all working together. Aunts and cousins help rear and take care of new babies. Often when a baby is struggling or complaining, the other members will go over and caress it. When a mother has a stillborn baby, the mother or other family members may be seen grieving for days. Scientists have documented many cases of elephants returning to a place where a baby has died to mourn, even as much as a year later. They do the same when poachers have killed a member of the herd.

When an elephant is ill or injured, other members of the herd gather around to protect it. They assist the sick elephant by lifting it to its feet with their tusks and then surrounding it to help it remain standing. Even while traveling, the other elephants walk close by the injured one to help it keep its balance and continue walking. They will support that elephant as long as it needs assistance, gradually giving it more room until it walks and functions on its own.

The way elephants care for each other is a good reminder of some of the qualities we as humans seek. We all desire to have the security and joy of sharing our lives in loving, caring relationships. Learning to be a good friend, a contributing family member, and a supportive member of the community contribute to our sense of connection to the world around us.

Typically, the relationship patterns learned in our homes shape our understanding of communication and behavior toward others. The concept of healthy and balanced relationships (where there is give and take and where physical and emotional boundaries are respected) is a particularly difficult challenge for many adolescents who live in unhealthy family environments. Additionally, young people who feel alone, misunderstood, and different from their peers will struggle with relationships and are vulnerable to getting into trouble. The more isolated and rejected young people feel, the harder it becomes for them to emotionally connect in healthy ways. We can help them by offering love and support and by teaching the core character qualities essential for building and maintaining healthy relationships.

In this section we will focus on three types of relationships—family, friends, and the community. Great effort is placed on helping young people to understand the behavioral dynamics and the feelings associated with healthy relationships. Too many youth have never learned the difference between loving and abusive or manipulative interactions. The activities are designed to help youth discover how to have healthy physical and emotional boundaries that are based on respect for themselves and for others. We encourage you to talk about your relationships and the lessons you have learned through the years. Good role modeling is a key to understanding relationships, and your honest discussions will be very motivational and instructional.

The Search for Intimacy

Author Tim Downs tells of a story he read in the *Los Angeles Times* one day about a very ordinary four-year-old girl from a very typical Southern California family.

The family was very busy, always on the go, and the little girl was often left to play by herself. She had everything she needed—except the love and attention that all four-year-olds crave.

One day the family went to a poolside barbecue and, as usual, the little girl was left to play by herself. Everything went as usual until the little girl wandered too close to the edge of the pool, slipped, and plunged in. One of the adults nearby saw her and realized in an instant that she could not swim. Immediately he dove in after her. As he pulled her, coughing and whimpering, to the edge of the pool, all of the other adults gathered around in great alarm. They wrapped her in warm blankets and soft towels, and a swarm of hands stroked her arms and legs and tangled hair. "Honey, what happened?" each one cooed in turn. "Sweetheart, are you all right?" The little girl just smiled and looked up into each loving, concerned face, and in that one moment she tasted all the love and affection she had longed for all her life.

And so the little girl began to develop the habit of "accidentally" falling into swimming pools.

Each time the family attended a poolside barbecue the little girl would wander a little too close to the pool's edge, slip, and fall in. She would float face down, waiting patiently for the big soft towels and the warm loving faces to come to her rescue. She did this again, and again, and again—until the day that no one saw her fall into the pool.

They found her body thirty minutes later lying face down at the bottom.

The coroner's death certificate listed the cause of her death as "drowning." But those who knew her—and her all-too-ordinary family—knew that she really died from something else.

She died from a lack of love.[1]

Many people are desperate for love and intimacy, and as this story illustrates, some will grab at anything to get it. If only the little girl's parents had understood that her actions were a desperate cry for love and attention. She was emotionally starving; "falling" into the pool was a way to get her legitimate emotional need met—even at the risk of drowning.

Countless young people are doing much the same thing, seeking intimacy and love in any way they can. The "pool" they fall into is someone else's bed, beer parties, or a gang. They may learn to be satisfied with any relationship even if it's an unhealthy or abusive one. Many are willing to trade their self-respect, character, and dreams for intimacy. Just as with the girl who drowned, the payment for moments of emotional connection is often greater than expected—babies out of wedlock, HIV/AIDS, alcohol or drug addiction, school failure, and other consequences. Unless someone shows these young people that life can be different, they never get the real thing; they just get more pain and loneliness.

Each of us has a profound need for love and intimacy—to be known and deeply loved by another. The word "intimacy" in Latin is *intimus,* which means "deepest" or "innermost." Psychologist Robert Sternberg defines intimacy as "the experience of warmth toward another person that arises from feelings of closeness, bondedness and connectedness to the other. Intimacy also involves the desire to give and receive emotional support and to share one's innermost thoughts with the other."[2] Intimate relationships are characterized by love, trust, commitment to the relationship and to the welfare of each other, good communication, self-control, and time to enjoy each other's company. We believe that long-lasting intimacy can be found only when two people of character choose to care for each other in a deep way. We must teach adolescents what true intimacy is and help them to seek it in healthy, character-based relationships.

Understanding Healthy Relationships

Our relationships can be just casual acquaintances, as with coworkers and people we meet in the community, or close, as with friends and family. In close relationships, we take on more responsibility for the other person's welfare; both are contributing to the relationship and are committed to serving, protecting, supporting, and challenging each other in positive ways. Building and maintaining these relationships is hard work, but it is worth every ounce of our strength, for it is the quality of our relationships that bring meaning and joy to life. The following are a few characteristics of close, healthy relationships.

Commitment to character: Can you imagine a healthy relationship without character? It is impossible. Healthy relationships are based on the Golden Rule and the commitment to be honest, respectful, kind, fair, and so on. Each person must make a commitment to be a person of character and to hold the other accountable.

"We" mentality: If "I" is the predominant focus of one or both persons, a self-seeking perspective, someone in the relationship is being either overpowered or neglected. A relationship focused on the needs of just one person becomes unhealthy very quickly.

Unconditional love: Healthy relationships are secure and not based on performance. We don't have to always agree with someone's behavior, but we choose to love despite the person's faults. There is security in knowing that we are loved, even when we know we have not been acting lovable.

Willingness to be vulnerable: Healthy relationships require sharing on the part of each person and the willingness to be vulnerable by laying feelings before each other. Being vulnerable demonstrates trust and the ability to be honest in the relationship.

Openness to grow: Healthy relationships must include two healthy people who are willing to change. Each person must be challenged to grow in character, and each must bring something new and fresh to the relationship. Without personal growth on the part of each person, relationships become boring and stagnant.

Characteristics of Healthy Relationships

- Commitment to character
- "We" mentality
- Unconditional love
- Willingness to be vulnerable
- Openness to grow
- Commitment to work through conflict
- Interdependence
- Time to play
- Ready forgiveness
- Balance

Commitment to work through conflict: All relationships will have conflict from time to time. Healthy relationships are characterized by people who can share their concerns and feelings in a respectful way. There is a commitment to work through conflict—not to ignore it or fight about it, but to listen and find a solution. Unresolved conflict is harmful to the relationship.

> *True forgiveness doesn't bury the hatchet while allowing the handle to remain exposed.*
>
> –Glen Van Ekeren, author and motivational speaker

Interdependence: Healthy relationships are composed of two healthy individuals who each have strengths, feelings, and dreams to bring to the relationship. Both individuals are capable of facing life's challenges by giving and receiving support and comfort to each other.

Time to play: Many relationships fail because people do not take the time to play. Too much work and stress will place the relationship into "survival mode," where it exists but does not thrive and grow. People in healthy relationships are able to balance work responsibilities and recreational time together.

Ready forgiveness: In healthy relationships, people assume the best of each other. When wrongs occur, there is a desire to work through the conflict and move forward. Many unhealthy relationships become bitter and vengeful, steeped in resentment because there is no true forgiveness.

Balance: Healthy relationships have a give-and-take mentality. No one person dominates by making all the decisions. In a healthy relationship the opinions, needs, and desires of both persons are given equal weight.

Personal Boundaries

All relationships should have boundaries. We typically think of boundaries in terms of designated space. Between nations, boundaries designate ownership of a particular area of land. Each government is responsible for its own land and is expected to respect the boundary separating it from its neighbors. Border guards patrol the boundary of their respective nations; these guards control the entrance and exit of all people and products, determining who and what can come in and go out.

In the same way, our personal boundaries delineate our personal space from that of others. Some have said, "It is where I end and you begin." We are the border patrol of our own lives, deciding who and what is allowed into or kept out of our personal space, physically and emotionally. Physical boundaries protect our body and determine who is given permission to touch us and how they are allowed to touch us. A physical boundary encompasses things such as how close we want people to sit by us and the physical limits we want to set in romantic situations. Emotional boundaries protect the privacy of our own thoughts and emotions. Just because someone wants to know our thoughts doesn't mean that they have a right to them. We determine what we want to share and what we want to keep private. Personal boundaries are an expression of the combination of trust we have in others and the respect we have for ourselves.

When people violate our boundaries, we usually have an uncomfortable feeling. Ron Herron and Kathleen Sorenson, in *Unmasking Sexual Con Games*, a great resource for teaching boundaries, describe the feeling this way:

> Think about riding in an elevator alone. You have all that space to yourself and you can move around as you please. Gradually, other people get on the elevator. You're not as comfortable as when you were alone. More people get on the elevator; someone steps on your foot, you feel scrunched in a corner. You smell someone's breath and body odor. You feel uneasy because other people have entered the space where you once felt comfortable. They are just too close. You feel crowded and uneasy. They have crossed one of your physical boundaries.[3]

You never know a line is crooked unless you have a straight one to put next to it.

–Socrates, Greek philosopher (469–399 B.C.)

Creating personal boundaries is difficult, especially for adolescents, but boundaries are essential for healthy relationships. Our boundaries define a safe place where we feel comfortable and free to be ourselves. Those with whom we have healthy relationships will understand and accept the boundaries we have established for ourselves. Those who don't respect us will always try to push our personal boundaries—and this is almost always for selfish reasons. In *Boundaries: A Guide for Teens*, Val J. Peter and Tom Dowd suggest that youth should understand the following information about personal boundaries:

1. There is a difference between your social information, superficial information about you that is commonly known, and your private or personal information; divulge private information only to trustworthy people.
2. Expect people to respect your beliefs and values (about drinking, physical touching, faith, and other issues of importance to you).
3. No one should tolerate being manipulated and controlled; ask for help if you are having trouble in this area.

4. Expect people to listen when you say "no."
5. Avoid taking responsibility to "fix" the problems of others, but offer reasonable help and support without taking on responsibilities that aren't yours.
6. Respect the boundaries of others.[4]

Boundaries keep us safe; they are essential to good mental and physical health. We want to help young people learn how to be close to others and interact freely in a relationship, yet be quick to perceive and react when others are attempting to intrude or take advantage of established personal boundaries. We can begin by encouraging youth to identify their own healthy boundaries and by teaching them the importance of respecting the boundaries of others. Each person has the right to say "no," and when they hear the word "no," it means "no" and they should stop what they are doing.

Evaluating Relationships

It can be particularly difficult for young people to understand healthy relationships, especially when they have no positive role models in their home or immediate environment. Adolescents are easily fooled into thinking that their relationships are healthy even when they are full of selfishness and lack character at their core. There is a great need for young people to learn a way to evaluate their own relationships honestly. Following are three important questions for them to consider.

1. What are my feelings in this relationship? Those involved in healthy relationships will experience times of both good and bad feelings. But overall, people feel good about themselves when they are in healthy relationships and bad about themselves when they are in unhealthy relationships. Here's how to tell the difference:

General Feelings in Healthy Relationships	General Feelings in Unhealthy Relationships
encouraged, understood, protected, nurtured, relaxed, joyful, supported, helped, motivated, loved, appreciated, optimistic, uplifted, safe, trusted, secure, valued, free, respected, equal, peaceful, content, energized	ashamed, fearful, inadequate, inferior, worthless, anxious, sad, embarrassed, burdened, blamed, used, criticized, lonely, ignored, judged, isolated, controlled, trapped, disappointed, depressed, insecure, discouraged, guarded

Healthy relationships affirm us and make us feel supported and emotionally connected to the other person. In contrast, unhealthy relationships involve control and manipulation; threats, intimidation, expectation of something (like sex) in return for a gift, and revenge are all means of control. Over time, unhealthy relationships can manifest numerous physical and emotional problems—broken spirits, depression, stress-related sicknesses, and escaping into harmful coping strategies. These are the result of the body trying to cope with many negative emotions. All relationships can have problems, but in healthy relationships there is a commitment to resolve the issues that lead to negative feelings, whereas in unhealthy relationships problems are typically ignored or denied.

2. Is character respected in this relationship? It is important to be aware of the role of good character in a relationship. Is there empathy, honesty, fairness, respect, loyalty, patience, and self-control? Is there trust? Do both persons in the relationship desire to do what is right, even if they fail from time to time? Or is the relationship full of one person's selfishness, hiding, or dishonesty? Someone with bad character does not make a healthy relationship partner.

3. Is there pressure to compromise? If there is integrity in the relationship, words will match behavior. In healthy relationships, people protect each other; in unhealthy relationships, people compromise their integrity for the other person in unhealthy ways. They find themselves doing things they have promised themselves and others they would not do, such as using alcohol, having sex outside of marriage, or being unfaithful. When others pressure us to do things we know are wrong, even after we have said we don't want to do them, there is reason to be concerned. Healthy relationships build us up and help us to grow in positive ways.

> Love is patient and kind.
> Love is not jealous or boastful or proud or rude.
> Love does not demand its own way.
> Love is not irritable, and it keeps no record of when it has been wronged.
> It is never glad about injustice but rejoices whenever the truth wins out.
> Love never gives up,
> never loses faith,
> is always hopeful,
> and endures through every circumstance.
>
> –1 Corinthians 13, *The Message*

No relationship will be perfect, but we must teach youth to be wise, particularly in relationships with the opposite sex. As we encourage them to answer these important questions honestly, it is essential that we be available to help them work through troubling issues. What may seem like frivolous emotions to us can be very painful for adolescents. They will be more likely to listen to our counsel if we truly take the time to show we care.

Building Healthy Relationships

Types of Relationships

Relationships, like people, come in all shapes and sizes. We have relationships with groups such as our family, work associates, faith communities, or community organizations. We also have individual relationships, such as with close friends, acquaintances, or romantic partners. We even have a relationship with ourselves. In this section we focus on helping youth to discover what it means to have healthy relationships with family, friends, and the community.

Relationships with Family

There are many things we get to choose in life, but family is not one of them. Parents don't choose their children, and children don't choose their parents or their brothers and sisters. Each person in a family must learn to love and adapt to each family member if the family is to be healthy. Young people tend to focus on friends more than family, yet we cannot overestimate the power of family members—particularly parents—in the lives of adolescents. Research by M. D. Resnick and colleagues clearly shows that youth who feel emotionally connected to their parents, and who believe their parents have high expectations for their performance in school, tend to make better choices. It is not so much the quantity of time spent with the parents, it is the affiliation and emotional connection young people have with their parents that is important.[5]

Encourage adolescents to talk with their parents, share their thoughts and feelings, and ask parents to share the story of their lives with them. It is through these interactions that young people can learn the values of the family, experience love and support, and learn vital life skills. As young people are challenged to invest in their families and to see their role in the family as important, it will have a powerful impact in their lives. Encourage youth to love and support their siblings, to celebrate their successes, and to avoid rivalry and jealousies, which are always hurtful and destructive. Families are society's glue. Healthy and happy families translate into a healthy and happy community.

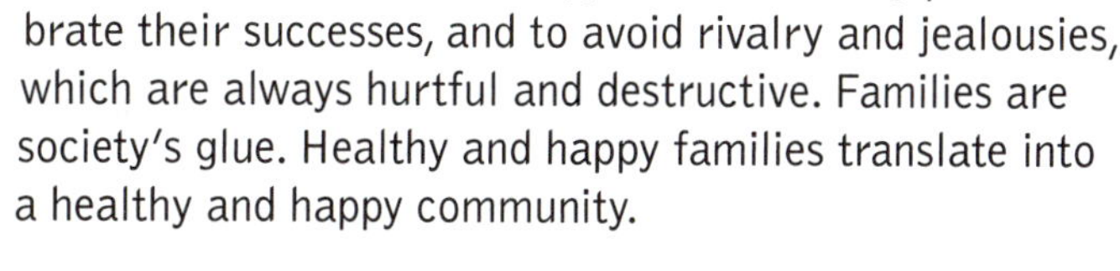

There are many ways to measure success; not the least of which is the way your child describes you when talking to a friend.

–Unknown

As we talk about family relationships, we must consider the emotional hurt that many young people face because they are living with emotionally absent or unhealthy parents in the home. The pain and embarrassment associated with unhealthy parents can overwhelm adolescents and make them feel different or isolated from their peers. It is important that we discuss the elements of healthy families, yet we must be supportive and sensitive as we do so. These youth need to understand that although they cannot change their family members, having their own healthy family is a possibility for them one day. Challenge them to dream about their future families and help them to develop the character traits that are essential for healthy relationships.

Helping youth to develop a "contributor" mentality and to learn the value of family will strengthen and enrich their family relationships. Each of us has an emotional bank account that needs to be rich with feelings of connection, trust, and support. Occasionally we may do things that hurt family relationships (withdrawals), and at other times we do things that make the family stronger (deposits). It is vital that the emotional bank account represents more deposits than withdrawals—more kindness than meanness, more selflessness than selfishness, and more gratitude than demands. The following chart lists some of the behaviors that constitute deposits and withdrawals.

Family Bank Account

Deposits	Withdrawals
◆ Show empathy	◆ Ignore the physical and emotional challenges of others ◆ Don't listen to the problems, interests, or joys of others
◆ Do small acts of kindness	◆ Don't show concern for others and what would make them happy or comfortable
◆ Show loyalty	◆ Talk bad about your family members in public ◆ Betray their confidences in you ◆ Put your friends before your family
◆ Apologize	◆ Don't take responsibility for your wrong attitudes and actions ◆ Blame others for your mistakes
◆ Express thanks	◆ Don't say thank you
◆ Be a contributor	◆ Develop a "taker" mentality and never help with work around the house
◆ Forgive	◆ Hold a grudge and act bitter, even when people apologize
◆ Keep promises	◆ Be unreliable ◆ Break your promises

Six Ways to Help Strengthen Families in Your Community

1. Encourage adolescents to talk with their parents.
2. Encourage parents to connect emotionally with their children.
3. Give youth opportunities to practice good character.
4. Teach effective communication and anger management skills.
5. Introduce youth in troubled families to healthy families in the community.
6. Offer parenting classes for those who are interested.

Healthy families have strong emotional bank accounts. If family members have invested well, they will be able to withstand life's challenges and help each other in times of need; they will also experience the joy and security of knowing that others love them and want them to succeed. It is very important that youth understand this principle and learn to practice it in their families. This principle works for other relationships as well. Whenever possible, we need to extend help and support to the family.

Relationships with Friends

Finding acceptance and emotional connection with their peers is the primary focus of adolescents; most youth will do just about anything to find it, even if it involves getting into trouble or placating a selfish person. Be sensitive to youth who are quite different in appearance or ability from their peers; they often experience excruciating emotional pain when left out. Without guidance from adults, many youth will stumble from relationship to relationship, learning very hard lessons.

Genuine friendship is based on a sincere interest in another and a concern for that person's welfare. Counterfeit friends are usually master manipulators and controllers, more concerned with what they want than with what is good for their friend or the relationship. Most counterfeits use some form of manipulation as a means of control: jealousy and possessiveness, anger, flattery, intimidation, bribery, threats, and occasionally outright physical abuse, especially in male-female relationships. Helping youth to discern the actions of true friends versus counterfeit friends will help them to invest wisely in their friendships and avoid people who take advantage of them.

The following chart contrasts the behaviors of genuine and counterfeit friends.

Genuine and Counterfeit Friends

Genuine Friends	Counterfeit Friends
◆ Listen and try to understand (empathy)	◆ Seem bothered by your problems and uninterested in what is going on in your life ◆ Discount your ideas, values, and beliefs
◆ Speak well of you in public	◆ Make jokes about you, even when they know it will hurt your feelings ◆ Talk with others about your inadequacies
◆ Keep confidences	◆ Tell others your secrets ◆ Betray you behind your back
◆ Tell you the truth about yourself in a loving way	◆ Tell you what you want to hear even if it isn't true ◆ Withhold valuable information from you ◆ Are critical and harsh
◆ Encourage personal growth	◆ Discourage healthy decisions ◆ Are jealous of your successes ◆ Delight in your failures
◆ Commit to working through conflict	◆ Either ignore or minimize conflict, or blame you for it ◆ Never apologize ◆ Seek revenge when they are wronged
◆ Make personal sacrifices for the sake of the friendship	◆ Consistently put their needs first in the relationship ◆ Take rather than give ◆ Help you only when they will get something in return
◆ Are loyal to you	◆ Will abandon you when it costs too much to stand by you
◆ Encourage and support other friendships and interests	◆ Expect your undivided attention
◆ Keep promises	◆ Leave a trail of broken promises
◆ Share their feelings honestly	◆ Lie to you

Building Healthy Relationships

Good friendships are not found, they are made. While it is possible to find a person who would make a good friend, actually becoming friends with that person will require effort. Making and keeping friends can be quite a challenge, which for some requires overcoming shyness or hurt from past relationships. Many young people greatly desire to have a close friend and to be part of a group, but they struggle because they don't understand friendship or have the skills to make it happen. Following are a few suggestions that can help youth to make and keep good friends:

1. *Be the type of person you would want your friend to be.* Learn to practice the Golden Rule with others around you. Be kind, encouraging, and interested in others. Be trustworthy and responsible by being honest and keeping your promises. Learn to say "I'm sorry," and be willing to forgive the mistakes of others.

2. *Learn to ask effective questions.* Isn't it refreshing to have someone ask questions about your life instead of talking on and on about themselves? Questions make a conversation two-way communication. They help others feel valued and that their opinion is important. Ask open-ended questions that require an explanation rather than just a yes or no answer. Inquire about the person's background, interests, and opinions, and seek the person's advice. When we ask good questions, people begin to see that we are interested in them, not just ourselves.

3. *Discover what you have in common.* Friends enjoy spending time together and sharing common interests. Find out what someone likes to do and invite the person to do it with you.

4. *Share your thoughts and feelings.* Deep friendships are built on trust. As people share their thoughts, feelings, and even troubles with each other, and as they find that the other person is caring and trustworthy, a friendship is built. If no one shares, the friendship may remain shallow and unfulfilling. Use discretion here, as trust needs to be built a little at a time; don't reveal deep personal information until you are relatively sure that the person is trustworthy.

5. *Work on a project together.* Many friendships are built when people work together. Invite someone to study with you, or find a way that the two of you can serve someone else in the community.

6. *Take time to care.* Friends enjoy helping and encouraging each other. Look for something you can do to make your friends' lives easier: help them with homework or chores, take time to listen to their problems, tell them they look nice or that they did a great job on a task. This shows that you are interested in them and that you care about the things in their world. These acts of kindness should not have expectations attached. Friends help because they care, not because of what they might get in return.

> *All people in the world are strangers. If you want a friend, you're going to have to go out and make one!*
>
> —Harville Hendrix, counselor

Six Ways to Help Adolescents Build Healthy Friendships

1. Clearly link character development with being a good friend.
2. Discuss specific behaviors associated with genuine friendship.
3. Help them discern when a friend really isn't a friend.
4. Reinforce friendship as a good investment and worth the effort.
5. Teach communications skills to help them express their feelings in the friendship.
6. Share how friends have been important to you.

Relationships with the Community

In addition to encouraging youth to pursue healthy relationships with their family members and friends, it is important to remind young people of their responsibility as members of the community at large. The values of trustworthiness, respect, responsibility, caring, and justice apply to all of our relationships, not just to the people we know. When we care about our community and choose to contribute to the life of the community, we are being good citizens. We don't have to run for public office or donate money to be community-minded; there are many ways to be contributors. Our job is to help youth to see that they have a responsibility to the community and that healthy communities are great places to live.

Serving others is a great way for adolescents to learn some of the character traits needed to develop and maintain healthy relationships. Organizing a group project will make it fun for youth to serve others, especially when they can see the results of their work. Ask youth to identify community needs and let them devise a plan to contribute to the solution. Whenever possible, pair adolescents with good adult role models to create natural mentoring relationships for them.

Listed below are four general ways to think about positively influencing the lives of others. Any of these types of actions, done on behalf of individuals in the community, or the community at large, are acts of good citizenship. As youth look for projects to do in the community, the following may give them ideas about how they can become involved in a positive way.

The friend who can be silent with us in a moment of despair or confusion, who can stay with us in an hour of grief and bereavement, who can tolerate not knowing, not curing, not healing-and face with us the reality of powerlessness-that is the friend who really cares.

-Henri Nouwen, Catholic priest

Serving: Serving others is simply seeing a need and doing something to help. There are innumerable ways we can serve others—making dinner or caring for a sick family in the community, cleaning up trash, watching someone's children for them, or helping at the scene of an accident are just a few examples.

Character Connection: Forgiveness

On an individual level, emotional hurt is not that different from physical hurt. If properly tended, flesh wounds will heal with time. But if the wound is constantly aggravated by picking and scratching, it will not heal and may even become worse. If the scab is disrupted, the wound bleeds anew and may become so inflamed and infected that healing cannot occur. When healing does finally take place, the resulting scars are larger than the original wound. Emotional injury can follow a very similar pattern.

There are two natural responses to being wronged, neither of which will allow emotional wounds to heal. These responses are very basic and have their origin in a basic physiologic level driven by the autonomic nervous system. When we are injured it is quite normal to experience an adrenaline surge that fuels the "fight or flight" response. We can either seek revenge or withdraw.

In revenge, an individual responds to emotional hurt by actively trying to even the score and inflict emotional damage on the offending individual or group. The motivation is, "You hurt me, so I am going to hurt you back." Revenge may take many forms and always has a potential for escalation. We have surely all seen this in action—for example, a child insults another child with a degrading name or comment. The injured child feels compelled to return an equally hurtful comment, and so a consuming process begins. Two wrongs can never make a right, and the wounds inflicted can fester and deepen over days, weeks, or years.

The other response to emotional injury is withdrawal. This is a passive response in which an individual attempts to avoid future injury by avoiding contact. The individual erects invisible walls around himself that grow higher with each additional injury, becoming increasingly effective in keeping others away. What is often unappreciated is that the same walls that keep others

(continued)

Character Connection: Forgiveness *(continued)*

out can lock the individual inside, isolating him from the interpersonal contact needed for growth. The fear, insecurity, and bitterness that result undermine character.

Neither of these choices brings freedom. Neither choice builds character. An alternative approach to revenge and withdrawal is forgiveness. Forgiveness is not a feeling; it is an intentional choice. It is making a decision to let go of the pain and injury caused by another. It is choosing to not punish the person for an offense. It means that someone who says "I forgive you" is making a commitment to the offender to never mention the hurt again. It doesn't mean that what was done is forgotten naturally, but that it will be *intentionally forgotten* and not brought up again.

Forgiveness involves risk. There is always a possibility that the offending party may not seek or accept your forgiveness. Fortunately, the freedom that comes from forgiveness is not dependent on its acceptance. A person who chooses to forgive is released from the bondage of bitterness and mistrust that can build with unforgiveness. Giving and receiving forgiveness are not natural responses but can be developed over time. Learning to forgive may be facilitated by drawing on one's faith. Framing the act of forgiveness in the broader spiritual context makes it easier to offer forgiveness unselfishly and can enhance the freedom that forgiveness offers.

Dare to be different. Dare to be a peacemaker when it is within your power. Put aside any hatred, bitterness, or anger you hold inside. These negative feelings can drain us and control us. They hold us back from reaching our dreams and achieving our full potential. We must have the courage and character to choose forgiveness. When we do, we will find that forgiveness yields compassion, kindness, patience, and peace in our relationships. Forgiveness is freedom.

Protecting: We can protect others by anticipating trouble and offering help or solutions. This can be done by pointing out dangers in the community, such as broken lights, unsafe streets, or walkways that are dangerous. It may even include reporting suspicious activity in your neighborhood, or telling authorities of someone's plans to commit a crime or hurt someone.

Supporting: Supporters encourage us when we are down, come alongside us when we need help, and celebrate with us the good things that happen in life. Cheering at a high school sports event, offering encouragement before a big test, listening to someone's troubles, or saying a kind word to a frustrated teacher are other examples of support.

Challenging: Helping others to see their potential and encouraging them to take risks is important. We can challenge people to learn new skills, grow in their talents, or make beneficial life changes. Try challenging friends to study hard for a test, take a risk and try something new, or change some negative attitudes or behaviors that are holding them back from success.

When our lives are nearing the end, whether we are rich or poor won't be in the forefront of our minds. If we are like others who get a chance to think on our deathbed, our thoughts will be consumed with the special relationships of close friends and family, not the things we acquired in life. The people who are remembered for their goodness live on after their deaths, especially in the minds of those honored few who had the chance to live in their presence.

It Takes Courage!

Have you ever considered how much courage it takes to build healthy relationships? It requires an immense amount of personal risk—sharing your heart at the risk of being ridiculed or ignored, initiating a friendship at the risk of rejection, standing by a friend when it is unpopular or costly, choosing to forgive even when others call you a coward. Setting personal boundaries and keeping them takes courage, as does walking away from unhealthy people who refuse to change. When we hold the hand of a sick person, stand up for people who are being mistreated, and are kind to those in need, we demonstrate the courage to believe that we can make a difference and the courage to dream that the community in which we live can be a better place. Relationships require a lot of hard work, especially within families, but as we grow in character and invest in positive ways in the people around us, we begin to experience the joy of loving and being loved.

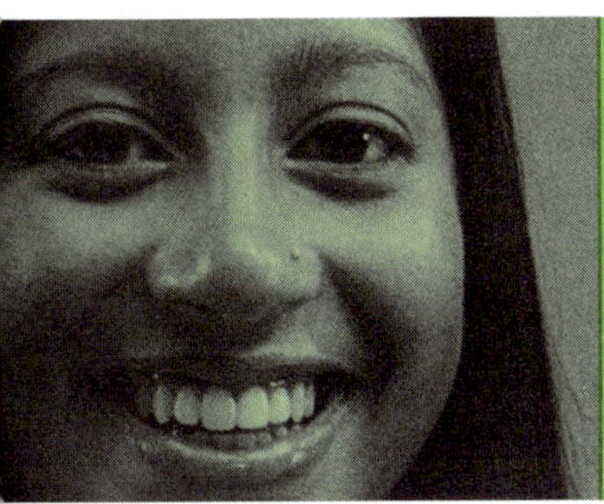

Building Healthy Relationships - Activities

29. Candle Burning 198
30. Community Circle of Trust 200
31. Opposite Poems 202
32. Putting It Into Practice 204
33. Web of Encouragement 206
34. Listen to Your Feelings 208
35. Boundaries 212
36. Parent Preferences 214
37. Family Bank Account 218
38. Genuine and Counterfeit Friends 222
39. The Giving Tree 224
40. The Comparison Game 226
41. Stereotypes 228
42. The Cold Within 232
43. What's Your Style? 236

Activity #29 Candle Burning

Variable Time

Character Connection
Kindness & Respect

Purpose To give participants an ongoing visual reminder of when their behavior is disrespectful or unkind

Overview Over an extended period of time, a single candle is used to keep track of how group members treat each other on a daily basis. A lit candle means the group is behaving with kindness and respect toward one another.

Life Skill Creating an environment that protects and affirms others

Group Size Any

Cultural and Age Considerations None

Materials One 10- to 12-inch, slow-burning taper candle (tall and thin); candleholder (try to find an unusual and creative holder); matches

Preparation Place the candle in the candleholder and draw a line around the candle about one inch from the bottom of the visible part of the candle (the line serves as a marker to indicate when the activity is completed). Place the candle in a prominent place in the room so it can be seen by everyone. Keep the matches handy.

Instructions

1. Explain the following:
    - The candle represents respect among members of the group.
    - The candle will be blown out each time something unkind or disrespectful is said or done in regard to a member of the group.
    - The candle will be relit at the beginning of the next session.
    - When the candle burns to the line at the bottom of the candle, the group will do something special.

    You may decide what that special activity is to be, or you may let the group decide.
2. When the rule is violated, blow out the candle.

Candle Burning

3. Relight the candle at the beginning of the next session.
4. When the candle burns to the line, arrange for the special activity to take place.
5. Begin the following session with a new candle, and repeat the process.

Application and Insight

Healthy and growing friendships require kindness and respect.

There are rewards for being consistently kind and respectful toward others.

Hurtful words can harm a relationship.

Going Deeper

How do you feel when someone else's behavior causes the candle to be blown out?

How has your thinking changed since we started using the candle?

What changes have you seen in your behavior toward one another?

A kind word is like a spring day.

—Russian proverb

It Takes Courage!

to be kind and not critical

Activity #30 Community Circle of Trust

Variable Time

Character Connection
Kindness & Loyalty

Purpose To help build trust and community within a group

Overview Participants form a circle in which they can share and discuss the real issues of their lives on an ongoing basis. Within this context, they learn to trust and support one another. This is a periodic activity as needed.

Life Skill Sharing honestly and protecting the confidences of others

Group Size Any

Cultural and Age Considerations None

Materials None

Preparation None

Instructions

1. Explain to the group that it is very important to build trust and community as they work together. There will be difficult times in all of their lives. As a group, they will encounter frustrations with each other. As the facilitator, you will sometimes get upset with the group. In order to build relationship bridges instead of walls, trust must be developed.
2. Ask the participants to sit in a circle (on the floor or in chairs).
3. Explain that this is a Community Circle of Trust. It is a circle where they will be able to listen to each other and openly discuss the problems or difficulties they are experiencing with each other.
4. It is important to emphasize that what is said around this circle is to be kept in confidence and not shared with others outside. This is one way that trust is built within the group.

Community Circle of Trust

5. A problem can be raised by a member of the group (for example, some of the others in the group have been teasing him at break time) or by the facilitator (for example, the group has been misbehaving and not listening as the facilitator teaches).
6. After the problem has been raised, each group member has the opportunity to make a statement that could help to solve the problem. While someone is speaking, no one else can ask questions or make comments about what that person is saying. Everyone has the choice to share their thoughts briefly. If they don't want to share, they can say "pass."
7. After all the participants have contributed, you can share your own thoughts and feelings.
8. After you have shared, ask the group to help you summarize all of the suggested solutions to the problem.

Application and Insight

For a group to function well, difficulties must be dealt with in a healthy way.

Trust is built when individuals feel safe enough to share their thoughts and feelings within a group.

Open, honest communication by everyone fosters a feeling of community and trust within a group.

Going Deeper

What are the things that make you afraid to share your honest thoughts?

What happens to a group when people don't share honestly and let problems go unresolved?

Trust is the result of a risk successfully survived.
—Jack Gibb, psychologist

It Takes Courage!
to trust others

Opposite Poems

30 Minutes

Character Connection
Empathy & Honesty

Purpose To help participants understand relational concepts through comparison and contrast

Overview Using pairs of opposite words, each participant will construct a simple poem that compares a positive character trait with its opposite negative trait.

Life Skill Discerning the effect of positive and negative qualities

Group Size Individual activity with any size group

Cultural and Age Considerations Participants must understand nouns, verbs, and adjectives.

Materials Pens or pencils, paper

Preparation Choose two opposite characteristics (unhealthy/healthy relationships, bad/good friends, etc.)

Instructions

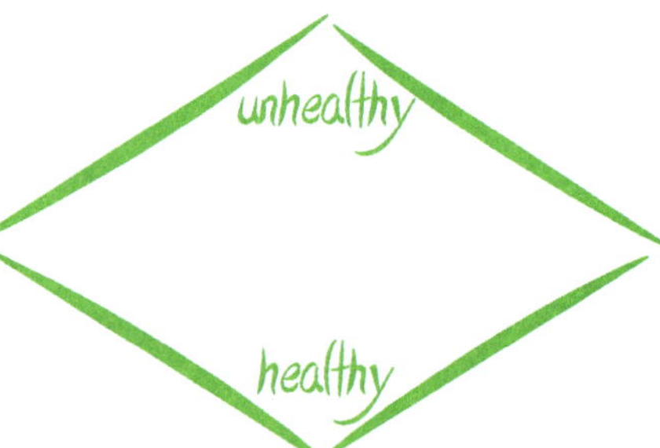

1. Ask participants to write the negative characteristic at the top of a sheet of paper. Then have them skip 6 lines and write the positive characteristic on line 7. Instruct them to write each set of words centered on the page.
2. Below the negative characteristic, ask them to list two nouns that come to mind when they think of that particular characteristic. Again, these words should be centered.
3. On the next line they will list three verbs related to that characteristic, and on the next line they will list four adjectives related to the same characteristic.
4. On the next line they should list four adjectives related to the positive characteristic written at the bottom of the page, then three verbs on the next line and two nouns on the next line, all related to the positive characteristic.

Opposite Poems

5. What they have written should be roughly in the shape of a diamond and should flow from the negative characteristic to the positive characteristic.
6. Ask a few participants to read their poems to the group.
7. Discuss what the participants have learned about the two opposite concepts from writing these poems.

Application and Insight

To understand one thing, it is helpful to compare and contrast it with its opposite.

The feel of an unhealthy relationship is totally different from the feel of a healthy one.

It is important to know the difference between a healthy and an unhealthy relationship or a good and a bad friend.

Going Deeper

What were some of the common words used for each opposite?

What are some of your overall impressions as the poems were read?

How did you feel as you changed from writing the negative words to writing the positive ones?

Keep company with those who make you better. —Unknown

Putting It Into Practice

15 Minutes

Character Connection
Responsibility & Self-control

Purpose To provide an ongoing opportunity to review how character is seen through our behavior

Overview This activity allows the group to explore practical ways they can show various character traits within the group. Taking time regularly to discuss these important issues will encourage participants to consider the character traits reflected in their own behavior.

Life Skill Putting positive character traits into practice

Group Size Any

Cultural and Age Considerations None

Materials Slips of paper (one per participant), pens or pencils, box or basket, chalkboard and chalk

Preparation *Refer to pages 47–48 to review the 15 Core Character Traits.* Write the 15 Core Character Traits on the chalkboard.

Instructions

1. Give each participant a slip of paper.
2. Instruct participants to choose one of the traits and write it on their paper. On the same paper, have them write two or three ways someone could display that characteristic within their educational environment.
3. Have each participant place the paper in the box or basket.
4. At each session, pull out one of the slips and read it. Briefly discuss how the trait written on the paper could be put into practice in the group.

Putting It Into Practice

Application and Insight

We can choose behaviors that reflect positive character qualities.

Growing as a person of character takes time and effort.

Group accountability and encouragement help us to develop good character.

Going Deeper

How have you seen examples of character traits demonstrated by members of the group?

If someone made a list of your character traits based on your behavior, what would be on that list?

What is one character trait you would like to develop in your life? How would it change the way you act now?

You must be the change you wish to see in the world. —Mahatma Gandhi, Indian statesman and spiritual leader

It Takes Courage!

to be accountable to a group for our behavior

Activity #33 Web of Encouragement

15–30 Minutes

Character Connection
Gratitude & Kindness

Purpose To build community within the group by giving participants the chance to give each other specific, positive feedback

Overview This fun group activity encourages participants to recognize the positive traits in one another. The group is asked to stand in a circle and throw a ball of string or yarn to each member while saying something positive about that person. This creates the web of encouragement and demonstrates how they can strengthen relationships in their lives.

Life Skill Publicly acknowledging the positive traits in others

Group Size Any (if more than 20 people, divide into smaller groups)

Cultural and Age Considerations None

Materials A ball of string or yarn

Preparation None

Instructions

1. Ask participants to stand in a large circle.
2. Hand the ball of string to an individual, instructing the person to hold onto the end and then throw the ball to another member of the group. At the same time, he or she should say one positive character trait about that person and explain how it is demonstrated in that person's life (for example, "You're loyal because you never say anything bad about your friends.").
3. The person who receives the ball should hold onto the string, throw the ball to another person in the group, and then say one positive thing about that person.
4. The process should be repeated until everyone has received the ball. The last person should throw the ball back to the first person. (Note: In a small group with fewer than 10 people, you may want to repeat the process, having each person throw the ball to a different person than before.)

Web of Encouragement

5. When the process is completed, have participants lay the string down on the ground and observe the web that has been created.
6. Ask the group to discuss what they learned about each other from the activity and how it affected the overall sense of community in the group.

Application and Insight

Encouragement is a powerful tool for building up one another and strengthening relationships.

Encouragement binds people together in a positive way.

Going Deeper

How did you feel about what was said about you?

How did you have to change your thinking about others in order to find something positive to say about them?

How can this apply to your relationships outside the group?

When spiders unite they can tie down a lion.
—Ethiopian proverb

It Takes Courage!
to accept affirmation

Activity #34

Listen to Your Feelings

45–60 Minutes

Character Connection
Kindness & Respect

Purpose To help participants understand the difference between healthy and unhealthy relationships

Overview Participants evaluate statements to determine if they are healthy or unhealthy and identify how those statements make them feel.

Life Skill Analyzing the health of a relationship

Group Size Any

Cultural and Age Considerations None

Materials Relationship Statements (Facilitator Notes), Analyzing Healthy and Unhealthy Relationships Handout, chalkboard and chalk

Preparation Make one copy of the Analyzing Healthy and Unhealthy Relationships Handout for each participant.

Instructions

1. Ask the group to think of signs that indicate a healthy relationship. What emotions do people feel in a healthy relationship? What are signs of an unhealthy relationship? Record some of the responses on the chalkboard.
2. Give each participant a copy of the Analyzing Healthy and Unhealthy Relationships Handout.
3. Read the Relationship Statements (Facilitator Notes) as examples of statements that individuals may say in a relationship. Ask participants to decide whether the relationship appears to be healthy or unhealthy and to circle the corresponding word on their handout.

Listen to Your Feelings

4. Instruct participants to match it to a specific emotion listed at the top of the handout, or write one of their own (for example, for the statement "My boyfriend made fun of my grades at a party the other night," unhealthy is circled. The feeling chosen might be "stupid.")
5. Once the handout is completed, review it and ask volunteers to explain their responses. Discuss in more depth the differences between healthy and unhealthy relationships.

Application and Insight

A healthy relationship builds up, while an unhealthy relationship tears down.

The relationships that a person chooses have a tremendous impact on his or her life.

Going Deeper

Why do people get into and choose to stay in unhealthy relationships?

What are some practical ways of getting out of an unhealthy relationship?

What relationships in your own life do you see as healthy? Unhealthy?

A leaky house may fool the sun, but it cannot fool the rain.
—Haitian proverb

It Takes Courage!
to walk away from unhealthy relationships

Relationship Statements

As you read each statement to the participants, they will evaluate whether it indicates a healthy or an unhealthy relationship.

1. You're my best friend, but I know you need time with other friends too.
2. You know, that gift you gave me for my birthday wasn't nearly as good as the one John gave me.
3. You're telling that stupid story again?
4. You helped me clean my room last time. It's my turn to help you.
5. I got an A on the math test yesterday. Did you fail again?
6. You did a good job answering that question in class today. I don't think I could have done as well as you did.
7. I don't care if you're tired. You said you'd help me, so get moving.
8. Why do you wear that jacket? It's so old and out of style. It's embarrassing to be with you when you're wearing it.
9. You're trying out for the soccer team this year? Sure, I'll be glad to help you. Maybe you can help me with my math. I'm having a tough time with it.
10. I'm sorry you were sick today. I've collected all your assignments and books for you. Do you need any help?

Write additional statements you would like to add:

Analyzing Healthy and Unhealthy Relationships

Emotions in a Healthy Relationship	Emotions in an Unhealthy Relationship
Peaceful Content Connected Stable Okay Motivated Excited Hopeful	*Discouraged Sad Fearful Insecure Insignificant Stupid Angry Neglected*

For each of the statements read, decide whether you think the statement shows a healthy or an unhealthy relationship. Then decide which emotion that statement would cause in the person it was said to (for example, "My boyfriend made fun of my grades at a party the other night." Unhealthy because it made me feel stupid). Choose an emotion from the lists above, or add one of your own that fits the category. You can use an emotion more than once.

	I think the relationship is...	Because the statement would make me feel... *(choose a word from above or add one of your own)*
1.	Healthy Unhealthy	
2.	Healthy Unhealthy	
3.	Healthy Unhealthy	
4.	Healthy Unhealthy	
5.	Healthy Unhealthy	
6.	Healthy Unhealthy	
7.	Healthy Unhealthy	
8.	Healthy Unhealthy	
9.	Healthy Unhealthy	
10.	Healthy Unhealthy	

Boundaries

45–60 Minutes

Character Connection
Respect & Self-control

Purpose To show the protective value of setting personal boundaries

Overview A blindfolded walk past fictitious "danger zones" sets the stage for a discussion on avoiding risk-taking behavior and setting healthy personal boundaries.

Life Skill Setting and maintaining personal boundaries

Group Size Large (10 or more)

Cultural and Age Considerations None

Materials Four signs that read: Alcohol and Other Drugs, Premarital Sexual Activity, Tobacco, Pornography; masking tape; blindfold

Preparation *Refer to pages 183–185 to review the Personal Boundaries section.* Make the signs. Clear a wide path through the room, or find an outdoor spot at least 30 feet long. Along the path, outline four small areas as "danger zones." These areas should overlap or be near the path. Label these areas with the four signs.

Instructions

1. Choose one participant to walk the path blindfolded. Divide the remaining participants into two groups: Good Guys and Bad Guys.
2. The blindfolded person will attempt to walk the path without stepping into any of the danger zones. He or she will walk the path twice.
3. The Bad Guys are to stand in the danger zones and attempt to talk the person into their zones.
4. The Good Guys are to position themselves around the danger zones to help protect the person from those areas.
5. Ask the blindfolded person to begin walking the path. Both groups should call out directions all at once to the blindfolded person.
6. On the first trip, the blindfolded person is not allowed to respond verbally and can only listen to what is being said.

Boundaries

7. On the second trip, the blindfolded person is allowed to ask for directions to be repeated. He or she can also set boundaries the following ways:
   - Raising a hand means the Bad Guys have to be quiet.
   - Touching the tape or the edge of a danger zone keeps the people quiet in that zone.
   - Stomping a foot means the person wants more directions from the Good Guys.
   - Touching someone means that only that person can talk.
8. After each trip, discuss how well the person did, what his or her body language communicated while walking the path, how successful the individual was at avoiding danger zones, etc. After the second trip, compare the difference it made when the person was allowed to set personal boundaries.
9. Discuss the issue of personal boundaries by asking such questions as:
   - What are examples of boundaries that people might set?
   - With whom do we need to set boundaries?
   - What are some boundaries you have set or you have observed others setting?

Application and Insight

Personal boundaries are necessary for healthy relationships.

Abuse happens when a person violates someone else's personal boundaries.

An individual is the only one who knows what boundaries are appropriate for him or her.

Going Deeper

What kind of boundaries do you have in your own life? Are they appropriate or not?

How do you feel when your boundaries have been violated?

Do you tend to push past the boundaries of others, or allow them to push through yours?

What steps can you take to establish better boundaries?

Adapted and used with permission from FRIENDS FIRST, Inc.

I'm not afraid of storms for I'm learning to sail my ship.
—Louisa May Alcott, author

It Takes Courage!
to set healthy personal boundaries and respect the boundaries of others

Parent Preferences

15–30 Minutes

Character Connection
Honesty & Respect

Purpose To build relationships within the home by fostering communication between parents and children

Overview A fun survey helps participants learn valuable information about their parents and becomes a catalyst for positive communication within the home. This activity is done over two sessions.

Life Skill Cultivating strong family ties

Group Size Individual activity with any size group

Cultural and Age Considerations Be sensitive to children who do not live with their parents or family members; substitute another adult they trust. You may need to change some of the questions to make the activity more culturally relevant.

Materials What's Your Guess? Handout, Discussion Questions Handout, pens or pencils

Preparation Make one copy of the What's Your Guess? and the Discussion Questions Handouts for each participant.

Instructions

1. Give each participant a copy of the What's Your Guess? Handout.
2. Ask participants to choose a parent, grandparent, or other caring adult for the activity.
3. Have participants complete the "My Guess" column of the handout.
4. As a homework assignment, ask the participants to interview the person they selected (without showing them the form) and record their answers.
5. In the next session, compare the "guesses" with the person's answers.
6. Distribute the Discussion Questions Handout to each participant. Ask them to answer the questions on their own.
7. Discuss the results as a group.

Parent Preferences

Application and Insight

Family members are more willing to discuss issues with one another when they know each other well. It is always surprising to discover how little a person may know about his or her family.

It helps to practice asking questions because it enhances active listening skills.

Going Deeper

If you were doing this activity over again, what would you do differently?

Interview other family members.

Develop some additional questions of your own.

It's in the shelter of each other that people live. —Irish proverb

It Takes Courage!
to build deep relationships with our parents

Handout

What's Your Guess?

Person Interviewed: ______________________________

Complete the first column, My Guess, before your interview. Complete the second column while you are conducting your interview.

Question	My Guess	Their Answer
What is your favorite food?		
What is your favorite thing to do?		
Who do you admire the most?		
What do you spend most of your day doing?		
What makes you sad?		
What is your favorite color?		
If you had the chance to go anywhere in the world, where would you go?		
What is your favorite memory as a child?		
What animal or object best describes your personality?		
If you could be anything in the world, what would you choose to be?		
What is your favorite piece of clothing?		
What was the hardest decision you had to make in your life?		
What is one of the funniest things that ever happened to you?		
When are you the happiest?		
Who is your closest friend?		
Where is your favorite place in the house?		

Discussion Questions

Answer the following questions after you have completed the What's Your Guess? Handout.

1. What surprised you the most while you were doing this activity?

2. Which question was the most difficult for the other person to answer?

3. Do you think the person enjoyed doing this activity with you?

4. How close were your answers to the other person's answers?

Activity #37 Family Bank Account

45–60 Minutes

Character Connection
Loyalty & Service

Purpose To help participants understand the importance of making investments in family relationships

Overview Participants create a "family bank account" record from their own family history as a way of finding out how well they are investing in their family relationships.

Life Skill Contributing to family in meaningful ways

Group Size Any

Cultural and Age Considerations None

Materials Dimensions of Health and Wellness (Facilitator Notes), Family Bank Account Summary Handout, 4 pieces of chart paper, marker, pens or pencils, chalkboard and chalk

Preparation *Refer to pages 35–37 in the Introduction to review the Dimensions of Health and Wellness, and to page 188 in Relationships to review the concept of the family bank account.* Draw the Dimensions of Health and Wellness (Facilitator Notes) on the chalkboard, leaving plenty of space to write in each section. Make one copy of the Family Bank Account Summary Handout for each participant. On each piece of chart paper, write one of the Health and Wellness Categories at the top. Below the category, write "Deposits"; halfway down the paper, draw a line and write "Withdrawals." Post these charts around the room where participants will have access to them.

Instructions

1. Ask participants to discuss the role of the family and how healthy families enrich our lives in each dimension. Write their ideas in the diagram on the chalkboard.
2. Introduce the concept that a healthy family is much like a healthy bank account (plenty of money in the bank to use as needed or desired). Spending all the available money leaves a person weak and vulnerable to problems. Money must be put into the bank (deposits) in order to take money out (withdrawals). Without deposits, most people will find an empty bank account one day.

Family Bank Account

3. Explain that each person is responsible for ensuring a healthy family bank account (there are strong, loving, supportive relationships among family members in each dimension). Explain the difference between the "contributor" and "taker" mentalities.
4. Ask the participants to choose one of the categories and go stand near the corresponding chart. They will need to take a pen or pencil to write on the chart.
5. Explain that the top of the chart is to record "Deposits" (a contributor mentality). The bottom of the chart is used to record "Withdrawals" (a taker mentality).
6. Give participants 10 minutes to write specific examples of how they can make "deposits" into and "withdrawals" from their family. Ask them to assign a value of 1–3 for each item. Use 1 for items that are of average importance, 2 for above average importance, and 3 for items that are seriously important.
7. When participants are finished, ask each group to share their responses.
8. Distribute the Family Bank Account Summary Handout and explain that participants will be creating a bank account based on their family interaction. Give them 10–15 minutes to record events that have occurred recently (in the last day or week).

Application and Insight

A healthy family is one in which each member is committed to contributing positively to the lives of every other member.

It is important to view family members as real people with personal needs and not just people to be used for gain.

It takes effort to value and treasure family members and not take them for granted.

Going Deeper

Why is it important to contribute to your family's well-being? What happens to a family when one member is constantly withdrawing and never depositing?

How is your personal family bank account? What are practical ways you can increase your deposits and reduce your withdrawals?

There was a man, some called him mad;
the more he gave, the more he had. —John Bunyan, author of *Pilgrim's Progress*

It Takes Courage!
to be a giver rather than a taker

Facilitator Notes

Dimensions of Health and Wellness

encompasses beliefs, values, ethics, and the ability to find meaning and purpose in life; for many, it includes issues of faith and hope

the ability to earn a living and enjoy it

social

the ability to interact in relationships with others; includes empathy, showing respect, and the ability to set relational boundaries

mental

logical thinking, creativity, mental alertness, and understanding

physical

the functions and activities of the body; includes muscular strength, endurance, flexibility, and body composition

emotional

the ability to experience a wide range of situations and feelings, give and receive love, cope with the spectrum of emotions, and enjoy life

Handout

Family Bank Account Summary

In each ledger below, list specific examples of the ways you have interacted in your family. Assign each item a value in terms of its importance:

1 = average importance *2 = above average importance* *3 = seriously important*

DEPOSIT SHEET

Physical		Mental		Social		Emotional		Spiritual		Occupational	
Total		Total		Total		Total		Total		Total	

WITHDRAWAL SHEET

Physical		Mental		Social		Emotional		Spiritual		Occupational	
Total		Total		Total		Total		Total		Total	

Add all the Deposit Sheet Totals: ______________________

Add all the Withdrawal Sheet Totals: ______________________

Subtract the Withdrawals from Deposits: ______________________

According to your ledger, are you more of a "Contributor" or a "Taker" in your family?

Genuine and Counterfeit Friends

30 Minutes

Character Connection
Humility & Loyalty

Purpose To encourage participants to evaluate their relationships with friends

Overview This group brainstorming activity will help participants identify the differences between genuine and counterfeit friends by analyzing examples.

Life Skill Recognizing genuine and counterfeit friendships

Group Size Any

Cultural and Age Considerations None

Materials Paper, pens or pencils, chalkboard and chalk

Preparation *Refer to page 190 to review examples of genuine and counterfeit friends.*

Instructions

1. Divide the participants into two groups, and give each person paper and a pen or pencil.
2. Assign each group one of the following statements:
   - Friends should . . .
   - Friends should not . . .

3. Give groups time to discuss and to complete their statement by listing at least 10 examples.
4. Ask the groups to report what they wrote, and record their answers on the chalkboard.
5. Lead a discussion about the difference between how a "genuine" friend acts and treats someone and how a "counterfeit" friend interacts with others.
6. Give participants a few minutes to evaluate and record what kind of friend they are to others.

Genuine and Counterfeit Friends

7. Ask participants to determine five ways they will improve how they treat their friends and to record these commitments on their paper.
8. Allow volunteers to share some of their commitments with the group.

Application and Insight

Real friends are people of good character.

It is important to be able to identify the difference between genuine and counterfeit friends.

People often judge others by the friends they choose; choose wisely.

Going Deeper

If you have any counterfeit friends, what can you do about it?

If you have any of the characteristics of a counterfeit friend, what can you do to become a true friend?

Challenge the group to make several commitments to treat each other as genuine friends and not as counterfeit ones. Write these commitments down on a sheet of chart paper and display it in the meeting room.

Hold on to a true friend with both hands. —Nigerian proverb

It Takes Courage!
to be a real friend

Activity #39 The Giving Tree

30 Minutes

Character Connection
Kindness & Service

Purpose To encourage participants who meet on an ongoing basis to get involved in community service projects as individuals and as a group

Overview A large paper tree constructed by the group is used to keep an ongoing record of the group's gifts of service to the local community.

Life Skill Helping others in effective ways

Group Size Any

Cultural and Age Considerations None

Materials Large sheets or roll of paper (brown paper, newspaper, etc.); brown paint (if brown paper is not used); green paper (for leaves); scissors; tape, tacks, or stapler (to attach tree and leaves to wall); pens or pencils; small box, basket, or envelope (to store unused leaves near tree). If paper and paint are not available, the tree and leaves can be drawn on a wall or on a chalkboard.

Preparation Decide where and how to attach the tree to the wall.

Instructions

1. Talk to the participants about the importance of serving the community. As a group it would be wonderful to be known as people of good character who serve others.
2. Introduce the Giving Tree idea:
   - The group will create a paper tree that will be used to keep track of all the ways the group helps the community throughout the year.
   - Once the tree is in place, each time the group or any individual in the group performs an act of service in the community, a leaf will be labeled with the action and placed on the tree. These actions may include volunteer activities like painting a building in the school, tutoring someone, babysitting for a friend, or cleaning house for an older person.

The Giving Tree

3. Give the group time to create the tree and hang it on the wall, and ask several participants to cut out a large pile of leaves for future use.
4. Put blank leaves, a pen, and tape in a container and place the container in a convenient area so members can fill out leaves whenever they have something to contribute to the tree.

Cook for a friend

Application and Insight

The group can demonstrate good character by extending a helping hand.

Taking responsibility for building a better community can truly make a difference.

As people reach out and touch the lives of others through kindness, the result is joy and satisfaction, and their self-esteem is enhanced.

Going Deeper

Challenge the participants to encourage their own families to be involved in a community service project.

Plant a live "giving tree" somewhere to serve as a reminder of the importance of giving to make the community more productive and beautiful.

Friendship is a sheltering tree. —Samuel Taylor Coleridge, British poet and philosopher

It Takes Courage!
to unselfishly serve the community without expecting anything in return

Activity #40 The Comparison Game

15 Minutes

Character Connection
Varies with the lesson topic

Purpose To review or introduce a new topic by using comparisons to stimulate participants' thinking on a topic

Overview This creative game of comparing everyday items to abstract concepts is an excellent way to introduce any topic and help participants begin to think in a certain direction. Participants will be given items to compare to the topic being discussed.

Life Skill None

Group Size Any

Cultural and Age Considerations None

Materials Any objects such as an egg, cell phone, piece of cloth, plate, toothbrush, CD, candle, pile of sticks, plant, candy, bar of soap, dirt, spatula, crayons, coin, photo, socks, watch, hair brush, etc. (two objects for each group); paper; pens or pencils

Preparation Gather the objects you want to use.

Instructions

1. Divide participants into groups of five to seven individuals. Give each group two objects.
2. Choose a topic such as Friends, Character, Relationships, Family, etc.
3. Explain that each group is to think of as many ways as possible that this object relates to the chosen subject. Instruct the groups to use *similes* to list their comparisons. (A simile is a comparison of one thing to another thing using the word "like." For example, "Friends are like crayons because they bring color into your life," or "Friends are like this candle because they help you when it's hard to see the right way.")

The Comparison Game

4. Ask each group to share a few of their ideas.
5. Use these comparisons to introduce the subject of the lesson.

Application and Insight

Comparisons can be helpful in providing a better understanding of deep concepts.

A tangible example can help bring clarity to a difficult concept.

Going Deeper

Choose whatever questions are appropriate for the subject to be discussed.

Participants can bring an item from home to talk about themselves so others can get to know them better.

Memories of our lives, of our works and our deeds will continue in others. —Rosa Parks, U.S. civil rights leader

It Takes Courage!

to be creative in front of other people

Stereotypes

45–60 Minutes

Character Connection
Empathy & Fairness

Purpose To help participants understand that stereotyping others is harmful to building successful relationships

Overview Stereotyping others prevents us from recognizing their unique qualities or helping them to reach their potential. It cripples relationships. We experience a feeling we do not soon forget. This activity enables participants to know the feeling of being labeled, misunderstood, and treated differently. Through this powerful learning experience, they can more readily identify with the feelings of others who are stereotyped.

Life Skill Treating all people with respect and dignity

Group Size Large (20 or more)

Cultural and Age Considerations This activity is best for participants 10 years of age and older. Use examples that will be appropriate for your cultural setting.

Materials Provide one of each of the following items for every participant: paper strip that will fit around the head like a headband, paper clip, name-tag-size pieces of paper, pen or pencil, safety pin; Survivors Handout

Preparation Make one copy of the Survivors Handout for each group. Think of six different roles from the local culture (banker, field worker, janitor, professor, lawyer, homemaker, maid, astronaut, etc.). Divide the headband strips into groups of six and write a different role on each headband. You should end up with several groups of the same six roles.

Group 1	Group 2	Group 3
Role 1	Role 1	Role 1
Role 2	Role 2	Role 2
Role 3	Role 3	Role 3
Role 4	Role 4	Role 4
Role 5	Role 5	Role 5
Role 6	Role 6	Role 6

Stereotypes

Instructions

1. Ask the group to define the word "stereotype."
2. After a brief discussion, suggest the following definition and ask for participants' reaction to it: "A mental category—a picture in our heads—that is based on exaggerated and inaccurate generalizations which are either favorable or unfavorable to a group of people. It is a prejudiced thought used to describe all members of the group."
3. Ask participants to stand in lines of six. Give each group a set of headbands and six paper clips. Make sure the headbands are handed to participants upside down, so the writing cannot be seen. Instruct participants not to look at what is written on the headbands until they are given permission to do so.
4. Once everyone has a headband and a paper clip, ask them to place the headband on the head of the person standing in front of them so the writing now shows, using the paper clip to fasten the headband in place. Explain that participants should not know what is written on their own headband. Ask them to sit in a circle in their groups.
5. Explain the following scenario:

   You were traveling for several hours on an airplane when a terrible storm forced the pilot to make an emergency landing in a desert far from civilization. Miraculously, no one was hurt, but the plane is beginning to burn so you must leave quickly. You and your group have time to grab 10 items from the plane before it explodes. Together you must agree on the items and then rank them in order of importance. As you interact with one another, treat each other as you would treat someone who fits the stereotype indicated on that person's headband. This should be done without letting the person know what is written on his or her headband.

6. Give each group a copy of the Survivors Handout, and then allow 10–15 minutes for the participants to interact with each other.
7. Once the time is up, give each person a piece of paper and a pen or pencil. Ask participants to write one word to describe how they felt as a result of how their group members treated them (stupid, important, ignored, smart, etc.). Ask participants to pin these pieces of paper onto their shirts.

Stereotypes

8. Instruct participants to look for others who felt the same way they did, and to form new groups based on these feelings.
9. Once everyone has found a new group, ask them to take off their headbands and see what stereotype they were given.
10. Lead the entire group in a discussion of stereotypes based on this activity.

Application and Insight

Stereotyping cripples relationships.

Stereotyping prevents people from recognizing their individual qualities and reaching their full potential. This leads them to seek the company of others who feel similarly labeled—creating boundaries that divide rather than unite us.

Even positive stereotypes are damaging. For example, suggesting that all women are feminine sets an unrealistic expectation on those who are more forceful, direct, and assertive.

Going Deeper

What were some of your frustrations during this activity?

In what ways have you been stereotyped by others? In what ways do you stereotype others?

Why is stereotyping destructive? What happens to someone when they are stereotyped?

No one can make you feel inferior without your consent. —Eleanor Roosevelt, former U.S. First Lady

It Takes Courage!
to treat all people kindly and respectfully

Survivors

You were traveling for several hours on an airplane when a terrible storm forced the pilot to make an emergency landing in a desert far from civilization. Miraculously, no one was hurt, but the plane is beginning to burn so you must leave quickly. You and your group have time to **grab 10 items** from the plane before it explodes. Together you must agree on the items and then rank them in order of importance.

As you interact with one another, treat each other as you would treat someone who fits the stereotype indicated on that person's headband. This should be done without letting the person know what is written on his or her headband.

✓		Rank
☐	Rope	______
☐	Bag of candy	______
☐	Mirror	______
☐	Flares	______
☐	Brandy	______
☐	Flashlight	______
☐	Laptop computer	______
☐	Knife	______
☐	Case of peanuts	______
☐	First-aid kit	______
☐	Case of diet soda	______
☐	Compass	______
☐	Matches	______
☐	Shovel	______
☐	Magazines	______
☐	Map	______
☐	Pen and note pad	______
☐	Fire extinguisher	______
☐	Batteries	______
☐	Two blankets	______
☐	Radio	______
☐	Umbrella	______
☐	Cell phone	______
☐	Floating seat cushions	______
☐	Oxygen	______

The Cold Within

30 Minutes

Character Connection
Empathy & Forgiveness

Purpose For participants to relate a poem to issues in society today and to evaluate the role of forgiveness in their own lives

Overview After reading "The Cold Within," participants will analyze the effects of unforgiveness in our society and evaluate their own efforts toward forgiveness.

Life Skill Recognizing the need for forgiveness and reconciliation

Group Size Individual activity with any size group

Cultural and Age Considerations None

Materials The Cold Within (Facilitator Notes), What Was the Cold Within? Handout

Preparation Make a copy of the What Was the Cold Within? Handout for each participant.

Instructions

1. Read aloud the poem "The Cold Within" (Facilitator Notes).
2. Distribute the What Was the Cold Within? Handout to each participant.
3. Ask participants to read the box on the left side of the handout, and in the box on the right describe the internal struggle of each man around the fire.
4. Discuss how these issues are reflected in society today.
5. Ask participants to answer the questions on the bottom of the handout and to discuss their answers in small groups.

Application and Insight

When people hold on to unforgiveness, they only destroy themselves.

Forgiveness leads to freedom.

The Cold Within

Letting go of prejudice and stereotypes and treating others with love and kindness brings satisfaction in relationships.

Forgiveness is not a one-time act but a process.

Going Deeper

Can you think of other examples of social issues—in your community, nation, or the world—that are associated with lack of forgiveness?

What are some practical ways to help address the lack of forgiveness seen in our society?

What are ways that we can show forgiveness?

Hatred paralyzes life; love releases it. Hatred confuses life; love harmonizes it. Hatred darkens life; love illuminates it.

—Martin Luther King, Jr., U.S. civil rights leader

It Takes Courage!

to forgive others

The Cold Within

Six humans trapped by happenstance, in black and bitter cold,
Each one possessed a stick of wood, or so the story's told.

Their dying fire in need of logs, the first man held his back,
For of the faces 'round the fire, he noticed one was black.

The next man looking 'cross the way saw one not of his church,
And couldn't bring himself to give the fire his stick of birch.

The third one sat in tattered clothes, and looking quite unhealthy,
Why should his log be put to use to warm the calloused wealthy?

The rich man just sat back and thought of the wealth he had in store,
And how to keep what he had earned from the lazy, shiftless poor.

The black man's face bespoke revenge as the fire passed from sight,
For all he saw in his stick of wood was a chance to spite the white.

The last man of this forlorn group did naught except for gain,
Giving only to those who gave to him was how he played the game.

Their logs held tight in death's still hand was proof of human sin,
They didn't die from the cold without, they died from the cold within.

What Was the Cold Within?

In the boxes below: 1. Identify the internal struggle of each man. 2. Describe how his struggle is reflected as an issue in our society today.

Six humans trapped by happenstance, in black and bitter cold,
Each one possessed a stick of wood, or so the story's told.

Poem	Response
Their dying fire in need of logs, the first man held his back, For of the faces 'round the fire, he noticed one was black.	
The next man looking 'cross the way saw one not of his church, And couldn't bring himself to give the fire his stick of birch.	
The third one sat in tattered clothes, and looking quite unhealthy, Why should his log be put to use to warm the calloused wealthy?	
The rich man just sat back and thought of the wealth he had in store, And how to keep what he had earned from the lazy, shiftless poor.	
The black man's face bespoke revenge as the fire passed from sight, For all he saw in his stick of wood was a chance to spite the white.	
The last man of this forlorn group did naught except for gain, Giving only to those who gave to him was how he played the game.	

Their logs held tight in death's still hand was proof of human sin,
They didn't die from the cold without, they died from the cold within.

How have you been affected by someone not offering forgiveness or not practicing the Golden Rule?

Is there someone you need to forgive? In what ways can you show forgiveness to this person?

What's Your Style?

30–60 Minutes

Character Connection
Honesty & Respect

Purpose To provide participants with an opportunity to identify their own interactive style and the interactive style of others

Overview Participants are introduced to and then choose from four different styles of interaction. Each style then gathers as a group to explore the uniqueness of their style.

Life Skill Select a life skill from the Life Skills Table

Group Size Large (20 or more)

Cultural and Age Considerations None

Materials What's Your Style? (Facilitator Notes); Group Interaction Styles Handout; signs labeled North, South, East, and West; tape

Preparation Make one copy of the Group Interaction Styles Handout for each participant. Place North, South, East, and West signs in four different locations in the room to identify where groups will meet.

Instructions

1. Explain that it is essential for people to understand each other and effectively communicate in order to be a productive team. We need to know our own style of interacting with other people and develop an appreciation for the styles of others.
2. Use What's Your Style? (Facilitator Notes) to describe the four styles of interaction.
3. Help participants to choose the style of communication they use in a group setting or on a team. Some people may feel that they function in two or more categories; ask them to choose the category that is most predominant.
4. Point out the four different stations where the signs are hanging and ask participants to go to the station of the style they have chosen.
5. Instruct the members in each group to work together to complete the Group Interaction Styles Handout.
6. While the participants are working, circulate around the room, taking notes about each group (for example, "The North group is on task and finished first." "The East

What's Your Style?

group is solving the world's problems." "The South group is being warm and kind to each other but there is no leader to keep the discussion focused." "The West group is quarreling over the perfect word and meaning to be written on their handout.") Look for unusual comments from each group that would distinguish their style. The more you "play" with the groups (especially as you walk around and write down specific examples from the group interaction), the more successful the outcome.

7. After 15 minutes, read some of the observations you jotted down. This always provides a lot of fun and laughter. Point out body language, noise level, and tone of the group (for example, the North group may have remained standing and were very forceful in their tone and gestures, whereas the South group may have been seated and all equally participating and agreeing with everyone).
8. Give each group a chance to report the results of their discussion.

Application and Insight

We are all different individuals with varying gifts and abilities.

It is important to understand how we function best in a group.

It is equally important to understand and to value the way others function best.

If everyone were the same, we would be very ineffective.

Going Deeper

How will understanding the interactive styles of others on your team help you work with them more effectively?

How will you use this knowledge to overcome obstacles to communicating effectively?

How will you maximize the strength of the interactive styles of your teammates to accomplish your goals?

Source: There are several different versions of this activity. We thank Marilyn Hale of the Irvine Unified School District in California for providing this idea.

The most important single ingredient in the formula of success is knowing how to get along with people. —Theodore Roosevelt, former U.S. President

It Takes Courage!

to value those who are very different from you

What's Your Style?

Use this diagram to explain each of the styles of interaction.

NORTH—Takes Immediate Action

- Completes a given task as quickly as possible
- Does not have a lot of attention to detail
- Views the end product as the main goal

WEST—Wants Every Detail

- Needs to see all the pieces and have great understanding of all the components before moving forward in discussion
- Wants to know who, what, when, where, why, and how

EAST—Sees All Possibilities

- Is not focused on the specific task
- Discusses all possible options
- Is creative in covering the topic, but often doesn't stay on the point
- Considers the process more important than the product

SOUTH—Seeks to Support

- Offers a lot of support to others
- Will not "push in" to have a voice unless invited
- Is agreeable
- Enjoys sharing thoughts among others

Group Interaction Styles

1. What four adjectives best describe the strengths of our style?

2. What four adjectives best describe the limitations of our style?

3. What group frustrates you the most, and why?

4. What do other people need to know about us so that we can work together more effectively?

5. In five words or less, the slogan that best describes our group is ______________

____.

Sand or Stone

Two friends were walking through the desert. At some point they had an argument, and one friend slapped the other in the face. The one who got slapped was hurt, but without saying anything, wrote in the sand:

"TODAY MY BEST FRIEND SLAPPED ME IN THE FACE."

They kept on walking until they found an oasis, where they decided to go for a swim. The one who had been slapped started to drown, but his friend saved him. After he recovered from the near drowning, he wrote on a stone:

"TODAY MY BEST FRIEND SAVED MY LIFE."

The one who had first slapped and later saved his friend said, "After I hurt you, you wrote in the sand and now, you write on a stone, why?"

His friend replied: "When a friend hurts us we should write it down in sand where the winds of forgiveness can erase it away. But, when a friend does something good for us, we should engrave it in stone where no wind can ever erase it."

Making Wise Decisions

The Decision to Grow	246
Managing Negative Emotions	247
Handling Conflict with Others	249
Choosing Wisely Under Pressure	250
Avoiding Risky Behavior	252
Character Connection: Rationalizing Behavior	259
It Takes Courage!	260

Making Wise Decisions

He who reigns within himself and rules his passions, desire, and fears is more than a king.

—John Milton, 16th century English poet

There is a great battle that rages inside me.
One side is a soaring eagle. Everything the eagle stands for is good and true and beautiful. It soars above the clouds. Even though it dips down into the valleys, it lays its eggs on the mountaintops.
The other side of me is a howling wolf. And that raging, howling wolf represents the worst that is in me. He eats upon my downfalls and justifies himself by his presence in the pack.
Who wins this great battle?
The one I feed.

-Native American tale

Wouldn't you love to kill that howling wolf once and for all? Just think how easy our lives would be if we could simply feed the eagle and starve that wolf to death. We would have it made, wouldn't we? But the reality is that the big, bad wolf won't die; he is part of our human nature, and his fierce attacks surprise us when we least expect them. The best we can hope for is to try to give healthy nourishment to the eagle while denying that old wolf as much as possible, keeping him weak and able to muster only feeble attacks that we can easily recognize.

As educators and youth service providers, we have the challenge of inspiring young people to see themselves as eagles—soaring, dreaming, fully capable, and able to navigate their lives. And yet so many of our youth feel like anything but an eagle. Many live in families where parents are feeding their wolves with drugs, sex, violence, and other forms of abuse; some are living with parents who care only about acquiring money and things; some live in families broken by divorce or death. Too many youth are surviving, not soaring. But despite this cruel reality, our challenge is to help all young people to realize that no matter what their circumstances, they can make choices that will positively invest in their future. This will require self-efficacy, which results from a combination of a sense of hope and an optimistic attitude.

According to psychologist C. R. Snyder, professor of psychology at Kansas University, "Hope is believing you have both the will and the way to accomplish your goals, whatever they may be."[1] Hopeful people share many of the same characteristics: they are able to motivate themselves; they feel capable of finding resources to accomplish what is important to them; they reassure themselves in difficult situations that things will improve; and they can adapt and regroup when things get off course. Hope usually accompanies optimism. Optimism is having a strong expectation that, in general, things will turn out all right in life, despite setbacks and frustrations. The following humorous story illustrates the contrast between optimists and their counterparts, pessimists.

There were two young boys who were identical twins. One was a hope-filled optimist. "Everything is coming up roses!" he would say. The other twin was a sad, hopeless pessimist who looked at the negative side of everything. Their worried parents took them to the local psychologist.

He suggested to the parents a plan to balance the twins' personalities. "On their next birthday, put them in separate rooms to open their gifts. Give the pessimist the best toys you can afford, and give the optimist a box of manure." The parents followed these instructions and carefully observed the results.

When they peeked in on the pessimist, they heard him complaining, "I don't like the color of these shoes! I'll bet this toy car will break. This game is boring. I know who's got a better soccer ball than this."

Tiptoeing across the corridor, the parents peeked in and saw their little optimist gleefully throwing the manure up in the air. "You can't fool me!" he giggled. "Where there's this much manure, there's got to be a pony!"

Optimists will find a way; pessimists claim there is no way. An optimist views the glass as half full; the pessimist views it as half empty. Optimists will fail and try again; pessimists are more likely to label themselves failures and cease to try. Hopeful, optimistic people believe in achievable goals and feel capable of reaching them.

He who does not hope to win has already lost.

-Jose Joaquin Olmedo, Ecuadorian politician and poet

When hope and optimism are combined, they create *self-efficacy*, the belief that one has the ability to meet life's challenges as they arise. People with a high sense of self-efficacy feel capable. For example, drug prevention programs tell youth to say no to drugs. Who is most likely to say no? It is those who feel capable of doing so because they have been taught the necessary resistance skills and have put them into practice. Young people who have a low sense of self-efficacy and are unsure about how to refuse drugs are therefore least likely to do so, even if they want to say no.

Youth learn hope and optimism from adults who challenge, encourage, and inspire them to discover their potential. When we help young people to discover their individual uniqueness

and talents and guide them to create a realistic vision for their lives, they begin to develop a sense of hope. When we teach them a skill—any skill—they learn to believe they are capable. When we support them when they fail, help them to gain perspective, and convince them to try again, we are building their sense of optimism. And, when we commend their ability to make good decisions and to manage their own lives, we are building their confidence.

Our goal is not simply to make children feel good about themselves but to make them feel good about being good.

–Michael Josephson,
Josephson Institute for Ethics

Research has shown time and again that the youth who are most likely to get into trouble lack self-esteem, a strong belief in oneself. Children with poor self-esteem feel inferior to those around them, are negative about their abilities, and lack a sense of hope. In contrast, youth with good self-esteem thrive—they experience the joys of success, feel a sense of competence, are comfortable with who they are, and are generally healthier.

Adults need to work hard to break down the stereotypes of racism, sexism, and economic disparities. All youth will benefit from hearing that they have infinite worth and are special and capable. But it will take more than words to build their self-esteem. Self-esteem is also a byproduct of making good decisions—avoiding drugs, treating others with respect, saying no to sexual activity, learning a skill, and studying hard in school. When we help young people learn to listen to their conscience, to use the critical thinking skills necessary to make good decisions, and to have the courage to take positive risks to reach their dreams, we are doing much more to develop their self-esteem than just giving them hollow accolades and talking about their worth. We are instilling a sense of personal pride that is a result of their ability to achieve small goals by maintaining self-control and delaying gratification. Our words of praise will then be an acknowledgment of their courage and perseverance to do the hard work of personal growth.

The activities in this section are designed to help youth to realize that life is full of things that they can and can't control and that ultimately their lives will be determined by their control of day-to-day decisions. They are free to make innumerable choices: whether to face the day with a positive or a negative attitude; to cheat or to study to pass a examination; to get drunk to avoid problems or to seek help in positively solving them; or to satisfy sexual urges when they arise or to control them and treat people respectfully. Each day is full of choices to invest in or to sabotage their lives, one decision at a time. These decisions, often very difficult ones, will determine and reflect their character. As they learn the valuable concepts of emotional self-control, delayed gratification, and the use of common sense in decision making, they will improve their self-esteem and will feel capable to manage their lives. When these elements are combined with a clear vision for life, they will have the wings to soar.

Good decisions feed the eagle; poor decisions strengthen the wolf. We are each free to choose which animal we feed.

The Decision to Grow

The popular Japanese carp, or koi, is a very interesting fish. Given good food and good water, this fish will happily remain 3–4 inches long while living in a small bowl. Place it in a tank, and it will grow to 6–10 inches. Placed in a small pond, it may grow to 18–24 inches. In a large lake, this fish will grow up to three feet long. Its size is dependent on the size of the body of water in which it lives. Its potential is therefore largely determined by its environment.

People are much the same. For us to grow to our full potential, we need to expand who we are by developing the physical, emotional, social, spiritual, occupational, and mental parts of our lives. Youth who choose to grow will become men and women of stature. Youth who do not choose to grow will just grow old. Unless we decide to grow, we will always be who we are today. Unlike koi, which just get put in an environment to live out their existence, humans have the freedom to determine much of what their lives will be. And because we are human beings, we are capable of and dependent on using rational choices to decide our futures.

To choose means to make a selection between two things over which we have some degree of control. We may choose ice cream over chips, assuming we can possess either. We could choose studying over cheating; it is possible to do both. Control is a key element in a choice. Learning what is within our control and clearly understanding what needs to be controlled will help us to focus our energies toward positive growth. Have you ever stopped to consider the things that we can and can't control about life? Following are a few examples:

> *The strongest principle of growth lies in human choice.*
>
> –George Elliott, Canadian novelist

Things we can control:

- *Personal habits:* Our grooming, makeup, clothing, accessories, tattoos, use of time, study habits, and community involvement
- *Personal growth:* Our character development, use of talents, and practice of faith
- *Attitudes:* Our emotional responses to others, communication style, treatment of others, and amount of effort we expend

Things we can't control:

- *Physical characteristics:* Our height, race, gender, hair, facial features, coloring, and physical handicaps
- *Other people:* Their thoughts, ideas, opinions, and lifestyle choices
- *Life circumstances:* Our family composition, place of birth, natural events, the economy, time, things in the past, and personal or family illnesses

> *If you don't like something, change it; if you can't change it, change the way you think about it.*
>
> –Mary Englebreit, artist and poet

The only thing we really have control over is ourselves—our own attitudes and behaviors. Everything else we must learn to adapt to—our physical characteristics, other people, and our life circumstances. We can't change them, but we are able to change our attitudes about them and learn to accept or manage them in positive ways. Youth have much more control than they realize. They will choose to be a person of courage or cowardice, to use or not use drugs, to get involved in or postpone sex, to respond calmly or lash out in anger. They will also decide whether to apply the Golden Rule in their relationships with others and whether they are going to take school seriously and invest in their future. These are all aspects of self-control—choosing activities and emotional responses based on common sense and on the principles of character rather than feelings. Without self-control, we cannot make wise decisions, especially under pressure.

Our perception of who is in control of our own lives will greatly influence our decision making. People who perceive that they are primarily responsible for what happens to them are more assertive and able to manage their lives in positive ways. Those who feel that their life circumstances are largely the result of external forces—whether the actions of others or outside life events—tend to blame others for circumstances that they themselves should control. For example, a student with this type of perception who fails a test would likely say things like, "The teacher gave an unfair test," "My parents made me stay up too late," or "I was distracted by the person sitting next to me." Who was the problem: the teacher, the parents, the person sitting beside the student, or the student herself? In the opposite scenario, students who feel that they determine most of their life events would likely say, "I didn't study the right material," or "I didn't take the test seriously enough." The problem was "I." By helping young people to understand what they can and can't control, and teaching them to take responsibility for what is within their control, we are increasing their ability to follow through on their personal decisions.

Managing Negative Emotions

One of the greatest challenges for a good decision maker is to refrain from letting negative emotions dictate a choice. Feelings such as boredom, stress, anger, and embarrassment often cause people to make life-changing decisions. Learning to recognize and master our emotions is very important. Good decision makers can recognize how they feel, manage how they feel in productive ways, and make wise decisions despite how they feel. This is certainly easier said than done; managing emotions under pressure is probably one of the greatest challenges in life.

A frazzled mother entered a grocery store with a crying child. "Emma," she said, "you can do this. We just have to get a few things." Moments later the child became more upset and the woman said calmly, "It's okay, Emma, just a couple more items." When the child became hysterical in the check-out line the mom took a deep breath and said, "Emma, hold it together. We'll be in the car in a few minutes." In the parking lot a woman stopped her. "Excuse me, I couldn't help but notice you in the store and I just wanted to compliment you on how patient you are with little Emma." The mother laughed. "Well, thank you, but the truth is, I'm Emma."[2]

This little story, told by Michael Josephson in his book *You Don't Have to Be Sick to Get Better*, is a great example of what is required to manage negative emotions: self-awareness. *Self-awareness* is a conscious recognition of our feelings and our thoughts about them. It is the ability to realize when feelings are becoming intense and to identify the thought pattern associated with that intensity. Persons who can identify their feelings, especially in the early stages of intensity, will be able to manage them most effectively. Some youth become mired in negative emotions, never fully aware that they are troubled or of how they came to feel that way. Before they realize it, they are enraged or completely distraught; they've missed the lesser emotions preceding an extreme feeling. It is impossible to manage feelings that we don't know exist.

Strong emotions feel like a takeover of our bodies and our thought process. We can literally feel "out of control." Reactions vary, but typical reactions would include a faster heartbeat, cold or wet palms, trembling, crying, overeating, or lack of appetite. People may begin to think of unkind things to do to others, may have trouble concentrating, or may begin negative self-talk that leads to thoughts of self-harm. These emotions can be very difficult, but youth need to understand that they are manageable, especially if they are stopped early. Youth can learn to respond to strong emotions in the following ways:

- **Think their way out:** Adolescents can catch negative emotions early by recognizing them and using positive talk to calm themselves down. This is what Emma did in the grocery store; as her frustration increased, she sent herself encouraging thoughts that enabled her to get through the difficult feelings.

- **Wait their way out:** Because many emotions involve an intense physiological response (such as increased adrenaline and raised blood pressure), sometimes it is best for youth just to leave the situation until they can calm down and think rationally rather than

emotionally. Going for a walk, taking deep breaths, or exercising may help them to release their stressful feelings and calm down so they can gain better perspective.

- **Work their way out:** At times it may be necessary for youth to do a positive activity to get their minds on something else and help them overcome these difficult feelings. We can teach them to create positive distractions, such as working on a project they've been meaning to do, reading a good book, or choosing to refocus by taking time to pray. Serving others is also a great way to get our mind off of our own troubles.

Handling Conflict with Others

The strongest emotions we feel are usually when we are in conflict with others. Managing our emotions at these times will help us to resolve many conflicts—or avoid them altogether. When in conflict, young people will need to be able to interpret the situation, choose not to act according to their feelings, and make a plan that is consistent with the goal of being a person of good character. We can help them understand this process using the analogy of a stoplight.

Red Light: "I'm over the edge."
- Stop! Don't act. Don't respond to the situation.
- Get harmful emotions under control by thinking it out, waiting it out, or working it out.

Yellow Light: "I'm figuring it out."
- Identify your feelings and what you think about them.
- Decide if the feelings are caused by something you can or can't control.
- Think of solutions for managing the emotions, the problem that caused them, or both.
- Discard solutions that are inconsistent with the Golden Rule and consider the consequences of the other options.
- If no solutions seem workable, ask for input from a trusted adult.
- Decide on a course of action.

Green Light: "I'm taking action."
- Execute your plan.
- Evaluate and learn from your experience.

In most cases, emotions won't cause harm; it is the negative actions because of those emotions that get youth into trouble. If young people learn to think their way out, wait it out, or work their way out of negative feelings, they can productively manage a difficult situation.

Choosing Wisely Under Pressure

"Come on, just take a sip." "What's wrong with you?" "This is no big deal." "No one will ever know." "You know I love you." "If you sleep with me we can tell everyone you are my girlfriend." "Prove it." These are just a few of the comments that young people may hear when they are being pressured. Manipulators use words designed to intimidate, anger, belittle, or flatter others to get what they want All too often young people are caught in situations that they didn't anticipate, and are often forced to respond in front of their friends. If youth can learn to anticipate a difficult situation, they will be better equipped to make a plan ahead of time.

We can help youth to become aware of manipulative phrases and to practice ways to get out *before* they get into trouble. They need to be able to quickly identify a manipulator's tactic and know how to respond. Withstanding this kind of peer pressure will require courage and communication skills to articulate an unpopular decision. The challenge is to take charge of the situation in an assertive and respectful manner. Following are some suggested responses we can teach young people to help them to get out of difficult situations with finesse.

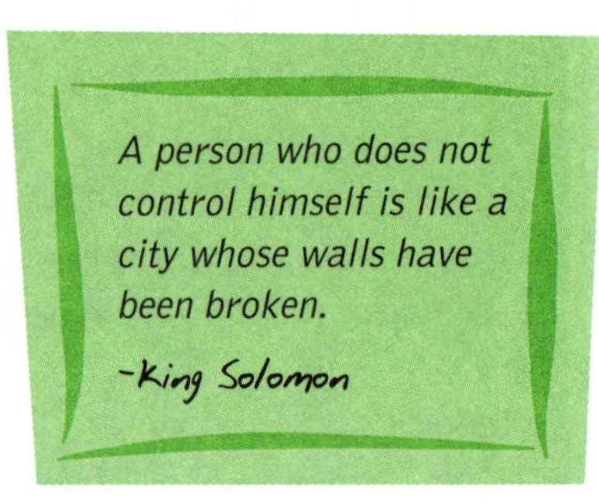

1. *Sound stunned and go on the offensive.* Expressing surprise at a suggestion can catch someone off guard. Acting stunned has a shock value that communicates just how ridiculous the suggestion is. Be quick to offer another, more positive solution: "What? I can't believe you suggested that! Let's just go and ________________."

2. *Use humor.* Humor is a great way to send an indirect message that communicates your feelings in a nonthreatening way. You may want to rephrase what the person said using paralanguage that changes the meaning. For example, repeat the phrase using inflection to convey the absurdity of the suggestion. Make jokes about the possibility of getting into trouble, ruining your life, or getting "killed" by your parents.

3. *Look to a friend for support.* If you're with others who might share your values, look to them for support. Talk directly to them and come up with a better suggestion, or choose to leave together. "You don't want to do this either, do you?"

4. *State your reason and stand your ground.* Say no and give a calm explanation of why. Don't lecture—just state why it is not a good idea. "It's not right, and I don't want to get into trouble."

5. *Leave.* When the pressure is too great and you can't talk your way out, just walk away. Run if you have to. It is better to be made fun of or be misunderstood than to compromise your beliefs or sabotage your dreams. You can say, "Hey, I can't do this. I've got to go."

Role-playing and drama are great ways to teach youth how to spot and respond to a manipulator. Manipulators will use any strategy that they believe will work—physically, emotionally, socially, occupationally, mentally, or spiritually. Let the youth tell you the phrases commonly used. You will be amazed by the stories they tell! Don't rush through this material. Young people will need to practice and practice before they will feel confident enough to handle these difficult situations. These quick-thinking resistance skills are critical.

Myself

Edgar Guest

I have to live with myself, and so,
I want to be fit for myself to know;
I want to be able as days go by,
Always to look myself straight in the eye;
I don't want to stand with the setting sun
And hate myself for the things I've done.

I don't want to keep on a closet shelf
A lot of secrets about myself,
And fool myself as I come and go
Into thinking that nobody else will know
The kind of man I really am;
I don't want to dress myself up in sham.

I want to go out with my head erect,
I want to deserve all men's respect;
But here in this struggle for fame and pelf,
I want to be able to like myself.
I don't want to think as I come and go
That I'm bluster and bluff and empty show.

I never can hide myself from me,
I see what others may never see,
I know what others may never know,
I never can fool myself and so,
Whatever happens, I want to be
Self-respecting and conscience free.

The Decision-Making Process

Many times when youth are challenged to do something that they shouldn't, they will have plenty of time to think about their response. For example, they may be encouraged to have sexual relations with their boyfriend or girlfriend during the upcoming weekend, go to a party in a few days, or cheat on tomorrow's test. Getting away from the peer pressure, having time to get emotions under control, and seeking advice will make a good decision more likely. The following are steps that many people use when they are faced with important or difficult decisions.

1. *Identify the problem.* When someone asks you to do something that is troubling, begin by identifying the request and what you believe is the motivation for the request. For example, if a friend dares you to steal some clothes at a store, the situation would be defined like this: "She wants me to *steal clothes*, because ______________." This method will allow you to clearly understand what is being requested and why.

2. *List the results of engaging in the action.* The next step is to make a list of possible consequences, positive or negative, for going along. "If I steal the clothes . . ."

3. *Consider the options.* Evaluate your options based on being a person of good character and whether the action would enable you to accomplish your vision for your life. Ask yourself some simple questions:
   - What does my conscience say I should do? If others found out, would I be ashamed of my actions?
   - Would I want someone to treat me this way?
   - Can anyone get hurt, including me?
   - Would most adults approve?
   - Could the result keep me from reaching my dreams?

4. *Choose the wisest course of action.* If at this point your answer is not clear, don't act! Find a healthy and trusted adult to advise you in the situation.

5. *Take action!* Once you are confident that your decision is wise, be courageous and take action. Being misunderstood, laughed at, or even losing a friend for a while is worth reaching your dreams—and protecting your character.

Avoiding Risky Behavior

A father took his young son walking through the woods one morning. As they walked and talked together, the father noticed a spot where there were four types of plants growing. He paused a moment, then pointing to the first plant, he said, "Son, can you pull this plant out of the ground?" His son reached down and pulled it out with no problem. Then the father pointed to the second plant, "This one? Can you pull this one out?" The son had to pull a bit harder, but the second plant came up rather easily too. Then the father said, "Good. Now what about this one? Can you pull this one out?" Sensing the challenge, the boy strained and

wiggled the plant back and forth; then, pulling with all of his weight, he plucked the plant out of the ground. He proudly presented it to his father. Laughing, the father then pointed to the fourth plant, a young tree, and said, "Okay, and what about this one?" The boy, ready to prove his strength to his father, grabbed the little tree trunk and pulled with all of his might. He pulled and pulled but finally gave up, frustrated and exhausted. The father smiled and put his arm around his son and said, "My son, it's the same with our bad habits. When we make a bad choice we can decide to change rather easily, but when we repeat bad choices they become bad habits, and then it takes much more effort to pull out their roots in our life."

Ten Decisions of Self-Sabotage

1. *Choose friends with bad character.*
2. *Get involved in sex outside of marriage.*
3. *Fight your way out of conflicts.*
4. *Never ask adults for advice.*
5. *Experiment with alcohol and other drugs.*
6. *Consider yourself more important than others.*
7. *Refuse to change.*
8. *Join a gang.*
9. *Just "get by" in school.*
10. *Ignore your parents or caregivers.*

Whether or not to get involved in risky activities—such as using alcohol or other drugs, smoking cigarettes, or having sex outside of marriage—are decisions that most youth have to wrestle with. Each decision builds on itself, creating positive and negative habits. As much as we hate to admit it, these types of decisions are theirs to make. No matter how much we want to protect young people, where there is the will, there can be a way—they are in control of their bodies. Most adolescents will fall into one of three broad categories: (1) those who won't get involved in dangerous behavior no matter what; (2) those who can be influenced one way or the other; and (3) those who are going to do the negative behavior no matter what they are told. By far, the largest group is the middle one—those who can be influenced.

If youth do not have a sense of hope, if they have nothing to live for or have no vision for what life could be, they are at high risk. Until they realize that they are special, unique, and have a reason to take care of themselves, they are likely to make decisions based on what they can see today—and for many of them, today carries burdens that are almost impossible to bear. They turn toward many of these harmful activities to escape from their emotional pain. We believe that talking *at* youth about these issues won't work. Coming alongside and talking *with* them, listening to them, and leading them through the decision-making process will make all the difference in the world.

We like to work with youth using the concepts of personal investments and self-sabotage. We begin with their dreams, which may be as simple as making the soccer team or as big as going to a university and becoming a doctor or successful businessperson. Next, we help them to think through what it will take for them to reach their dreams, the investments they must make in order for their dreams to come true. Then we ask them to consider the types of things that are likely to sabotage their dreams—drugs, sex, and poor performance in school are usually at the top of their lists. Walk adolescents through the decision-making process. You'll be amazed that when you give them correct information and link it to their dreams, without lecturing to them, they are open to listen. At the same time, if we work to provide healthy ways for youth to build relationships and find positive recreation, many will choose healthy behaviors.

The remainder of this section contains basic information to help you discuss the issues of sexual activity and the use of alcohol and other drugs. These two issues are responsible for shattering the dreams of millions of young people. We've designed this information as a quick reference for you to use as you process the activities in this section. It should not be considered to be the comprehensive information that would be addressed in formal instruction on these topics. Our focus is on the decision-making process and on helping adolescents to choose personal investments instead of self-sabotage.

Sexual Activity

Discussing the topic of sex and sexuality with an adolescent audience makes many adults feel quite uncomfortable. Some adults find it easy to talk to other adolescents, but almost impossible to talk with their own. Cultural norms surrounding sexual conduct vary from culture to culture, as do the roles and responsibilities of men and women. Images and stories on television challenge traditional norms. Many youth are confused and looking for answers, and if healthy adults don't provide answers, youth will learn about sex from their friends or from adults who manipulate adolescents for their own sexual gratification. Our messages to youth about sex greatly influence their sexual choices. As difficult as it is, we must break the silence when it comes to sex and help adolescents think through the purpose of sex and the dangers of engaging in sex outside of its intended purpose.

Many of the activities in this section are designed to raise various issues about sexual activity, giving youth the opportunity to hear accurate information and to think through the issues of

Common Reasons Why Youth Become Sexually Active

- To experience pleasure
- To feel loved
- Curiosity
- Pressure from friends
- Fear of losing a boyfriend or girlfriend
- To feel powerful
- To prove one's manhood
- To prove heterosexuality
- To prove fertility
- To have fun
- To be popular
- To get money or things
- To show love
- To get attention

The Freedoms of Postponing Sexual Involvement

Freedom from:

- Sexually transmitted infections
- Fear of unintended pregnancy
- Experiencing the trauma of abortion
- Pressure to get married before you are ready
- Deep emotional scars
- Guilty feelings
- Social stigma
- Worries about getting caught

Freedom to:

- Focus energy on reaching goals
- Enjoy being a teenager
- Experience that special relationship found only in marriage
- Be able to bear children when the time comes
- Experience greater self-esteem

sex in a safe learning environment and with adults who can positively influence their thinking. While their interest in and desires for sex are positive and healthy, it is vital for them to understand that their lack of self-control in this area may sabotage many of their dreams, as well as the dreams of others. Listed below are some of the common reasons why youth choose to become sexually active. Discuss these reasons with them. Help them to see that the Golden Rule applies to sexual activity also.

We are committed to teaching the concepts of abstinence before marriage and faithfulness in marriage as the healthiest sexual choices. The reality is that sex outside of a mutually faithful marriage relationship carries with it enormous emotional as well as medical risks; HIV/AIDS and other sexually transmitted infections cause pain, discomfort, infertility, death, abnormalities in newborn babies, and many other consequences. Postponing sexual involvement until marriage brings enormous freedom—freedom from the pain of negative consequences and freedom to focus on achieving dreams and goals.

Our job is to help make these freedoms a reality in the lives of all youth, not just for those who are currently abstaining. We have seen hundreds of young girls and boys who have already been sexually active seize an opportunity to choose abstinence once more. They long for a chance and permission to change their lifestyle. Many youth live with regret, and they need you to tell them that making a new start is possible.

They also need to know that you will be there to support their efforts. As in our story of the plants, it may be impossible to pull out deep roots alone. If the father had helped, the son could have yanked the young tree from the ground. We may need to get our hands around the problems of youth who cannot help themselves. The son had more strength available than he was using—his father's strength was right beside him.

We can help adolescents to make wise sexual choices, but we can't choose for them. The pull of cultural norms, even unhealthy cultural norms, is difficult to overcome. Our job is to give clear and accurate medical information about the dangers of early sexual involvement, teach sex within the context of the Golden Rule, and set healthy expectations. In the process, we must convey an attitude that communicates our belief in marriage and that waiting until marriage is both possible and in their best interests. We can also help by teaching youth the skills to say no, provide healthy ways for them to interact with the opposite sex, and encourage them when they succeed and when they fail. Finding the will and the courage to stand up against peer pressure and to learn self-control when it comes to sexual desire is a personal choice; each of us must choose for ourselves.

Alcohol and Other Drugs

Another quick way for youth to sabotage their lives is to get involved in the use of drugs. Whether the drugs are legal, such as alcohol and prescription medications, or illegal, such as cocaine, heroin, and marijuana, drugs (natural or manmade) can affect a person's body structure and functions, behavior, and feelings. People use drugs for many reasons. Some individuals use drugs to enhance a social situation, typically where others are present. Some people are looking for a different mood. For example, they may consume alcohol after work because of stress or use a drug to eliminate feelings of sadness, depression, or anger. Many others use drugs to treat or cure conditions or illnesses.

Most drugs abused by youth fall into two categories: *depressants*—drugs that slow the body down, and *stimulants*—drugs that speed the body up. Depressants are typically used to reduce anxiety, tension, or anger, whereas stimulants cause an increase in energy. These drugs are administered in one of three ways:

- *Oral ingestion:* The most common method of drug ingestion is swallowing, whether in pill form, as with amphetamines, or in liquid form, as with alcohol.
- *Inhalation:* Inhalation includes breathing substances into the lungs, such as tobacco and marijuana, as well as snorting drugs, such as cocaine, so that they get into the bloodstream via mucous membranes in the nose. Other substances that are inhaled include various household and industrial products, such as glue and paint thinner.
- *Injection:* Drugs such as heroin and cocaine can be injected into muscles or directly into the bloodstream by using a syringe. Injecting these drugs directly into the bloodstream produces a very fast response. Of particular concern with injection drug use is HIV/AIDS and hepatitis transmission; these diseases are easily spread when needles are shared.

Drug Tolerance and Dependence

Many youth begin using drugs out of curiosity and recreational interests, but all too often the fun turns into a nightmare of dependence—physically, psychologically, or both. This begins with an increased tolerance to a drug, in which more and more of the drug is needed to achieve the desired high. Where four beers used to cause a pleasant feeling, it now may take six to eight beers to get the same effect. A true *physical dependence* results when the drug has been used so extensively that the body has adapted to its presence. The drug then becomes necessary for the body to function "normally." Youth who become physically dependent find that without the drug, they have great physical discomfort and an inability to function compared to their nondrugged peers. A *psychological dependence* occurs when a person begins to crave the drug. This craving is not necessarily associated with anything physical, but the individual begins to believe that the drug is needed in order to function—even if there is no physical dependence on the drug.

As the physical or psychological dependence grows, the addict's life is reduced to planning the next drug-taking event. This craving clouds the person's judgment, and all of life's responsibilities take second place to drugs. Sometimes addicted users steal, rob, or harm others to get drugs. They often forget about their friends, families, and communities because overwhelming drug-seeking behaviors consume their lives. While they should be enjoying life as teenagers, young addicts go from one problem to the next. The following are common outcomes of youth involved with drugs:

- Failure in school
- Poor self-esteem
- Family problems
- Automobile accidents
- Social isolation
- Physical ailments
- Financial problems
- Inability to manage difficult emotions
- Diseases such as HIV/AIDS and hepatitis C
- Overdose resulting in long-term impairment or death
- Newborn birth defects (fetal alcohol syndrome)
- Incarceration for lawbreaking
- Inappropriate sexual behavior
- Sexual abuse

Alcoholism

One of the most common drug addictions is alcoholism. It is easy to spot an older alcoholic on the street, but spotting an adolescent who is developing alcoholism is a much greater challenge. The signs are frequently overlooked. Persons addicted to alcohol typically have four symptoms:

- *Craving:* A strong need or compulsion to drink
- *Loss of control:* The inability to limit one's drinking on any given occasion
- *Physical dependence:* Withdrawal symptoms, such as nausea, sweating, shakiness, and anxiety, when alcohol use is stopped after a period of heavy drinking
- *Tolerance:* The need to drink greater amounts of alcohol in order to "get high"

People sometimes do not understand why an alcoholic can't utilize willpower to stop drinking. However, alcoholism has little to do with willpower. Alcoholics are in the grip of powerful biological and psychological "cravings" and have an urge for alcohol that overrides their desire to stop drinking. This urge can be as strong as the urge for food and water.

Although a small percentage of people are able to recover from alcoholism without help, the vast majority of alcoholics need assistance. With professional treatment and the support of families and friends, many individuals are able to stop drinking and rebuild their lives.

Detecting an Alcohol or Drug Problem

Many youth worry about friends or family members who seem to be experiencing problems with alcohol or other drugs. Some worry about their own behavior. Knowing the signs of danger can help with early intervention and treatment.

Signs of an Alcohol or Drug Problem

- Getting high on drugs or getting drunk on a regular basis
- Lying about the amount of alcohol or drugs being consumed, or about other things
- Avoiding others in order to get high or drunk
- Giving up usual activities, such as sports, homework, or hanging out with friends who don't use alcohol or drugs
- Having to use more alcohol or drugs to get the same effect
- Constantly talking about using alcohol or drugs
- Believing that alcohol or drugs are necessary to have fun
- Turning to alcohol or drugs after a confrontation or argument, or to relieve uncomfortable feelings
- Pressuring others to use alcohol or drugs
- Getting into trouble with the law
- Taking risks, including sexual risks or driving under the influence of alcohol or drugs
- Remembering how last night began, but not how it ended
- Feeling alone, miserable, hopeless, depressed, or even suicidal
- Having trouble at work or in school because of alcohol or drug use
- Making promises to stop using alcohol or drugs

Someone who drinks too much at a party and gets pulled over by the police and charged with a drunk driving violation is not necessarily an alcoholic. The person simply made a horrendously bad mistake by driving while intoxicated. A healthy person would be extremely embarrassed and make a major life change; they would never drink and drive again. On the other hand, someone who is experiencing problems with alcohol would blame the occurrence on something other than their drinking and would be more likely to make that mistake—and others like it—again. When drinking causes a problem, healthy people adjust their drinking.

Character Connection: Rationalizing Behavior

It is very common to try to rationalize actions that are inconsistent with good character. Teaching about character is easy; living it consistently is another issue. Through our teaching about character, we have become much more aware of the rationalizations that we catch ourselves trying to use. It is so easy to do, but wrong is wrong, and we are obliged to admit it when we catch ourselves trying to justify our wrongs because of our special circumstances. Here are some of the common methods for rationalizing wrong behavior.

The Payback: We justify our wrong actions because someone has wronged us. "Look, what goes around comes around." "She's only getting what she's done to others."

The Comparison: We look around and evaluate our actions based on what others are doing. "I'm not doing anything that everybody else isn't doing."

The Reward: This one is used when we believe we are owed. "I know I lied, but I deserve this. I worked hard for that promotion."

The Need: This is the old argument that the end justifies the means; the greater good negates the wrong in the process. "I had to cheat or I would have failed, and getting a job will help my family."

The Law: We determine what is right or wrong based on "rules." If there is no rule that says something is wrong, then it's justified. "I didn't break any laws." "No one said I couldn't do it."

The Damage Assessment: The wrong is minimized by its failure to damage others. If no one gets hurt, then it can't be wrong. "Look, I'm only hurting myself if I get caught." "Nobody got hurt; nobody is going to get hurt either."

None of these reasons for doing wrong is right. But it is human nature to pull them out when our conscience speaks to us. What is wrong is wrong, and we usually know it, whether we admit it or not. We need to teach young people to understand these rationalizations and help them to see that they are not appropriate justifications for wrong. It is in the little areas of life where it is so easy to compromise our integrity for something that we want or think we need.

Persons who have problems with alcohol can't seem to manage their drinking behavior, even when they want to.

We must remember that many of the signs—sudden changes in mood, difficulty in getting along with others, poor job or school performance, irritability, depression—might be explained by other causes. When determining whether a person may need to seek treatment, it is important to look for multiple problems and to substantiate the link to alcohol versus some other life event or physical problem. Denial is a common symptom of addiction. Do not be surprised if those with a problem deny it, even when it is evident to everyone around them. As we help youth to think through these issues, we must be ready with a list of community resources where they can seek help for themselves or their loved ones.

Unfortunately, many of the youth with whom you work will experiment with alcohol or other drugs at least once. Many will get involved in sex before marriage. Too often we are left in the position of intervention rather than prevention. Still, preventing negative behavior from beginning is much easier than intervening later, so talk candidly about these issues and listen carefully. Gently challenge unhealthy thoughts and opinions, even if they are tied to cultural norms. Help young people to see that although we can't change the past, we can and will choose our tomorrows by the decisions we make today.

It Takes Courage!

Making a decision does not require courage; anyone can make a decision. But making the right decision at the right time can take an enormous amount of courage. A rare form of courage is moral courage, seen in persons who choose to act or to refrain from acting because it is the right thing to do. Moral courage is displayed when youth confront their friends in defense of a person who is being mistreated. It is displayed when someone takes responsibility for wrong actions, even when no one would ever know what happened. People with moral courage are willing to weather the storms of ridicule, criticism, and rejection in order to do what is right. It takes courage to forge upstream when it is easy to float with the crowd, even if they are going the wrong way.

It takes an act of the will to choose to learn how to manage angry emotions and to endure painful ones. Morally courageous people think through the consequences of their actions and take the time to ensure that their decisions are consistent with being persons of good character. We all fail in doing what is right, but courageous people take responsibility for their mistakes. An immense amount of courage is needed to admit bad choices and to humbly ask for forgiveness when we have wronged another person.

Making Wise Decisions – Activities

44. The Choices We Make 262
45. Processionary Caterpillars 264
46. Rescue Mission 268
47. The Cake 272
48. Hidden Squares 274
49. The Problem Box 278
50. Red Light, Yellow Light, Green Light 282
51. What's Your Opinion? 286
52. Drama-in-a-Bag 290
53. Step by Step 294
54. A Crowded Bed 298
55. Sex in the Media 302
56. Pressure Points 306
57. Sex Pros and Cons 310
58. My Most Courageous Moments 314
59. When Is It Okay to Lie? 318
60. Nine Dots 320
61. Appointments 324
62. In the Court Today 328

Activity #44 The Choices We Make

15–30 Minutes

Character Connection
Perseverance & Responsibility

Purpose To illustrate the fact that decisions and actions always have consequences

Overview We face many decisions every day. Even our smallest decisions have consequences, though they may not be initially apparent. This activity using paper clips is designed to help participants understand that every decision they make has either a positive or a negative impact on their lives.

Life Skill Linking choices to results

Group Size Any

Cultural and Age Considerations None

Materials 3 paper clips, overhead projector, chalkboard and chalk

Preparation Set up overhead projector.

Instructions

1. Ask three volunteers to come to the front and assist you with an activity.
2. Give each of them a paper clip.
3. Tell them they will be in competition with one another. They will have 10 seconds to make the paper clip as straight as possible using only their hands.
4. Start the time and see how well they do in carrying out their assignment.
5. When the time is up, place the paper clips on the overhead projector and turn it on.
6. Take an informal vote to see whose paper clip is the straightest.
7. Thank the participants, but then tell them they are not finished yet.
8. Return the paper clips to them and explain that you will give them an additional 10 seconds to rebend their paper clips into their original shape. After 10 seconds, again place the paper clips on the overhead so everyone can see the results.
9. Let the group decide who did the best job of restoring his or her paper clip to its original shape.

The Choices We Make

10. Give each volunteer a small gift, such as a piece of candy, for participating in the activity.
11. Ask the group to share some of their thoughts or lessons they have learned from this activity. You may want to record their answers on the chalkboard.
12. Discuss with the group the following questions:
    - Why is it so difficult to restore the paper clip to its original shape?
    - If you knew you needed to return the paper clip to its original shape, would you have done anything differently?
    - What have you learned from this activity about the consequences of decisions?
    - How can you apply this lesson to your life?

Application and Insight

When making a decision to do something, a person is changed and is never quite the same again.

Some decisions enrich a person's life, whereas other decisions have negative consequences that cannot be completely mended.

Unwise decisions in the past do not prevent a person from choosing to make wiser decisions in the future.

Going Deeper

Can you think of decisions you have made that had a negative impact on your life? What can you learn from these decisions?

How can you encourage each other to make good choices?

Character is much easier kept than recovered. —Thomas Paine, British political theorist

It Takes Courage!
to make wise decisions

Activity #45 Processionary Caterpillars

15 Minutes

Character Connection
Responsibility & Self-control

Purpose To illustrate the danger of following others without questioning their vision, purpose, or direction

Overview This story about processionary caterpillars illustrates the dangers of following the crowd and failing to make good personal decisions.

Life Skill Thinking before following

Group Size Any

Cultural and Age Considerations None

Materials Processionary Caterpillars Story (Facilitator Notes)

Preparation None

Instructions

1. Share the Processionary Caterpillars Story with the group.
2. Divide participants into pairs. Read the following questions one at a time, giving pairs time to discuss, then have them report their answers to the group.
   - In what ways are you like the processionary caterpillars? How are you unlike them?
   - How can you avoid being like them?
   - How would your life change if you were to truly think independently and make decisions for yourself?
   - How would our society change if most people thought for themselves?

Application and Insight

Every person needs to think through decisions and not blindly follow others.

One must make personal decisions without depending on others to make that choice.

Processionary Caterpillars

Going Deeper

Why do you find it difficult to make decisions on your own?

Why do we decide to follow people who are a bad influence on us even though we know they will lead us into trouble?

Where your heart goes, there your feet will go. —Afghan proverb

It Takes Courage!
to think independently

Processionary Caterpillars Story

The Pine Caterpillar is a follower by nature. Where the first one goes, all the others follow. These furry insects march in single file, so close together that the head of one is touching the fuzzy rear of the other. Thus, the name "processionary" is given to these pine-gnawing creatures.

The processionary caterpillar who chances to be at the head of the procession dribbles a silken thread fixing it on the path wherever he wishes to go. The thread is so tiny that a grain of sand will cause it to break. The second caterpillar in the line steps on the thread and doubles it with his thread, each caterpillar following the silken thread and spitting out more. Their roads, literally made from silk, will lead them through the night and back to their nest in the morning.

In 1896, a French scientist, J. Henri Fabre, discovered a large troop of processionary caterpillars beginning to circle the outer rim of a flowerpot. He waited until all the space at the top of the pot was closed and then he cut the thread so no more caterpillars could join. In the uninterrupted circular procession there was no longer a leader. The scientist was quite intrigued. What will the caterpillars do? Will they walk endlessly round and round until their strength gives out entirely, or will the caterpillars, in order to survive, leave the line to go look for food? Dr. Fabre predicted the caterpillars would scatter and reassemble somewhere else.

To add interest to his experiment, he placed their favorite food, pine needles, on the table less than 9 inches away. Even hungry, these furry creatures never stopped walking. They were relentless—around and around they went, hour after hour, day after day, night after night. They walked, a total of 335 times around the top of that flower pot—over a quarter of a mile (453 meters)! Distressed, starved, shelterless, and chilled with cold at night, these little caterpillars literally walked a total of 84 hours before each one fell off the rim of the pot and died.

Notes

The definition of insanity is doing the same thing over and over and expecting a different result.

–Benjamin Franklin, author and diplomat

Rescue Mission

45–60 Minutes

Character Connection
Perseverance & Respect

Purpose To help participants learn to work together to solve problems

Overview Cooperation is essential to healthy relationships. This highly interactive activity gives participants an extended experience of working through a problem situation together. Participants learn how they function in a group and which approaches are most effective for promoting good group dynamics.

Life Skill Collaborating well with others

Group Size Large (10 or more)

Cultural and Age Considerations You may want to change the scenario to be more appropriate to the group's age and culture.

Materials Rescue Mission Storehouse List Handout, pens or pencils

Preparation Make one copy of the Rescue Mission Storehouse List Handout for each participant.

Instructions

1. Divide participants into groups of five to eight individuals.
2. Explain the following scenario:

   It has just come to the attention of the local authorities that a new infectious disease has been identified in several remote towns in your region. The government is asking you to help deliver some badly needed medicine to these towns to keep this new strain from becoming an epidemic. Each group will be carrying 20 units of medicine to a different town.

   Due to the terrain, the trip will have to be made on foot, so you will have to carry everything you need for the trip in backpacks. The trip should last no more than four days and will entail hiking over fairly rocky terrain.

   Your first task is for each person to choose what you will need to take with you on the trip. You are allowed 20 items each. You can choose only from this list.
3. Distribute the Rescue Mission Storehouse List Handout to each participant.

Rescue Mission

4. Give participants time to choose their 20 items. Continue with the scenario:

   Now, to make your load lighter, compare your lists to see if you can decrease the number of items you are taking as a group. Remember that you are going to have to carry everything on your backs, including the 20 units of medicine.

5. Give groups time to complete this second task. Add this new element to the scenario:

   We have just learned that another 20 units of medicine is available for each town. You are not obligated to take any of it, but obviously, any extra you can take could make a huge difference for the people of the town as well as the whole region, should the infection spread. So decide what your group can do to make room for this extra medicine. Consider one smaller item on the list to be equivalent to one unit of medicine, and one larger item to be equivalent to two units of medicine—for example, a bottle of water equals one unit, and a sleeping bag equals two units.

6. Give groups time to complete this task. Then discuss the following questions:
   - What were some of the problems you encountered as your group tried to work through each portion of the activity?
   - What were some of the ways you were able to resolve the problems?

Application and Insight

It takes cooperation and flexibility to accomplish a group goal.

For a group to be productive, each member must be considerate of the needs of the other members in the group.

Going Deeper

What are some general principles of problem solving that you've seen demonstrated in this activity?

In what kinds of problem-solving situations do you find yourself?

How can this activity help make your approach to problems more productive?

We are not primarily put on this earth to see through one another, but to see one another through. —Peter De Vries, author

It Takes Courage!
to collaborate with others to help people in need

Rescue Mission Storehouse List

Choose up to 20 items from this list to take with you on the rescue mission.

✓	
	Plastic sheet or tarp
	Underwear
	Sleeping bag
	Blanket
	Toothbrush/toothpaste
	First aid kit
	Soap
	Candle
	Washcloth
	Mosquito net
	Hairbrush/comb
	Shoes/boots
	Deodorant
	Swimsuit
	Hair products
	Fly swatter
	CD player
	Umbrella
	Pocket knife
	Bug repellent
	Matches
	Watch
	Bottled water
	Compass

✓	
	Lantern
	Hammock
	Kerosene
	Tent
	Reading book
	Fishing rod
	Flashlight
	Hunting rifle/ammunition
	Shirt
	Hat
	Trousers
	Firewood
	Laundry detergent
	Rope
	Coat hanger
	Snack food
	Hairdryer
	Reading glasses
	Coat
	Writing paper
	Socks
	Pen/pencil
	Cell phone
	Eating utensils kit (plate, cup, knife, fork, spoon)

People are often unreasonable, illogical, and self-centered;
Forgive them anyway.
If you are kind, people may accuse you of selfish, ulterior motives;
Be kind anyway.
If you are successful you will win some false friends and true enemies;
Succeed anyway.
If you are honest and frank, people may cheat you;
Be honest and frank anyway.
What you spend years building, someone could destroy overnight;
Build anyway.
If you find serenity and happiness, they may be jealous;
Be happy anyway.
The good you do today, people will often forget tomorrow;
Do good anyway.
Give the world the best you have, and it may never be enough;
Give the world the best you've got anyway.
You see, in the final analysis, it is between you and God;
It was never between you and them anyway.

–Mother Teresa

The Cake

15–30 Minutes

Character Connection
Patience & Perseverance

Purpose To demonstrate the necessity of challenges and adversity for character development

Overview Character is tested in the crucible of experience. This is a simple illustration of the importance of the "heat" of adversity and challenging events in shaping character. All the ingredients of a cake are combined, but the cake is never baked.

Life Skill Choosing short-term pain to achieve long-term gain

Group Size Any

Cultural and Age Considerations None

Materials Mixing bowl, basic cake recipe, ingredients to make a cake

Preparation None

Instructions

1. Place the mixing bowl in front of the group.
2. Ask a volunteer to read the recipe to you as you add each ingredient. (Alternatively, you can read the recipe and ask individuals to come forward to add each item.) Do not mix the ingredients as they are added to the bowl.
3. Once the list is complete, hold the bowl for the group to see. Tell them the cake is ready, and ask who wants a piece.
4. When they express disinterest, ask the participants what needs to happen next. Discuss the fact that the cake must be baked before it is edible—as it is submitted to high heat, it undergoes a beneficial change. Explain the need for character to be molded in the fire of struggles and difficulties.
5. If an oven is available, bake the cake and share it with the group.

The Cake

Application and Insight

The "ingredients" of good character need to be mixed and refined by the fire of experience.

Adversities and challenges are opportunities to grow.

Going Deeper

Can you think of a trial or challenge that you overcame? What did you learn about yourself?

How did this experience equip you for similar experiences in the future?

What did this experience teach you about facing challenges or trials?

What choices can you make when you face a challenge or trial?

I gain strength, courage and confidence by every experience in which I must stop and look fear in the face . . . I say to myself, I've lived through this and can take the next thing that comes along . . . We must do the things we think we cannot do. —Eleanor Roosevelt, former U.S. First Lady

It Takes Courage!

to endure hardship

Hidden Squares

15 Minutes

Character Connection
Excellence & Self-control

Purpose To illustrate that one's perception is not always reality

Overview By analyzing a simple geometric pattern, participants are challenged to look beyond the obvious and consider alternate perspectives in problem solving.

Life Skill Meeting challenges in a creative way

Group Size Individual activity with any size group

Cultural and Age Considerations None

Materials Hidden Squares Diagram (Activity Materials), chalkboard and chalk

Preparation Copy the Hidden Squares Diagram onto the chalkboard.

Instructions

1. Point out the diagram to the group.
2. Ask participants to quickly count the number of squares they see in the diagram and then say that number out loud.
3. Explain that the correct answer is 30. Use chalk to show the squares.
4. Discuss the following questions:
   - What factors prevent us from easily obtaining the correct answer? (For example, we may stop at the first answer, we may not take time to think it through, etc.)
   - How is this diagram like other problem situations we face? (Problems consist of many different parts.)
   - What can we learn from this illustration that can be applied to other problems?

Hidden Squares

Application and Insight

Give thought and consideration to discovering different options and then making the best choices.

When making a decision, look at all the possibilities first.

Going Deeper

What has this activity taught you about your problem-solving skills?

How can you apply what you have learned to larger, more personal and critical problems?

Never, never, never give up. —Winston Churchill, former British Prime Minister

It Takes Courage!

to solve problems

Hidden Squares Diagram

Solution

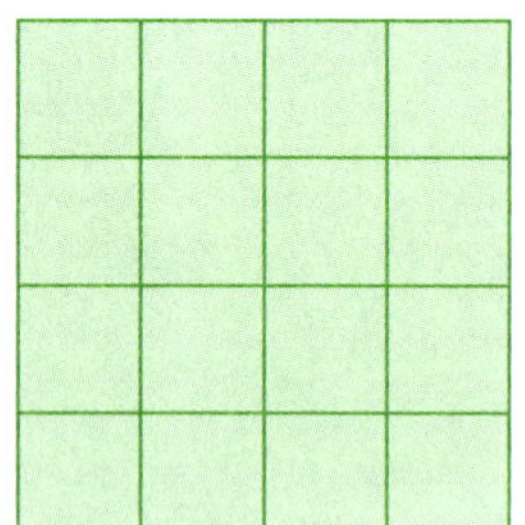

1 whole square

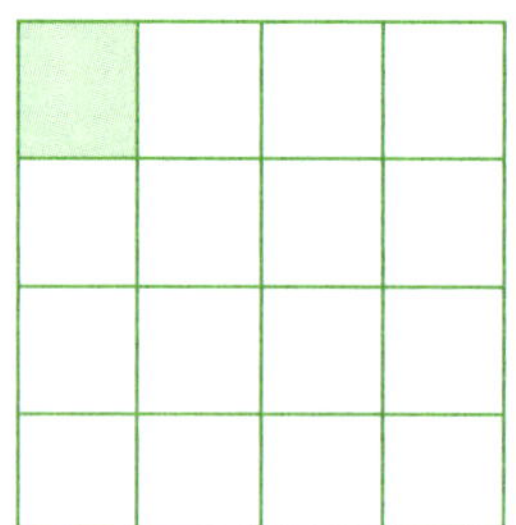

16 individual squares

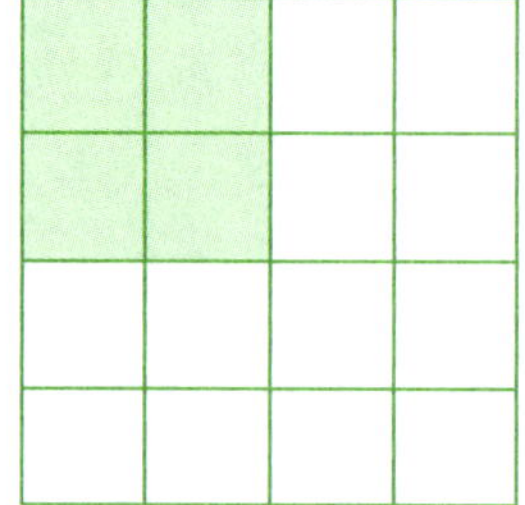

9 squares of 4 units each (one in the middle)

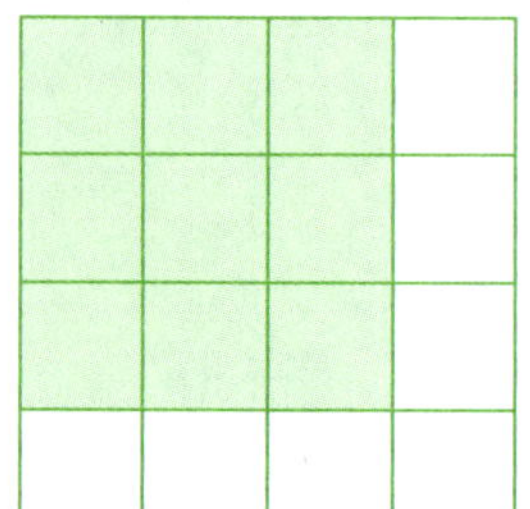

4 squares of 9 units each

Notes

Weakness of attitude becomes weakness of character.

—Albert Einstein, scientist

The Problem Box

Variable Time

Character Connection
Excellence & Patience

Purpose To help participants determine which factors we can control and which we cannot and how that affects the decision-making process

Overview This activity is a great way to facilitate group discussion. It illustrates that, although we may not have all the answers, we can look to others for help and guidance. It helps participants to analyze situations that they can and cannot control in life. This can be used as a one-time activity or as an ongoing project in which one problem is tackled in each meeting.

Life Skills Building strong support systems

Group Size Any

Cultural and Age Considerations None

Materials Things We Can and Cannot Control (Facilitator Notes), small pieces of paper (for a small group, you may want to have several pieces per person), pens or pencils, small box

Preparation *Refer to page 246 to review the Things We Can and Cannot Control.* Decorate the box and label it "Problem Box."

Instructions

1. Give each participant a piece of paper.
2. Ask the participants to write down a specific problem that has been bothering them. Inform them that the problem will later be discussed with the group, but participants will remain anonymous. Some examples include "My parents won't let me stay out late," "Everyone makes fun of me because of my curly hair," or "My boyfriend is pressuring me to have sex."
3. Pass around the Problem Box and ask participants to place their paper pieces in it.
4. Discuss Things We Can and Cannot Control (Facilitator Notes).
5. Pull a piece of paper out of the box and read it to the group.

The Problem Box

6. Ask participants to discuss whether the problem is controllable or not. Then identify the problem based on a category, such as personal habits, personal growth, physical characteristics, etc.
7. If it is a controllable problem, ask for suggestions on how the person could approach solving the problem. If the problem is uncontrollable, brainstorm ideas to help the participant accept or manage the situation.

Application and Insight

Resolving a problem is often easier when collaborating with trusted friends.

It is important to analyze whether a particular problem is something one can or cannot control.

Discussing problems with others helps one realize that many people struggle with some of the same issues.

Going Deeper

Have you ever realized that others might have the same problems as you do?

Will you actively commit to the things you can control?

How will you communicate this concept to friends and family?

How will you make controllable factors work to your advantage?

God grant me the serenity to accept the things I cannot change, the courage to change the things I can, and the wisdom to know the difference. —Serenity Prayer

It Takes Courage!

to share your problems with others

Things We Can and Cannot Control

Things We Can Control

Personal habits: Our grooming, makeup, clothing, accessories, tattoos, use of time, study habits, and community involvement

Personal growth: Our character development, use of talents, and practice of faith

Attitudes: Our emotional responses to others, communication style, treatment of others, and amount of effort we expend

Things We Cannot Control

Physical characteristics: Our height, race, gender, hair, facial features, coloring, and physical handicaps

Other people: Their thoughts, ideas, opinions, and lifestyle choices

Life circumstances: Our family composition, place of birth, natural events, the economy, time, things in the past, and personal or family illnesses

Notes

You've got to do your own growing, no matter how tall your grandfather was.

–Irish proverb

Red Light, Yellow Light, Green Light

30–45 Minutes

Character Connection
Empathy & Self-control

Purpose To identify the process of managing negative emotions in a three-step approach that is easy to remember

Overview This activity teaches empathy and consideration for other people, their emotions, and how they cope. Three steps are used to help participants think through their negative emotions using a familiar object, the traffic light.

Life Skill Managing anger in constructive ways

Group Size Any

Cultural and Age Considerations None

Materials Traffic Light Explanation (Facilitator Notes), Traffic Light Handout, traffic light prop (cardboard, construction paper, markers, glue), slips of paper, pens or pencils, small box or jar, chalkboard and chalk

Preparation *Refer to pages 247–249 to review Managing Negative Emotions.* Copy one Traffic Light Handout for each participant. Cut one slip of paper for each participant. Make a large traffic light prop. In the middle of the red circle, write "Over the Edge." In the yellow circle, write "Figure it Out." In the green circle, write "Take Action."

Instructions

1. Discuss the types of negative emotions (fear, anger, disgust, sadness) and write examples on the chalkboard.
2. Pass out the slips of paper. Ask the participants to identify a strong negative emotion they have felt recently and to write down the situation in which it occurred. For example, "A time I felt angry was when . . . ," or "I felt scared when . . ." Explain that this should be done anonymously because the situations will be read by others in the class. If a particular negative emotion is hard to address, let them choose another emotion that is easier to talk about.

Red Light, Yellow Light, Green Light

3. Pass around a box or a jar to collect all the paper slips.
4. Review the three-step process for managing negative emotions, referring to the traffic light prop.
5. Give each participant a copy of the Traffic Light Handout.
6. Ask participants to form groups of two or three and ask one person to select a slip of paper from the jar.
7. Instruct groups to work through the emotion and the situation according to the three-step process.
8. If time permits, ask the participants to share their situation and solution with the entire group.
9. Keep the traffic light prop in the meeting room to remind participants of the three-step process. Refer back to this activity throughout the year if you meet on a regular basis.

Application and Insight

It is helpful to understand the three-step process to cope with negative emotions.

Remember to stop, figure it out, and then take action before responding to a conflict.

Keeping one's emotions under control instead of reacting in anger takes skill and character.

Going Deeper

When have you lost control of your emotions?

What were the consequences?

How could you have handled it differently?

How did your actions affect other people?

Speak when you are angry and you'll make the best speech you'll ever regret. —Lawrence J. Peter, author

It Takes Courage!
to exercise self-control

Traffic Light Explanation

"I'm over the edge."

- Stop! Don't act. Don't respond to the situation.
- Get harmful emotions under control by thinking it out, waiting it out, or working it out.

"I'm figuring it out."

- Identify your feelings and what you think about them.
- Decide if the feelings are caused by something you can or can't control.
- Think of solutions for managing the emotions, the problem that caused them, or both.
- Discard solutions that are inconsistent with the Golden Rule and consider the consequences of the other options.
- If no solutions seem workable, ask for input from a trusted adult.
- Decide on a course of action.

"I'm taking action."

- Execute your plan.
- Evaluate and learn from your experience.

Traffic Light

Read through the scenario. In the **red circle**, write how you would physically react if you were in the other person's position. In the **yellow circle**, write whether you can control it and how you would handle the situation (how you would think it out, wait it out, or work it out). In the **green circle**, write your plan of action.

15–30 Minutes

Character Connection
Honesty & Responsibility

Purpose To provide an interactive method for participants to share their opinions about controversial or difficult issues

Overview This group question-and-answer exercise is a simple way to elicit individual responses from all the members of a group, providing a safe environment for participants to express their opinions as well as to hear the opinions of others.

Life Skill Expressing thoughts and opinions appropriately

Group Size Large (10 or more)

Cultural and Age Considerations Although this activity can be applied to any age group or culture, the questions provided in this activity are of a sexual nature and are more appropriate for ages 12 and older. Adapt the questions to whatever issues are relevant within your culture.

Materials Opinion Statements (Facilitator Notes), one piece of chart paper, six different colored plastic chips (or colored paper, if chips are not available)

Preparation Make Opinion Lines by cutting chart paper into four long strips; write one of the following words across each one: Strongly Agree, Agree, Disagree, Strongly Disagree. Divide chips or paper into sets (one set per small group, each set having all different colored chips).

strongly disagree | agree

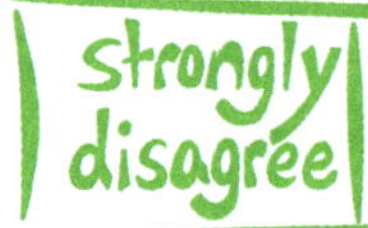

Instructions

1. Divide participants into groups of six individuals. Give each group an Opinion Line and a set of chips.
2. Ask each participant to take a different color plastic chip, which will be used to represent his or her opinion. Tell participants that you will read a series of statements to which they must give their opinion.
3. Before each statement is read, have the participants raise their chips over their heads.

What's Your Opinion?

4. After each statement is read, give participants 10 seconds to think about their answers (if they strongly agree, agree, disagree, or strongly disagree). Then, on the count of three, have all participants (at the same time) place their chip on the words that best represent their opinion about the statement.
5. After all the chips are on the opinion lines, ask the participants, one at a time, to pick up their chips from the line and share their opinions with the group in one or two statements. These answers should be brief—no speeches allowed!
6. During the discussions, walk around the room and glance at the participants' responses. This will provide informal feedback about their attitudes.
7. After participants have given their opinions on all the statements, lead the whole group in a discussion about the importance of forming and expressing your own opinion, as well as having respect for differing opinions.

Application and Insight

Listening to others' opinions and views on a subject helps to bring clarity to the discussion.

It is important to learn to respectfully participate in group discussions about difficult or controversial subjects.

Explaining why you made a certain decision helps you to solidify your own beliefs and understanding.

Going Deeper

How can you apply the listening skills you have learned to all aspects of your life?

What have you learned about your decision-making skills?

What would you like to do to improve your decision-making skills?

What can you do to help create a safe environment for group discussions?

A wise man makes his own decisions; an ignorant man follows the public opinion. —Chinese proverb

It Takes Courage!
to publicly take a stand

Opinion Statements

Read each statement to the participants, allowing them to give their opinion on it.

- The success of a date can be judged by how sexual it was.
- When someone says "no" to sex, it means that he or she does not like the other person.
- If a lot of money is spent on a date, sex should be given in return.
- When a female says "no" to sex, it really means "maybe," and "maybe" really means "yes."
- A real man is one who has had sex with a woman.
- Someone who dresses in a sexy way wants to have sex.
- By accepting an invitation to go to somebody's house alone, a person would be expected to have sex.
- It is the female's responsibility to decide how sexual a relationship will become.
- Boys who decline a girl's sexual advances are homosexual.

Notes

Act like a mouse and a large cat may try to eat you.

–Anonymous

Activity #52 Drama-in-a-Bag

30–60 Minutes

Character Connection
Honesty & Self-control

Purpose To equip participants to remove themselves from potentially dangerous situations

Overview These five dramas are a creative way for young people to consider the ways in which they can talk themselves out of a bad, and perhaps potentially dangerous, situation without ruining a relationship. It also helps participants to consider when it is best to leave a dangerous situation using any means possible.

Life Skill Avoiding unhealthy behaviors

Group Size Large (20 or more)

Cultural and Age Considerations It is very important to be sensitive to the varying communication strategies that are considered rude in different cultures. Be sensitive to the male-female dynamic in this activity. Modify any of the items to make the activity fun and more appropriate for your cultural group.

Materials Drama-in-a-Bag Strategy Cards (Activity Materials); five different bags filled with various items such as these: Violence Bag (frying pan, bandage, soda, tree branch, reading glasses, dirt); Alcohol Bag (empty beer bottle, tie, chewing gum, pair of old shoes, hat, keys, towel); Cheating Bag (notebook, ball, small box, CD, watch or clock, tissues, fake money); Stealing Bag (dress, pack of cigarettes, trash bag, book, pillow, cup, comb or brush); Sex Bag (empty beer bottle, T-shirt, candle, matches, fishing pole, sea shell, piece of jewelry)

Preparation Copy and cut out the Strategy Cards. Fill the bags and label each one.

Instructions

1. Divide participants into five groups and assign each group one of these topics: violence, alcohol, cheating, stealing, or sex.
2. Explain that each group will have 10 minutes to create a drama that demonstrates peer pressure associated with their topic (engaging in violence; being coaxed into

Drama-in-a-Bag

drinking alcohol, cheating, or stealing; or getting talked into sex outside of marriage). The drama must be 2–4 minutes long, include every person in the group, and use all items in the bag.

3. Hand each group their designated bag of items. Give them 10 minutes to create their dramas.
4. Ask each group to perform their drama for the others. After all the groups have finished, have each group choose one Strategy Card from your hand. Explain that their task is to modify their drama so the persons involved can get out of trouble using the strategy shown on their card.
5. You may have the groups perform the dramas again or simply state what their solution was to their assigned problem.
6. Discuss with the group the importance of developing effective verbal strategy skills. Highlight the strategies listed on the cards.

Application and Insight

There is great value in learning how to say "no."

There are many ways to say "no" without looking weak or being unkind.

It is always important for our verbal communications to match up with the nonverbal messages we are sending.

Whenever necessary, use anger to leave the situation immediately and free yourself from the conflict or struggle.

Going Deeper

What are some potentially dangerous or harmful situations you may face in your life?

Consider ways you can be prepared to confront those situations safely and tactfully.

How can you and your friends encourage each other to avoid these situations?

What is right is right, even if no one is doing it. What is wrong is wrong, even if everyone is doing it. —Unknown

It Takes Courage!

to resist negative peer pressure

Drama-in-a-Bag Strategy Cards

Copy and cut out one card for each group.

Strategy Card

Use humor

Strategy Card

Look to a friend for support

Strategy Card

State your reason and stand your ground

Strategy Card

Leave the situation

Strategy Card

Sound stunned and go on the offensive

Notes

The Challenge

Let others lead small lives,
but not you.
Let others argue over small things,
but not you.
Let others cry over small hurts,
but not you.
Let others leave their future in someone else's hand,
but not you.

–Jim Rohn, author and motivational speaker

Step by Step

30–45 Minutes

Character Connection
Patience & Responsibility

Purpose To illustrate the importance of thinking through tough decisions in order to make wise choices

Overview This activity is designed to introduce the five-step decision-making process. Participants work in groups to resolve a scenario, utilizing each step of the five-step process. While they are solving the problem, they will receive a twist to the scenario, making the problem-solving process even more challenging. This activity will teach participants that some problems can be solved on their own, some problems require the help of peers, and other problems need immediate attention from adults.

Life Skill Anticipating and avoiding negative consequences

Group Size Large (15 or more)

Cultural and Age Considerations Scenarios may need to be adapted to make them more relevant to the cultural and age group setting. The class can be divided by gender, with females working on female scenarios and males working on male scenarios.

Materials Decision-Making Process (Facilitator Notes), Scenarios and Challenges (Activity Materials), chalkboard and chalk, paper, pens or pencils

Preparation Copy and cut out each Scenario and Challenge Card. Keep the Scenario and Challenge cards separated. The Challenge Cards will be used later in the activity.

Instructions

1. Referring to the Facilitator Notes, discuss the five-step decision-making process. Write the five steps on the chalkboard.
2. Divide participants into groups of four to five individuals. Give each group a piece of paper and ask each to designate one person to write their ideas.
3. Give one Scenario Card to each group. Ask the groups to carefully read their cards and work together to create each step of the five-step decision-making process using their scenarios.

Step by Step

4. After the groups have worked for a few minutes, give them the Challenge Cards that correspond to their scenario. These cards contain a twist to each scenario, an uncontrollable factor in the process. Remind participants that you will offer assistance if they need it.
5. When everyone has finished the activity, reassemble all the groups. Ask each group to describe their scenario and the steps taken to make a decision. Allow groups to give feedback and discuss other options.

This Way
Go Here

Application and Insight

A person's choices help form personal character.

When making a decision, it is important to understand the decision-making process.

It is wise to consult a trusted friend or an adult when making a difficult decision.

Going Deeper

Was it easier to make tough decisions with the support of your peers?

Was it easier to make tough decisions with adult support?

How will using the five-step decision-making process help you in the future?

How would this exercise help develop good character?

The journey of a thousand miles begins with a single step. —Lau Tzu, Chinese Imperial Court librarian (604–531 B.C.)

It Takes Courage!
to ask others for advice

Decision-Making Process

1. **Identify the problem.** When someone asks you to do something that is troubling, begin by identifying the request and what you believe is the motivation for the request. For example, if a friend dares you to steal some clothes at a store, the situation would be defined like this: "She wants me to *steal clothes*, because _______________." This method will allow you to clearly understand what is being requested and why.

2. **List the results of engaging in the action.** The next step is to make a list of possible consequences, positive or negative, for going along. "If I steal the clothes . . ."

3. **Consider the options.** Evaluate your options based on being a person of good character and whether the action would enable you to accomplish your vision for your life. Ask yourself some simple questions:
   - What does my conscience say I should do? If others found out, would I be ashamed of my actions?
   - Would I want someone to treat me this way?
   - Can anyone get hurt, including me?
   - Would most adults approve?
   - Could the result keep me from reaching my dreams?

4. **Choose the wisest course of action.** If at this point your answer is not clear, don't act! Find a healthy and trusted adult to advise you in the situation.

5. **Take action!** Once you are confident that your decision is wise, be courageous and take action. Being misunderstood, laughed at, or even losing a friend for a while is worth reaching your dreams—and protecting your character.

Scenarios and Challenges

Copy and cut out one Scenario Card and corresponding Challenge Card for each group.

Nami Scenario: Nami is not satisfied with her friends. She would rather be included in the popular group that everyone admires. They have wild parties on weekends and seem to be more grown up. Nami has managed to get herself invited to one of their parties, where there are no parents around. Most of the boys and girls start pairing off and going on walks together.

Natasha Scenario: Natasha and her new friend are shopping. Natasha sees something she wants but cannot afford. Her friend suggests that she put the item in her bag when no one is looking. Her friend says it's easy, and she does it all the time without getting caught. Natasha looks around to see if anyone is looking. She really wants the item, but she has never thought of stealing before.

Muno Scenario: Muno is about to graduate from high school. He has been offered a job nearby where he can remain close to his family and friends. However, he has also been accepted to a college far away from home. The thought of leaving his family and friends really scares Muno, because he has never been separated from them for long.

Vitale Scenario: Vitale often has sex with many different girls. One of the girls he had sex with recently informed Vitale that she has HIV. She tells Vitale that it's in his best interest to get tested.

Nami Challenge: An attractive guy begins to flirt with Nami and asks her to go for a walk with him.

Natasha Challenge: A policeman walks into the store and grabs Natasha's arm.

Muno Challenge: Muno's mother has recently been diagnosed with a terminal illness. Her doctor has told her that she has less than a year to live.

Vitale Challenge: Vitale is engaged to be married.

A Crowded Bed

30–45 Minutes

Character Connection
Honesty & Self-control

Purpose To illustrate the importance of understanding how sexually transmitted infections are spread via multiple sexual partners

Overview This is a very effective way to illustrate the concept that each new sexual partner greatly increases one's chances of being exposed to a sexually transmitted infection. This activity also provides an excellent opportunity to discuss decision making and character, as the absence of certain character traits can cause significant damage in a relationship.

Life Skill Controlling sexual desire

Group Size Large (25 or more)

Cultural and Age Considerations You may want to vary the scenarios to make them more relevant to the age of your group. If you choose, you can easily incorporate more volunteers in this activity by adding more scenarios. If the use of a bed sheet is too vivid of a "picture" for your audience, ask the participants to stay standing and place their hand on the shoulder of the partner to represent the intimate relationship.

Materials A Crowded Bed Guidelines (Facilitator Notes), large sheet with a fun print, two large pillows

Preparation None

Instructions

1. Ask for eight males and six females to volunteer to participate in the activity and join you in the front of the room—males on one side of you and females on the other side of you.
2. Conduct the activity using the Crowded Bed Guidelines (Facilitator Notes).
3. Thank volunteers and ask them to return to their seats.
4. Discuss the following questions:

A Crowded Bed

- Do you think this could be a realistic scenario?
- What does this demonstrate about the danger of multiple sexual partners?
- What were some of the reasons why people engaged in sexual contact?

Application and Insight

Multiple sexual partners allow sexually transmitted infections to quickly spread from person to person.

It is probably impossible to know someone's complete past history. They may not know it themselves!

Prostitution, drug use, and same-sex relationships were all occurring without Juan or Lydia having any idea about them.

Going Deeper

What promises will you make to yourself about engaging in sexual activity? Are you willing to say "no" to sexual relations outside of marriage?

What can you do to keep your pledge?

How will you communicate your understanding of this concept to those you love? Your family? Your friends?

Adapted and used with permission from Life at the CrossRoads, © 2002 New Life World Aid, Inc.

He who is master of his thirst is master of his health. —French proverb

It Takes Courage!
to take responsibility for our choices

A Crowded Bed Guidelines

Note: We have used an adult example for this activity. You may want to change the scenarios to fit your youth culture. Choose scenarios based on when, where, and why youth engage in sexual activity. For example, you could choose situations such as a dance, alcohol and drug use, a party, at college, or going for a walk in an isolated area.

Eight male and six female volunteers are needed for this activity.

Step 1: Choose a male and a female to step forward and stand in the center facing the audience. It is best to choose people who are least likely to be embarrassed and most likely to add humor to the activity. Ask the group to pretend that the two volunteers are adults: Juan is 30 years old, and Lydia is 28 years old. (Be sure to use fictitious names.)

Step 2: Tell the group that Juan and Lydia met a few months ago when they were taking the same class at a university. They are hopelessly in love and think that they are ready to make the decision to begin sexual relations with each other.

Step 3: Pull out the sheet and ask Juan and Lydia to help you make the bed. Invite them to come and sit on the front of the sheet, facing the class. Hand each of them a pillow to hold.

Step 4: Explain the following scenario using the volunteers in the front of the room.

- "During their conversations, Juan told Lydia that he has had one previous sexual partner, his former wife." Select another volunteer to represent Juan's ex-wife and ask her, "Would you please come over here and sit on Juan's side of the bed?"
- "Lydia needs to be told a few things that she is not aware of. Juan doesn't know this, but while he and his wife were still married and he was on an extended business trip, she had a sexual relationship with another man." Choose a male volunteer to represent this person, and ask him to sit on Juan's side of the bed.
- "What Juan's wife didn't know is that this man had sexual relations with three women before his relationship with her." Choose three female volunteers to represent these people; ask them to sit on Juan's side of the bed.
- "Oh, and one more thing: Juan wasn't completely honest about his sexual past. While he was away on his extended trip, he had too much to drink one night and had sex with a prostitute." Choose another volunteer and ask her to sit on Juan's side of the bed.

A Crowded Bed Guidelines *(continued)*

- "And years ago in high school, Juan's first sexual experience was with this girl." Choose another volunteer to represent this person. Ask her to sit on Juan's side of the bed.
- "We have some news for Juan, too. Lydia told Juan that she had been involved with only one sexual partner, a boyfriend in high school." Choose another volunteer to represent this person. Ask him to sit on Lydia's side of the bed.
- "Lydia has led Juan to believe that she is sexually inexperienced because she has never been in love before. But even though she wasn't in love, she had sexual relations with this man and this man." Choose two volunteers to represent these people, and have them sit on Lydia's side of the bed.
- "What Lydia didn't know is that this man had sex with this woman. She also didn't know that he was an injection drug user. And the other man had sex with this man and this man." Choose three volunteers to represent these people. Ask them to sit on Lydia's side of the bed.
- "Now, let's think about this situation between Juan and Lydia. The bed is quite full, isn't it? Juan and Lydia, we have a question for you. Considering everything we've discussed about the spread of sexually transmitted infections, do you still think it would be wise to have sex together? Obviously not."

Sex in the Media

30–45 Minutes

Character Connection
Honesty & Responsibility

Purpose To challenge participants to be discerning in their choice of media

Overview This activity is designed to challenge participants to properly evaluate the information they are exposed to in the media. The activity spans two sessions: after the assignment is given, participants complete the handout at home, and then the material is discussed in a subsequent session.

Life Skill Recognizing negative influences

Group size Individual activity with any size group

Cultural and Age Considerations You may need to revise this assignment based on the media choices available to participants in your culture.

Materials Sex in the Media Evaluation Handout

Preparation Make one copy of the Sex in the Media Evaluation Handout for each participant.

Instructions

1. Distribute the Sex in the Media Evaluation Handout.
2. Explain that each participant is to complete the handout at home, together with a caring adult. Give participants a due date for the handout to be completed.
3. On the due date, ask the group to share their evaluations.
4. Discuss what was learned from the activity:
   - How many situations depicted in the media were an accurate portrayal of life?
   - What did this exercise teach you about choosing media to listen to or to watch?

Sex in the Media

- What did this exercise teach you about being discerning?
- What did this exercise teach you about making healthy choices?

Application and Insight

A person's belief system is influenced by the media.

Making wise choices about what to watch helps us to develop good decision-making skills.

Often what the media portray about life is not true or real.

It is important to choose media that encourage one to lead a purposeful and healthy life.

Going Deeper

Did you decide to stop watching or listening to certain media?

Did you decide to continue watching or listening to certain media?

How do the media affect the way you think, feel, and act?

Why is it important to be discerning?

Nothing is more difficult and therefore more precious than to be able to decide. —Napoleon Bonaparte, French general (1769–1821)

It Takes Courage!
to live our convictions

Sex in the Media Evaluation

Choose a television show or a movie that is known to have some sexual content. After watching the show or movie, answer the following questions about it.

1. How does it portray men's attitudes about sex?

2. How does it portray women's attitudes about sex?

3. What positive character qualities does it highlight?

4. What negative character qualities does it highlight?

5. If you decided to do what these people did, would it make you a better, stronger person? Why or why not?

6. If everyone in your community acted this way, what would the community be like? Would you want to live there?

Notes

The Flies and the Honey Pot

A number of flies were attracted to a jar of honey which had been overturned in a housekeeper's room, and placing their feet in it, ate greedily. Their feet, however, became so smeared with the honey that they could not use their wings, nor release themselves, and were suffocated. Just as they were expiring, they exclaimed, "O foolish creatures that we are, for the sake of a little pleasure we have destroyed ourselves."

—Aesop, legendary fable author

Pressure Points

30–45 Minutes

Character Connection
Honesty & Perseverance

Purpose To help participants become acquainted with the various ways people pressure others to have sex

Overview This lively group activity is a light, fun way of unveiling the very serious ways in which people are drawn into having sex.

Life Skill Planning to avoid personal harm

Group Size Large (10 or more)

Cultural and Age Considerations For certain cultural and age group settings, it may be appropriate to instruct boys and girls separately.

Materials Dimensions of Health and Wellness Diagram (Facilitator Notes), chalkboard and chalk, paper, pens or pencils

Preparation Draw the Dimensions of Health and Wellness Diagram on the chalkboard.

Instructions

1. Briefly review the Dimensions of Health and Wellness Diagram with the group.
2. Explain that they will be playing a game involving the ways people try to get others to have sex by applying pressure in each dimension (physical, emotional, mental, social, occupational, and spiritual).
3. Divide participants into groups of three to five individuals.
4. Ask each group to designate one person to record the ideas generated by the group throughout the game.
5. Choose a category from the Dimensions of Health and Wellness Diagram and announce it. Give each group one minute to generate as many ways as possible that people apply pressure in that particular dimension to get others to have sex.
6. When the time has expired, ask one of the groups to read its list. All items that are duplicated on any other group's list should be crossed out on everyone's list. When

Pressure Points

the first group finishes reading their list, instruct them to circle the remaining items (those that have not been crossed out). These are the items unique to their list that no one else thought to include.

7. One by one, ask each group to read its list, mentioning only the items that have not yet been crossed off.
8. Repeat the process with the remaining five categories of the diagram, asking groups to total their unique answers after each round. The group with the most items at the end of all six rounds wins the game.

Application and Insight

There are many ways in which people will pressure others to have sex with them.

Each person has the power to say "no" to the pressure to have sex.

Going Deeper

Why do people pressure others to have sex? Why is it wrong to do so?

How do you feel when you sense someone is pressuring you to have sex with them?

In what area are you the most vulnerable to pressure? How can you protect yourself in that area?

To be nobody but yourself—in a world which is doing its best, night and day, to make you everybody else—means to fight the hardest battle which any human being can fight; and never stop fighting.

—Marie Curie, Polish-French chemist

It Takes Courage!
to avoid risky situations

Dimensions of Health and Wellness Diagram

Notes

Some boys, playing near a pond, saw a number of frogs in the water and began to pelt them with stones. They killed several of them, when one of the frogs, lifting his head out of the water, cried out: "Pray stop, my boys: What is sport to you, is death to us."

One man's pleasure may be another's pain.

–Aesop, legendary fable author

Sex Pros and Cons

45–60 Minutes

Character Connection
Empathy & Self-control

Purpose To challenge participants to consider the reasons for abstaining from or engaging in sexual behavior

Overview This group activity challenges participants to consider the varied reasons for choosing to abstain from or to engage in sex before marriage. They will also discuss the concept of healthy sexual behavior for individuals and the community as a whole.

Life Skill Articulating personal values to others

Group Size Any

Cultural and Age Considerations This activity assumes that saving sex for marriage is the healthiest choice. Sexual norms may vary among cultures; yet, from a medical perspective, it is imperative that we challenge young people to save sex until marriage and then to remain faithful in marriage. Use your judgment as you explore these issues and challenge cultural norms that are not healthy.

Materials Sex Before Marriage Pros and Cons Handout, pieces of chart paper, markers, pens or pencils

Preparation Make one copy of the Sex Before Marriage Pros and Cons Handout for each participant.

Instructions

1. Distribute the Sex Before Marriage Pros and Cons Handout to each participant.
2. Divide the group by gender, and give each group a piece of chart paper and a marker.
3. Ask each group to choose one person to record the group's responses on the chart paper. Instruct the other participants to write the same answers on their handout.
4. Give groups 10 minutes to discuss the pros and the cons of sex before marriage and to write their answers in the columns. Some examples might include the following:

Reasons to Have Sex:

- Peer pressure
- Curiosity
- Fun
- Want to have a baby
- Lonely
- Want to feel loved
- Don't want to lose the relationship
- Act like an adult
- Hate having others tell them what to do or not do

Sex Pros and Cons

Reasons to Postpone Sex:
- Honor faith teachings
- Honor parents' wishes
- Afraid of being caught and getting in trouble
- Afraid of getting a sexually transmitted infection
- Afraid of getting pregnant
- Don't want to complicate the relationship
- Don't want to hurt parents
- Want to protect reputation
- Want to make sure they achieve goals

5. Reassemble as a group, and ask each group to share the answers they have written on their paper. Remind the participants to be respectful of each other during feedback.
6. After both groups have shared their answers, send participants back to their groups and give them 10 minutes to discuss the three questions at the bottom of the handout.
7. Ask one new person from each group to share some of the main points discussed.
8. Ask questions to help the group identify and discuss healthy and respectful sexual behavior. Also, be aware that some participants may be victims of sexual abuse, making sure all comments are kind, gentle, and noncondemning.

Application and Insight

Discussing these issues and the answers to these questions is difficult in a group setting of peers. Learning to participate in a caring and responsible way is an important skill.

Abstaining from sexual behavior until marriage and remaining faithful in marriage is the safest, healthiest form of sexual behavior.

Going Deeper

How will you determine the sexual behavior that is best for you?

What will you do to prepare yourself to engage in the safest, healthiest behavior?

What can you do to have meaningful discussions about this topic with your friends?

How can you encourage one another to make good choices about sexual behavior?

Everything can be taken from a man but one thing: the last of the human freedoms—to choose one's own way. —Dr. Viktor Frankl, author, Holocaust survivor

It Takes Courage!

to postpone sexual involvement

Sex Before Marriage Pros and Cons

PROS	CONS
Reasons people have sex before marriage	Reasons people postpone sex until marriage

What were the similarities and differences between the male and female groups?

How does our culture view sexual behavior?

Do you think our cultural norms are healthy and consistent with what it means to be a person of good character? Why or why not?

The Freedoms of Choosing Abstinence

Freedom from:

- Sexually transmitted infections
- Fear of unintended pregnancy
- Experiencing the trauma of abortion
- Pressure to get married before you are ready
- Deep emotional scars
- Guilty feelings
- Social stigma
- Worries about getting caught

Freedom to:

- Focus energy on reaching goals
- Enjoy being a teenager
- Experience that special relationship found only in marriage
- Be able to bear children when the time comes
- Experience greater self-esteem

My Most Courageous Moments

30–45 Minutes

Character Connection
Patience & Perseverance

Purpose To give participants the opportunity to reflect on occasions when they exercised courage and to identify ways these moments of courage have helped them to become better people

Overview Participants plot and illustrate points on a timeline to indicate their most courageous moments. They then recognize how these moments have helped them to become better people.

Life Skill Coping positively with life's challenges

Group Size Individual activity with any size group

Cultural and Age Considerations None

Materials My Most Courageous Moments Timeline Handout, pens or pencils

Preparation Make one copy of the My Most Courageous Moments Timeline Handout for each participant, or draw the diagram on the chalkboard and ask participants to copy it on plain paper.

Instructions

1. Distribute the My Most Courageous Moments Timeline Handout to each participant.
2. Ask participants to close their eyes and think of some of the defining moments in their lives—at least four decisions or events that changed the direction of their lives in some way. Instruct them to record each of these moments on their timeline.
3. Ask participants to think of at least four of the most courageous moments of their lives. Instruct them to graph these moments onto the timeline. They may illustrate or decorate their timelines however they wish.
4. When the timelines are completed, instruct participants to answer the questions at the bottom of the handout.

My Most Courageous Moments

5. Ask participants to share their timelines in small groups. They should reflect on and discuss the role of courage in developing good character.

Application and Insight

Developing and demonstrating good character requires moments of courage.

People overcome personal fears by walking through them.

Going Deeper

What similarities did you notice as people shared their most courageous moments?

How did courageous moments shape their character?

How have your courageous moments influenced later decisions that you have made?

A most insidious form of fear is that which…condemns as foolish and futile the small, daily acts of courage which help preserve man's self-respect. —Aung San Suu Kyi, Burmese civil rights leader

Timeline

My Most Courageous Moments

On the timeline below, record and illustrate at least four defining moments of your life. Then record at least four of the most courageous moments in your life.

BIRTH

PRESENT

Describe how these courageous moments have helped you to become a better person.

Is there a time you wish you had shown courage but did not? How would you do things differently now?

What Will Matter

Ready or not, some day it will all come to an end.
There will be no more sunrises, no minutes, hours or days.
Your wealth, fame and temporal power will shrivel to irrelevance.
It will not matter what you owned or what you were owed.
Your grudges, resentments, frustrations and jealousies will finally disappear.
So too, your hopes, ambitions, plans and to-do lists will expire.
The wins and losses that once seemed so important will fade away.
It won't matter where you came from or what side of the tracks you lived on at the end.
It won't matter whether you were beautiful or brilliant.
Even your gender and skin color will be irrelevant.

So what will matter? How will the value of your days be measured?

What will matter is not what you bought but what you built,
not what you got but what you gave.
What will matter is not your success but your significance.
What will matter is not what you learned but what you taught.
What will matter is every act of integrity, compassion, courage or sacrifice that enriched, empowered or encouraged others to emulate your example.

What will matter is not your competence but your character.
What will matter is not how many people you knew,
but how many will feel a lasting loss when you're gone.
What will matter is not your memories but the memories of those who loved you.
What will matter is how long you will be remembered, by whom and for what.

Living a life that matters doesn't happen by accident.
It's not a matter of circumstance but of choice.
Choose to live a life that matters.

—Michael Josephson

Activity #59

When Is It Okay to Lie?

15–30 Minutes

Character Connection
Honesty & Self-control

Purpose To help participants assess what it means to be a truth teller and to look at the reasons why individuals choose to lie

Overview This individual activity, in which participants are on both the giving and receiving ends of a lie, prompts them to consider the acceptability of lying from both perspectives.

Life Skill Maintaining personal integrity

Group Size Individual activity with any size group

Cultural and Age Considerations None

Materials Paper, pens or pencils, chalkboard and chalk

Preparation None

Instructions

1. Give each participant a piece of paper.
2. Ask participants to list some reasons why they would lie to someone.
3. Ask volunteers to share some of their reasons. Write their answers on the chalkboard.
4. Instruct participants to write their answers to the question, "When is it okay to lie to someone?"
5. Elicit feedback and write their answers on the board.
6. Finally, ask the following question: "If the roles were reversed and someone lied to you, would you be okay with that person lying to you for the same reasons?" Allow participants time to think about the question and to record their thoughts.
7. Ask for volunteers to share their answers, then discuss the following questions:
   - Is it okay to lie?
   - Why would it not be okay for someone to lie to you for the same reasons?

When Is It Okay to Lie?

- How do you feel when someone lies to you?
- What happens in a relationship when someone lies to you?

8. Allow time for discussion and write down some key thoughts on the chalkboard.

Application and Insight

Lying is often rationalized as okay; however, lying:

- *Always breaks trust in a relationship*
- *Makes people feel like they have to hide out of fear of "being caught"*
- *Labels that person as a liar*
- *Can hurt employment possibilities*
- *Destroys self-esteem*

The Golden Rule is an important factor to consider when discussing being a "truth teller."

One lie often leads to another in order to cover up the original one. This is bondage. A person who tells the truth is free.

Going Deeper

Ask participants to keep a journal reflecting on each day for the next month. They should note the times that they may have lied or "shaded the truth," and write down the reasons they made that choice. Ask them to also note the times when they were tempted to lie but chose not to, and how that wise choice made them feel.

How many times do you have to lie to be called a liar?
—Michael Josephson, founder of the Josephson Institute of Ethics

It Takes Courage!
to be a truth teller

Nine Dots

15 Minutes

Character Connection
Patience & Perseverance

Purpose To provide an opportunity for participants to develop or sharpen their creative and critical-thinking skills

Overview Participants are challenged to stretch their perception and critical-thinking skills by solving a fun geometric puzzle.

Life Skill Finding creative alternatives

Group Size Individual activity with any size group

Cultural and Age Considerations None

Materials Nine Dots Diagram Handout, pens or pencils, chalkboard and chalk

Preparation Copy one Nine Dot Diagram Handout for each participant.

Instructions

1. Give each participant a copy of the Nine Dots Diagram Handout.
2. Ask the participants to try to connect all nine dots using only four straight, continuous lines—without lifting up their pencils or retracing a previous line.
3. Allow a few minutes for them to make several attempts, and then ask how many completed the task successfully.
4. If any participants have solved the puzzle, ask them to show their solution to the class. If no one has solved the puzzle, draw the solution diagrams on the chalkboard.

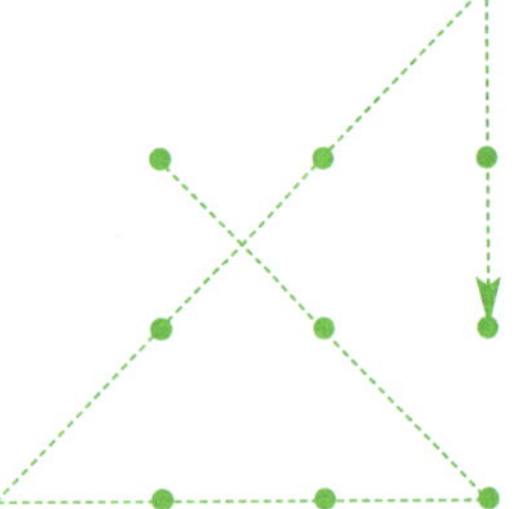

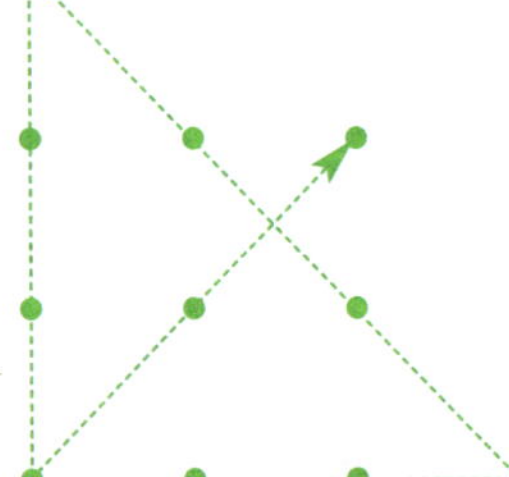

Nine Dots

5. Discuss the following questions:
   - What does our mind tend to do with the configuration of the nine dots? (We mentally create a square and end up not being able to figure out how to incorporate the middle dot.)
   - What is the key to solving the puzzle? (Try to think past the obvious solutions that automatically come to our minds and begin to think of new possibilities.)
   - In what ways do we tend to think "inside the box"—considering only the usual ways of doing things? How can we begin to think "outside the box"—looking beyond the normal concepts we're used to considering?

Application and Insight

Developing creativity, critical-thinking skills, and problem-solving skills is essential to making good decisions.

Going Deeper

Can you think of a problem you solved that required creative thinking? Do you have an example you can share with the group?

What can you do to stretch your ability to perceive things from different perspectives? How can you best develop this habit?

You have brains in your head and feet in your shoes. You can steer yourself in any direction you choose. —Dr. Seuss, children's author

It Takes Courage!
to think creatively

Nine Dots Diagram

Try to connect all nine dots using only four straight, continuous lines, without lifting up your pencil or retracing a previous line.

Notes

If you want to slide, you must carry your sled.

—Ukrainian proverb

Activity #61 Appointments

15–30 Minutes

Character Connection
Kindness & Respect

Purpose To get to know other people and to hear their opinions

Overview This easily adaptable activity is designed to help people interact with others in the group. By changing the questions, you can adapt the activity to explore different topics.

Life Skill Socializing in healthy ways

Group Size Large (10 or more)

Cultural and Age Considerations For variety, one way to adapt the activity is to let each time represent a meeting place—such as the lake, the store, the church, and so forth. You can also use different times of the day such as breakfast, lunch, and dinner, or you could use different days of the week.

Materials Appointment Questions and Statements (Facilitator Notes), Appointment Schedule Handout, pens or pencils

Preparation From the Appointment Questions and Statements (Facilitator Notes), decide which questions you will use during the activity. Make one copy of the Appointment Schedule Handout for each participant.

Instructions

1. Give each participant a copy of the Appointment Schedule Handout.
2. Explain that each person will need to make "appointments" with several other group members. On the handout, ask each participant to write the name of one person next to the time of the appointment. Each name may be used only one time.
3. Allow five minutes for individuals to arrange all of their appointments. Ask them to return to their seats as soon as they have finished.

Appointments

4. Explain that you will call out an appointment time at random. Each person must stand up and go find the person with whom they made an appointment during that time.
5. When most people have found their partner for that appointment, read a question from your list and explain that they will have exactly two minutes to discuss the answer.
6. At the end of two minutes, call out the next appointment time (it is more fun if you do this at random instead of going down the sheet one by one) and then read the next question on the list.
7. Follow the same procedure until all of the appointments have been completed.

Application and Insight

Questions are an effective way to get to know someone.

Listening to others is a crucial aspect of communicating well.

Going Deeper

Did you find any of these questions offensive?

Did you learn anything new about yourself or your friends?

What types of questions would help you to see someone's true character?

The good things in life are not to be had singly, but come to us with a mixture. —Charles Lamb, English poet

It Takes Courage!

to meet new people

Appointment Questions and Statements

Choose up to nine statements to use in the activity.

- ☐ What was the happiest moment in your life?
- ☐ What is the ugliest thing that you have ever seen?
- ☐ If you could visit any place in the world, where would you go?
- ☐ If you were stranded on a desert island, which three people would you like to have along?
- ☐ Would you want to know the exact date of your death? Why or why not?
- ☐ What is the best gift you've ever received?
- ☐ If you could interview any person who has already died, who would you want to interview?
- ☐ What is your biggest worry?
- ☐ What is your favorite way to relax?
- ☐ What one thing about yourself would you change if you could?
- ☐ If you were going to be changed into a scientist, baby, or president of a country for one day, which would you prefer to be and why?
- ☐ What four words best describe you?
- ☐ What one thing do you hope to accomplish in your life?
- ☐ If love were a color, what color would it be?
- ☐ Explain one thing you do not understand about the opposite sex.
- ☐ What is your favorite joke or story?
- ☐ What do you want to be doing five years from now?
- ☐ If you could change anything about the world, what would it be?
- ☐ Who do you think is the most important person who has lived in the last few years?
- ☐ What is your most prized possession?
- ☐ What is the first thing that comes to mind when you think about God?
- ☐ If your life were turned into a movie, what would be the title of the movie?
- ☐ How do you act when you are angry?
- ☐ If anger were a color, what color would it be?
- ☐ What makes you really angry?
- ☐ What would you do if your best friend had a problem with alcohol or other drugs?
- ☐ List three things you wish you could control but can't.
- ☐ If a friend were pressuring you to do something that you didn't want to do, how would you try to get out of it?
- ☐ Name three sure ways to sabotage your life.
- ☐ Describe your ideal spouse.
- ☐ Name one thing that you could control, but you usually don't.
- ☐ Describe the problems of an alcoholic.

Appointment Schedule

Make appointments with one person for each of the times listed below. Names should not be repeated.

Time	Name
9:00 a.m.	______________________
10:30 a.m.	______________________
11:00 a.m.	______________________
12:00 p.m.	______________________
1:30 p.m.	______________________
2:00 p.m.	______________________
4:30 p.m.	______________________
5:30 p.m.	______________________
6:00 p.m.	______________________

Activity #62 In the Court Today

45–60 Minutes

Character Connection
Honesty & Responsibility

Purpose To help participants understand the concept of rationalizing wrong behavior

Overview This activity helps to explain the concept of rationalization, or justifying a wrong behavior. A fun and exciting courtroom drama is used to identify and discuss the five common ways people rationalize their behavior.

Life Skill Accepting responsibility for our actions

Group Size Large (10 or more)

Cultural and Age Considerations This activity works best with an age group that understands courtroom procedures. Change the court case to one that is familiar and relevant to make it age-appropriate and culturally relevant.

Materials Court of Rationalization (Facilitator Notes), Role Cards (Activity Materials), In the Court Today Handout, props for the courtroom (desk or table for the judge, several chairs for the courtroom players, and a witness stand)

Preparation Make one copy of the In the Court Today Handout for each participant. Copy and cut out the Role Cards. Assemble additional props.

Instructions

1. Using the Court of Rationalization (Facilitator Notes), explain the concept of rationalizing and the five common ways this is done to excuse wrong behavior.
2. Ask for eight volunteers to pick from the eight Role Cards. The roles are defendant, defense attorney, two defense witnesses, victim, prosecuting attorney, prosecution witness, and jury foreman. As the facilitator, you will serve as the judge.
3. The remaining group members will serve as members of the jury. Give each of these participants a copy of the In the Court Today Handout.
4. Allow time for the actors to meet together to review their roles. The rest of the group can help set up the courtroom.

In the Court Today

5. As the judge, begin the court session by introducing the case and explaining that this is the sentencing phase of the trial. Read: "The defendant has been found guilty of stealing money from a neighbor. We are here today to hear comments before the jury decides the punishment." The more creative the story, the more fun the group will have with it.
6. The judge will then ask to hear from different members in the courtroom. Follow the script on the In the Court Today Handout as participants follow along.
7. Following the case, conduct a group discussion:
   - How many rationalizations were used throughout the case? (Refer to the Court of Rationalization list.)
   - How would the case have ended differently if the defendant had faced the facts and told the truth?
   - What are some examples of poor character in the scenario?

Application and Insight

Rationalization is twisting the truth and making excuses for wrong behavior.

When someone rationalizes wrong behavior, it can hurt others as well as the individual.

Making the choice to be honest and not rationalize builds self-esteem and character.

Going Deeper

Explain why rationalizing is equivalent to lying, to yourself and to others.

Think about how often you rationalize in your daily life. What are some other examples of rationalization?

Will you commit yourself to telling the truth and not justifying your wrong behavior in the future?

Those who can't dance blame it on the flute and drum. —Thai proverb

It Takes Courage!
to admit when we are wrong

Court of Rationalization

Review the following points with the group.

Five Common Methods of Rationalization

1. **The Payback:** Justifying our wrong actions because someone has wronged us. *"She's only getting what she's done to others."*
2. **The Comparison:** Evaluating our actions based on what others are doing. *"I'm not doing anything that everyone else isn't doing."*
3. **The Reward:** When we believe we are owed. *"I know I lied, but I deserve this. I worked hard for that promotion."*
4. **The Need:** The end justifies the means. *"I had to cheat or I would have failed."*
5. **The Law:** If there is no rule that says something is wrong, then it's justified. *"I didn't break any laws."*
6. **The Damage Assessment:** If no one gets hurt, then it can't be wrong. *"Nobody got hurt; nobody is going to get hurt, either."*

Court Case Ideas

Driving a friend's car without permission
Drinking and driving
Beating his wife
Stealing food from a local market
Cheating on a college entrance examination
Vandalizing school property
Speeding and hitting a child on a bicycle
Attending a party where people were using drugs
Failing to pay their taxes for two years
Throwing a rock at a car and breaking a window
Carrying a hidden bag of drugs at the airport
With a gang when someone was shot and killed
Committing date or acquaintance rape
Stealing clothes at a department store

In the Court Today

Title of the Court Case ______________________________

Courtroom Procedure

1. Judge enters the courtroom and states the case.
2. Judge asks the prosecuting attorney to interview the victim and the prosecution witness.
3. Judge asks the defense attorney to interview the defendant and each of the two defense witnesses.
4. Judge asks the prosecuting attorney to summarize his or her arguments.
5. Judge asks the defense attorney to summarize his or her arguments.
6. Judge asks the jury to deliberate.
7. Jury Foreman announces the sentence.
8. Judge will make summary comments and end the case.

What rationalizations did you hear in the court room? Give specific examples.

Role Cards

Copy and cut out cards for each person in the drama.

Victim
When called to take the stand, the victim will be asked to explain the crime and how he or she has been hurt by the situation.

Defendant
When called to take the stand, the defendant admits to the crime, but asks for leniency, defending his or her behavior and actions using rationalizations.

Defense Attorney
The defense attorney represents the defendant, calls the witnesses for the defense to the stand, asks questions, and makes a summary argument asking for leniency (using rationalizations).

Prosecuting Attorney
The prosecuting attorney calls the victim and the prosecution witness to the stand, asks questions, and makes a summary argument for why the defendant should be held accountable for his or her actions and punished accordingly.

Defense Witness 1
This witness will testify for the defense, with the goal to rationalize the defendant's actions and ask for leniency.

Prosecution Witness
This witness will testify for the prosecution, with the goal to discredit the defendant's rationalizations with facts.

Defense Witness 2
This witness will testify for the defense, with the goal to rationalize the defendant's actions and ask for leniency.

Jury Foreman
The leader of the jury consists of the rest of the group members. The jury foreman leads a brief deliberation to decide the fate of the defendant. The foreman announces the jury's decision in the courtroom.

Preventing HIV/AIDS

HIV/AIDS Overview 338
Associated Symptoms 339
Voluntary HIV Counseling and Testing 340
Ways HIV is Spread 342
Discussing HIV Transmission 346
Preventing the Spread of HIV 347
Universal Precautions 354
Living Longer with HIV 358
HIV Infection and Sexual Relations 361
Treatments and Cures 361
Character Connection: Empathy and Compassion 363
Community Involvement in HIV/AIDS 365
It Takes Courage! 367

Preventing HIV/AIDS

He who heareth has hope; he who has hope has everything.

—Arabian proverb

Many young adults today have never known a world without grim reports and statistics about HIV/AIDS. Despite our best efforts, HIV infection continues to enter and ravage new communities and people groups. In just a little over two decades, AIDS has become the largest health problem in the world, a disease disproportionately affecting young people in developing nations.

All nations are touched by this pandemic, but in many developing nations HIV/AIDS has become one of the primary causes of death. We have spent the last nine years traveling to many of these nations leading conferences on preventing the spread of HIV/AIDS and other sexually transmitted infections, and we have met wonderful educators and professionals who work tirelessly to protect and care for their communities. Our hearts are heavy with the accounts of pain and suffering of their own families and those with whom they work. What a privilege it has been to walk alongside these dear friends and colleagues, offering support as they search for answers for their own communities.

There has been progress in the fight against HIV/AIDS on many fronts. Research has revealed critical information about HIV and how it attacks the immune system. New medicines are now available to treat many of the infections associated with a weakened immune system. Mother-to-child transmission can be greatly reduced with drugs such as AZT and Nevirapine. Antiretroviral therapies have slowed the disease progression in many (but not all) patients, giving them unexpected hope. Even though there is a long way to go, great advances have been made in reducing the stigma of AIDS. Political leaders and faith-based organizations are entering the fight, mobilizing prevention and care efforts like never before. Difficult issues such as sexual abuse and rape are being acknowledged and condemned. And an emphasis on behavioral change has led to a striking reduction in new HIV infections in a few countries.

The greatest single success to dramatically decrease new cases of HIV is represented in the ABC (Abstain, Be faithful, Condoms) approach to prevention first introduced in Uganda. In this practical approach, President and First Lady Museveni passionately encouraged Ugandans to Abstain before marriage, Be faithful in marriage, and use Condoms as a last resort. President Museveni mobilized the nation and called the people to their "patriotic duty" to stop the spread of AIDS. Faith communities and other groups, schools, and many sectors of the media were trained to deliver public health messages focusing on the concepts of abstinence before marriage and faithfulness in marriage. It made a huge difference!

The security of communities is under threat, as a generation of young people grows up without adequate adult guidance, nurturing, care, or love. The loss of every breadwinner's income makes it harder for his or her dependents to obtain health care, education, and nutrition—thus leaving them more vulnerable to infection. This cycle need be repeated only a few times and AIDS destroys an entire community.

-Kofi Annan, Secretary-General of the United Nations

According to "Evidence That Demands Action,"[1] published by the Medical Institute for Sexual Health, there were amazing results when it came to changing sexual behavior. In the first decade of promoting the ABC philosophy, the HIV/AIDS prevalence rate among pregnant women dropped from 21 percent to 6 percent. Men and women dramatically decreased their number of sexual partners and both boys and girls delayed the onset of sexual behavior. This is exciting news in HIV prevention, because both of these factors are critical for the prevention of HIV/AIDS and other sexually transmitted infections.

From Uganda's experience, we have learned a valuable lesson: people can and will make changes in their sexual behavior. Yet the challenge of sustaining the new healthier behavior is still before us. Recent data in Uganda suggests that the early changes in behavior are beginning to slide. Some have suggested that condom promotion and the introduction of antiretroviral medications may be causing a misperception of safety. Finding the right combination of messages for the right people, at the right time, and in such a way that causes lifelong change is a formidable challenge.

Controlling HIV is complex because circumstances surrounding the epidemics vary in different parts of the world. You may be living in a community where HIV has had little impact, or you could be teaching in an area where 10 percent of the precious students in your classroom are HIV-positive. In some areas, such as Eastern Europe, the epidemic is raging because of injection drug use. Other areas of the world deal with epidemics driven by sexual activity. Researchers have watched countries explode in the growth of HIV infection rates in just a few short years. No nation is immune.

Therefore, halting the spread of HIV/AIDS is dependent on political and personal will to coordinate and implement behavior change programs in schools, faith communities, and throughout all segments of society. We must teach and promote healthy sexual behavior—both partners waiting until marriage to begin sexual involvement, and both partners choosing to be faithful in marriage. This is essential, but certainly not an easy task. These messages challenge the roles of men and women and are counter to today's popular culture. Delivery of these messages is particularly challenging within cultures where issues such as sexual abuse

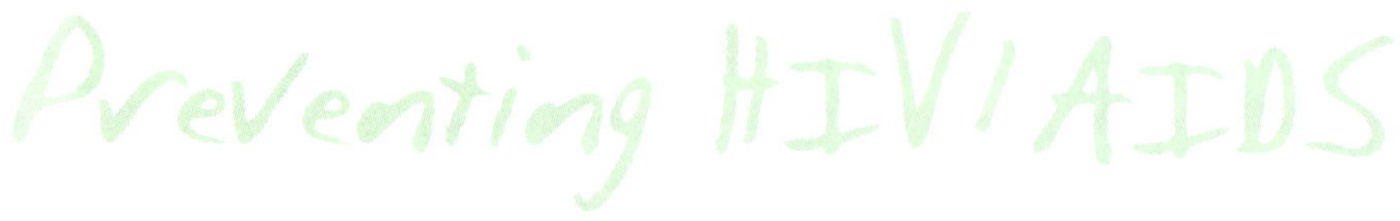

and survival sex are widespread. Success will require a multifaceted approach within a context of hope. There must be hope that life can be different.

A comprehensive public health approach to HIV/AIDS must address prevention, treatment, and care issues. Those who are infected need access to antiretroviral drugs and medicines to treat opportunistic infections. They need to be able to live in communities free of stigmatization and discrimination. Families need financial assistance. And particularly daunting and troubling is the need to care for the millions of orphans left behind. These little ones struggle to survive and are often homeless victims of violence and sexual abuse. Teachers struggle to meet their needs; many children never even make it to school.

We have strived to make this section easy to read, although it is quite technical and lengthy compared to the others. Giving information about HIV/AIDS and correcting misinformation about HIV/AIDS is central to our task. Misinformation can be very dangerous. But information alone will not change behavior! Prevention success will be achieved when we change attitudes about sex and alcohol and other drug use and teach the skills to say "no" to them. As educators and youth service providers, our work is never done. There is always a new group of young people—and the education begins anew.

The information in this section is consistent with the ABC approach to prevention. Because our intent for this text is to prevent premarital sexual behavior, this guide does not advocate condom distribution for educational settings. The activities therefore focus solely on the A and B components of the model. However, we have included facts about condoms and their use for individuals who are working in HIV counseling centers with married couples and for those who are working with the highest risk groups.

Our goals in this section are to:

- Facilitate opportunities to teach practical and medically accurate information about the spread of HIV
- Present abstinence until marriage and mutual faithfulness in marriage as essentials to avoiding sexually transmitted infections
- Impart a sense of duty to be actively involved in fighting the spread of HIV and reducing the stigma and discrimination in the community
- Promote caring for others by presenting practical ways to help those who are HIV-infected
- Present information on learning how to live with HIV infection

Note that the practical skills to say "no" are presented in the sections "Communicating Effectively" and "Making Wise Decisions."

We've designed this section to supplement existing HIV/AIDS programs. If you are just beginning your involvement in AIDS education, we strongly encourage you to obtain additional educational materials and take advantage of educational programs and HIV prevention specialists in your area. Your local health department can assist you with issues specific to your locale and can point you to excellent resources.

Take the time to know your facts and learn techniques for teaching in a sensitive and compassionate way. This will help you to feel confident and relaxed and will enhance your learning environment. Young people want to know about issues related to sex and its consequences, but they want to hear accurate and relevant information from compassionate and kind adults who are willing to listen, too.

HIV/AIDS Overview

HIV: Human Immunodeficiency Virus

HIV is the virus that causes a condition called AIDS (Acquired Immune Deficiency Syndrome). Science has learned more about HIV than any other virus in history! The cause and effect relationship of HIV to AIDS has been firmly established. HIV is a very complex virus and is particularly destructive in the human body as it slowly destroys the immune system's ability to fight off disease. When people are initially infected with HIV, they may experience flu-like symptoms which go away in a few days. Most people are unaware that they have been infected. Yet, ever so slowly, HIV destroys their body's ability to fight off disease, and eventually they experience serious medical problems. At this point they have progressed to the condition called AIDS.

Once people are infected with HIV, they can pass it to others, whether they are feeling ill or well.

AIDS: Acquired Immune Deficiency Syndrome

We use the term AIDS to describe the symptoms of an immune system that has been so damaged by HIV that it becomes extremely difficult for the body to fight off simple infections. People with AIDS struggle to stay healthy. They are plagued by opportunistic infections (pneumonia, cancer, tuberculosis, fungal infection, etc.) that are rarely seen in persons with strong immune systems. Although there are medicines and treatments that can prolong the life of someone who has AIDS, it is believed that most persons with AIDS will die prematurely. Whenever discussing HIV or AIDS, it is important to emphasize that once people are infected with HIV, they can pass it to others, whether they are feeling ill or well, whether they are on treatment or not, and whether they believe that they are safe or not.

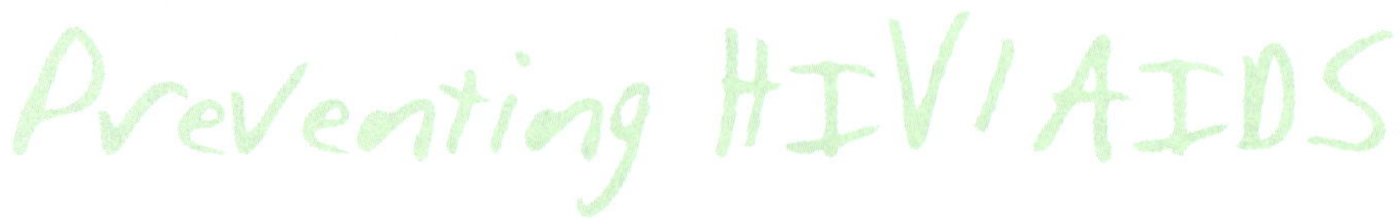

Associated Symptoms

A person who has been infected with HIV will likely feel normal for quite a few years. As the immune system is slowly destroyed, the person will notice any number of persistent and unexplained symptoms that cause concern. It is important to emphasize that having one or more of these symptoms does not mean that someone is HIV-positive. Many people get diarrhea, skin rashes, or symptoms from sexually transmitted infections, and many women experience yeast infections. Infections such as herpes are relatively common in people without HIV infection, but they are usually limited in extent and duration. While most of the following symptoms can occur in the absence of HIV infection, when these symptoms are severe or persistent, a medical evaluation with an HIV test is indicated.

- periods of extreme and unexplained fatigue that may be combined with headaches
- loss of more than 10 pounds (4.5 kilos) over a couple of months, not due to increased exercise or nutrition changes
- long-lasting diarrhea (greater than a month)
- prolonged fever
- neurological abnormalities
- a thick, whitish coating of the mouth or tongue (thrush), sometimes accompanied by a sore throat or pain and difficulty swallowing
- severe or recurring vaginal yeast infections
- chronic pelvic inflammatory disease
- severe frequent infections like herpes zoster, which causes shingles, or Human Papilloma Virus (HPV), which causes genital warts (These are relatively common in people without HIV infection; however, they are usually small and limited in extent.)
- recurring lightheadedness or dizziness
- unexplained bleeding; bruising more easily than normal
- recurring fevers or night sweats
- swelling or hardening of glands in the throat, armpit, or groin
- periods of continued, deep, dry coughing
- increasing shortness of breath
- the appearance of discolored or purplish growths on the skin or inside the mouth

- recurring or unusual skin rashes
- unexplained lack of muscular strength
- mental deterioration or unexplained personality change

Voluntary HIV Counseling and Testing

Voluntary HIV Counseling and Testing (VCT) is an opportunity for individuals to receive counseling so that they can make informed choices about being tested for HIV.[2] These programs are quite successful in identifying and encouraging individuals to seek medical care. They also educate the community about HIV infection. While VCT programs vary, there are some standard principles that they follow:

- **Confidentiality:** Personal identifiers are collected but all test results and identifying information stays between the client and health care professionals. (Clients may choose to involve family or close friends for support.)
- **Voluntary:** Counseling and testing are provided entirely at the client's initiative.
- **Pre-test/Post-test Counseling:** Clients are offered trained counselors to explain the importance of HIV testing; ways to reduce the risk of HIV infection; the next steps for persons who have a positive test result, which will vary depending on access to medical services; and the need for additional testing of people whose test results are negative but who have had recent exposure to HIV.
- **Respect:** Clients receive assurance that no one will be discriminated against based on their test results.
- **Access to a variety of prevention, care, and support services:** Services vary but may include antiretroviral medications, treatment for opportunistic infections, family planning information, social support groups, prenatal and delivery care, ongoing mental health care, and other services.

Many people are afraid to be tested for HIV. They fear the stigma of AIDS—the judgment and rejection by their friends, community members, even their own family members. Many are afraid to face the realities that the knowledge of having HIV/AIDS would bring to their lives. They know a positive test result will change their lives forever.

The public needs to understand that there are many personal advantages to knowing one's HIV status. These include (1) the opportunity to receive drug therapies that may slow the progression of disease; (2) the awareness of the need to make healthy lifestyle choices that

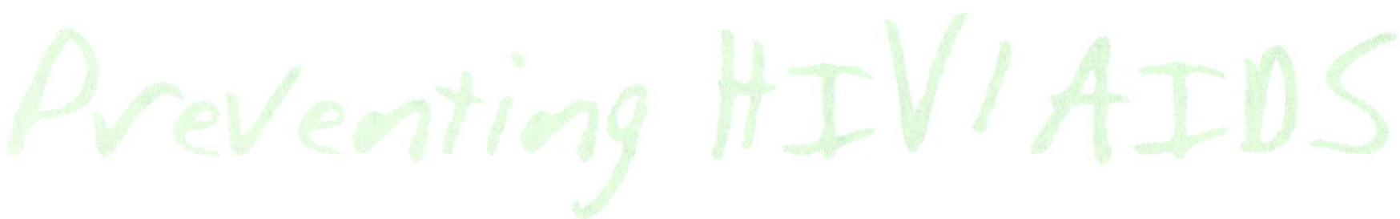

will strengthen and preserve the immune system; (3) the ability to drastically reduce the risk of HIV transmission to an infant through the use of antiretroviral therapy in pregnancy and during labor; (4) the knowledge of ways to prevent loved ones (especially spouses) from becoming infected; (5) information on avoiding the medical complications of acquiring other sexually transmitted infections; (6) the opportunity to refrain from passing the virus through risky behaviors such as injection drug use and sex; and (7) time to prepare financially, emotionally, and spiritually for difficult times ahead.

The Advantages of Knowing One's HIV Status

- Receive drug therapies that may slow the progression of disease
- Make healthy lifestyle decisions that will strengthen and preserve the immune system
- Reduce the risk of HIV transmission to an infant
- Prevent loved ones from becoming infected
- Avoid the medical complications of other sexually transmitted infections
- Refrain from passing the virus to others through risky behaviors such as injection drug use and sex
- Time to prepare financially, emotionally, and spiritually for difficult times ahead

Who Should Be Tested?

The following persons should go for voluntary counseling and testing for HIV:

- Anyone who is donating blood
- Anyone who is pregnant (HIV should be a routine part of all prenatal care.)
- Anyone who has used injection drugs
- Anyone who is experiencing many of the symptoms of HIV infection, such as unexplained weight loss, diarrhea, coughing, fever, or unusual recurrence of sexually transmitted infections such as sores and genital warts
- Anyone who believes there is a possibility that he or she has been exposed to HIV
- Anyone who becomes involved sexually with a new partner
- Anyone whose sexual partner has sexual relations with any new sexual partner, as in a situation of marital unfaithfulness (In such cases, both partners should be tested.)

Antibody Testing

The most common test used to detect the presence of HIV in the body is called the ELISA test. The ELISA test does not detect the virus itself but rather the immune system response—specific antibodies that the immune system creates to fight HIV. The ELISA test is a very accurate and effective screening tool for HIV. Most individuals without prior chronic illness who become infected with HIV will test positive on an ELISA test within three months of the initial infection.

There are two problems with traditional antibody testing. First, for the test to work, a sufficient amount of antibodies needs to be present in a measurable quantity. This usually occurs within three to six weeks after the initial infection, but it may take up to three to six months.

The time period between the point of HIV infection and the ability of the test to detect the antibodies is called the *window period.* People who are infected with HIV and have an ELISA test in the window period will test negative, even though they are infected and will test positive in a few weeks or months. An accurate test result may require a three- to six-month risk-free period (avoiding any activity involving an exchange of body fluids or sexual secretions) before testing.

The second problem with traditional antibody testing is that it typically takes one to two weeks to obtain the results of an ELISA test. Most patients worry during this period, and must take more time away from home or work and make arrangements to return to the testing site to learn their HIV status. Many never return. A new antibody test now available in some areas is helping to solve these problems. This test can give results within 30 minutes, so patients can remain in the facility while awaiting their results. This new rapid HIV-1 antibody test is not available in all clinics and is approved only for testing for the B Subtype of HIV-1. As is true for all screening tests, a positive HIV test must be confirmed before a final diagnosis of infection can be made.

Some tests are actually able to identify the presence of the virus itself within a few days after exposure. These tests are not used in general screening because they are very expensive. However, they are often used after incidents involving unintentional needle sticks in a clinical setting, in cases of rape, or to track the effectiveness of antiretroviral therapies.

Ways HIV Is Spread

There are many ways that HIV is spread from person to person. When infected body fluids, particularly blood or sexual secretions (semen in men, vaginal secretions in women), have an opportunity to pass from one person to another, there is a risk of infection. Most people are infected as a result of sexual choices (either their own or their partner's) or injection drug use. It is very important for adolescents to understand that many people are infected because of the actions of others. Some become infected when their spouse engages in sex outside of the marriage relationship. Mothers who are HIV-positive can pass the virus to their babies. Others are infected because they received a blood transfusion with HIV-positive blood. Occasionally people become infected through everyday accidents.

Helping adolescents to learn exactly how HIV is spread and challenging them to take responsibility to refrain from passing HIV to others is vital for their health and the health of others in their community. Yet they need to be cautioned to refrain from judgmental attitudes that cause social stigmatization and discrimination of those persons who are suffering with

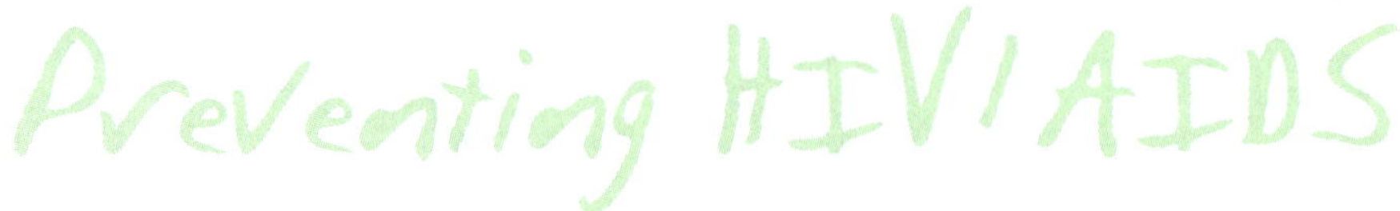

HIV/AIDS. Remember to integrate these concepts with a discussion of the character traits of kindness, empathy, forgiveness, and compassion. How someone got infected is not our business. How we treat them as our neighbor, even though they are infected, is of utmost importance and will reveal our true character.

The following explains the most common ways people become infected with HIV.

Sexual Activity

Any sexual activity involving an exchange of sexual fluids (semen in men and vaginal secretions in women) can transmit HIV. These fluids are most likely to enter the body of another person via mucous membranes, the moist tissues of the bodies. For men, the particularly vulnerable area is the tip of the penis, and for women it is the entire vaginal area.

A history of multiple sexual partners—which increases one's chances of coming in contact with HIV—and beginning sex at an early age—which typically leads to more lifetime sexual partners—result in increased risk of exposure to HIV and other sexually transmitted infections. Teaching abstinence until marriage and fidelity in marriage delays the onset of sexual behavior and reduces the number of lifetime sexual partners. Many people still believe that HIV/AIDS is primarily a disease among homosexuals, and yet worldwide HIV is most often spread during sexual relations between males and females. Anal intercourse, vaginal intercourse, and oral sex all carry risk for HIV infection.

Anal sexual intercourse is the insertion of the penis into the anal cavity of another person. This is a typical sexual practice among homosexuals. Some heterosexual couples also engage in anal intercourse for different reasons, such as pleasure, because "technically" it is not "having sex," or as a way to avoid pregnancy. Anal intercourse is an extremely efficient way to pass HIV from one person to another. The anal lining can be easily torn because it neither stretches nor lubricates as does the vaginal lining.

Vaginal sexual intercourse is the insertion of the penis of the male into the vagina of the female. Both partners are susceptible to HIV infection through the mucous membranes, males through the tip of the penis and females throughout the lining of the vagina. HIV is transmitted when infected sexual secretions are passed from one partner to another. It is believed that women are more likely to acquire HIV from men than they are to pass it to men.

How someone got infected is not our business. How we treat them as our neighbor, even though they are infected, is of utmost importance and will reveal our true character.

Oral sex is the sexual stimulation of one partner by using the mouth of the other partner. This can be done male-to-female or female-to-male or by partners of the same sex. Although this practice may not be accepted from culture to culture, many people have turned to this type of sexual activity believing it is a "safe" way to give or receive sexual pleasure without "having sex." Obviously, this is erroneous thinking. Oral sex is sex and the few studies available reveal that this can spread HIV.[3] Oral sex should never be considered a safe activity for either partner. The receiver may be exposed to blood from bleeding gums or small cuts in the mouth. The giver may be exposed to HIV via the sexual fluids of the receiving partner (semen or vaginal secretions).

Many people are not aware that the presence of other sexually transmitted infections influences HIV transmission.

Many people are not aware that the presence of other sexually transmitted infections influences HIV transmission. People who have another sexually transmitted infection—particularly an ulcerative disease such as herpes, chancroid, or syphilis—are more likely to be infected if their sexual partner is HIV-positive. HIV enters through ulcerated skin. A person who is HIV-positive and who has an ulcerative sexually transmitted infection is also much more likely to pass HIV to others. This is because there are numerous immune system cells at the site of the sore trying to fight the infection. Many of these cells are infected with HIV. Adolescents need to keep in mind that anyone who has experience with multiple sexual partners is likely to be infected with one or more sexually transmitted infections.

Injections

Any activity involving the sharing of needles is very dangerous. When a needle used by someone who is infected with a virus (such as HIV or Hepatitis B or C) is then used by someone else, there is a significant chance that the second person will receive a small amount of tainted blood. This happens most often in the injection drug culture. Injection drug users share "equipment" in order to save money. Infection via needles can also happen when receiving tattoos or in hospital or clinical settings where needles are not sterilized properly. It is always wise to teach people to insist on new or properly sterilized needles when receiving any type of injection.

Mother to Child

We know that without treatment there is approximately a 30–35 percent chance that a mother who is HIV-positive will pass HIV to her child. If the baby is not breastfed by its mother, the risk of infection is about 20 percent.[4]

Unfortunately, many mothers do not even know they are infected with HIV until their babies test positive for HIV antibodies. This is a devastating situation for a family. Mothers can infect their babies while they are in the womb, during the birthing process, or during breastfeeding. In recent years, the medicines AZT and Nevirapine have successfully lowered the rate of transmission to infants from 30–35 percent to approximately 8 percent. Wherever possible, HIV-infected pregnant women should receive three anti-HIV drugs for the duration of the pregnancy. For this reason it is critical that all mothers be tested for HIV infection as part of normal prenatal medical care and that they be given access to these important medications.

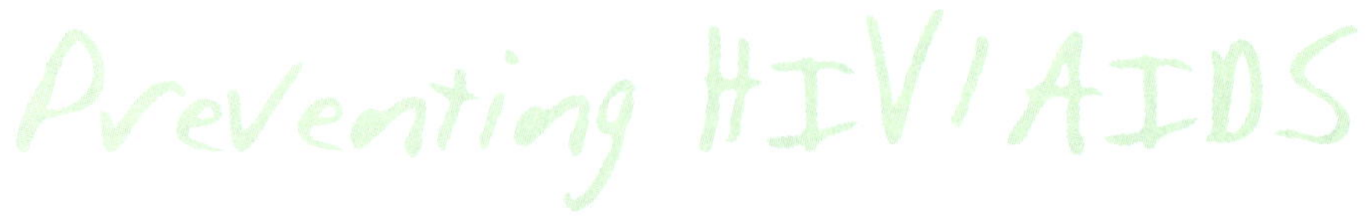

According to current United Nations recommendations, infants should be exclusively breastfed for the first six months of life. Thereafter, infants should receive nutritionally adequate and safe complementary foods while breastfeeding continues up to 24 months or beyond. Mothers who do not know their HIV status should always follow this practice. Any nursing mother who suspects that she could be HIV-positive should go to a clinic and participate in a voluntary counseling and testing program. If she is HIV-positive, she will be encouraged to use replacement feeding, but only if it is determined to be acceptable, feasible, affordable, sustainable, and safe. If infant formula is used, it is extremely important to mix the formula according to the directions and to use sterilized water.

The children born to mothers who are HIV-positive will usually test positive for HIV on an antibody test. This does not mean that the newborn is infected with HIV. The test is looking for antibodies (the response to the virus) that are shared between the mother and child. The mother could be HIV-positive, but the baby has only her antibodies, not HIV. If the baby continues to test positive 18 months after birth, it is believed that the baby is infected with HIV, too. Typically, children with HIV struggle to survive and live only a few years.

Blood Transfusions and Organ Donation

Although it is possible to get HIV from receiving a blood transfusion, it is unlikely. Hospitals around the world routinely screen donated blood for the presence of HIV. To eliminate any risk, however, patients can ask about donating their own blood before having elective surgery. An HIV-negative person can never be infected by donating blood. It is possible for someone to become infected through receiving a donated organ. Donated organs should always be tested for HIV before being placed into another person. Additionally, donated semen for artificial insemination must also be tested for the presence of HIV.

Skin Cuts and Accidents

HIV can be transmitted when someone has a break in the skin and the infected blood of another person is able to get into the bloodstream. This break in the skin can be intentionally caused, such as in scarification rituals, circumcisions, or in some methods of tattooing. The break in the skin can also be caused from disease, such as sores associated with sexually transmitted infections or bleeding gums due to poor dental hygiene. Accidents on the playground, in the kitchen, etc., can cause a break in the skin and make it vulnerable. Any time there is a break in the skin, it is important to make sure that someone else's infected body fluids, especially blood, cannot get on the broken skin area.

Ways HIV Is *Not* Spread

- Hugging
- Holding or shaking hands
- Closed-mouth kissing (social expressions of endearment or family affections)
- Living in the same household
- Touching shared food, cups, or plates
- Eating food prepared by someone else
- Clothing or towels
- Toilet seats or shower facilities
- Combs or brushes
- Animal or insect bites
- Swimming in a pool, river, lake, or ocean
- Drinking fountains

Five Common Misconceptions about HIV/AIDS

Myth: *HIV does not cause AIDS.*
Fact: Not true! AIDS has been studied for over 20 years, and the cause and effect relationship of HIV to AIDS has been firmly established. Persons acquire HIV before they develop AIDS. HIV destroys the immune system, and this causes AIDS.

Myth: *HIV/AIDS is only a homosexual disease.*
Fact: Not true! HIV can infect any human. It does not discriminate based on sexual orientation, age, religion, or race. Most persons around the world are infected via heterosexual contact.

Myth: *Having sex with a virgin will cure HIV or other sexually transmitted infections.*
Fact: Not true! There is no cure for AIDS. Having sex with a virgin will only result in infecting the virgin, too.

Myth: *It is dangerous to live with someone who is suffering from AIDS.*
Fact: Not true! Millions of people have cared for persons suffering from AIDS in their homes and have never been infected. There is no danger as long as proper precautions for handling blood and other body fluids are followed. (See the section "Caring for Someone with AIDS at Home.") People who are infected with HIV and need special care should inform their caregivers so that proper precautions can be followed.

Myth: *There is a cure for AIDS.*
Fact: Not true! There is no cure for AIDS, only treatments to help people live healthier for longer periods.

Discussing HIV Transmission

Many people become frightened during discussions about HIV transmission. It is important that we recognize that this fear can be a fear for oneself or fear for a loved one who is making unwise choices. There is usually much misinformation and many myths that need to be clarified about HIV. These myths vary all over the world. When youth possess a clear understanding of where HIV is located in the body (primarily blood and sexual fluids) and how HIV enters the body (via the bloodstream or contact with mucous membranes), they will be able to differentiate many myths from fact.

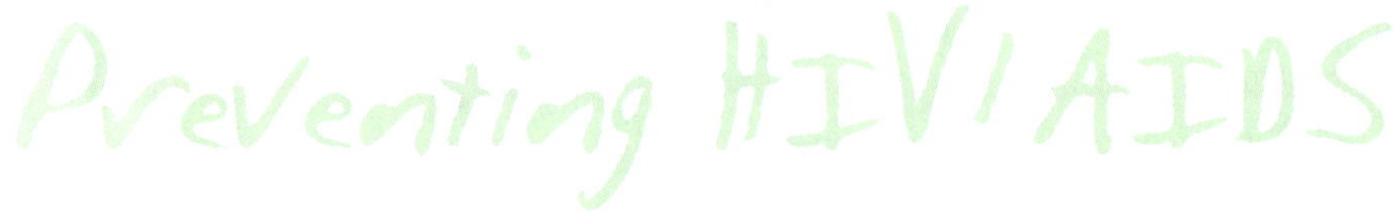

People also grow concerned about what they read in the newspapers and hear on television. They hear of stories where individuals have purposely infected others because they are angry with them. There are such cases, but they are rare. People worry about car accidents, and going to the barber or the dentist. They worry about needless things like sharing a meal, shaking hands, or attending school with a person who is infected with HIV. It is important that we patiently and compassionately help people understand the differences between safe activities, accidents, and unhealthy lifestyle choices. Give clear information and keep the discussion focused on the most important topics. In our experience, we have found that adults, especially unmarried young adults, usually focus on "accidents" instead of their own sexual choices.

Preventing the Spread of HIV

Adolescents are particularly vulnerable to a variety of sexually transmitted infections. Most adolescents do not know the basic facts about sex and disease transmission. They are less likely to have the skills to avoid sexual pressure, less able to negotiate any type of risk-reduction strategy, and they typically believe that bad things will never happen, especially to them. Adolescents are very curious about sex and often engage in high-risk sexual behaviors. In addition, adolescents are more likely to mix the use of alcohol and other drugs with their sexual activities, thus reducing inhibitions and the ability to think clearly. Each year young adults 15 to 24 years of age make up over 50 percent of all new cases of HIV.

Young girls are particularly vulnerable to sexually transmitted infections. They are often propositioned for sex by older boys and men, many of whom have had multiple sexual partners and are carriers of disease. Many girls live in cultures which fail to support a woman's right to say "no" to sex; others believe in their right to say no but lack the skills to do so. There are also gender-specific biological disadvantages when it comes to sexually transmitted infections. The female's cervical tissues are not fully developed until approximately 18 years of age. These under-developed tissues are particularly vulnerable to infections, resulting in greater risk of infection simply due to one's age. Additionally, a female's body has a greater surface area of mucous membranes, which increases vulnerability to infection with HIV. And finally, when females are infected, they are less likely to have symptoms and are more likely to experience severe and lifelong complications such as infertility, cervical cancer, and chronic abdominal pain.

When talking with youth about sex, it is important to keep in mind that adolescents have had very different sexual experiences. There are (1) those who have never had sex, (2) those who have had sex but are not sexually active now, (3) those who are sexually active now but who may be open to changing their behavior, and (4) those who will be sexually active no matter what information they receive. We need to encourage those who are making good choices to continue to do so and motivate those who are impressionable to choose wisely. Access to medical services and counseling should be made available to help those who fail to listen, never forgetting that they may be interested in changing their behavior in the future.

> *Sex is not a manifestation of a biological drive; it is socially directed . . . I have been emphasizing a return to our time-tested cultural practices that emphasized fidelity and condemned premarital and extramarital sex. I believe that the best response to the threat of AIDS and other STDs is to reaffirm publicly and forthrightly the respect and responsibility every person owes to his or her neighbor.*
>
> –Yoweri Museveni, President of Uganda

We must also be aware that many adolescents, boys as well as girls, have experienced or are currently experiencing sexual trauma such as rape or incest. Research indicates that those who are the most sexually active are typically those who have been sexually abused. We need to be sensitive to troubles and hurts in the lives of young people; a judgmental attitude is guaranteed to be met with closed ears, whereas compassion is always attractive.

Preventing the spread of HIV/AIDS requires good personal decision making skills as well as medical strategies to control infectious diseases. These strategies include monitoring the blood supply, sterilizing medical instruments, and using gloves during medical procedures involving body fluids. They also involve avoiding pregnancy for women who are HIV-positive; sterilizing instruments used for tattooing, circumcision, and scarification rituals; and avoiding sharing needles for injection drug use. But the most important thing we can do to prevent the spread of HIV/AIDS is to help people make decisions to avoid trouble altogether.

You may have heard the story of a wealthy businessman who needed to hire a driver for his wife and family. He showed each applicant the treacherous, winding road they would have to drive between his home and the town. He then asked the question, "How close can you drive to the edge of the cliff and keep my family safe?"

The first applicant, certain of his driving ability, responded confidently to the question. "I will be able to drive 12 inches from the edge without falling off." The second driver likewise boasted, "I can drive within 6 inches of the edge without falling off." Finally, the last applicant quickly replied, "I would drive as far from the edge as I could." Who was hired? The third driver.

The ABC Approach

In some ways the ABC approach, which was first implemented in Uganda, represents the philosophy of that story. This approach to prevention focuses on a risk-avoidance message for the general public: choose abstinence before marriage and remain faithful in marriage. For some persons who would be identified as members of high-risk groups (prostitutes and their

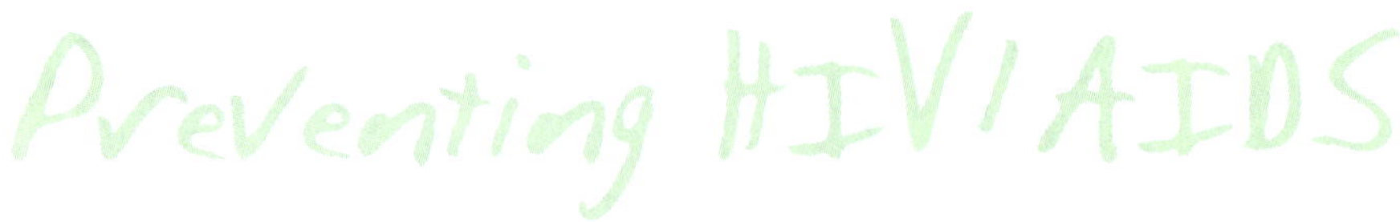

customers), a risk-reduction message is offered: use condoms correctly for each and every act of sexual intercourse.[5] The ABC philosophy is explained in further detail below.

Abstinence

The Medical Institute for Sexual Health defines abstinence as *the calculated decision and deliberate action of a person to refrain from sexual activity.* Abstinence is not merely technical virginity—everything but intercourse. It is a decision to refrain from any exchange of body fluids or touching of genital areas by any two persons before marriage. Abstinence eliminates the risk of infection with HIV and other sexually transmitted infections. Millions of young people around the world are adopting abstinence until marriage as their lifestyle choice.

Young people who have already been sexually active can choose abstinence again! This is sometimes referred to as *secondary virginity.* We need to kindly and compassionately challenge adolescents to once again choose a wise lifestyle. Abstinence is the only lifestyle for unmarried adolescents and adults that is free from the risk of HIV/AIDS and other sexually transmitted infections caused by sexual relations. Choosing abstinence lowers two very important risk factors for acquiring a sexually transmitted infection by delaying the onset of sexual activity and by reducing the number of sexual partners.

Choosing and maintaining abstinence as a lifestyle isn't easy, but it works! Millions of adolescents are realizing that sex is not worth the risks and that it has great potential to sabotage life dreams. But many adults are skeptical about whether adolescents can successfully remain abstinent. They sometimes promote misconceptions that are not based on fact. Here are a few examples:

1. *Abstaining from sexual intercourse will make someone psychologically unstable.*
   Not true! There is no evidence to support an association with poor mental health; however, there is considerable evidence to the contrary. Youth who engage in early sexual involvement are more likely to report lower self-esteem and psychological distress such as depression.

2. *Once people get sexually excited, they must complete the act of sex.*
   Not true! Although there may be some sexual discomfort, there is no physical damage caused by unexpressed sexual arousal. Adolescents need to know that they can say "no" even after they've become sexually aroused.

3. *Refraining from sexual intercourse until marriage may cause an inability to bear children.*
   Not true! This is an absurd claim with absolutely no basis in fact. Again, the opposite may be true. Those engaging in sex with multiple partners are likely to be exposed to sexually transmitted infections that can lead to infertility.

Helping adolescents to choose abstinence as a lifestyle is a very difficult task. Some youth will listen and some will not, no matter how you try to influence them. A "just say no" approach to abstinence is likely to fail. But an approach that encompasses each of the dimensions of a person and is delivered with acceptance and compassion will at least be considered by most youth. Until young people learn respect and responsibility for themselves and others, and until they have a sense of hope for the future, they will struggle in this area. Here are some things we can do to help them:

10 Ways to Help Adolescents to Choose Abstinence

1. Clearly communicate your expectation for them to wait until marriage.
2. Discuss reasons for delaying sexual activity until marriage.
3. Help them practice skills to say "no" to sex but "yes" to relationships.
4. Provide safe recreational activities to enjoy with the opposite sex.
5. Link young people to healthy adult role models.
6. Provide counseling and support for sexually abused children.
7. Help youth to develop character.
8. Encourage relationships with parents.
9. Help youth to develop a skill—music, sports, drama, etc.
10. Create a positive school environment.

Be Faithful

The only safe sexual relationship is a relationship between two uninfected persons who both choose to have sexual relations only with each other for a lifetime. This type of relationship has been traditionally known as marriage. If both partners are disease-free and are faithful, there is no risk of infection! Of course, the ability to remain faithful will require character on the part of both partners. They will need to exercise some basic character traits such as respect, self-control, and loyalty.

In many countries where HIV/AIDS is spread throughout the general population, it is important for couples to consider HIV testing before marriage. If each partner has refrained from sex and other high-risk behaviors for the previous six months, this will give both partners accurate information about the health status of each partner before the wedding. If either person is found to be infected, he or she should be evaluated to identify the stage of infection and whether or not treatment is indicated.

Even if a sexually active couple do not marry, it is very important that both partners remain faithful to each other. Persons who choose to have multiple sexual partners, whether married or not, are at greatest risk for HIV infection. Data from Uganda suggests that the greatest

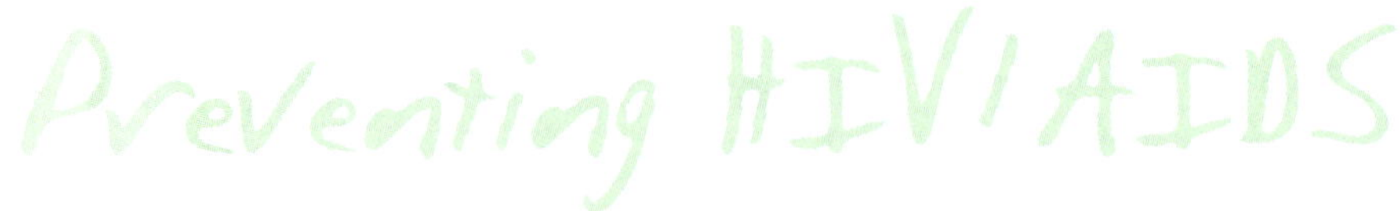

reduction in the spread of HIV was due to the reduction of multiple sexual partners in the general population.

Condoms

One of the most controversial topics in HIV/AIDS prevention is the use of condoms and their role in the prevention of HIV/AIDS and other sexually transmitted infections. In the ABC approach to prevention, condoms are a part of the prevention strategy, but the heaviest emphasis is on the A and B messages, abstain and be faithful. The condom message is reserved for people who refuse to follow the wisdom of the A and B messages or for special circumstances where one marriage partner is HIV-infected. The Uganda approach encourages condom use only for select high-risk groups, such as commercial sex workers and truck drivers who choose to have multiple sexual partners when traveling for work.

The A, B, and C messages are not equivalent messages. Abstinence and being faithful to one's marriage partner are risk-elimination strategies, while condoms are merely a risk-reduction strategy.

Condoms play a secondary role in the prevention strategy for two main reasons. First, although condoms help to reduce the risk of transmission of some sexually transmitted infections when used consistently and correctly, most people do not comply with consistent and correct use. This can be due to lack of education, lack of cultural acceptability, a dislike for how condoms feel during sex, impairment of judgment due to alcohol and other drug use, or lack of self-control when condoms are not available. Second, even when condoms are used properly, they offer little to no risk reduction for other sexually transmitted infections; significant risk for acquiring life-threatening infections still remains. Thus the condom's risk reduction role is secondary in disease prevention. The primary role must be behavior change—risk elimination.

Condom Facts

A condom is a barrier that keeps the male's semen from coming into contact with his sexual partner. Condoms may be made of different materials: natural skin, latex (rubber), or polyurethane (used when people are allergic to latex). Latex condoms are the best choice for preventing the spread of infections. Although condoms need to fit properly and are available in various sizes, shapes, and styles, most condoms will fit most men.

> *You just can't tell people it's all right to do whatever you want as long as you wear a condom. [AIDS] is just too dangerous a disease to say that.*
>
> —Harold Jaffee, Chief of Epidemiology, U.S. Centers for Disease Control and Prevention

In order for condoms to help reduce the spread of HIV/AIDS, they must be used consistently and correctly. Consistent condom use means using a condom every single time someone engages in intimate sexual activity. The people who tend to do best at wearing condoms every time they have sex are adults who are in stable relationships.

Condoms must also be used correctly. Using a condom correctly is quite complicated. The condom must be put on the male's penis correctly and then taken off and thrown away correctly. Of course, the use of alcohol or other drugs makes using condoms correctly much more difficult.

Here are some important facts to remember in order to use condoms correctly:

- Condom packages need to be opened and handled carefully. Ragged or sharp fingernails, rings, or other jewelry can tear the condom. If the package is damaged or condoms are past their expiration date, the condoms should not be used. Heat weakens the texture of condoms; therefore, they should not be stored in a wallet or in hot or sunny places (for example, in a car or near a window). A new condom should be used for every act of intercourse.
- Plenty of water-based lubricant should be put *on* the condom—never *in* it—to reduce the friction that can cause breakage. Oil-based lubricants like Vaseline, some hand creams, Crisco, butter, mineral oil, or other oils can dissolve or weaken latex and lead to breakage. Water-based lubricants are available in many pharmacies that sell condoms. Saliva can also be used.
- The condom must be put on after erection and before any sexual contact. If the penis is uncircumcised, the foreskin should be pulled back before putting on the condom. The tip of the condom should be squeezed while the condom is unrolled in order to leave an airless pocket to collect semen. (Unrolling a condom before putting it on does not work!)
- If the condom breaks during sex, sex should stop immediately and a new condom put on the penis before continuing.
- After intercourse, the penis should be withdrawn while still erect, and while the condom is held around the base of the penis to prevent it from slipping off or spilling semen.
- The used condom should be wrapped in a tissue and thrown in the trash where others won't handle it. Condoms should never be flushed down the toilet (they can plug up the toilet).
- Afterward, the male's hands and genitals should be washed with soap and water. This prevents sexual fluids from remaining on the penis or dripping from the penis after intercourse.

It is easy to suggest that using condoms provides "protection," but actually getting people to use them all the time and use them the right way every time is very, very challenging. Anytime people are sexually active outside of a committed marriage relationship, with or without a

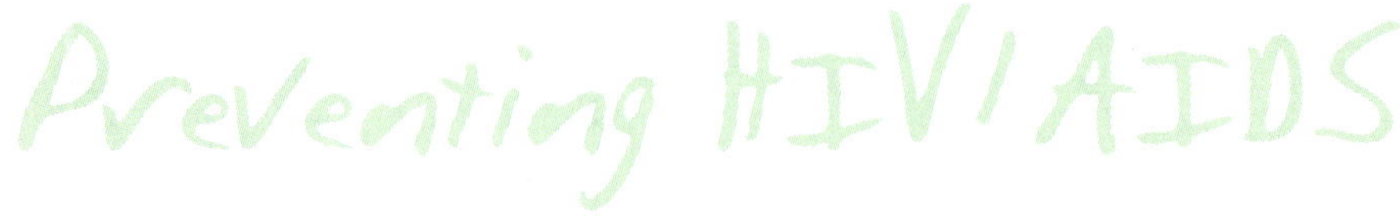

condom, there is a very good chance that they may come in contact with a sexually transmitted infection.

If worn consistently and correctly, as described above, condoms do a good job of reducing the risk of HIV transmission—about 88 to 90 percent of the time. And there is scientific evidence that condoms may help prevent the spread of gonorrhea and herpes about 50 percent of the time, but there is also evidence that condoms do very little to protect against Human Papilloma Virus (HPV) in females, the virus that causes genital warts and cervical cancer.[6]

There is value for individuals who are engaging in unwise behavior to use a condom, but sex using a condom should never be considered a safe activity. Sex outside of marriage is always risky. Even when condoms are used perfectly and used every time, there can be problems—the higher the number of sexual encounters and the higher the number of sexual partners, the more potential for infection.

We believe that condom use should not be presented to adolescents as an alternative to abstinence; the messages just do not equate. What happened in Uganda is proof that an abstinence message can change sexual behavior for both adolescents and adults! Here are some of our reasons:

1. An abstinence message is much more culturally acceptable and leaves no risk for infection.

2. A condom message undermines our belief that it is possible for adolescents to abstain. As we teach about disease prevention, we need to do everything in our power to convince adolescents that they can control the sexual area of their lives.

3. We also believe that due to lack of condom availability and the reality that youth are unlikely to use condoms for each act of sex, condoms are ineffective as a prevention strategy for youth.

4. Even when a condom is used consistently and correctly, there is still enormous risk for the transmission of sexual infections.

Abstinence is possible, but youth will consider it to be possible only if adults believe it, too. Adolescents need to hear that abstinence is in their best interest as well as the community's best interest. We need to instill a sense of personal and public responsibility when it comes to sexual decision making. Knowledge alone does not change behavior. The life skills and concepts discussed in the rest of this manual are integral to empowering adolescents to choose wisely.

Universal Precautions

Since HIV is passed through blood, fluids containing blood or pus, semen, or vaginal secretions, it is wise to take precautions around these fluids. *Universal precautions* means protecting oneself from exposure to blood or body fluids by following basic safety recommendations.[7] Because it is impossible to know who may be infected with HIV, these are safety precautions that should be implemented—whenever blood or other body fluids are present—regardless of the situation. We highly recommend that each home and school have a universal precautions kit so individuals can be ready to deal with accidents in a safe manner.

Managing Accidents and Injuries

The following are recommended guidelines for handling injuries and accidents to avoid contact with blood or other body fluids.

Helping the Injured Person

- If blood is present, immediately create a barrier between your body and the injured person's body fluid by using gloves. If gloves are not available, a thick layer of paper towels, cloth, or plastic shopping bags can be used. Make sure there are no holes!
- In the case of a car accident, extreme care should be taken around glass and other sharp objects in the car (heavy gloves are better than latex gloves in this situation).
- Stop the bleeding. Whenever possible, have the injured person apply pressure to the area and clean their own wounds (such as scratches, minor cuts, and nosebleeds).
- Place any soiled clothes or possessions of the person in a bag and seal it.
- Throw trash and used gloves in a plastic bag (to protect others from exposure).

Accidental Exposure to Another's Blood

- Promptly clean the area with soap and running water.
- Clean the area with an antiseptic; or use 1 part bleach to 9 parts water.

Universal Precautions Kit

- Large resealable container for the kit
- Assorted bandages for cleaning and covering wounds
- Scissors and tape for securing dressings
- Four pairs of latex gloves (2 medium and 2 large)
- Alcohol wipes
- Moist towelettes
- Absorbent paper towels or rags
- Four pairs of rubber (household) gloves (2 medium and 2 large)
- Antibacterial gel or lotion

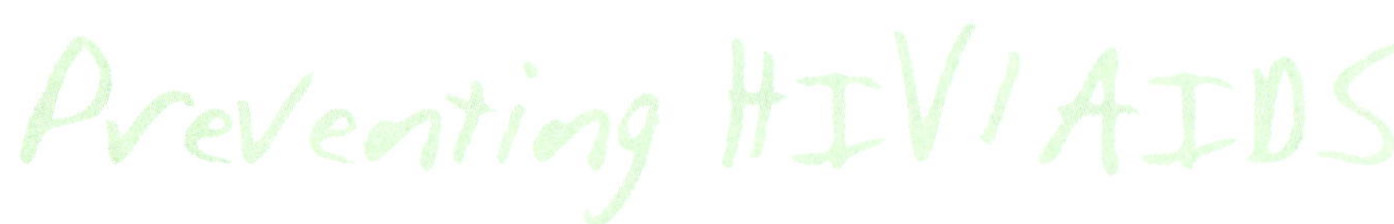

- If blood was splashed in the eyes or mouth, flush with running water for at least three minutes.

Cleanup

- Wear thick rubber gloves when cleaning and disinfecting environmental surfaces.
- Use disposable paper towels or cloth to remove blood or other body fluids.
- After cleaning the spill, disinfect the area by using ¼ cup of bleach to 1 gallon of water (store brand disinfectants can be used as well). Allow the surface to stay wet for several minutes.
- Remove gloves and place all used cleaning materials in a plastic bag for disposal.
- *Wash hands with soap as soon as possible!* Make sure fingernails are cleaned as well. An antibacterial cleaner or towelette may be used *until there is soap and water available.*

Caring for Someone with AIDS at Home

Although HIV can be transmitted between family members in a household setting, this type of transmission is rare. These transmissions are believed to have resulted from contact with the infected body fluids of the person with HIV via broken skin or mucous membranes of the caregiver. To prevent such rare occurrences, precautions need to be followed. Once persons with AIDS become sick and need assistance, it is always wise and important for them to reveal their HIV status to their caregivers.

This section offers practical recommendations that will protect everyone in the home when they are living with a person who has AIDS. These recommendations appear in the first person in order to add emphasis and clarity, and they have been modified for cross-cultural application. They have been adapted from a guide produced by the United States Centers for Disease Control and Prevention titled "Caring for Someone with AIDS at Home."[8] The focus of each recommendation is the avoidance of HIV-infected body fluids and reducing the potential for the spread of infectious diseases.

1. **Wash your hands.** Everyone in the household should wash their hands often. It is the best way to kill germs. Hands should be washed after going to the bathroom, before preparing food, and before and after feeding, bathing, providing bathroom assistance, or giving other care to someone with HIV. You should also wash your hands if you sneeze or cough; touch your nose, mouth, or genitals; handle garbage or animal litter; clean the house; or touch anybody's blood, semen, vaginal fluid, urine, or feces. If you are caring for more than one person, wash your hands after helping one person and before helping the next person. Wash your hands with warm, soapy water for at least 15 seconds. Clean under your

fingernails and between your fingers. If your hands become dry or sore, apply hand cream or lotion, but keep washing your hands frequently!

2. **Use gloves when touching body fluids or when cleaning.** Use *disposable, hospital-type latex or vinyl gloves.* You can buy hospital-type gloves by the box at most pharmacies, along with urinals, bedpans, and many other medical supplies. Gloves need not be worn when giving medicine or food to someone with AIDS, but only if there is no chance that you might touch blood or sexual fluids (semen, vaginal fluid, cuts or sores, or bloody feces). It is wise to wear gloves when giving care to the mouth, rectum, or genitals of the person with AIDS, as well as when changing diapers or sanitary pads and emptying bedpans or urinals. In order to avoid a variety of germs, wear gloves to clean up urine, feces, or vomit.

   Household rubber gloves, which are sold at any pharmacy or grocery store, are recommended for cleaning blood or bloody fluids from floors, bed, etc. These gloves can be cleaned and reused. Clean the gloves with hot, soapy water and with a mixture of about ¼ cup of bleach to 1 gallon of water. Be sure not to use gloves that are peeling, cracked, or have holes in them. Don't use the rubber gloves to take care of a person with AIDS; they are too thick and bulky.

   To take gloves off, peel them down by turning them inside out. This will keep the wet side on the inside, away from your skin and other people. When you take the gloves off, wash your hands with soap and water right away.

3. **Cover sores.** Any cuts or sores, especially on the hands, need to be bandaged well in order to avoid passing on infections. Those who have cold sores, fever blisters, or any other skin break should not touch others or their things. If it is necessary to give care, cover the sores with bandages and wash your hands before touching the person. If the rash or sores are on your hands, wear disposable gloves. If at all possible, those with boils, impetigo, or shingles need to be kept away from the person with AIDS until well.

4. **Treat early signs of tuberculosis.** If the person with AIDS has a cough that lasts longer than a week, a doctor should check him or her for tuberculosis (TB). If the patient does have TB, then everyone else living in the house should be checked for TB infection too, even if they aren't coughing.

5. **Use needles and syringes carefully.** A person with AIDS may require needles and syringes to take medicine. If you have to handle these needles and syringes, you must be careful not to stick yourself.

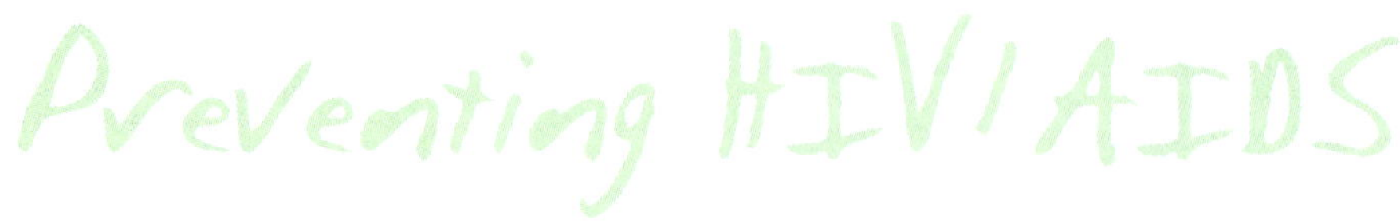

Use a needle and syringe only one time. Do not put caps back on needles, take needles off syringes, or break or bend needles. If a needle falls off a syringe, use something like tweezers or pliers to pick it up; do not use your fingers. Touch needles and syringes only by the barrel of the syringe, holding the sharp end away from you.

Put the used needle and syringe in a puncture-proof container, such as a coffee can. Keep the container well out of the reach of children or visitors. When the container gets nearly full, seal it and get a new container. A doctor or nurse can tell you the best way to dispose of the container with the used needles and syringes.

If you are stuck by a needle that was used on the person with AIDS, don't panic. Since there would be such a small amount of blood on the tip of the needle, the chances are excellent (better than 99 percent) that you will not be infected. This is a different situation than when drug users inject a substance into the body. However, you need to act quickly to get medical care. Put the needle in the used needle container, then immediately wash the area where you stuck yourself, using warm, soapy water. Right after washing, call the doctor or the emergency room of a hospital, no matter what time it is, explain what happened, and ask what else you should do. Your doctor may want you to take medicine, such as AZT and other anti-HIV medicines. If you are going to take medication, you should begin taking it as soon as possible, certainly within a few hours of the needle stick.

Protecting the Caregiver and Family Members

1. Wash hands regularly.
2. Wear gloves when touching body fluids and cleaning.
3. Cover sores.
4. Treat early signs of tuberculosis.
5. Use needles and syringes carefully.
6. Dispose of waste and waste products properly.
7. Clean laundry regularly.
8. Do not share personal items.
9. Avoid sexual relations that exchange body fluids.

6. **Dispose of waste and waste products properly.** All liquid waste (urine, vomit, diarrhea, etc.) and paper and tissues that may contain blood can be washed down the toilet, taking care not to splash. Paper towels, sanitary pads and tampons, wound dressings and bandages, diapers, and other items with blood, semen, or vaginal fluid on them should be put in plastic bags. Seal the bags and discard them in the trash.

7. **Wash clothes and bed linens regularly.** Clothes and bed linens used by someone with AIDS can be washed the same way as other laundry. If clothes or sheets have blood, vomit, semen, vaginal fluids, urine, or feces on them, disposable gloves must be worn when handling them. Items should be kept in plastic bags until they are washed. Bleach is not necessary to kill HIV; normal washing will kill the virus. If stains from blood, semen, or

vaginal fluids are on the clothes, soaking them in cold water before washing will help remove the stains.

8. **Do not share personal items.** No one in the home should share razors, toothbrushes, tweezers, nail or cuticle scissors, earrings or other "pierced" jewelry, or any other item that might have even a small amount of blood on it.

9. **Avoid sexual relations that result in the exchange of body fluids.** If at all possible, avoid sexual relations with anyone who is infected with HIV/AIDS. Talk to your spouse (or sex partner) about what will need to change. If you decide to have sexual intercourse (vaginal, anal, or oral), use condoms. Latex condoms can considerably reduce the risk of HIV infection if they are used the right way every time you have sex. However, condoms will not eliminate the risk of infection.

Living Longer with HIV

Many people want to know how long someone can live with HIV/AIDS. That is a hard question to answer, because it depends on many variables, such as the type and subtype of HIV the person was exposed to, access to good nutrition and medical care, and general lifestyle issues. The focus of treatment is threefold: keeping the immune system strong, treating infections, and, when possible, using antiretroviral therapies to slow the progression of the disease. Following are a number of practical things a person with HIV can do.[9]

1. Take advantage of good medical/social services.

- Choose a doctor with experience in treating HIV.
- Keep your appointments and take your medicines exactly as prescribed.
- Call your doctor for advice—don't follow the medical "advice" of friends.
- Get immunizations (injections) to prevent infections such as pneumonia and flu (your doctor will tell you when to get these injections).
- Antiretroviral therapies improve the quality and extend life. While they do not benefit everybody, they are effective for most.
- Get information and support from a local AIDS organization.

2. Follow general health recommendations.

- Eat plenty of healthy foods, even if you do not feel hungry.

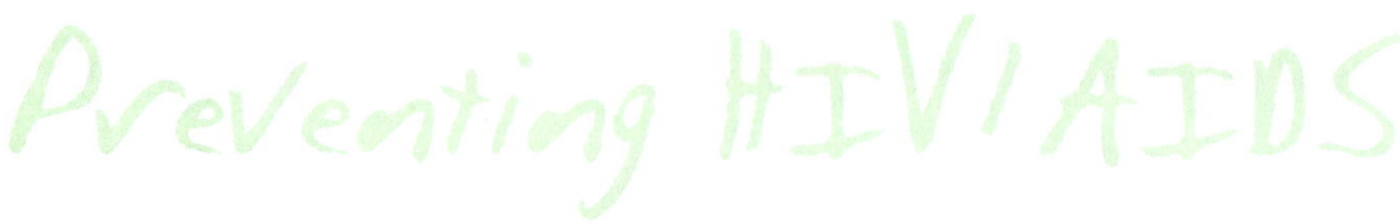

- Exercise regularly to stay strong and fit.
- Get enough sleep and rest.
- Avoid stressful situations.
- Nurture your spirit through prayer or meditation.

3. Avoid risk-taking behavior.

- Do not use alcohol, drugs, or tobacco products.
- Avoid sexual relations even if the partner is also infected with HIV, whether or not you use a condom. This reduces exposure to other sexual infections, and lessens the likelihood of getting a second HIV infection that makes your present infection worse.

Tips for Living Longer with HIV

1. Take advantage of good medical/social services.
2. Follow general health recommendations.
3. Avoid risk-taking behavior.
4. Minimize exposure to infectious disease.
5. Eat a healthy diet.

4. Minimize exposure to infectious disease.

- *Keep sick people away.* A person with AIDS often can't fight off colds, flu, or other common illnesses. If the caregiver for the person with AIDS is sick and cannot find help, he or she should wear a well-fitting, surgical-type mask that covers the mouth and nose.
- *Keep people with chickenpox or shingles away.* Never let anyone with chickenpox or shingles in the same room as a person with AIDS until all sores are healed. Don't let anyone who recently has been near someone with chickenpox in the same room as a person who has AIDS. After three weeks, the person who was exposed to the chickenpox can visit, if they aren't sick. If the caregiver was near someone with chickenpox and there is no one else to help, he or she needs to wear a well-fitting, surgical-type mask and wash his or her hands before caring for the person with AIDS. Time in the room should be minimal. There is a medicine that can make chickenpox less dangerous, but it must be given very soon after the person has been around someone infected with chickenpox.
- *Make sure all childhood immunizations have been received.* Everyone living with or helping to care for a person with AIDS should make sure they have received all their childhood immunizations. Children or adults who live with someone with AIDS and who need to get vaccinated against polio should get an injection with "inactivated virus" vaccine. The regular oral polio vaccine has weakened polio virus that can spread from the person who got the vaccine to the person with AIDS. Similarly, Measles, Mumps and Rubella (MMR) vaccination are live virus and can spread from the vaccinated person to someone with AIDS over the subsequent 14–17 days.

  Everyone living with a person with AIDS should get a flu shot every year to reduce the chances of spreading the flu to the person with AIDS. Everyone living with a person with AIDS should be checked for tuberculosis every year. All children should get the hepatitis B vaccine regardless of whether they are around a person with AIDS.

- *Take precautions with pets.* Having a pet around can make a person with AIDS feel better and enjoy life more. However, many pets carry germs that don't affect healthy people but can make a person with AIDS very sick. A person with AIDS can have pets but must wash their hands with soap and water after handling the pet. Someone who does not have HIV infection must clean the litter boxes, cages, fish tanks, pet beds, and other pet areas. Wear rubber gloves when you clean up after pets, and wash your hands before and after cleaning. Pets need yearly checkups and current vaccinations. If the pet gets sick, take it to the veterinarian right away.
- *Be careful when gardening.* There are germs even in garden or potting soil. People with HIV can garden, but they must wear work gloves while handling dirt and must wash their hands before and after handling dirt. When they have AIDS, they should wear a surgical-type mask that covers their nose and mouth when in a dusty environment.
- *Clean house thoroughly.* Cleaning removes germs that may be dangerous to the person with AIDS. Tubs, showers, and sinks need to be cleaned with household cleaners, then rinsed with fresh water. You may want to mop floors and clean the toilet at least once a week and decontaminate by using a mix of bleach and water or a commercial cleaner. Urinals and bedpans need to be decontaminated with bleach after each use. About ¼ cup of bleach mixed with 1 gallon of water makes a good disinfectant. Make a new mixture every 24 hours.

5. Eat a healthy diet.

People with AIDS can eat almost anything they want; in fact, the more the better. A well-balanced diet with plenty of nutrients, fiber, and liquids is healthy for everybody. Preparing food for a person with AIDS takes a little care, although you should follow these same rules to prepare food for anyone. A person living with AIDS does not need separate dishes, knives, forks, or spoons. All the dishes can be washed together with soap or detergent in hot water. A person with AIDS can also prepare food for other people.

Ten Rules for Food Preparation

1. Don't use raw (unpasteurized) milk.
2. Don't use raw eggs or products made with raw eggs.
3. All meats should be cooked well done, with no pink in the middle.
4. Don't use raw fish or shellfish (like oysters).
5. Wash your hands and utensils before handling different foods.
6. Use a clean spoon every time you taste.
7. Don't let blood from any meat or seafood touch other food.
8. Wash fresh fruits and vegetables thoroughly.
9. Serve hot foods hot and cold foods cold.
10. Place leftovers in the refrigerator as soon as possible.

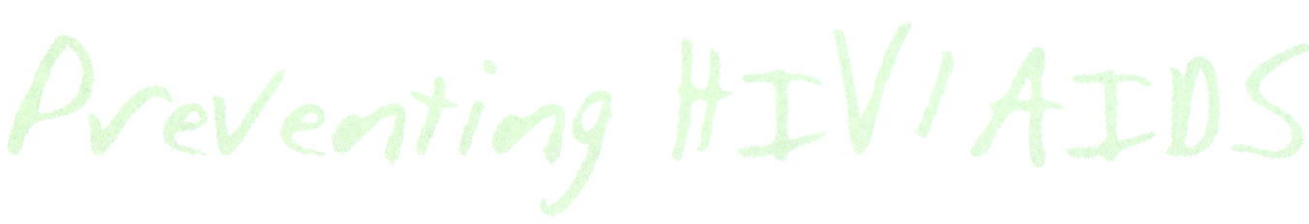

HIV Infection and Sexual Relations

A primary responsibility of every person who is infected with HIV is to avoid passing the infection to others. The hard truth is that there is no way to engage in intercourse and completely eliminate the possibility of spreading the virus to someone else. For this reason, physicians will always recommend that in order to protect the noninfected partner, sexual relations involving the exchange of body fluids must cease. This is a difficult decision, especially in the context of marriage. The Golden Rule needs to be applied, yet all too often partners hide their HIV status or demand their "rights."

At the very least, it is the responsibility of every HIV-infected person interested in having sexual relations to do the following:

1. Inform any potential sex partner (including marriage partner) of your HIV status.
2. Clearly explain that there is no way to eliminate the possibility of infection for them.
3. Give a sexual partner the freedom to say "no" to sex.
4. If both partners are willing to take the risk, learn to use condoms correctly and use them every time in order to reduce the risk of infection.

It is important to reemphasize that sexual infections are unusually problematic for someone who is HIV-infected. Typically the infections are more severe, especially viral infections such as herpes (which causes genital sores) and HPV (which causes genital warts). It is extremely important for someone who is infected with HIV to know the sexual habits of any sexual partner! Unfaithful partners are likely to be exposed to other sexually transmitted infections, even if they are using condoms. This is very dangerous for someone with AIDS.

Treatments and Cures

It is crucial that people understand the difference between a treatment and a cure. There are many treatments available for HIV/AIDS illnesses, but there is no cure. A *treatment* is the *use of medicines to lessen the symptoms of a condition or disease.* For example, the common cold has many symptoms—headache, runny nose, fever, etc. One treatment is to take aspirin, which will reduce the headache and help the fever to disappear. The person still has the virus that causes the common cold, but aspirin helps the person to feel better while the body's immune system fights off the virus. Eventually the body kills the virus, and the person feels well again.

A *cure*, on the other hand, is *the use of medicines to eliminate the infectious agent from the body*. We can cure bacterial diseases, such as gonorrhea and chlamydia, by killing them with antibiotics. After administering antibiotics, harmful bacteria are no longer present in the body. The body's immune system can kill some viruses, but for the most part we can only *treat* viral infections because we don't have any medicines that can *cure* them.

Persons suffering from HIV/AIDS are susceptible to many types of germs. Tuberculosis is one example. If someone with HIV/AIDS gets tuberculosis, we can cure that disease with drugs that fight the germs that cause tuberculosis. Killing the tuberculosis germs will allow the person with HIV/AIDS to live longer. However, the drugs for tuberculosis will not kill HIV, so the person will continue to have AIDS and will likely become ill with another infection. That is one reason why it is so expensive to treat patients with AIDS—they continually get sick and need treatment.

All over the world, people talk about cures for AIDS. Some people offer natural medicines like eating bark from special trees or drinking water from a particular lake. In some areas people insist that having sex with a virgin (a girl who has never had sex) will cure AIDS. Other people appear on television programs claiming to have been cured. Some people who were close to dying started taking antiretroviral medications, and they started to feel much better. They gained weight, and it looked liked they were healthy again. Nonetheless, these drugs are not a *cure*. They are, however, one of the most exciting *treatments* for HIV.

Antiretroviral Therapy

Although there is no cure for AIDS, much progress has been made in maintaining health and prolonging life by using medications that decrease the growth of HIV and thus slow down the destruction of the immune system. These medicines are commonly called *antiretroviral therapy*, or ARV (or ART) for short. The medicines do not kill HIV, rather they reduce HIV's ability to reproduce, which decreases the amount of virus in the body. Because ARVs do not eliminate HIV from the body, they cannot cure HIV infections. They are limited to keeping HIV under control. It is important to note that ARV currently available does not work for all patients.

Antiretroviral therapy is very exciting and much effort is focused toward making the medicines available to people all over the world. Thousands of people who were close to death are feeling healthier and are enjoying more years of life. But as exciting as it is, there are serious issues and challenges surrounding the use of antiretroviral therapy.[10]

Administering ARV treatment is quite complicated. It requires a medical infrastructure, which currently does not exist in most countries with a severe HIV epidemic. Patients require extensive counseling and education; they must take ARV for the rest of their lives; many will

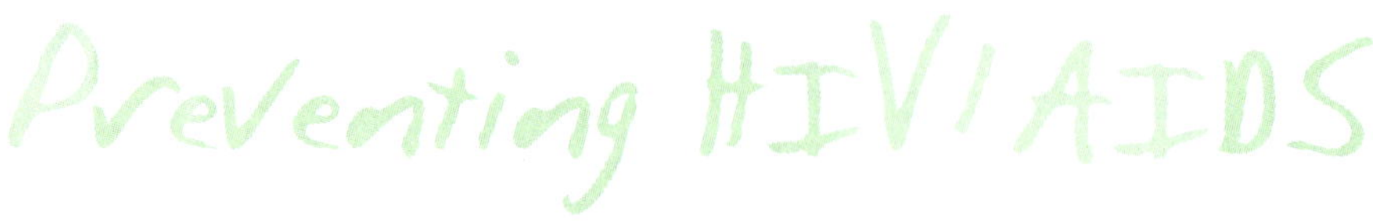

Character Connection: Empathy and Compassion

One day a busy mother sent her young daughter to the market to purchase some items for the family. Hours went by, and the mother became angry that her daughter had not returned. When the daughter finally returned home, her mother asked for an explanation. The nervous child explained that her friend down the street had fallen and broken her new doll and that she had stopped to help her. The mother, still frustrated, replied, "And what did you do to help?" The little girl gave an astounding reply: "I just sat down and helped her cry."

This little girl had a quality essential for being a person of character—empathy. Empathy is the capacity to recognize how situations and events make someone feel. While some people are more naturally empathetic, empathy is also learned as we purposely and unselfishly take the time to consider and understand the feelings of others. Daniel Goleman, accomplished author in the field of emotional intelligence, tells us that the root of altruism (unselfish concern for others) is empathy, the ability to read emotions in others. Goleman suggests that where there is no sense of another's need or despair, there is no caring. The little girl also demonstrated compassion. The Latin origin of the word means *com*, together + *pati*, suffer—"together suffer." It is beyond empathy; it is to feel so deeply that we are moved to do something on behalf of the one suffering. In the story the little girl didn't just look at the sadness and keep going —she stopped and joined in the suffering, doing the best thing she knew to do to help.

When it comes to people who are suffering from AIDS, many people choose to judge and punish with social stigmatization and discrimination rather than empathize and show compassion. Judgmental attitudes become blinders from the excruciating pain and suffering associated with AIDS. People forget that there are millions who suffer from AIDS through no fault of their own, and that many whose choices have resulted in their infection are really no more fallible than the rest of us. The difference is that their mistakes can't be rectified; they are forced into a horrific nightmare of emotional and physical suffering. As we learn to empathize, to think from another's perspective, we begin to understand. By reflecting on our own harmful choices, we realize that we too have made serious mistakes and are in no place to judge. We will begin to see with our hearts, becoming able to treat others with the dignity and respect that we ourselves would want to have shown to us. "How" becomes less important. Our compassion will begin to flow! We may not know exactly what to do in response, but at the very least we can sit quietly, hold a hand, and show someone that we care.

need some sort of refrigeration in their home (or village) so ARVs do not rapidly deteriorate; all must make a commitment to take ARV despite side effects (which are common). Patients need to be tested regularly both to find harmful side effects before serious damage occurs and to make sure the medicines are working. This requires extensive training of medical personnel, development of laboratory facilities, and personnel with appropriate quality controls so laboratory values are valid. Also required is long-term commitment of financial resources to maintain continuity of ARV supply, high-quality laboratory support, and reliable service delivery.

Regardless of what they may have done, each of the 40 million men, women, and children worldwide who are infected with HIV are precious to God. And if they're precious to God, then by God, they should be precious to us.

-Franklin Graham, founder of Samaritan's Purse

Of utmost importance is the issue of compliance. These medicines must be taken exactly as prescribed to avoid resistant strains of HIV. While the accessibility of ARV and the education to use them properly may seem to be formidable challenges in developing nations, studies indicate that patients are willing to cooperate fully with programs. Over 90 percent of African patients participating in the first African studies took their ARV properly.

There are many ethical issues surrounding the use of ARVs. Despite the dramatic drop in the price of medications, the average person who needs them still cannot afford them. Needs greatly exceed available resources, thus the allotment of funds presents difficult ethical and political problems. Judgments must be made about who gets ARV and who does not.

In recent years researchers documented an increase in risky sexual behavior among persons receiving ARV, including the non-use of condoms to decrease the risk of HIV spread. The existence of effective ARV, which slow the HIV multiplication and delay the development of AIDS and death, caused many people to believe that HIV infections are not serious. They view HIV infection as a normal or treatable disease with a normal life expectancy. No longer do they worry about acquiring HIV, because they believe, "I can always take treatment and everything will be all right." Unfortunately, this ignores the personal and societal cost, the frequent side effects, and the development of resistance. The term *disinhibition* is used to describe this trend towards riskier activity based upon perceived lack of high risk.

ARV medications may not reach many of the poor for whom they were intended. Too often ARV, whether donated to the national health service by an international organization or by a non-governmental organization, find their way to politically favored families or into open markets for sale. Fake medications are sold as ARV because of the inability of the health care system to monitor the distribution of ARV.

Before beginning to take these drugs, people must commit to take them for the remainder of their lives. Many people experience serious side effects from ARV treatment, including liver

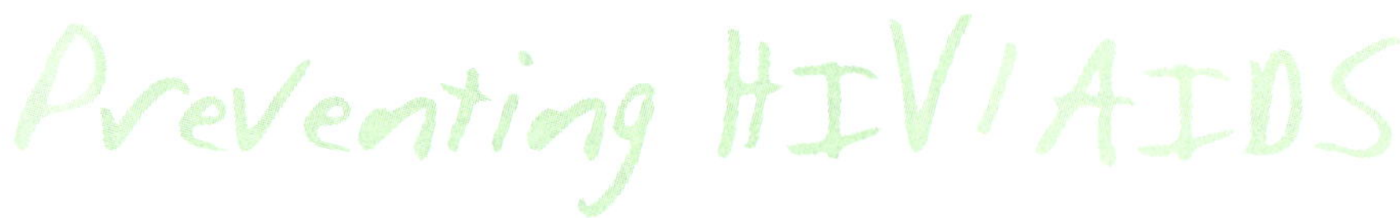

and cardiovascular problems. The longer people are on ARV, the more likely they are to develop an HIV strain resistant to ARV and thus, treatment becomes less effective. Resistance occurs even when people follow the drug regimen exactly as prescribed. If people stop taking antiretrovirals, their AIDS-related symptoms return, usually within a month or two. At best, antiretroviral drugs prolong life; thus, they are not the best answer to the HIV/AIDS problem.

Once infected, at no time is a person totally free from the potential of infecting someone else. While the ARV may decrease the virus in the blood, often it does not decrease the level of virus in male semen or in female vaginal secretions. *People who are taking antiretroviral drugs still have HIV in their genital fluids as well as low levels in their blood.* The amount of virus in the body at any given time is unpredictable, so it is impossible to know just how infectious a person may be.

Every claim of a cure for AIDS is either a misunderstanding about a specific therapy or a claim made by someone trying to get money from desperate people. Many people exploit the fear and pain of AIDS to make money. Some have suggested that drinking special potions or eating special foods will help. These claims are not true. All money spent on a so-called "cure" is wasted. But money spent on antiretroviral treatment and nutritious food may restore the quality of life and increase longevity for many individuals, at least for a time.

To date, antiretroviral drugs have not been widely accessible to most people around the world. It will be years before functional systems can meet the demands of ARV delivery on national levels. ARVs are exciting and should be made available to everyone who needs them, but we must use wisdom. As money and attention shifts to ARVs, the messages of prevention can easily become secondary to treatment. This is dangerous and begins a vicious cycle which focuses on controlling the symptoms instead of treating the core of the problem, unhealthy sexual practices. ARVs are not the solution to the AIDS epidemic. Even with the use of ARVs, it is believed that almost everyone who is infected with HIV will die from an AIDS-related illness. We must not wane in promoting behavioral changes which include risk-elimination through abstinence and being faithful in marriage.

Community Involvement in HIV/AIDS

HIV/AIDS involves more than just the problems of the person who is infected—it is a family problem, too. Families who are caring for infected loved ones are under great mental, emotional, physical, social, spiritual, and financial stress, and they need help. Don't just teach your youth about HIV/AIDS—get them involved! Although they have limitations as youth, there is much they can do to help.

In his book *Helping the Hurting*, author Philip Yancey tells a beautiful story of giving:

The story is about Beethoven, a man not known for his social grace. Because of his deafness, he found conversation difficult and humiliating. When he heard of the death of his friend's son, Beethoven hurried to the house, overcome with grief. He had no words of comfort to offer. But he saw a piano in the room. For the next half hour he played the piano, pouring out his emotions in the most eloquent way he could. When he finished playing, he left. The friend later remarked that no one else's visit had meant so much.[11]

There are many things youth can do to make a difference. Encourage them to make a commitment as an individual or as a group to assist people in need. Following are some suggestions for helping families who are struggling with HIV/AIDS.

- Wash clothes
- Go shopping
- Take flowers or other encouraging gifts
- Offer comfort
- Help clean their house
- Cook a meal
- Sit and talk
- Read a book or the newspaper out loud
- Collect water
- Help in the garden
- Take care of pets or other animals
- Provide transport to the clinic
- Provide company at the hospital
- Pray for and with them
- Go for a walk with them
- Bring healthy food and drinks
- Write a note of encouragement
- Sing to or play games with the family

It Takes Courage!

Fear is an underpinning of the AIDS pandemic—fear of infection, of speaking out about the risks, of death, of being orphaned, of leaving children behind, of pain and suffering, of stigmatization, of hospitals, of poverty... to name just a few. It is important that we do not confuse the presence of fear with cowardice, the opposite of courage. Courage is not the absence of fear; it is reflected in what we choose to do even in spite of our fear.

As we have traveled extensively around the world speaking on the topic of HIV/AIDS and promoting character-based abstinence education programs, we have had the privilege of meeting children, women, and men who possess great courage. We meet groups of boys publicly encouraging their peers to say "no" to sex, persevering despite sneering; adolescent girls and boys courageously caring for their siblings as the head of the home; women and men taking orphans into their homes, even when they don't know how they will feed them. We observe courageous people in hospital waiting rooms awaiting their test results; we meet principals and government officials willing to put their careers at risk to promote abstinence. They believe abstinence will work, and they choose to promote abstinence because they believe it is the right thing to do.

If ever there was a time for courageous people to take a stand, it is now. We need healthy people to kindly challenge unhealthy social norms, to care for those who are infected, to speak out against stigmatization and discrimination, to protect vulnerable children, and to try new techniques of prevention and treatment. People with HIV/AIDS need to courageously acknowledge their infection and actively participate in prevention strategies. World leaders such as Yoweri Museveni of Uganda are needed to support what others would label "unrealistic" approaches to prevention. And we need leaders from various faith communities to courageously talk about HIV/AIDS and lead the way with compassion.

Our task as we work with adolescents is to instill a sense of responsibility to be part of the solution to HIV/AIDS. We need to call on youth to demonstrate the courage to act on what they know is right and to give them a sense of hope that their lives can be different from many who have gone before them. It is important that we call on them to consider a source of strength greater than themselves. We have observed many courageous people around the world reaching out to God for direction, compassion, and strength and finding the courage to face another day. The world needs compassionate men and women of character and courage to end this horrible pandemic. We believe your youth can lead the way!

Preventing HIV/AIDS - Activities

63. Fast Facts 370
64. Dr. Truth 372
65. Know the Risk 378
66. What Do You Know? 382
67. Story Problems 384
68. Looks Can Be Deceiving 392
69. Reach and Teach 394
70. Forbidden Fruit 398
71. How Can We Help? 400
72. That's Not True 404
73. Spread the Word 412
74. Make a Statement T-Shirts 416
75. Safety First 420
76. Where's the Risk? 426
77. A Quick Check 430

Fast Facts

15–30 Minutes

Character Connection
Excellence & Responsibility

Purpose To assess participants' knowledge of basic facts about HIV/AIDS.

Overview This activity illustrates the importance of understanding basic concepts and facts related to HIV/AIDS. A competition is conducted within small groups to allow maximum participation. It is beneficial to use this activity twice, just before and right after teaching the HIV/AIDS material.

Life Skill Finding accurate information concerning health issues

Group Size Any

Cultural and Age Considerations None

Materials None

Preparation *Refer to pages 342–345 to review basic facts related to HIV transmission.* Identify topics to include, such as: ways HIV is and is not transmitted, risky behavior that could lead to contracting HIV, and symptoms of HIV.

Instructions

1. Divide participants into groups of six or eight. Divide each group in half, making two teams per group.
2. Explain to the participants that this activity will test their knowledge about HIV. They will be competing to see which team can give the most facts for each topic you name. In each group, one team will give a fact and then the other team will give a fact until all of their knowledge on that topic is shared. Emphasize the importance of quick, correct answers.
3. Call out a topic and the amount of time the teams will have to compete against one another (the time given will depend on the topic).
4. The teams should continue to call out facts to each other until the time is up. If a team calls out a false

Fast Facts

fact or cannot add another fact in a reasonable amount of time (10 seconds or so), that team is out for the round.

5. Instruct participants to raise their hands if they need help deciding whether answers are correct or incorrect. Walk around the room to monitor the activity.
6. Repeat with different topics.
7. After the desired topics have been covered, ask participants to reassemble, then discuss the activity with the entire group.

Application and Insight

Myths about HIV/AIDS can be very dangerous, so it's important to identify and dispel them.

By talking with others about HIV/AIDS, we can help to correct any misinformation.

Going Deeper

How will you help others to learn the facts about HIV?

Would you ask an adult if you had questions about HIV/AIDS?

Where did you learn most of the information you know about HIV/AIDS?

AIDS is a war no one wants to lose but no one yet knows how to win. —Dr. Gerald J. Stine, U.S. author

It Takes Courage!
to challenge myths or misinformation

Dr. Truth

45–60 Minutes

Character Connection
Respect & Service

Purpose To identify healthy solutions and correct information for common questions about HIV/AIDS

Overview This activity gives participants the opportunity to answer questions based on what they have learned about safe and risky behaviors associated with HIV/AIDS. Posing as the wise and knowledgeable "Dr. Truth," each group will respond to real-life dilemmas through an advice column format.

Life Skill Giving accurate advice to others

Group Size Any

Cultural and Age Considerations None

Materials Dear Dr. Truth Questions (Activity Materials), Dr. Truth Answers (Facilitator Notes), chalkboard and chalk, paper, pens or pencils

Preparation Select the questions you want to use from the Dear Dr. Truth Questions (Activity Materials). Write the selected questions on the chalkboard.

Instructions

1. Divide participants into groups of three or four, and give each group a piece of paper. Ask them to select one person to record their answers.
2. Explain that each group will pretend to be "Dr. Truth," a wise and knowledgeable advice columnist who responds to letters asking questions about HIV/AIDS. As a group, they should write an answer to their assigned question based on what they have learned. Emphasize that in each scenario, there are many possible healthy solutions. However, some solutions may be better than others, so they should try to identify the best one.
3. Assign each group a different question, and allow them 20 minutes to write their responses.

Dr. Truth

4. Ask each group to share their Dr. Truth solutions with the large group.
5. After each presentation, ask participants in the large group to evaluate the answers and give additional suggestions. Offer other suggestions as needed to add important information, correct, or clarify. Refer to the Dr. Truth Answers (Facilitator Notes) to help you guide the discussion to the most important points.
6. Allow time for further discussion and questions when the activity is finished.

Application and Insight

It is important to ask the right person when you don't know the answer to an important question.

It is wiser and safer to say you don't know the answer to a question than to give someone an answer that is incorrect and possibly life-threatening.

Going Deeper

Do you ever admit that you don't know the answer to a question?

How can you give advice to others when they are involved in unhealthy or risky behaviors?

Ask participants to explore opportunities to share this information with others, such as in the local newspaper, over the public address system at school, etc.

He who heareth has hope; he who has hope has everything. —Arabian proverb

It Takes Courage!
to fight the stigma of HIV/AIDS

Dear Dr. Truth Questions

1. My mom has AIDS and she's pregnant. Will the baby die from AIDS?
2. Is it possible to get AIDS without having sexual relations?
3. Why do so many adults have AIDS?
4. My uncle has AIDS and is very sick. He stays at our house and my mom takes care of him. Will my mom get AIDS?
5. My dad is very sick. Is he going to die from AIDS?
6. Can you tell if a baby has AIDS?
7. My brother has tuberculosis. Does that mean he has AIDS, too?
8. My sister and I visited a lady with AIDS. While we were there, the lady's dog bit my sister. Will my sister get AIDS?
9. I want to get married soon. How can I tell that the person I will marry does not have AIDS?
10. Who is a risky sexual partner?
11. How can I know whether or not I have HIV?
12. My friend says her dad has HIV, not AIDS. Is this possible?
13. My friend says that only people who are homosexual get AIDS. I want to have sex, but I'm scared. Will I get AIDS if I have sex?
14. My friend's father is dying from AIDS. Is she dangerous to be around?
15. My dad drinks a very expensive tea every night. He says it has special herbs that will cure his AIDS. Will this tea cure his AIDS?
16. My boyfriend is pressuring me to have sex with him, but I am afraid. He promises to practice safe sex. Should I go ahead and have sex with him? If I don't, he says he will find another girlfriend.
17. I am visiting a country where many people have AIDS. It is the time of year when there are lots of mosquitoes. Do I need to worry about getting AIDS from a mosquito bite?
18. There was a bad accident and my father helped the victims get to the hospital. One man was bleeding heavily. People say the man in the accident has AIDS. Will my father get AIDS?
19. I heard that my barber recently died from AIDS. He had cut my hair for years. Should I be tested for AIDS?
20. I have had bad diarrhea for a week. Do I have AIDS?

Dr. Truth Answers

The following basic facts are the main points that should be incorporated into any answer of these questions. Work with your youth to frame the answer in a culturally appropriate way.

1. My mom has AIDS and she's pregnant. Will the baby die from AIDS?

   It is possible for the mother to pass HIV to her baby. She should go to the doctor for voluntary counseling and testing. There are medications (Nevirapine) the mother can take to greatly reduce the chances of the baby becoming infected with HIV.

2. Is it possible to get AIDS without having sexual relations?

   Any activity involving the exchange of blood (injection drug use, accidents, etc.) or sexual fluids can transmit AIDS.

3. Why do so many adults have AIDS?

   The reasons vary. In some areas of the world, the primary means of transmission is injection drug use, while in other areas it is the result of having multiple sexual partners or having sex with someone who has had multiple sexual partners. It also takes up to 7–10 years for the signs of infection to show. Many adults with AIDS were infected as adolescents or young adults.

4. My uncle has AIDS and is very sick. He stays at our house and my mom takes care of him. Will my mom get AIDS?

   Few people who care for persons with AIDS become infected with HIV. However, it is very important to follow universal precautions when caring for someone who is infected.

5. My dad is very sick. Is he going to die from AIDS?

   It's impossible to tell from this little bit of information. The father could be sick for a variety of reasons. If AIDS is suspected, he must go to a clinic to be tested for HIV/AIDS.

6. Can you tell if a baby has AIDS?

   Because the baby shares his or her mother's antibodies, if the mother is HIV positive, the baby will typically test positive too, even if that isn't the case. Therefore, physicians cannot know for sure if the baby is infected with HIV until the baby is 18–24 months old.

7. My brother has tuberculosis. Does that mean he has AIDS, too?

   Not necessarily. Many people have tuberculosis without HIV infection. However, many people who have AIDS are sick with tuberculosis. The brother needs to see a physician who will prescribe antibiotics to cure the tuberculosis, and he must take these medications exactly as prescribed. If the brother or physician suspects he may be infected with HIV/AIDS, he should be tested.

Dr. Truth Answers *(continued)*

8. My sister and I visited a lady with AIDS. While we were there, the lady's dog bit my sister. Will my sister get AIDS?

   Animals do not transmit HIV. HIV is only spread from one human to another.

9. I want to get married soon. How can I tell that the person I will marry does not have AIDS?

   There is no way to know for sure, unless the person is tested AND is trustworthy. A test may reveal the current HIV status, but someone who is not trustworthy may be having sexual relations with others and would therefore put you at risk. Also, it is possible to have a negative HIV test and still be positive, due to the "window period."

10. Who is a risky sexual partner?

    Outside of marriage, everyone should be considered a risky sexual partner. How could you know for sure that you were someone's first partner? The risk of infection increases with the number of sexual partners. Having sex with someone who has had multiple sexual partners is dangerous too. Sex within marriage is a protection only if both partners are faithful.

11. How can I know whether or not I have HIV?

    The person should go to a clinic and request an AIDS test. For an accurate test result, there must be a six-month period where there has been no risk for acquiring HIV, prior to receiving the test.

12. My friend says her dad has HIV, not AIDS. Is this possible?

    Many people are infected with HIV but are not experiencing any symptoms. They look and act like anyone else. The father may be newly infected or may be receiving anti-retroviral medications that slow the destruction of the immune system. Most people live 7–10 years without experiencing noticeable symptoms of HIV infection. A person has AIDS when he or she is chronically ill due to HIV infection. This is the latter stages of HIV infection.

13. My friend says that only people who are homosexual get AIDS. I want to have sex, but I'm scared. Will I get AIDS if I have sex?

    The friend is misinformed—any two human beings can pass this virus. Anyone who exchanges blood or sexual secretions with someone who is infected may acquire this disease. The person should be scared; HIV is not the only consequence of sex. There is the risk of pregnancy and other serious sexually transmitted infections to consider too. A sexual partner who has had sex with anyone could be infected with HIV or other sexually transmitted infections.

14. My friend's father is dying from AIDS. Is she dangerous to be around?

    The friend would not be infected just because the father is ill. There is no danger of acquiring AIDS via casual contact.

Dr. Truth Answers *(continued)*

15. My dad drinks a very expensive tea every night. He says it has special herbs that will cure his AIDS. Will this tea cure his AIDS?

    There is no known cure for AIDS; there are only treatments that help people to feel better. The father should go to a clinic and ask about available medications that might help him. He should also resist spending the family's valuable resources on unproven claims.

16. My boyfriend is pressuring me to have sex with him, and he promises to practice safe sex. Should I go ahead and have sex with him? If I don't, he says he will find another girlfriend.

    These are not the words of a loving boyfriend; these are the word of a manipulator. There is no safe sex, even if a condom is used. Condoms do not eliminate the risk for acquiring a sexually transmitted infection or pregnancy. Withdrawing the penis prior to ejaculation will not prevent the transmission of HIV/AIDS. She should be encouraged to talk to him about waiting until marriage to get involved in sex. If he doesn't respect that decision, she should look for a new boyfriend. No one should ever be coerced into sex.

17. I am visiting a country where many people have AIDS. It is the time of year when there are lots of mosquitoes. Do I need to worry about getting AIDS from a mosquito bite?

    Many studies have shown that mosquitoes and other insects do not transmit HIV/AIDS. However, mosquitoes do transmit malaria, so care should be taken to prevent malaria.

18. There was a bad accident and my father helped the victims get to the hospital. One man was bleeding heavily. People say the man in the accident has AIDS. Will my father get AIDS?

    There would be no danger unless the victim's blood had an opportunity to get into the father's body through cuts on his hands. If he suspects this was possible, he should talk to his physician. The father could be tested for AIDS 6 months after the incident to be sure.

19. I heard that my barber recently died from AIDS. He had cut my hair for years. Should I be tested for AIDS?

    This would not be necessary, since barbers do not bleed on their patients. However, if there are any instruments that may be exposed to blood (such as razors), barbers should clean and sterilize them between uses.

20. I have had bad diarrhea for a week. Do I have AIDS?

    Many things can cause diarrhea—flu, parasites, etc. If there has been no risk for acquiring HIV, there is no need to be concerned. A physician should be consulted for a medical evaluation. If AIDS is suspected, the person should be tested for HIV.

Know the Risk

30–45 Minutes

Character Connection
Empathy & Responsibility

Purpose To teach the risks associated with the exchange of body fluids in various situations

Overview This activity uses drama to teach about common situations where it is possible for body fluids to be passed from one person to another. Six scenarios are presented to help participants identify and discuss the risk of exposure to HIV/AIDS.

Life Skill Applying basic facts to real-life situations

Group Size Large (10 or more)

Cultural and Age Considerations None

Materials Know the Risk Drama Scenarios (Activity Materials), two cups of water, one plastic bag, one pair of surgical gloves

Preparation Two to four actors (participants) should be briefed ahead of time. The facilitator can also be one of the actors. In either case, *the actors must know the dialogue and their actions well.* A rehearsal is recommended.

Instructions

1. Invite the actors to come to the front of the room to act out the scenarios.
2. Give each actor a cup of water, and explain that the cups of water represent a person's body fluids.
3. Ask participants to observe the various scenarios and be ready to discuss them.
4. After each scenario is presented, emphasize the italicized points on the Risk Drama Scenarios (Activity Materials).
5. Discuss the following questions:
   - At the end of this exercise, who was infected?

     We do not know! You can't tell whether people are infected with HIV just by looking at them. Many people who are HIV-infected don't even know it themselves. In these scenarios, each person could have been infected beforehand.

Know the Risk

- Are there times when the risk of exposure is justified?

  When offering help to someone who is physically injured, there is acceptable risk.
- Is "protected" sex safe?

  No. Abstinence offers the only true protection. It eliminates risk, while "protected" or "safe sex" merely reduces the risk of getting HIV or some of the other sexually transmitted infections.

Application and Insight

We can never know someone's HIV status for sure unless the person is tested.

The risk of HIV infection is associated with exposure to body fluids (blood and sexual secretions).

It's important to follow the universal precautions at the scene of an accident.

Going Deeper

How can you control your risk for acquiring HIV or other sexually transmitted infections?

How does this activity show us that stigmatization and discrimination of people with HIV is wrong?

Freedom is not in our circumstances but in ourselves. —Unknown

It Takes Courage!

to know what is safe or risky

Know the Risk Drama Scenarios

Scenario 1: Living a Normal Life

Actors 1 and 2 both hold their cups of water in one hand and tightly cover the cup with the palm of the other hand. The actors should talk, touch, rub against one another, and interact. They can freely move their cups around without fear of spilling the water. It is not known if Actor 1 or Actor 2 has HIV/AIDS or any other Sexually Transmitted Infection (STI).

Point out that there is no risk of exchanging body fluids and thus contracting HIV/AIDS, because both parties are intentional about containing body fluids. Stress that this scene represents normal life.

Scenario 2: Helping an Accident Victim

Actor 1 has been in an accident and has an open, bleeding wound and needs help. Actor 2 arrives on the scene of the accident and stops to assist. However, when Actor 2 observes the bleeding wound, she becomes very concerned about the possibility of contracting a disease. Again, it is not known if Actor 1 or Actor 2 has HIV/AIDS or any other STI. To represent the break in the skin and the exposure of body fluids, Actor 1 should cover his cup with his hand but allow space between the fingers, and should move around enough to show some water escaping the cup.

Stress the dilemma. If Actor 2 helps Actor 1, there is exposure to body fluids (blood), and thus there is a potential for infection. There is no certainty of either protection or infection, but risk is present. Ask the group, "What can Actor 2 do to protect herself?" If no answer or an incorrect answer is given, suggest that Actor 2 protect herself by wearing surgical gloves. If gloves are not available, a person could use a plastic bag or something similar to help create a barrier against the entry of body fluids. Display each of these items.

Have Actor 2 place the glove or plastic over her hand. If these are not available, Actor 2 needs to show the audience that her fingers are tight across the mouth of the cup, representing the gloves or bag. Actor 2 then proceeds to help Actor 1.

Stress that there is still risk because Actor 2 is not 100 percent sure that she has covered all open wounds (entry points for body fluids). It is also important to emphasize that, even though there cannot be 100 percent confidence of no risk, Actor 2 has taken all known precautions to protect herself and has decided this is an acceptable risk to save the life of another. Hands should always be thoroughly washed with soap afterwards.

Scenario 3: Engaging in Sexual Activity

In the next three scenarios, set the scene by explaining that Actor 1 and Actor 2 represent two people who meet each other in a bar. As they talk, there is the suggestion by Actor 1 to engage in intimate sexual activity. It is not known if either one of them has HIV/AIDS or any other STI. The two actors need to "play up" the situation to the crowd—to the point of overemphasis!

In Scenario 3, both Actor 1 and Actor 2 are willing participants in unprotected sexual activity. This is demonstrated by a conversation in which both express the desire to "play" by holding their cups with one hand and casually flipping water out of it with their other hand. As the "play" continues, the cups get closer and closer, illustrating intimate activity. The water should spill into the other person's cup and

Know the Risk Drama Scenarios *(continued)*

in the surrounding area. Again, the actors need to use an exaggerated, fun style in their words and actions to emphasize the point.

Explain that, in this situation, body fluids (sexual secretions) are freely exchanged between the actors. The fluids have easy access to the other person's body (represented by the cup). Again, because it isn't known if either actor is infected, there is a high risk of infection.

At this point, risk needs to be differentiated. There was a risk in Scenario 2, but the risk was justified to save a life. There is a greater risk in Scenario 3, and it is only for the pleasure of a single sexual encounter.

Scenario 4: Practicing Safer Sex

In this scenario, Actor 2 is unwilling to participate in unprotected sexual activity. To appease Actor 2, Actor 1 agrees to wear a condom. This is again demonstrated through a conversation of "play," as Actor 2 responds with hesitation. To demonstrate the condom, Actor 1 covers his cup with slightly spread fingers, allowing the passage of some water. As the two actors discuss "playing," Actor 2 holds her cup with one hand and casually flips water out of her cup with the other hand. Actor 1 moves his cup around with spread fingers "covering" the opening. Water should get into the other person's cup and in the surrounding area, though primarily from Actor 2's "flipping."

Emphasize that while the actors are not as exposed as in the previous scenario, they have merely reduced risk. People often mistakenly call this "safe sex" and refer to a condom as "protection," but it merely reduces the risk of contracting certain STIs. Ask if this risk is acceptable and if this one sexual encounter is worth the associated risk.

Scenario 5: Practicing Abstinence

In this scenario, Actor 1 makes strong overtures toward Actor 2. However, Actor 2 is unwilling to engage in any intimate sexual activity. Actor 1 assumes the role of "play" by flipping water out of his open cup. Actor 2 says "No" strongly, covers her cup with the palm of her hand, then turns and walks away.

Point out that there is no way for fluids to be exchanged when there is an unwilling participant who flees the situation. The abstinence message is stressed not as a source of risk reduction but rather as the only method of risk elimination.

Scenario 6: Having Multiple Sexual Partners

This scenario can be a quick continuation of Scenario 5. After Actor 2 runs out of the room, Actor 1 can speak to the audience as he flips water over them and asks what happens if he shares fluids with all these people.

Because it is not known if he is infected, every time body fluids are shared there is a risk of infection. Emphasize the dangers of multiple sexual partners. The greater the number of partners, the greater the risk and spread of the epidemic.

Activity #66 What Do You Know?

30–45 Minutes

Character Connection
Honesty & Respect

Purpose To provide an interactive way to introduce new information and discover the participants' knowledge of and interests in a topic

Overview This activity can be used to introduce a new topic. It can also be used at the end of a lesson or unit to informally assess the knowledge gained. Participants will work in pairs and identify the existing knowledge and questions they have about various topics.

Life Skill Thinking critically

Group Size Any

Cultural and Age Considerations None

Materials Six large pieces of paper, two different colored pads of Post-It Notes (or slips of colored pieces of paper with tape), masking tape, pens or pencils

Preparation Tape the six pieces of paper together in two rows of three so they form a chart. Label each section with general topics associated with HIV/AIDS, such as HIV, AIDS, Transmission, Testing, Treatment, Prevention, etc. Hang the chart on the wall.

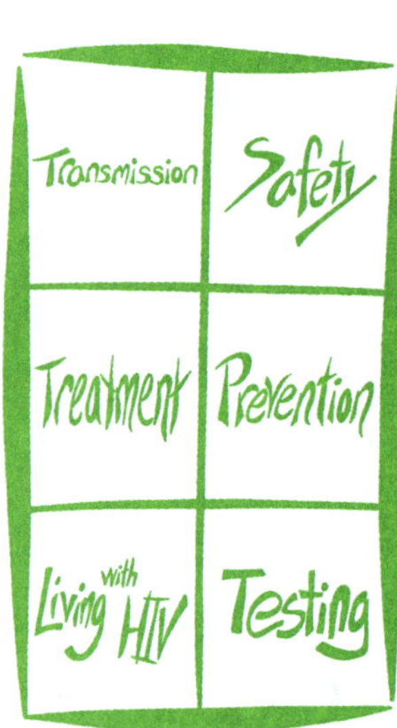

Instructions

1. Ask participants to divide into pairs, and give each pair four Post-It Notes (two of each color).
2. Give pairs 10 minutes to briefly discuss the topics listed on the chart and choose two sections. On each Post-It Note of the first color (name one of the colors), ask them to write down one thing they already *know* about each of the two topics.
3. Now ask pairs to choose two sections they *want to learn more about* and record their questions on the other two Post-It Notes.
4. When they have finished writing, instruct them to place their notes on the chart in the appropriate sections.

What Do You Know?

5. Invite a volunteer to come to the front to read all the notes listing *what is already known* about the topic. *Note: Do not use this time to correct misinformation, as this can be done later during the instruction time.*
6. Invite another volunteer to come to the front to read all the questions or topics the participants *want to learn.*
7. Reinforce and commend the participants on the information they have already acquired, and discuss your plans for the next sessions. It is important to acknowledge your desire to incorporate their questions and interests into the learning activities on HIV/AIDS.

Application and Insight

We need to share what we know about HIV/AIDS with others.

Many people have the same questions and concerns that we do.

We need to be open to learning from others.

There is much misinformation about HIV/AIDS.

Going Deeper

What new information have you already learned from this activity?

What additional questions do you want us to add to the chart?

Every person in this life has something to teach me—and as soon as I accept that, I open myself to truly listening. —Catherine Doucette, author

It Takes Courage!
to admit you don't know an answer

Activity #67 Story Problems

45–60 Minutes

Character Connection
Honesty & Responsibility

Purpose To help develop the critical-thinking skills related to HIV/AIDS by analyzing potential real-life situations

Overview This activity describes three different scenarios and uses discussion questions to stimulate thought and interaction among participants.

Life Skill Using facts in a practical way

Group Size Any

Cultural and Age Considerations None

Materials Story Problems Handouts, Story Problem Answers (Facilitator Notes), pens or pencils

Preparation Make one copy of each of the three Story Problem scenarios (Nathaniel, Margaret, Lewis).

Instructions

1. Divide participants into three groups of two to eight persons each. Create additional groups if necessary.
2. Give each group one story. Instruct them to read the story and then take 20 minutes to answer the questions.
3. Ask each group to read their story to the other groups and present the results of their discussion.
4. Provide any clarification, additions, or corrections as necessary to ensure that correct information has been presented.

Story Problems

Application and Insight

It is important to think through the implications of real-life situations and how one could appropriately respond.

Our choices today can greatly influence our tomorrows.

Going Deeper

What have you learned from this activity?

What are some additional situations we could analyze as a group?

Why is it almost impossible to know how some people got infected with HIV?

I believe that we are here on the planet Earth to live, grow up and do what we can to make this world a better place for all people to enjoy freedom. —Rosa Parks, U.S. civil rights leader

It Takes Courage!
to show true compassion

Story Problems

Nathaniel

Nathaniel has lived most of his life in a small town near a large city. He is 30 years old and lives in a house with his wife. His son and daughter-in-law and their three children live in the house, too. When Nathaniel was a teenager he used to inject drugs, but he went to a rehabilitation center and he is better now. A few years ago, Nathaniel had a bad fall when he was fixing the roof on the house. He got a large cut on his leg that bled a lot. His son took him to the local hospital, where he stayed for three days. While Nathaniel was at the hospital, the doctor gave him a blood transfusion because Nathaniel had lost a lot of blood. Nathaniel got well quickly and was back at work. This year, Nathaniel developed severe diarrhea and began to lose a lot of weight. Then he got tuberculosis. The doctor says Nathaniel has AIDS. His family does not understand. Nathaniel has always been strong and healthy, and they know he does not have sexual relations with other women.

- Based on the facts of the story, how do you think Nathaniel got AIDS? Can you think of any other ways he may have been infected?

- What are the signs that Nathaniel has AIDS?
- Will Nathaniel's wife get HIV from him?
- Will his son's family get HIV from Nathaniel?
- What are the chances that Nathaniel will recover?

Story Problems

Margaret

Margaret is 19 years old. She and her husband, John, live in a small village and have two children. John goes to a nearby town each day to work. Margaret works on a plot of land and grows food for the family. Last year, Margaret had a third child. Margaret was healthy, but the baby was sick with AIDS when it was born. The baby died within three months. Margaret wants to have more children, but she is afraid they will die also. She wants everyone in her family to get an injection against HIV/AIDS.

- How did the baby get AIDS?
- Does Margaret have AIDS?
- Should Margaret try to get pregnant again?
- Will Margaret die of AIDS?
- Should the family get an injection to protect them against HIV/AIDS?

Story Problems

Lewis

Lewis is the oldest son in a family of five. His parents are very proud of him. He went to the university and became a lawyer in a large city. Many of his clients have HIV/AIDS, but he tries to help them anyway. He is a smart young man, and he is good to his parents. Lewis loves the nightlife in the city and likes to dance. He has had sexual relationships with many girlfriends, but now he is interested in a special girl. He plans to marry next year. A year ago, Lewis began to have swollen glands in his neck and under his arms. Many nights he has a fever and sweats a lot. He sometimes gets a skin rash. He finally decides to go to the doctor to see what is wrong. After testing, the doctor tells him that he is infected with HIV. Lewis tells the doctor that he is wealthy and can pay for the cure.

- How do you think Lewis got infected, based on the facts in the story?
- What cure will the doctor suggest to Lewis?
- How can Lewis keep from spreading HIV to other people?
- Should Lewis still consider marriage?
- Will Lewis die or get better?

Story Problem Answers

Story 1: NATHANIEL

Based on the facts of the story, how do you think Nathaniel got AIDS? Can you think of any other ways he may have been infected?
Nathaniel was likely infected with HIV when he shared syringes with other drug users. Even if he had been exposed to HIV through his blood transfusion, which is rare, he would not typically show severe health problems for many years.

What are the signs that Nathaniel has AIDS?
Severe diarrhea, significant weight loss, and tuberculosis are symptoms that may indicate Nathaniel has AIDS. Up to this point, he has been strong and healthy.

Will Nathaniel's wife get HIV from him?
Nathaniel's wife may have already gotten HIV from Nathaniel if they had sexual relations. She should be tested. If Nathaniel's wife is not infected, it would be wise for them to stop having sexual relations. If they choose to have sex, it is important for them to use a condom correctly every single time to reduce the risk of transmission.

Will his son's family get HIV from Nathaniel?
No, Nathaniel's family will not get HIV from him. HIV is not spread in social ways such as sharing meals, using the toilet, or living in the same household with a person who has AIDS. The family needs to learn universal precautions to safely care for Nathaniel.

What are the chances that Nathaniel will recover?
A doctor or health worker can treat the symptoms of Nathaniel's illness, such as the diarrhea, but Nathaniel can never get rid of the virus. He will probably die from one of the diseases associated with AIDS. New antiretroviral medications may slow the destruction of the immune system and allow Nathaniel to feel better for quite some time.

Story 2: MARGARET

How did the baby get AIDS?
The baby was infected with HIV either in the mother's womb, during childbirth, or when breastfed. We do not know how Margaret got the virus.

Does Margaret have AIDS?
Margaret may not have AIDS yet, but she is infected with HIV, the virus that causes AIDS.

Should Margaret try to get pregnant again?
Margaret should probably be discouraged from trying to get pregnant again. Because she has the virus, any new baby is at risk for infection in the womb, during childbirth, or when breastfed. Margaret is fortunate to have two healthy children. If she had no children, it could be very hard for her to choose not to become pregnant. She should receive counseling and information so she can make her own decision. The drug Nevirapine could reduce but not eliminate the risk of infection for the baby.

Story Problem Answers *(continued)*

Will Margaret die of AIDS?
Margaret is infected with HIV, but right now she does not have any of the diseases linked with AIDS. If she takes good care of her health and has access to good medical treatment, she may live for many years without developing an AIDS-related disease.

Should the family get an injection to protect them against AIDS?
The family cannot get an injection to protect them against AIDS because no vaccine exists right now. However, they will not get HIV from social contact, so Margaret does not need to worry. Margaret's husband should also be tested for HIV. If he is not already infected with HIV, they should decide to refrain from sex involving an exchange of body fluids. If that is not acceptable, condoms may help protect him from becoming infected with the virus. Used correctly 100 percent of the time, condoms may reduce his risk of infection up to 85–90 percent.

Story 3: LEWIS

How do you think Lewis got infected, based on the facts in the story?
By being sexually involved with many women, Lewis increased his chances of having sexual contact with a woman infected with HIV.

What cure will the doctor suggest to Lewis?
The doctor cannot suggest a cure for Lewis, because there is no cure. Lewis may be able to take antiretroviral medications to slow the progression of HIV, but they may or may not work for Lewis.

How can Lewis keep from spreading HIV to other people?
Lewis can spread HIV to others during sexual intercourse. He can also spread it to others if he gives his blood for transfusions. The only responsible decision for Lewis is to stop his lifestyle of multiple sexual partners. There is no safe way for Lewis to engage in sex anymore. Even with a condom, there is a chance that Lewis can infect a sexual partner.

Should Lewis still consider marriage?
Lewis should be advised to be honest with his wife-to-be about the fact that he is HIV-positive. If they marry, it is best if they can avoid intimate sexual activity involving an exchange of sexual secretions.

Will Lewis die or get better?
Lewis will have HIV for the rest of his life. He may not get sick right away, and if he takes good care of himself, he may not get sick for many years. Eventually, the chances are that Lewis will die of AIDS.

Notes

People who don't help others in trouble "because they got into trouble by their own fault" would probably not throw a lifeline to a drowning man until they learned whether he fell in through his own fault or not.

–Sydney J. Harris, U.S. journalist and author

Activity #68 Looks Can Be Deceiving

15–30 Minutes

Character Connection
Honesty & Responsibility

Purpose To illustrate that refusing to participate in sexual behaviors is the primary way to be safe from HIV and other sexually transmitted infections

Overview This activity allows participants to choose from three seemingly identical cookies, two of which have been tampered with beforehand. Choosing from among the cookies represents the risk taking that occurs when choosing sexual partners.

Life Skill Making wise decisions that promote a healthy lifestyle

Group Size Any

Cultural and Age Considerations None

Materials Three identical cookies (or choose another special food participants would enjoy), three napkins or paper towels, pen or pencil

Preparation Write one of these phrases on the bottom of each napkin: "All Around the Room," "Three People," and "Safe." Place a cookie on each napkin. Make sure the writing on the bottom of the napkins is not visible to participants.

Instructions

1. Ask for two or three volunteers and send them out of the room.
2. Select the cookie on the napkin marked "All Around the Room" and pass it around the group, explaining that participants can do anything to the cookie (touching, smelling, licking, etc.) as long as the cookie does not look any different.
3. Ask for three participants to come to the front of the room. Select the cookie on the napkin labeled "Three People" and pass it around to them, explaining that they should only touch it with their hands.

Looks Can Be Deceiving

4. Do not do anything to the third cookie. Place it next to the first two cookies.
5. Before the volunteers come back into the room, encourage the group to try to influence the volunteers' decisions in any way they can.
6. Ask the volunteers to come back into the room. Show them the three cookies and explain that one of the cookies has been tampered with by the whole group, one has been touched by three people, and the other one has not been touched at all.
7. Allow the volunteers to choose any one of the cookies, or to decline all three. After making their decisions, ask why each person made that choice.
8. Discuss with the group how this activity relates to the choice of sexual partners and the risk of contracting HIV/AIDS.

Application and Insight

Every choice of a sexual partner involves a risk. Although someone may look "safe," it is impossible to determine that person's sexual history or infection status.

Sexual abstinence is the best way to prevent HIV/AIDS.

Short-term pleasure can result in a lifetime of hurt.

Going Deeper

What factors might affect the volunteer's choice?

How does peer pressure influence decision making?

Why are some people greater risk takers than others?

Freedom is the ability to say no. —Unknown

It Takes Courage!

to say no to harmful temptation

Activity #69 Reach and Teach

30–45 Minutes

Character Connection
Excellence & Fairness

Purpose To determine factors that spread or inhibit HIV infection

Overview This is a team competition in which members of each team take turns drawing an item from a bag and then correlate that item to a fact about HIV/AIDS as a way to help clarify misinformation about HIV/AIDS.

Life Skill Sharing life-saving knowledge with others

Group Size Any

Cultural and Age Considerations Vary the items in the bag to address HIV/AIDS topics that are appropriate for the age and culture of your group.

Materials HIV Associations Grab Bag Items (Facilitator Notes); large, opaque bag containing any or all of the following items. (Individual cards with the name of each item can be substituted for the actual items.)

1. Drinking glass
2. Toilet seat
3. Doorknob
4. Bathing suit
5. Bug repellent
6. Bleach bottle
7. Birth control pills
8. Condoms
9. Toothbrush
10. Razor
11. Latex gloves
12. Work gloves
13. Beer can
14. Syringe
15. Baby doll
16. Soccer ball
17. Pierced earrings
18. Stuffed animal
19. Fake tattoo
20. Telephone
21. Dental floss
22. Comb

Preparation Place the chosen items in the large bag.

Instructions

1. Divide the class into two teams. Instruct each team to sit together on opposite sides of the room.

Reach and Teach

2. Ask a member of Team 1 to reach into the grab bag and pull out an item. Give the team 30 seconds to explain what that particular item has to do with HIV/AIDS transmission. If the team answers correctly, award them one point.
3. If a team answers incorrectly, give the other team an opportunity to answer the question. If their answer is correct, award them a point.
4. Now ask a member of Team 2 to reach into the grab bag and pull out an item. Give them 30 seconds to explain how that item relates to HIV/AIDS transmission. Again, if the team answers correctly, award them one point.
5. Continue alternating teams until all of the items in the bag have been identified.
6. Give the winning team a prize.

Application and Insight

Everyone has a responsibility to learn as much as possible about HIV/AIDS.

It is important to clarify and correct misinformation about HIV/AIDS.

Going Deeper

What are some other items we could have placed in the bag?

How would you link those items with HIV/AIDS transmission?

What are some of the common myths related to HIV/AIDS transmission that people believe in this community?

How can we help inform people with correct information on HIV/AIDS?

Do all the good you can, by all the means you can, in all the ways you can, in all the places you can, at all the times you can, to all the people you can, as long as you ever can. —John Wesley, English clergyman and founder of Methodism

It Takes Courage!
to tell others about HIV/AIDS

HIV Associations Grab Bag Items

1. **Drinking glass:** There is no risk from casual contact.
2. **Toilet seat:** There is no risk from casual contact.
3. **Doorknob:** There is no risk from casual contact.
4. **Bathing suit:** There is no risk from casual contact. HIV is not transmitted in swimming pools, rivers, or lakes.
5. **Bug repellent:** People do not get HIV from insects.
6. **Bleach bottle:** A solution of 1 part bleach to 9 parts water kills HIV on surfaces contaminated by body fluids.
7. **Birth control pills:** These offer no protection against HIV or other sexually transmitted infections.
8. **Condoms:** Condoms can help reduce the risk of HIV infection by 85 to 90 percent *if used consistently and correctly every time someone has sex.*
9. **Toothbrush:** Never use someone else's toothbrush; it may be contaminated with blood.
10. **Razor:** Never use someone else's razor; it may be contaminated with blood.
11. **Latex gloves:** These form an effective barrier against HIV; use when handling body fluids such as vomit and when cleaning the wounds of others.
12. **Work gloves:** These are the best gloves to use when cleaning surfaces where HIV may be present.
13. **Beer can:** Alcohol may impair judgment and increase risky behaviors.
14. **Syringe:** Syringes are a likely way to transmit blood; always use sterilized needles.
15. **Baby doll:** Babies can get infected by their mothers in the womb, during birth, or when breastfeeding.
16. **Soccer ball:** It's safe to play soccer unless someone is bleeding.
17. **Pierced earrings:** Any item used to pierce the body must be sterilized.
18. **Stuffed animal:** Animals do not transmit HIV.
19. **Fake tattoo:** Unsterilized needles used to make tattoos can transmit HIV.
20. **Telephone:** Phones carry no risk of HIV transmission. HIV hotlines are a good source of information.
21. **Dental floss:** People who don't floss have poor oral hygiene, increasing the risk that HIV can be spread through prolonged kissing.
22. **Comb:** There is no risk from casual contact.

Notes

Hope is like a road in the country; there was never a road, but when many people walk on it, the road comes into existence.

–Lin Yutang, Chinese novelist and philosopher

Forbidden Fruit

15–30 Minutes

Character Connection
Responsibility & Self-control

Purpose To illustrate that it is impossible to determine from an outward appearance whether an individual has HIV or another sexually transmitted infection

Overview This activity uses pieces of fruit, some injected with food coloring, to represent the unforeseen risks associated with choosing a sexual partner.

Life Skill Waiting until marriage to have sex

Group Size Any

Cultural and Age Considerations None

Materials One whole apple for each participant; one *brand new, sterilized* syringe; dark blue or green edible food coloring

Preparation Inject 30 percent of the apples with a significant amount of food coloring. (You may need to practice on a few apples to determine the best method and amount of coloring to inject into the apples.) Alternatively, use three apples, place food coloring in only one apple, and select three volunteers to come to the front of the room to perform the activity.

Instructions

1. Hand an apple to each participant, asking them not to begin eating until everyone has received one.
2. When everyone has an apple, invite them all to bite into their apples.
3. As some of the participants begin to notice that their apples have been dyed, ask the group to stop eating and give you their attention.
4. Explain that some of the apples were injected with food coloring, the same substance used in cake icing, and that this dye won't hurt them. Allow participants to continue eating their apples.
5. Explain that this illustration demonstrates how people may look the same on the outside, but some of them may be carriers of HIV. They look like everyone else, but

Forbidden Fruit

just like the apples, there is no way of knowing whether someone has been exposed to HIV.

Application and Insight

It is important to look beyond appearance when it comes to choosing a sexual partner.

You can never know for sure whether someone is infected with HIV.

Most people around the world who have HIV do not even know that they are infected.

Character is an essential element in choosing a sexual partner.

Going Deeper

Can you think of a situation where you thought someone or something was healthy that turned out to be unhealthy?

Do you think people are usually truthful about their previous sexual experiences? Why or why not?

What are some practical ways to avoid risky sexual behavior?

You have to sacrifice something to get something. —Thai proverb

It Takes Courage!
to abstain from sex until marriage

How Can We Help?

30–45 Minutes

Character Connection
Empathy & Service

Purpose To consider practical ways to help people affected by or infected with HIV/AIDS

Overview In this activity, participants brainstorm ideas for serving the community. Participants compete in teams to think of original ways to help people affected by or infected with HIV/AIDS.

Life Skill Increasing self-respect by giving to others

Group Size Large (20 or more)

Cultural and Age Considerations None

Materials How Can We Help? Handout, pens or pencils, chart paper, marking pen, chalkboard and chalk

Preparation Make one copy of the How Can We Help? Handout for each team. Draw the How Can We Help? Handout on the chart paper and post in the room.

Instructions

1. Divide participants into at least three teams (seven or eight people per team). Give each team a copy of the How Can We Help? Handout.
2. Ask participants to think of ways to help each category of people (listed on the left) in each of the dimensions of wellness (listed at the top).
3. Inform groups that each idea must be different; answers cannot be repeated in multiple boxes. Give participants 10 minutes to fill in as many boxes as possible.
4. Place the large How Can We Help? chart at the front of the room.
5. Write the name of each team on the chalkboard (one column per team) for scorekeeping.
6. As a large group, work through the entire chart. For every box, ask each team to

How Can We Help?

read their idea aloud. Every appropriate answer is awarded one point. Each appropriate answer that is also an original idea (one that no other team suggested) receives two points.

7. When the entire chart has been reviewed, the team with the most points wins.
8. Challenge the group to put a plan into action and to help serve the community.

Application and Insight

There are many different ways to help people affected by and infected with HIV/AIDS. Various groups and individuals may have different resources, but everyone can help in some way.

Going Deeper

Challenge the group to do a community service project related to caring for persons and families affected by HIV/AIDS.

Why is it important to help other people?

What kind of service projects have you seen that showed the best results?

Too often we underestimate the power of a touch, a smile, a kind word, a listening ear, an honest compliment, or the smallest act of caring, all of which have the potential to turn a life around.

—Leo Buscaglia, U.S. author

It Takes Courage!

to devote your time to helping others in need

How Can We Help?

How Can We Help?	Emotionally	Physically	Mentally	Spiritually	Socially
A person with HIV/AIDS					
A family caring for someone with HIV/AIDS					
Children orphaned due to HIV/AIDS					

1. What are three ways you can get involved as a group in caring for people who are sick with AIDS or their families?

2. What are three ways you can individually use your time, energy, or talents to help care for people who are dealing with HIV/AIDS?

Notes

To complain that life has no joys while there is a single creature whom we can relieve by our bounty, assist by our counsels or enliven by our presence, is . . . just as rational as to die of thirst with the cup in our hands.

–Thomas Fitzosborne, 18th-century author

That's Not True

30–45 Minutes

Character Connection
Honesty & Responsibility

Purpose To correct misinformation and give accurate information about HIV/AIDS

Overview This activity involves a competition among four teams. Participants will classify statements about HIV/AIDS as either true or false.

Life Skill Discerning truthful statements from false ones

Group Size Large (10 or more)

Cultural and Age Considerations None

Materials True Statements and False Statements (Activity Materials), True Statement Answers and False Statement Answers (Facilitator Notes), large jar or bowl, two large cards or pieces of paper for each group

Preparation Choose the desired number of items from the True Statements and False Statements (Activity Materials). Fold all the statements and place them in a jar. Make pairs of answer cards—one pair for each team. Write the word *TRUE* in large letters on one card and the word *FALSE* on the other.

Instructions

1. Divide participants into four teams and ask each team to select a representative.
2. Label the teams A, B, C, and D, or allow teams to make up their own names. Write the name of each team on the chalkboard (one column per team) for scorekeeping.
3. Invite Team A's representative to come to the front of the room and select a statement from the jar.
4. Ask Team A's representative to read that statement aloud to all the participants, then give teams 30 seconds to decide whether the statement is true or false.

That's Not True

5. When the time is up, have each team hold up either a *TRUE* card or a *FALSE* card. Each team that is correct receives one point.
6. Team A has the opportunity to support the statement if it is true or disprove the statement if it is false. If they give an appropriate piece of information, they receive two points.
7. After each question, ask the next team to send their representative to the front to read the next question. After all the slips are drawn, the team with the most points wins.

Application and Insight

Statements that seem to be true or sources that seem to be credible may actually be providing false information.

It is important to keep up to date with new information on HIV/AIDS.

Going Deeper

Give the participants one week to collect written examples of misinformation about HIV/AIDS. Set aside time so their findings can be presented to the group.

Why does false information about HIV/AIDS exist?

What can you do to make sure you are receiving accurate information?

Knowledge has never been known to enter the head via an open mouth. —Doug Larson, 1924 Olympic Gold Medalist

It Takes Courage!
to share truth with others

True Statements

Copy and cut out each statement.

1. A baby can be born without HIV but get infected by the mother's breast milk. true	*2. A person with AIDS may be able to live longer by taking antiretroviral drugs.* true	*3. If a person with AIDS gives someone a long open-mouth kiss, he or she can pass HIV to the other person.* true	*4. If condoms are used consistently and correctly, they can reduce the risk of HIV.* true
5. People with AIDS can pass tuberculosis to others just by coughing on them. true	*6. HIV causes AIDS.* true	*7. If you have a sexually transmitted infection, you are more likely to become infected with HIV.* true	*8. A person can easily get AIDS by having sex with a prostitute (commercial sex worker).* true
9. Women are more likely to get AIDS from men than they are to give it to men. true	*10. Elderly women can get AIDS too.* true	*11. It is dangerous for someone who has AIDS to be in the presence of people who have a cold or the flu.* true	*12. It is not dangerous for people with AIDS to play soccer with others.* true
13. Gloves should always be worn at the scene of a car accident. true	*14. Donated blood is usually tested for the presence of HIV.* true	*15. Mosquitoes cannot transmit HIV.* true	*16. It is okay to eat food prepared by someone who has AIDS.* true

False Statements

Copy and cut out each statement.

1. You can tell if a person is infected with HIV. false	2. It is best to not eat dinner at a friend's house if someone with AIDS lives there. false	3. It is best to always refuse a blood transfusion. false	4. Bed bugs or cockroaches can spread HIV. false
5. Children can catch AIDS by using the same toilet as their sick mother who has AIDS. false	6. There are very expensive medications that can cure HIV/AIDS. false	7. Since HIV is found in all body fluids, a girl with AIDS can infect her boyfriend if she cries and her tears get on his hands. false	8. You should never swim in a pool with someone who has AIDS. false
9. Brothers and sisters of persons with AIDS usually get AIDS too. false	10. There is a new treatment in the United States that can cure AIDS. false	11. Doctors and nurses who treat people with AIDS often get infected by their patients. false	12. Antiretroviral drugs can help everyone who has AIDS. false
13. Traditional healers can cure people with AIDS. false	14. Kids with AIDS should be asked to leave school because they are a danger to others. false	15. Sharing a toothbrush with someone who you know doesn't have AIDS is okay. false	16. Having a negative HIV test is sure proof that someone is not infected with HIV. false

True Statements Answers

1. A baby can be born without HIV but get infected by the mother's breast milk.

   This is because the virus is present in the mother's breast milk—this does not happen all of the time. Mothers who think they are infected with HIV should consult a doctor.

2. A person with AIDS may be able to live longer by taking antiretroviral drugs.

   These drugs are expensive, but they help to prolong the life of many people who take them as prescribed.

3. If a person with AIDS gives someone a long open-mouth kiss, he or she can pass HIV to the other person.

   Sometimes people have broken teeth or small cuts in their mouths and the virus can enter. People can also have bleeding gums due to poor dental hygiene.

4. If condoms are used consistently and correctly, they can reduce the risk of HIV.

   "If" is the main word. Condoms used consistently and correctly can reduce the spread of HIV by as much as 85 to 90 percent.

5. People with AIDS can pass tuberculosis to others just by coughing on them.

   Tuberculosis germs act very different from the HIV. They are present in sputum and can be transferred to others, especially when they are not in a well ventilated area. AIDS is not transmitted this way, but many people who have AIDS suffer from tuberculosis infection. Medicines can treat tuberculosis.

6. HIV causes AIDS.

   Almost all scientists recognize the link between HIV and AIDS.

7. If you have a sexually transmitted infection, you are more likely to become infected with HIV.

   This is especially true if it is an ulcerative disease such as syphilis, chancroid, or herpes. The break in the skin makes it easier for HIV to enter a person's body.

8. A person can easily get AIDS by having sex with a prostitute (commercial sex worker).

   A prostitute has had many sexual partners and has likely been exposed to HIV and other sexually transmitted infections.

9. Women are more likely to get AIDS from men than they are to give it to men.

   Women have more mucus membranes (in the vaginal area) that are exposed to infected body fluids.

True Statements Answers *(continued)*

10. Elderly women can get AIDS too.

    Any human being can get AIDS.

11. It is dangerous for someone who has AIDS to be in the presence of people who have a cold or the flu.

    Persons with AIDS are very prone to infection due to a weakened immune system.

12. It is not dangerous for people with AIDS to play soccer with others.

    If they are not bleeding, there is no danger.

13. Gloves should always be worn at the scene of a car accident.

    There may be glass and broken metal at the scene of an accident. People may be bleeding. Gloves help to protect the hands. People should still be very careful.

14. Donated blood is usually tested for the presence of HIV.

    Almost every country tests donated blood before giving a transfusion. There is a risk, but it is very small.

15. Mosquitoes cannot transmit HIV.

    Many studies prove that mosquitoes do not transmit HIV.

16. It is okay to eat food prepared by someone who has AIDS.

    Touching food will not transmit HIV.

False Statement Answers

1. You can tell if a person is infected with HIV.

   Most people who are infected with HIV do not know it. People may be very healthy for years, even though they are carrying HIV in their bodies.

2. It is best to refrain from eating dinner at a friend's house if someone with AIDS is living there.

   Being around someone who has AIDS is not dangerous. Blood and sexual secretions are the modes of transmission.

3. It is best to always refuse a blood transfusion.

   A doctor knows the risk and would never recommend a transfusion unless it is absolutely necessary.

4. Bed bugs or cockroaches can spread HIV.

   Animals and insects do not transmit HIV. HIV is passed from human to human.

5. Children can catch AIDS by using the same toilet as their sick mother who has AIDS.

   The dangerous body fluids are blood and sexual fluids. If the mother is very ill with diarrhea, care must be taken to clean the toilet regularly, for hygienic reasons, not to prevent the spread of AIDS.

6. There are very expensive medications that can cure HIV/AIDS.

   There is no cure for AIDS. Once infected with HIV, a person is infected for the rest of his or her life!

7. Since HIV is found in all body fluids, a girl with AIDS can infect her boyfriend if she cries and her tears get on his hands.

   The virus in the tears has no means of entering the intact skin of the boyfriend. There are no known cases of anyone becoming infected with HIV via tears.

8. You should never swim in a pool with someone who has AIDS.

   Chlorine kills most infectious agents.

9. Brothers and sisters of persons with AIDS usually get AIDS too.

   AIDS is not hereditary. Living with someone does not cause AIDS.

10. There is a new treatment in the United States that can cure AIDS.

    There is no cure for AIDS anywhere in the world.

False Statement Answers *(continued)*

11. Doctors and nurses who treat people with AIDS often get infected by their patients.
This only happens in rare cases due to an accident like a needle stick.

12. Antiretroviral drugs can help everyone who has AIDS.
This treatment only works for some people. Many people have taken these medications and have not received benefit.

13. Traditional healers can cure people with AIDS.
There is no cure for AIDS anywhere in the world.

14. Kids with AIDS should be asked to leave school because they are a danger to others.
Normal school activities do not put others at risk for HIV transmission.

15. Sharing a toothbrush with someone who you know doesn't have AIDS is okay.
Since it is impossible to know someone's HIV status, it is always unwise to share a toothbrush—with anyone.

16. Having a negative HIV test is sure proof that someone is not infected with HIV.
The person could've been tested in the window period. A negative test result is only true if the person tested refrained from any AIDS associated risk-taking behavior for six months prior to the test.

Activity #73

Spread the Word

45–60 Minutes

Character Connection
Responsibility & Service

Purpose To provide an opportunity for youth to educate others about HIV/AIDS

Overview This activity gives participants the opportunity to work in groups to create public service announcements that could be broadcast on a local radio station.

Life Skill Influencing a community with healthy life messages

Group Size Any

Cultural and Age Considerations None

Materials Public Service Announcement Topics (Activity Materials), paper, pens or pencils, empty jar, tape recorder

Preparation Ask if your local radio station will sponsor a contest for the best public service announcement. Copy and cut out Public Service Announcement Topics (Activity Materials). Select the topics you want to use, or add your own topics as desired. Put all the slips of paper in the jar.

Instructions

1. Divide participants into groups of three to four individuals. Give each group paper and a pen or pencil.
2. Explain the definition of a Public Service Announcement (a two- to three-minute educational audio segment), and ask if participants can share some examples of public service announcements they have heard on the radio.
3. If arranged, explain that the local radio station is sponsoring a contest for the best public service announcement. Announce the judging methods and the prize to be won. Allow participants one or two days to prepare and practice, so they will be ready to make their presentations at the next session. If not arranged, allow 20 minutes or so for participants to prepare, then let them select the winner.
4. Ask someone from each group to come up and pick a slip from the jar. Give each group paper and a pen or pencil to write their script.

Spread the Word

5. Allow groups time to create a public service announcement about their topic for the people in their community. The two-minute presentation should use a role-play so everyone can be involved, and can include singing, sound effects, etc.
6. During the preparation, walk around to assist participants in their creative process.
7. Give group time to present their public service announcements to the others, and tape record their presentations.
8. As each group finishes their presentation, discuss the information presented in their public service announcement.
9. If the radio station is not judging the ads, ask participants to choose the top three presentations.

Application and Insight

A peer group can greatly affect the surrounding community by applying their knowledge and learning.

Creatively sharing good ideas can help to foster acceptance of new information and promote understanding about HIV/AIDS.

Going Deeper

Ask the youth to explore opportunities to present their announcements for a parent meeting, student groups, churches, or assemblies.

What important information is missing in existing advertising about HIV/AIDS prevention, abstinence, etc.?

Do you feel the people in your community are accurately targeted in these ads?

How can you influence the surrounding community to learn more about HIV/AIDS?

Kindness in words creates confidence, kindness in thinking creates profoundness, kindness in feeling creates love. —Lao Tzu, Chinese philosopher

It Takes Courage!

to really contribute to the community

Public Service Announcement Topics

Copy and cut out each statement.

If you are pregnant, see your doctor for early care

Importance of voluntary testing and counseling

Common ways people get HIV

We don't need to fear a person with AIDS

Wait for marriage to have sex

Be faithful to your spouse

Ways to help your neighbor who is sick

Don't discriminate against people with AIDS

It's not your business how someone got infected

Drugs and alcohol cloud your judgment

AIDS kills

There is no cure for AIDS

You can't tell if someone is infected with HIV

You can help prevent AIDS

Safety precautions for preventing HIV/AIDS transmission

Notes

Hope works in these ways: it looks for the good in people instead of harping on the worst; it discovers what can be done instead of grumbling about what cannot; it regards problems, large or small, as opportunities; it pushes ahead when it would be easy to quit; it "lights the candle" instead of "cursing the darkness."

–Anonymous

Activity #74 Make a Statement T-Shirts

30–45 Minutes

Character Connection
Honesty & Respect

Purpose To allow participants to creatively express the reasons why people should abstain from sex before marriage

Overview In this activity participants will create T-shirt designs to express their personal reasons for not engaging in premarital sexual activity.

Life Skill Sharing beliefs with others

Group Size Individual activity with any size group

Cultural and Age Considerations Select a topic that is appropriate for the age of your group.

Materials T-shirt Design Handouts, paper, pens or pencils, art supplies (markers, paint, glitter, etc.)

Preparation Make one copy of the T-shirt Design Handouts for each participant. If possible, arrange with a business or group of local leaders to sponsor a T-shirt design contest. Set a time and place for the judging. Ask the local leaders to print T-shirts with the winning design for all participants.

Instructions

1. If arranged, explain the T-shirt contest and announce the judging methods.
2. Give each participant paper and a pen or pencil.
3. Either pick one of the following statements for participants to use, or read all three and allow them to choose one: "Abstain from sex because . . ." "I'm waiting until marriage because . . .," or "It Takes Courage! to . . ." You may also want to allow participants to make up their own slogans. Instruct participants to write down their creative responses to one of these statements.
4. Ask participants to choose their favorite response and show it to you. Be sure the responses are appropriate and acceptable.

Make a Statement T-Shirts

5. Distribute the T-shirt Design Handout to each participant and make the art supplies available.
6. Allow participants time to produce a creative T-shirt design of their response.
7. Invite volunteers to share their ideas with the rest of the group. Discuss the different responses written on the T-shirts.
8. Collect the T-shirt designs for judging.

Application and Insight

Good decision-makers can be role models for their peers.

There are a number of strong reasons for abstaining from sex until marriage.

Sharing one's beliefs with others builds character.

It Takes Courage!

Going Deeper

Explore options to print and sell the T-shirts as a fundraising activity.

In the other T-shirt designs, were there responses you had not thought of before?

What responses apply to your age group? To everyone?

The strongest oak tree of the forest is not the one that is protected from the storm and hidden from the sun. It's the one that stands in the open where it is compelled to struggle for its existence against the winds and rains and scorching sun. —Napoleon Hill, author

It Takes Courage!

to take a stand for what you believe

T-shirt Design

Front

T-shirt Design

Back

Safety First

30–45 Minutes

Character Connection
Humility & Responsibility

Purpose To practice making decisions about HIV/AIDS safety

Overview This easily adaptable activity is designed to help people interact with others in the group. By changing the questions, you can adapt the activity to explore different topics. In this situation, we are reviewing safety tips and precautions for living in a world with AIDS.

Life Skill Choosing to act in safe ways

Group Size Large (10 or more)

Cultural and Age Considerations For variety, one way to adapt the activity is to let each time represent a meeting place—such as the lake, the store, the church, etc. You can also use different times of the day such as breakfast, lunch, and dinner, or you could use different days of the week.

Materials Safety First Appointment Topics (Facilitator Notes), Appointment Schedule Handout, pens or pencils

Preparation Choose questions from the Safety First Appointment Topics (Facilitator Notes) to use during the activity. Make one copy of the Appointment Schedule Handout for each participant.

Instructions

1. Distribute the Appointment Schedule Handout to each participant.
2. Explain that each person will need to make "appointments" with several different group members. On the handout, ask each participant to write the name of the person next to the time of the appointment. Each name may be used only one time.
3. Allow five minutes for individuals to arrange all of their appointments. Ask them to return to their seats as soon as they have finished.

Safety First

4. Explain that you will call out an appointment time at random. Each person must stand up and go find the person with whom they made an appointment during that time.
5. When most people have found their partner for that appointment, read a topic from the Safety First Appointment Topics (Facilitator Notes) and explain that they will have two minutes to discuss the answer.
6. At the end of two minutes, call out the next appointment time (it is more fun if you do this at random instead of going down the sheet one by one) and then read the next topic on the list.
7. Follow the same procedure until all of the appointments have been completed.

Application and Insight

It is impossible to know who is infected with HIV.

Preventing accidents is not very difficult.

HIV is found in infected blood and sexual secretions.

Going Deeper

Should people who live with you tell you their HIV status?

Should children in school be required to reveal their HIV status?

When is it important for people to reveal their HIV status?

Good health and good sense are two great blessings. —Latin proverb

It Takes Courage!

to help others in an emergency

Safety First Appointment Topics

Choose any of the following topics for this activity.

1. Your friend severely cuts himself with a large knife while you are preparing dinner together. He asks for your help. How do you safely deal with the situation?

   Put on gloves immediately; apply pressure to the wound; seek help; wash hands as soon as possible.

2. While driving, you encounter a terrible car accident. A woman is unconscious and bleeding. What precautions should you take to help her and keep yourself out of danger?

   Put on gloves. If not available, protect hands with something like a plastic bag, shirt, etc.; wash hands as soon as possible.

3. You are caring for a sick AIDS patient who urinates on his bed linens. What is the proper method for cleaning the laundry?

   Put on gloves, then wash linens as usual.

4. A classmate sitting beside you suddenly vomits on you and your belongings. How do you react? (This is a hygienic issue, not an AIDS issue.)

   Seek the help of an adult, and keep others away. Someone should clean areas with rags and a mop using a solution of water and bleach. Wash any skin in contact with the vomit.

5. What should be included in a universal precautions kit?

   Assorted bandages, scissors, tape, latex gloves, alcohol wipes, towelettes, absorbent paper towels or rags, household gloves, anti-bacterial gel or lotion.

6. A bag of trash containing used needles, gloves, and syringes spills onto the floor. How do you clean the area?

   Seek help from an adult; put on thick gloves; use EXTREME caution when handling sharp objects; place in a container impervious to needles and sharp objects (i.e., thick cardboard or plastic) and seal tightly—being careful that a handler won't get stuck; wash area with bleach solution; clean hands with soap and water as soon as possible.

7. What everyday items should not be shared with other people?

   Toothbrush, razor, etc.

Safety First Appointment Topics *(continued)*

8. While playing on the playground, a friend falls. His knee is bleeding quite a bit. How do you help him without endangering yourself?

   If at all possible, let him cover his own wound with a clean cloth. If the wound is serious, take him to an adult. Do not let him resume playing until after his wound is covered and bandaged so blood cannot get onto others.

9. You are a preparing a large dinner for some friends. One person is sick with AIDS. What types of precautions do you take with foods?

   No precautions are necessary.

10. You were volunteering your time to help at a youth program for a week. At the end of the week, you discover that one of the children has acquired chicken pox. You have never had the chicken pox, but you feel fine. Should this affect your weekend visit with your cousin who has HIV?

    Stay home! People with chicken pox are contagious for at least one day before they have symptoms. Chicken pox is a very dangerous illness for people with HIV infection —their immune system is weak and they are likely to become infected and very ill as a result.

11. What are safe ways to show affection and love for person who is infected with HIV?

    Shaking hands, holding hands, hugging, a kiss on the cheek, sitting close to each other, etc. Any activity that does not exchange body fluids would be considered a safe activity.

Appointment Schedule

Make appointments with one person for each of the times listed below. Names should not be repeated.

Time	Name
9:00 a.m.	______________________
10:30 a.m.	______________________
11:00 a.m.	______________________
12:00 p.m.	______________________
1:30 p.m.	______________________
2:00 p.m.	______________________
4:30 p.m.	______________________
5:30 p.m.	______________________
6:00 p.m.	______________________

Notes

You give little when you give of your possessions. It is when you give of yourself that you truly give.

–Kahlil Gibran, Lebanese poet and philosopher

Activity #76 Where's the Risk?

30–45 Minutes

Character Connection
Responsibility & Self-control

Purpose To increase discernment about risky scenarios and risky people

Overview In this activity, participants evaluate all aspects of individuals' lives in various scenarios and identify the potential risks involved.

Life Skill Analyzing risk factors

Group Size Large (20 or more)

Cultural and Age Considerations Carefully choose the scenarios in this activity. Some scenarios may not be culturally relevant or appropriate for your group.

Materials Where's the Risk Scenarios? (Activity Materials), Risks and Issues (Facilitator Notes), paper, pens or pencils

Preparation Copy and cut out the Where's the Risk? Scenarios.

Instructions

1. Divide participants into six groups of three or four individuals.
2. Give each group a Where's the Risk? Scenario card, paper, and a pen or pencil.
3. Ask each group to identify all the risks in their scenario.
4. Reconvene as a large group and ask groups to share their thoughts.
5. Ask participants if they see any other risks.

Application and Insight

Even though a person may practice healthy sexual behavior, there are several other HIV/AIDS risk factors.

There is a certain amount of risk involved in any sexual encounter.

There is no stereotypical risky partner.

Where's the Risk?

Going Deeper

What risks are most often overlooked in relationships?

Have you ever noticed risk and chosen to ignore it? Why or why not?

Square your shoulders to the world,
be not the kind to quit,
it's not the load that weighs you down
but the way you carry it.

—Unknown

It Takes Courage!

to walk away from dangerous situations

Where's the Risk? Scenarios

Copy and cut out each card.

Rachel Scenario: Rachel is a teenager who works on the weekends at a department store. Her boss noticed injection marks on her arm, but she has never been a problem. She is always kind to customers and is trustworthy. Her parents like her boyfriend who is studying at the university. When she came in last Saturday, her parents suspected she had been drinking alcohol. She went straight to bed and her parents decided not to make it an issue.

Emanuel Scenario: Emanuel has been married for 15 years, and is not really in love with his wife. He works on a cruise ship, where he pursues other women when he is away. His wife has been so lonely. Last week a man's car was seen in their driveway. Emanuel suspects there is another man, but doesn't say anything. He knows his wife is probably using condoms and besides she knows he's been with other women too.

Dave Scenario: Dave is getting older, and people are wondering why he isn't married. Religion is very important to Dave; he believes people should be virgins when they marry. He has had girlfriends but recently became engaged. He decided not to tell his fiancée that one time he visited a prostitute. He didn't have intercourse, but he did engage in oral sex. He felt really bad about it and has never done it again.

Carla Scenario: Carla came from a very poor family. Her father died when she was a baby and her mother worked evenings to make money. An older businessman in the neighborhood used to buy her mother nice clothes and groceries if she would give him sexual favors. Carla is very active in school. She has a new boyfriend. She has explained to him that she intends to wait until she is married to get involved in sex.

Tom Scenario: Tom is a 40-year-old doctor. He is a homosexual, but no one knows. Tom used to date women and even now will occasionally do so, mostly to keep his homosexuality a secret. Tom loves having parties at his house and cooking for all of his friends. He is known as one of the nicest doctors in town, and he always gives his patients a hug when they leave his office.

Angela Scenario: Angela is in love with Frances, a university student. Frances told Angela that he loves her and wants to have sex together. He said he wanted to be honest about his sexual history. He told her he had sex only once when he was at a bar and ended up going home with someone he didn't know. Angela was embarrassed and didn't know what to say. She told Frances she was a virgin.

Risks and Issues

In addition to the items listed below, use this opportunity to create discussion and spotlight examples of good, questionable, and poor character.

Rachel Scenario

By using injection drugs, Rachel is at risk for HIV infection. Her older boyfriend is likely to have had additional sexual partners. Her alcohol use impairs her judgment.

Emanuel Scenario

Multiple sexual partners increase the risk for sexually transmitted infections, for the individual as well as for the spouse; unfaithfulness in marriage puts both partners at risk.

Dave Scenario

Oral sex is sex, and can transmit sexually transmitted infections. Even though Dave had only one sexual partner, his partner has had many partners, which increases the chances that he was exposed to a sexually transmitted infection.

Carla Scenario

Carla's mother's multiple sexual partners put her at high risk for sexually transmitted infections, but her mother's behavior poses no physical risk for Carla.

Tom Scenario

Given his age, a history of multiple partners is likely (but we can't tell for sure from this scenario). Unless Tom is honest about not being interested in the women he goes out with, he is using them for his advantage; he is a man with secrets. There is no risk to others with his cooking, working at the clinic, or hugging patients.

Angela Scenario

Knowing that Angela was a virgin, Frances may have lied about his past in order to convince her to have sex. He may have had other sexual encounters.

Activity #77 A Quick Check

15–30 Minutes

Character Connection
Honesty & Humility

Purpose To assess the thoughts and feelings of participants after a discussion about HIV/AIDS

Overview This written activity creates an opportunity for individuals to quickly reflect on a talk or series of talks about HIV/AIDS and give anonymous feedback. The participants will also have an opportunity to share their thoughts with others, if desired.

Life Skill Taking the time to assess personal thoughts and feelings

Group Size Individual activity with any size group

Cultural and Age Considerations This activity may be easily adapted by changing the phrases on the handout.

Materials Quick Check Handout

Preparation Make one copy of the Quick Check Handout for each participant.

Instructions

1. Begin by empathizing with the difficulty of discussing a difficult topic like HIV/AIDS.
2. Explain to the participants that writing down our thoughts help to clarify our thoughts and feelings.
3. Distribute the Quick Check Handout and tell the participants that this is an anonymous activity so they should not make any identifying marks on their paper.
4. Ask them to write down the first thoughts that come to mind, and point out that there are no right or wrong answers.
5. After 15 minutes, ask if any volunteers would like to share their thoughts and feelings with the class by reading their paper. After interested participants have shared, collect all the papers.

A Quick Check

Application and Insight

It is good to stop and reflect on our thoughts and feelings.

It is important to act on what we learn.

Going Deeper

Introduce the value of recording thoughts in a journal.

Identify and share counseling resources in the community.

No money can replace courageous leadership. —Dr. Peter Piot, UNAIDS executive director

It Takes Courage!

to be vulnerable with others

Quick Check

I learned ______________________________

I feel ______________________________

I was surprised by ______________________________

I'm wondering ______________________________

I wish ______________________________

I've decided to ______________________________

I appreciated ______________________________

I can't ______________________________

It hurts me ______________________________

I hope ______________________________

I need others to ______________________________

I want ______________________________

Teaching Through Storytelling

A Father's Love 437
A Glass of Milk 440
All God's Creatures Have Work to Do 441
Are You Going to Help Me? 444
Appointment with Love 446
Father Kolbe 449
Gather Your Gossip 451
Nails in a Tree 452
Mandela: The Long Walk to Forgiveness 455
One at a Time 458
Puppies for Sale 459
Racheltjie De Beer 461
Sacrifice of a Champion 463
S. T. 466
The Ambulance in the Valley 468
The Little Girl Who Waited 470
The Man, the Boy, and the Donkey 472
The Man Who Would Not Drink Alone 474
The Merchant and the Builder 475
The Oxpecker and the Giraffe 478
The Purse of Gold 480
The Two Gifts 481
Three Fish 483

Teaching Through Storytelling

Tell me a fact and I'll learn.
Tell me a truth and I'll believe.
But tell me a story and it will live in my heart forever.

—Indian proverb

Stories are everywhere—in books, movies, music, and in our conversations. Stories have been used down through the centuries and are one of the oldest forms of teaching. Even in our media-driven culture, stories are as useful today as they were thousands of years ago.

We see reflections of ourselves in a good story and can see the effects of positive and negative choices through story characters. We can actually feel the difference between right and wrong actions, the joy of a just reward, the sadness of betrayal. We experience the humor in our humanness, the pain of an insensitive remark, or the admiration of an act of extravagant love. Stories move life concepts from the head to the heart. A good storyteller can in one brief moment leave a lifelong reminder. Sermons and lectures are soon forgotten, but a story that touches our soul can be as strong as the waves of the ocean crashing on the shore, making a huge body of water come to life with sound, beauty, and force.

Many of the stories included in this section have been handed down from generation to generation. They have stood the test of time because they are both entertaining and effective in conveying valuable life lessons. As you use these stories to teach and reinforce good character qualities, it is our desire that young people will embrace character traits as essential to obtaining many of the things they wish for and are not just rules that take all the fun out of life. Stories can help them to see that being a person of character will bring freedom, contentment, self-esteem, and healthy relationships, and will empower them to make wise decisions that positively affect their future—and maybe even save their lives.

This section is full of powerful stories that friends from around the world have either submitted or written. We have also included many of our personal favorites. In addition to teaching character traits, these stories can be used to teach about other places in the world. We encourage you to pull out a map and show your youth the country represented in the story. Explore the actions of the characters and how they are similar or different from your cultural traditions. Add your favorite stories from your culture too!

We have organized this section into two parts to help you maximize the use of these stories in your teaching sessions: (1) generic activities you can use to process just about any story, and (2) a collection of 23 stories, each of which identifies two character traits that are either present or clearly lacking in the story characters. We have also suggested discussion questions to get your youth to think critically about the situations and to tie the story line to other concepts taught in this guidebook. A chart is provided so that you can easily select stories that illustrate specific character traits.

Life is a profound, inspiring, and passionate journey and our youth desperately need us to take a strong interest in them, care deeply about them, and help guide them on a positive path of life. We hope these stories inspire you and will be helpful tools as you do just that!

Story #1

Forgiveness & Humility

A Father's Love

By Philip Yancey

It takes courage and humility to admit our mistakes, and it takes a person of character with a loving heart to offer forgiveness when it is not deserved.

A young girl grows up on a cherry orchard just above Traverse City, Michigan. Her parents, a bit old-fashioned, tend to overreact to her nose ring, the music she listens to, and the length of her skirts. They ground her a few times, and she seethes inside. "I hate you!" she screams at her father when he knocks on the door of her room after an argument, and that night she acts on a plan she has mentally rehearsed scores of times. She runs away.

She has visited Detroit only once before, on a bus trip with her church youth group to watch the Tigers play. Because newspapers in Traverse City report in lurid detail the gangs, the drugs, and the violence in downtown Detroit, she concludes that is probably the last place her parents will look for her. California, maybe, or Florida, but not Detroit.

Her second day there she meets a man who drives the biggest car she's ever seen. He offers her a ride, buys her lunch, and arranges a place for her to stay. He gives her some pills that make her feel better than she's ever felt before. She was right all along, she decides: her parents were keeping her from all the fun.

The good life continues for a month, two months, a year. The man with the big car—she calls him "Boss"—teaches her a few things that men like. Since she's underage, men pay a premium for her. She lives in a penthouse, and orders room service whenever she wants. Occasionally she thinks about the folks back home, but their lives now seem so boring and provincial that she can hardly believe she grew up there.

She has a brief scare when she sees her picture printed on the back of a milk carton with the headline "Have you seen this child?" But by now she has blond hair, and with all the makeup and body-piercing jewelry she wears, nobody would mistake her for a child. Besides, most of her friends are runaways, and nobody squeals in Detroit.

After a year the first sallow signs of illness appear, and it amazes her how fast the boss turns mean. "These days, we can't mess around," he growls, and before she knows it she's out on the street without a penny to her name. She still turns a couple of tricks a night, but they don't pay much, and all the money goes to support her habit. When winter blows in she finds herself sleeping on metal grates outside the big department stores. "Sleeping" is the wrong word—a teenage girl at night in downtown Detroit can never relax her guard. Dark bands circle her eyes. Her cough worsens.

One night as she lies awake listening for footsteps, all of a sudden everything about her life looks different. She no longer feels like a woman of the world. She feels like a little girl, lost in a cold and frightening city. She begins to whimper. Her pockets are empty and she's hungry. She needs a fix. She pulls her legs tight underneath her and shivers under the newspapers she's piled atop her coat. Something jolts a synapse of memory and a single image fills her mind: of May in Traverse City, when a million cherry trees bloom at once, with her golden retriever dashing through the rows and rows of blossomy trees in chase of a tennis ball.

God, why did I leave? she says to herself, and pain stabs at her heart. *My dog back home eats better than I do now.* She's sobbing, and she knows in a flash that more than anything else in the world she wants to go home.

Three straight phone calls, three straight connections with the answering machine. She hangs up without leaving a message the first two times, but the third time she says, "Dad, Mom, it's me. I was wondering about maybe coming home. I'm catching a bus up your way, and it'll get there about midnight tomorrow. If you're not there, well, I guess I'll just stay on the bus until it hits Canada."

It takes about seven hours for a bus to make all the stops between Detroit and Traverse City, and during that time she realizes the flaws in her plan. What if her parents are out of town and miss the message? Shouldn't she have waited another day or so until she could talk to them? And even if they are home, they probably wrote her off as dead long ago. She should have given them some time to overcome the shock.

Her thoughts bounce back and forth between those worries and the speech she is preparing for her father. "Dad, I'm sorry. I know I was wrong. It's not your fault; it's mine. Dad, can you forgive me? She says the words over and over, her throat tightening even as she rehearses them. She hasn't apologized to anyone in years.

The bus has been driving with lights on since Bay City. Tiny snowflakes hit the pavement rubbed worn by thousands of tires, and the asphalt steams. She's forgotten how dark it gets at night out here. A deer darts across the road and the bus swerves. Every so often, a billboard. A sign posting the mileage to Traverse City. *Oh, God.*

When the bus finally rolls into the station, its air brakes hissing in protest, the driver announces in a crackly voice over the microphone, "Fifteen minutes, folks. That's all we have

here." Fifteen minutes to decide her life. She checks herself in a compact mirror, smooths her hair, and licks the lipstick off her teeth. She looks at the tobacco stains on her fingertips, and wonders if her parents will notice. If they're there.

She walks into the terminal not knowing what to expect. Not one of the thousand scenes that have played out in her mind prepare her for what she sees. There, in the concrete-walls-and-plastic-chairs bus terminal in Traverse City, Michigan, stands a group of forty brothers and sisters and great-aunts and uncles and cousins and a grandmother and great-grandmother to boot. They're all wearing goofy party hats and blowing noise-makers, and taped across the entire wall of the terminal is a computer-generated banner that reads "Welcome home!"

Out of the crowd of well-wishers breaks her dad. She stares out through the tears quivering in her eyes like hot mercury and begins the memorized speech, "Dad, I'm sorry, I know..."

He interrupts her. "Hush, child. We've got no time for that. No time for apologies. You'll be late for the party. A banquet's waiting for you at home."

Discussion Questions

1. Did the ending surprise you? If so, what would you have expected a typical father or family to do in this situation?
2. Did the daughter deserve to be forgiven? Why or why not?
3. What are your requirements for extending forgiveness to others?
4. Who do you think demonstrated the most courage in this story?
5. When someone loves you or forgives you, even though you don't deserve it, how does it make you feel?

Story #2

Gratitude & Kindness

A Glass of Milk

Retold by Deborah M. Garrick

True kindness seldom expects a reward. However, sometimes the recipient of the deed is given the opportunity to express gratitude in a significant way.

A young medical student was selling books to help pay his way through medical school. One hot, summer day, he stopped at a farmhouse and asked a bright young girl if she cared to buy a book. "No, thank you," she replied. "My mother is a widow, and we cannot afford to buy books." Then the student asked for a glass of water. The girl replied, "We have cold milk in the spring house. Would you care for a glass of milk?" The student thanked her, and gratefully drank his glass of refreshing cold milk. When he offered to pay for the milk, she refused, saying, "Mother has taught me to be kind to strangers."

A number of years passed. One day, a very ill woman was brought to a hospital. She was too sick to notice anyone, but the chief surgeon saw her and recognized her as the girl who had once given him a glass of milk. He took a special interest in her case. She was placed in a private room and special nurses were assigned to care for her during her lengthy hospital stay.

One morning a nurse informed her, "You are going home tomorrow!" "Oh," replied the woman, "I am so glad. But the hospital bill worries me. It must be very large." The nurse said, "I will bring it to you." As the woman looked over the bill and saw the large amount owed, she began to weep. Then, she looked at the bill again and, down at the bottom, she read these words: "PAID IN FULL BY A GLASS OF MILK!" Thus it was that Dr. Howard A. Kelley returned the kindness that a country girl showed to a stranger!

Discussion Questions

1. Why do you think kindness came naturally to the young girl?
2. Do you look for opportunities to show kindness? In what ways?
3. Name some easy ways to show kindness in daily contacts.
4. Can you think of someone who has extended kindness to you who you have not thanked?

Story #3

Excellence & Responsibility

All God's Creatures Have Work to Do

Retold by Deborah M. Garrick

In this Southeast Asia tale, we are reminded that being responsible and striving for excellence yield dividends.

There once were two cousins who lived in the same town. Being the same age, they became constant companions, growing up more as beloved brothers than cousins.

As time went on, however, their paths began to diverge—one finding his fulfillment in books, the other in play. The first cousin studied hard year after year, learning his lessons and passing his exams at the head of his class. The second cousin enjoyed his freedom too much to devote such time to his schoolwork, and more often chose swimming and games over attending class. Not surprisingly, he learned little and failed his exams.

The diligence of the first cousin did not go unnoticed, and he was eventually chosen by the king to be one of his advisors. The second cousin was chosen as well, and was assigned to be one of the oarsmen on the king's royal yacht.

One day, on a trip down the river, the king and his advisors sat up on the top deck, enjoying the cool air and discussing affairs of state. Far below, in the hold of the yacht, the oarsman toiled away, untouched by the breezes above. Aware that his cousin was seated by the king's side, he became jealous. "Why does he get to sit by the king while I must work so hard below? What makes him better than me? Are we not both God's creatures?"

His jealousy soon turned to anger, and he began to complain to his fellow oarsmen, "What's so special about those men? What good are they anyway? All they do is sit and talk while we do all the real work. Maybe they should come down here some time and try doing something useful for a change. It's just not fair! After all, aren't we all God's creatures?" As the oarsman bellowed, a shadowy form lurked just around the corner, listening to every word he said.

That night, after they had gone ashore and set up camp, the oarsman lay asleep in his tent. Suddenly he was shaken awake by an insistent hand. The king knelt over him, beckoning him to come outside. "I need your help, oarsman. There are strange noises coming from the woods over there, and I cannot sleep for worry of what it might be. It is not safe for me to enter the woods by myself. Our enemies are everywhere. Would you please investigate?"

Pleased that the king would choose him for such a task, the oarsman quickly ran into the woods, coming back in just a few moments. "A mother cat has just given birth to a litter of kittens, Your Majesty. They are hungry and cry for food."

"I see," said the king. "And what type of kittens are they?"

Not quite sure, the oarsman returned to the woods. "They are Siamese kittens, Your Majesty," he reported.

"And how many are in the litter?" the king inquired.

"I'm not sure. I'll check," said the oarsman, embarrassed that he must once again trek back into the woods. Upon his return he informed the king that there were six kittens.

"Male or female?" the king asked.

The oarsman turned and ran back to the litter of kittens. "Two males and four females, Your Majesty . . . and they are a beautiful gray with white on their paws," he reported, adding the last fact with pride that he had noticed something the king had not yet asked about.

"Thank you," the king said. "Now, come with me."

He led the oarsman to a small tent on the far side of the camp, where he shook the oarsman's cousin awake.

"I hear something in the trees just inside the forest," the king told him. "Go and find out what it is."

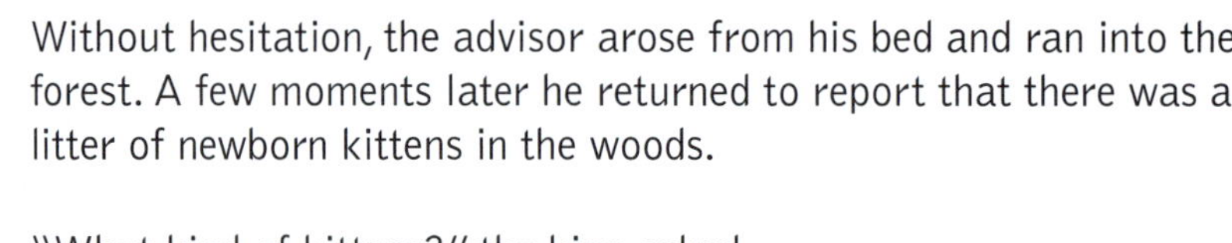

Without hesitation, the advisor arose from his bed and ran into the forest. A few moments later he returned to report that there was a litter of newborn kittens in the woods.

"What kind of kittens?" the king asked.

"They are gray Siamese, Your Majesty, with white on their paws."

"And how many are there?"

"There are six kittens—two males and four females. The mother cat belongs to the mayor of the small village just over the hill. She ran away last night to give birth to her kittens. The mayor is grieved that his cats have caused you to lose sleep and offers any of the newborns as a royal pet, if Your Majesty so desires."

Once the cousin had returned to his tent, the oarsman stood in silence, waiting for the king to speak.

"I heard you complaining today as you rowed," the king began. At this revelation, the oarsman cringed. "You are right. We are all God's creatures and are equal in value. However, we are not all equal in our abilities. Each of us is suited to a different task. Your cousin has devoted his life to developing his mind, and you have devoted yourself to building your physical strength. Today you helped me by rowing my boat down the river. Your cousin would have been hard-pressed to accomplish that task. For this reason, you are my oarsman. Tonight I asked for your help in solving a mystery. It took you four trips into the woods to find out what your cousin discovered in one trip. For this reason, he is my advisor. Tomorrow when you return to your duties, know that each of you is doing exactly what your choices have skilled you to do."

Discussion Questions

1. How does this illustrate that early habits set the stage for different destinies?
2. Was there an element of truth in the oarsman's complaints? Why or why not?
3. What other character traits, or lack thereof, do you see in this story?
4. The king said, "We are all God's creatures and are equal in value. However, we are not all equal in our abilities. Each of us is suited to a different task." Do you agree with his statement?

Story #4

Loyalty & Perseverance

Are You Going to Help Me?

By Jack Canfield and Mark Victor Hansen

In the midst of utter devastation and chaos, a father seeks to rescue his son. This is a true story of undaunted courage and perseverance born out of loyalty.

In 1989 an 8.2 earthquake almost flattened Armenia, killing over 30,000 people in less than four minutes.

In the midst of utter devastation and chaos, a father left his wife safely at home and rushed to the school where his son was supposed to be, only to discover that the building was as flat as a pancake.

After the traumatic initial shock, he remembered the promise he had made to his son: "No matter what, I'll always be there for you!" Tears began to fill his eyes. As he looked at the pile of debris that once was the school, it looked hopeless, but he kept remembering his commitment to his son.

He began to concentrate on where he walked his son to class each morning. Remembering his son's classroom would be in the back right corner of the building, he rushed there and started digging through the rubble.

As he was digging, other forlorn parents arrived, clutching their hearts, saying, "My son!" "My daughter!" Other well-meaning parents tried to pull him off of what was left of the school, saying:

"It's too late!"

"They're dead!"

"You can't help!"

"Go home!"

"Come on, face reality—there's nothing you can do!"

"You're just going to make things worse!"

To each parent he responded with one line: "Are you going to help me now?" And then he proceeded to dig for his son, stone by stone.

The fire chief showed up and tried to pull him off of the school's debris saying, "Fires are breaking out, explosions are happening everywhere. You're in danger. We'll take care of it. Go home." To which this loving, caring Armenian father asked, "Are you going to help me now?"

The police came and said, "You're angry, distraught, and it's over. You're endangering others. Go home. We'll handle it!" To which he replied, "Are you going to help me now?" No one helped.

Courageously he proceeded alone because he needed to know for himself, "Is my boy alive or is he dead?"

He dug for 8 hours . . . 12 hours . . . 24 hours . . . 36 hours . . . then, in the 38th hour, he pulled back a boulder and heard his son's voice. He screamed his son's name, "ARMAND!" He heard back, "Dad?"

"What's going on in there? How are you?" the father asked.

"There are 14 of us left out of 33, Dad. We're scared, hungry, thirsty, and thankful you're here. When the building collapsed it made a wedge, like a triangle, and it saved us."

"Come on out, boy!"

"No, Dad! Let the other kids out first, 'cause I know you'll get me! No matter what, I know you'll be there for me!"

Discussion Questions

1. What do you think gave the father the courage and perseverance to dig when all the other adults had lost hope?
2. Who demonstrated loyalty in this story?
3. Can you give an example of loyalty you have experienced?
4. Are acts of loyalty always rewarded?

Story #5

Loyalty & Respect

Appointment with Love

By Sulamith Ish-Kishor

This is an intriguing love story demonstrating one woman's determination to choose character over passion.

Six minutes to six, said the clock over the information booth in New York's Grand Central Station. The tall, young Army officer lifted his sunburned face and narrowed his eyes to note the exact time. His heart was pounding with a beat that shocked him. In six minutes he would see the woman who had filled such a special place in his life for the past 13 months—the woman he had never seen, yet whose written words had sustained him unfailingly.

Lt. Blandford remembered one day in particular, the worst in the fighting, when his plane had been caught in the midst of a pack of enemy planes.

In one of his letters, he had confessed to her that he often felt fear, and only a few days before this battle, he had received her answer: "Of course you feel fear... all brave men do. Next time you doubt yourself, I want you to hear my voice reciting to you: 'Yea, though I walk through the valley of death, I shall fear no evil, for Thou art with me.'" He had remembered, and it had renewed his strength.

Now he was going to hear her real voice. Four minutes to six.

A girl passed close to him, and Lt. Blandford started. She was wearing a flower, but it was not the little red rose they had agreed upon. Besides, this girl was only about 18, and Hollis had told him she was 30. "What of it?" he had answered. "I'm 32." He was 29.

His mind went back to the book he had read in the training camp. *Of Human Bondage*, it was; and throughout the book were notes in a woman's writing. He had never believed that a woman could see into a man's heart so tenderly, so understandingly. Her name was on the bookplate: Hollis Maynell. He got hold of a New York City telephone book and found her address. He had written; she had answered. Next day he had been shipped out, but they had gone on writing. For 13 months she had faithfully replied. When his letter did not arrive, she wrote anyway, and now he believed he loved her, and she loved him.

But she had refused all his pleas to send him her photograph. She had explained: "If your feeling for me has any reality, what I look like won't matter. Suppose I'm beautiful. I'd always fear that you were taking a chance on just that, and that kind of love would disgust

me. Suppose I'm plain (and you must admit that this is more likely), then I'd always be haunted that you were going on writing because you were lonely and had no one else. No, don't ask for my picture. When you come to New York, you shall see me and then you shall make your own decision."

One minute to six. He flipped the pages of the book he held. Then Lt. Blandford's heart leaped.

A young woman was coming toward him. Her figure was long and slim; her blonde hair lay back in curls from her delicate ears. Her eyes were blue as flowers, her lips and chin had a gentle firmness. In her pale green suit, she was like springtime come alive.

He started toward her, forgetting to notice that she was wearing no rose, and as he moved, a small, provocative smile curved her lips.

"Going my way, soldier?" she murmured.

He made one step closer to her. Then he saw Hollis Maynell.

She was standing almost directly behind the girl, a woman well past 40, her graying hair tucked under a work hat. She was more than plump; her thick-ankled feet were thrust into low-heeled shoes. But she wore a red rose on her rumpled coat. The girl in the green suit was walking quickly away.

Blandford felt as though he were being split in two, so keen was his desire to follow the girl, yet so deep was his longing for the woman whose spirit had truly companioned and upheld his own; and there she stood. He could see that her pale, plump face was gentle and sensible; her gray eyes had a warm twinkle.

Lt. Blandford did not hesitate. His fingers gripped the worn copy of *Of Human Bondage*, which was to identify him to her. This would not be love, but it would be something precious, a friendship for which he had been and must ever be grateful . . .

He squared his shoulders, saluted, and held the book out toward the woman, although even while he spoke he felt the bitterness of his disappointment.

"I'm Lt. Blandford, and you—Miss Maynell. I'm so glad you could meet me. May... may I take you to dinner?"

The woman's face broadened in a tolerant smile. "I don't know what this is all about, son," she answered. "That lady in the green suit begged me to wear this rose on my coat. And she said that if you asked me to go out with you, I should tell you she's waiting for you in that restaurant across the street. She said it was some kind of test."

Discussion Questions

1. Is lifelong happiness based on passionate love or on other qualities?
2. Were Miss Maynell's actions fair or were they dishonest and manipulative? What was she trying to find out?
3. What would your prediction be for this couple's future?
4. Would you be interested in either character in this story as a marriage partner? Why or why not?

Story #6

Empathy & Humility

Father Kolbe

By Steven V. Cannizzaro

This is a compelling true account of a courageous Polish man who during the Second World War chose a painful death to spare the life of another.

The trembling prisoners stood fearfully beneath the summer sun in 1941 as their cruel captors randomly selected ten of them to die by starvation. As the Nazi guards walked down the line of prisoners, selecting the weakest for a slow and painful death, one of the men chosen, a Polish farmer, fell to his knees weeping in despair, "Oh! My poor wife! My poor children! I shall never see them again. What will they do?"

In the midst of this horrific scene, prisoner Number 16670—Father Kolbe, clad in his soiled striped uniform—humbly stepped forward. All eyes turned to him in stunned silence as the commandant screamed, "Halt! What does this Polish pig want of me?"

* * * * *

When Nazi Germany invaded Poland on September 1, 1939, Father Kolbe, a 45-year-old Catholic priest, was presiding over the monastery at Niepokolanow, a village near Warsaw. Though he was a journalist, publisher, and an intellectual, he was known for his joy, compassion, and humor and loved by his plainspoken brethren. During the next two years, the monastery at Niepokolanow became a shelter for Jews and members of the Polish resistance seeking refuge from the German persecution.

On February 17, 1941, the Nazis arrested Father Kolbe for aiding the Jews and Polish resistance. On May 28, 1941, he was sent to Auschwitz, a German labor and death camp run by Commandant Karl "Butcher" Fritsch. Father Kolbe was tattooed with the number 16670, made to wear a uniform, and put to work carrying heavy stones to build a crematorium—a place for the Nazis to burn the bodies of those they executed.

During his imprisonment, Father Kolbe cared for the needs of his fellow prisoners. He shared his meager rations of food with those who were hungry. He secretly heard their confessions, prayed for them, and held Mass for them. He encouraged them and urged them to forgive their persecutors and to overcome evil with good.

On August 3, 1941, three prisoners escaped from Auschwitz. One of them was from Barracks #18 where Father Kolbe was imprisoned. To penalize and warn the prisoners not to escape, the Nazis chose to execute ten prisoners by starvation.

* * * * *

"I would like to go in place of one of the men you have condemned," Father Kolbe said, softly and calmly to the Nazi commandant staring at him in anger and disbelief.

"In whose place do you want to die?" asked the commandant.

"For that one," Father Kolbe responded, pointing to Franciszek Gajowniczek, the prisoner who had fallen to his knees and cried out in despair.

The commandant agreed, and Father Kolbe was thrown into an airless, underground cell with the other nine victims, where one by one they died of hunger and thirst. After two weeks, the cell was needed for more prisoners. The Nazis opened the cell to find Father Kolbe still alive—merely a skeleton propped up against a wall, his eyes fixed on some faraway vision, and smiling faintly. He was dragged out and executed by lethal injection.

Father Kolbe had told his fellow prisoners, "Hate is not creative. Our sorrow is necessary that those who live after us may be happy." Franciszek Gajowniczek never forgot Father Kolbe—his words, his deeds, and his sacrifice. After his release from Auschwitz, he considered it his duty to tell people about Father Kolbe's heroic act of love. For the rest of his life, nearly 53 years, Gajowniczek told the world of this simple yet profound story of forgiveness, of good overcoming evil, of the greatest demonstration of love—one who lays down his life for others.

Discussion Questions

1. How did Father Kolbe expect his fellow prisoners to overcome evil with good?
2. How did Father Kolbe demonstrate sacrifice early in the story?
3. What do you believe was the source of Father Kolbe's courage?

Story #7

Humility & Self-control

Gather Your Gossip

Retold by Deborah M. Garrick

A gossip learns to think before he speaks as a wise teacher shows him that words, once spoken, can never be recovered.

A peasant with a troubled conscience went to a wise teacher for advice. He said he had circulated a vile story about a friend, only to find out that the story was not true. The wise man said, "If you want to make peace with your conscience, fill a bag with goose down. Go to every door in the village, and drop one fluffy feather!" The peasant did as he was told. Finally, he came back to the teacher and announced that he had finished.

The teacher said, "You have not finished yet. You must now take your bag and make the rounds again. Gather up every feather you have dropped." Greatly dismayed, the peasant said, "But I cannot gather up the feathers. The wind must have blown them all away!" "My son," said the wise teacher, "so it is with gossip!"

Words, good and evil, are easily dropped. But no matter how hard you try, you can never get them back again!

Discussion Questions

1. Have you ever made a comment, perhaps without thinking, that you later regretted? What were the consequences?
2. How did the monk demonstrate his wisdom in allowing the peasant to discover for himself the effects of his folly?
3. How do you think the gossiping peasant felt after his encounter with the monk?
4. What do you think the peasant should have done after he left the monk's presence?

Story #8

Forgiveness & Patience

Nails in a Tree

Retold by Deborah M. Garrick

The story of a loving father's patience and forgiveness has a surprising happy ending.

There once was a farmer who had a son named John, a boy who desired nothing more than his own happiness. He filled his days with boyish pursuits—climbing the neighbor's fence to steal fruit from his trees, hiding in the bushes to throw stones at passersby, and taunting the elderly people in the village. His duties on the farm, though minimal, were attended to only when he was forced to do so, and the lies to cover his indiscretions mounted to the point where no one believed his words—least of all his father, who was dismayed at his son's carelessness with life.

John's favorite place was a beautiful tree that grew in the meadow behind his house. He called it his dreaming tree. He would climb its majestic trunk and perch in its flowing branches and think. Mostly his thoughts were of his future. He thought about the marvelous things he would do when he grew up, imagining wild adventures and heroic feats that would take him far away from the confines of their small farm. Instead of stealing fruit, he would imagine himself a wealthy landowner who would benevolently provide fruit for the entire land. Instead of throwing rocks at riders, he saw visions of himself astride a magnificent steed with a flowing mane, named Thunder, galloping down the road to rescue a village in distress. Every day John would climb up in the tree and dream of being someone different, and every day he would climb back down to the boy he was. Occasionally he would think about this and wish that he were more like the boy in the tree.

One day his exasperated father sat beside him and said, "John, I am concerned about who you are becoming. I know that in your heart, you are a good boy and that you have many dreams. But I am afraid that the decisions you are making now will keep you from your dreams, and your dreams are important to me. What can I do to help you?" Although he did not fully understand his father's words, he knew he needed to change, and somewhat hesitantly accepted his father's help. Together they devised a plan. It was important that John have a visual reminder of his actions and so it was decided that every time John made a selfish or hurtful decision, he and his father would drive a nail into the trunk of his beloved tree. And every time he chose wisely, a nail would be removed from the tree.

In the coming days, they worked together to carry out their plan. Before dinner each night, they would meet at the tree and review the day. Each day they had at least one nail and sometimes a great many to drive in, but very seldom one to draw out.

After a long time, John noticed that a large section of the trunk was now quite covered with nails. His spirit sank as he saw the trunk of his beloved tree disappearing beneath a blanket of nail heads, and he resolved to do better. The next day he was so good and industrious that several nails came out. The day after, it was the same thing and so on for a long time, till at last only one nail remained. That night, as they met at the tree, John's father, with a look of pride on his face, said to him, "Look, son, here is the very last nail, and now we're going to draw it out. This is a day we have looked forward to for many months. Are you not glad?"

John looked at the proud tree trunk, now riddled with nail holes, and instead of expressing joy, as his father expected, his eyes welled with tears. "Why," asked his father, "what's the matter? I should think you would be delighted. You've worked hard to change your ways, and you've done so. The nails are all gone."

"Yes," cried John, choking back the tears, "the nails are gone, but the holes are there yet. I have marred my beautiful tree by my own selfish choices."

Wishing to ease his son's grief, the concerned father put his arm on John's shoulder and assured him that the tree would heal itself and that in time the holes would mend. Little comforted by his father's words, John said, "But I will always know what I have done to my tree. I will always know it could have been better." And with that, John walked away for the last time from his dreaming tree.

Time went by, and John proved that he had indeed become a different man. He grew up, left home and, in time, became a doctor. As he rode from village to village, attending to the sick and aged, he often reflected on his boyhood dream. His horse, a beautiful charcoal gray stallion, he had named Thunder, and he did indeed find himself, at times, riding like the wind down the dusty road to rescue some poor soul in need. At these moments, he would think of his tree and wonder what had become of it.

John's duties kept him from the farm for many years, but finally one day he received word that his father was ill and dying. He immediately saddled his horse and began the long journey home. As he rounded the last bend and the farm came into view, he was astounded at how beautiful it had become. The small house was beautifully painted and awash in a sea of lush flower bushes and colorful gardens. The little barn, barely big enough for the few cows his father kept, had been replaced by a spacious, lofty structure that could easily house the stock of the entire village. He stopped and stared, unable to take it all in.

After dinner that night, he inquired as to the incredible changes that had taken place. With a look of mysterious delight on his face, John's father said, "Come with me, son. I want you to see something."

Slowly and haltingly, John's father led him out the back door and into the meadow. John could see his dreaming tree towering over the landscape at the end of the meadow. Although his father said nothing, it soon became apparent that the tree was their destination. Coming around to the flawed side of the tree, John prepared himself for the pain of seeing the visual reminder of his past mistakes. But what he saw, instead of an ugly backdrop of nail scars, was the most intricate design of curls and curves he had every seen, as if a master weaver had chosen the tree bark itself for his loom. So unusual was the pattern, his father told him, that the tree had become a favorite visiting site for people throughout the entire region. Every day, a stream of curious visitors would come to the farm, asking to see the tree's unique design—and willing to pay for the privilege.

Thus it was that John understood that the scars, far from destroying his dreams, had become a part of what made them come true. The struggles of his past had become a source of beauty and prosperity, not only for him, but for his family as well. As John and his father turned and walked away from the tree, a sense of gratefulness flooded his heart, and he found himself truly thankful for the nails . . . and for the holes that they had left.

Discussion Questions

1. In helping his son devise a plan for discipline, how was the exasperated father demonstrating forgiveness and patience?
2. John found himself "truly grateful for the nails . . . and for the holes," but in reality, who deserved the gratitude? Explain your answer.
3. How is this story an example of building character?

Story #9

Forgiveness & Self-control

Mandela: The Long Walk to Forgiveness

By Johan Mostert (Johannesburg, South Africa)

Rising from prison to the presidency is a remarkable feat indeed. Choosing forgiveness over revenge, Nelson Mandela modeled the way toward reconciliation and unity in South Africa.

On Sunday afternoon, February 11, 1990, the most famous political prisoner in the world walked out of a prison close to Cape Town, a free man for the first time in 27 years. No one would have blamed him if he had become a bitter old man. He had sacrificed his entire adult life because he believed in a system of democratic equality for all races. He was imprisoned by a government whose policies were rejected by the entire world. Millions of people waited with baited breath to hear what he was going to say.

At the age of 21, Nelson Mandela was already an advocate for the rights of his people. His activities on campus got him kicked out of college and he had to finish his law degree through correspondence. He became even more involved in non-violent resistance and defiance campaigns against the brutal laws of the South African apartheid government as he grew older. In 1952 he and his friend Oliver Tambo opened the first black law practice in Johannesburg. But it wasn't long before they were branded as Communists by the government and were banned from attending any public gatherings.

During those days, South African society was being restructured according to a philosophy designed by a white politician named Hendrik Verwoerd. This social restructuring was called "apartheid" and was a race-based classification system that dictated where people could work, how much they could earn, where they were allowed to live, and in which line they were to stand when they wanted to mail a letter.

As the South African government began to enforce this classification system, thousands of black people were forcibly removed from the homes they had occupied for decades, simply because they were living in areas designated for "white" housing. Everything in society became segregated according to race: buses, schools, hospitals, restaurants, and government offices. Resistance to this inhumane social system started to become violent and culminated in the 1960 Sharpeville massacre where well-armed security forces killed 67 black protesters. In the bloody build-up after Sharpeville, Nelson Mandela and many of his friends were arrested and charged with sabotage and treason, and in June 1964 he was sentenced to life imprisonment with hard labor on Robben Island.

In the almost three decades that followed, South African society became increasingly violent and approached a state of civil war. Thousands of lives were lost as bombs exploded in towns, and police invaded the townships in attempts to restore order. In the 27 years that he was in prison, Nelson Mandela became a symbol for oppressed people all over the world.

The government and Mandela's African National Congress Party negotiated his release to begin a process of putting South Africa on the road to democracy. By the time he was released, no one knew what he would say. He was 72 years old. He had spent almost half of his life imprisoned by a system that was universally condemned as being inhumane. The civil rights that he had fought for were being trampled under foot, and his nation was torn apart in bloody racial confrontations. He was an icon, and the undisputed leader of the new South Africa. In the eyes of the world, and of his millions of followers, he had earned the right to be angry and bitter for the hardship and persecution he had suffered.

But from the day of his release from prison when he addressed the world from the steps of the Cape Town City Hall, through his term as the first President of a united, democratic South Africa, to this very day, Nelson Mandela has been a symbol of racial reconciliation. He refused to entertain the thought of a "Nuremburg" style inquisition of apartheid-era criminals. He established a government of national unity with his former captors, and at every opportunity he proclaimed a message of forgiveness. He charmed his enemies into submission. In his first speech to the new Parliament he quoted a poem in Afrikaans, the language of his political foes. He dined with his jailers. He flattered his adversaries and gave a job to his former torturer on Robben Island.

In 1995, a year after achieving democracy, South Africa was the host nation for the Rugby World Cup. Rugby was generally associated with whites and Afrikaners, and previously had elicited boos from black South Africans. Against great odds, the South African team beat all the teams and won the Cup. In the electric atmosphere of that final win, Mandela walked onto the field wearing the Springbok rugby uniform. In front of a virtually all-white capacity crowd, he stood next to the Springbok captain, and with a proud, exultant smile, raised the winner's trophy into the air. The ecstatic crowd went into a thunderous rapture and began to chant, "Nelson! Nelson!"

In that same year, he made what could be considered one of his most dramatic symbolic statements on forgiveness. He learned that Betsy Verwoerd was celebrating her 94th birthday. She was the widow of Hendrik Verwoerd, the architect of apartheid and his greatest political foe. She had moved to Orania, a small rural town in the northwest of the country, far removed from airports and major highways. The town had been established by a group of Afrikaners who still felt that they wanted to separate themselves to maintain their culture, language, and

traditions. On the Sunday afternoon, he arranged for the presidential jet to fly him to the nearest airport and for a car to transport him and his entourage to this small, dusty town, so that he could have tea with Betsy Verwoerd and pay his respects to the widow of the former South African leader.

Nelson Rolihlahla Mandela, once the symbol of the oppressed masses, has become the undisputed, international symbol of reconciliation and forgiveness. While it was in his power, and moral right, to retaliate and punish his enemies, he has consistently decided to forgive. In his actions he has consistently displayed the qualities of what we consider to be "good character."

Discussion Questions

1. What specific actions of Nelson Mandela demonstrated self-control?
2. Why do you think Nelson Mandela chose forgiveness instead of hate and revenge?
3. How does this story apply to you and the conflicts or challenges you face with others?
4. If you applied the lessons of this story in your personal life, would your friends perceive you as weak or strong? Would you be praised or ridiculed? Why?

Story #10

One at a Time

Empathy & Perseverance

Author unknown

This brief tale illustrates the difference one person can make.

An old man was strolling along the ocean shoreline one morning after a very high tide. As he walked along, he saw hundreds of starfish that had been washed ashore and he realized that they would die if they were not returned to the sea. But because there were so many, there was no way he could save them.

In the distance, he saw a young boy who was bending over, picking something up, and throwing it into the water. As he drew nearer, he realized that the boy was methodically bending down, picking up a starfish, throwing it into the ocean, and then repeating the process again and again.

The old man stopped the boy and asked him why he was bothering. What difference would it make? There were simply too many starfish. The boy looked up at the old man, bent down and picked up another starfish and threw it into the ocean. As he did so, he answered, "It makes a difference to that one."

Discussion Questions

1. What character traits are represented in this story?
2. Is there someone who has personally touched your life by reaching out and helping you?
3. How does this story apply to attitudes about HIV/AIDS?

Story #11

Empathy & Kindness

Puppies for Sale

By Dan Clark

This little incident goes beyond a small boy's desire for a dog. It will touch your heart.

As a storeowner was tacking a sign in his store window which read PUPPIES FOR SALE, a little boy appeared. "How much are you selling the puppies for?" he asked.

The man told the lad he didn't expect to let any of them go for less than $50.

The boy reached in his pocket, pulled out some change, looked up at the storeowner and said, "I have two dollars and thirty-seven cents. Can I look at them?"

The storeowner smiled and whistled. From the kennel, a dog named Lady came running down the aisle, followed by five tiny balls of fur. One puppy lagged behind. Immediately, the little boy asked about the limping puppy.

"What's wrong with that doggie?"

"The veterinarian told us the dog is missing a hip socket," said the storeowner. "He'll always limp like that."

"That's the one I want to buy," the lad said quickly.

The storeowner replied, "No, you don't want to buy that dog. If you really want him, I'll just give him to you."

The boy came close to the storeowner's face and said angrily, "I don't want you to just give him to me. That doggie is worth just as much as all the other puppies and I'll pay the full price. I'll give you $2.37 now and 50 cents a month until I have him paid for!"

The storeowner replied, "No, no, no. You don't want that dog. He's never going to be able to run and jump and play like the other dogs."

In response, the little boy pulled up his pant leg to reveal a badly twisted left leg, supported by two steel braces.

"Well, sir," he said, "I don't run so well myself, and the puppy will need someone who understands."

Discussion Questions

1. Can you blame the storeowner for his lack of empathy? Why or why not?
2. What do you think the storeowner will learn from this encounter?
3. Why was the little boy so adamant about paying full price for the puppy?

Story #12

Loyalty & Responsibility

Racheltjie De Beer

Retold by Marthie Erasmus (Durban, South Africa)

This true story from South Africa tells of a young girl's love and self-sacrifice in order to save her brother's life.

This story took place in the 1840s on a farm in South Africa, on the Transvaal's side of the Drakensberg mountains. A friendly farmer allowed the De Beer family to stay over on his farm while Mr. De Beer was looking for land to build their own home.

It was a very cold winter's night with bone-chilling winds and rain. Snow began to fall. No human or animal could survive in the open, so all the creatures hid as best they could against the elements.

But by the river, a lonely girl of 12 named Rachel was wandering around with her little brother. They were lost and walking in circles. The little brother could not stop crying. She kept trying to comfort him, promising him that she would keep him warm. They were out looking for a little calf that was left behind when the cattle were brought to safety. Her father had told Rachel to look near the river while he looked elsewhere. The little brother insisted on going with her.

Although they did not find anything, they were fine until night fell and the snowstorm overwhelmed them. The little boy could not walk any further, so Rachel picked him up. She was hoping for some sign of hope, a fire or a gunshot, that could point her toward home. After walking awhile and feeling completely exhausted, she stumbled over an anthill. By then she realized that she could not save herself out in the open in that weather, but she could help her brother. He was as cold as ice and was still crying, so she again assured him that she would keep him warm.

With stiff, icy fingers, she took a sharp rock and scooped out the anthill, like her mother taught her when they made bread ovens in the field. She then took off her clothes and put them on her brother. Carefully she placed him in the scooped out anthill with her clothes on over his own. She then did the last thing she could do before she could rest herself. She laid her naked body down to cover the opening. By then, the wind had stopped and there was less snow. She did not feel anything, though.

By dawn they found Rachel's body. Her brother was alive and warm . . . she had kept her promise.

Discussion Questions

1. How can you explain the sense of responsibility shown by this young girl?
2. Can you think of another example where someone showed loyalty to this extent?
3. How do we respond to challenges in our daily lives?
4. Do you think Rachel's brother knew what she was doing? How do you think he felt when he realized his sister had saved his life at the expense of her own?

Story #13

Excellence & Perseverance

Sacrifice of a Champion

Retold by Jessie Hannebury

Submitted by Tatiana Korolkova, Elena Khomchenko, and Marina Semenova (Samara, Russia)

This much-loved true story of heroism in Russia is an example of lifelong excellence and the sacrifice of a champion swimmer.

It happened several years ago, but Sharvarsh Karapetjan still remembers even the smallest details of that September evening.

Sharvarsh, a dedicated and competitive swimmer, was finishing his daily exercise. He had run twenty kilometers along the bank of Erevan Lake. As usual, Sharvarsh completed his run using all his energy, not holding anything back. He believed that laziness is a quality not possessed by a true sportsman.

Suddenly, he noticed an overcrowded trolley bus lose control and, in just a few seconds, hit the barrier of the dam and fall into the water. Because it happened so quickly, only a few people had time to get off the trolley. Sharvarsh immediately threw off his loose clothing and jumped into the water.

They say fate is blind, but it seems no accident that Sharvarsh Karapetjan, part of an entire family of highly competitive swimmers, was the very person on the scene when the trolley fell. Even Sharvarsh, the most experienced swimmer, had hardly enough air to dive the ten-meter depth to the trolley, break the window with his feet, and drag a breathless person to the surface.

Sharvarsh acted quickly. In the dark depths of the water, he had to rely on touch to find the submerged victims. On one of his dives, he returned to the surface with an empty trolley seat—a mistake that cost someone's life.

Without an oxygen tank, flippers, or any other kind of diving equipment, Sharvarsh submerged himself into the water again and again. Even though he began to feel sharp pains in his stomach, Sharvarsh disappeared once more into the water and this time he returned with two passengers! When he re-entered the water this time, drops of blood were left on the surface. Sharvarsh had cut himself on the trolley's shattered windows.

At long last, help arrived. A lifting crane was set up to retrieve the trolley. However, Sharvarsh would have to return to the trolley one more time to secure the crane's steel rope to the vehicle. The athlete was faint and had lost a great deal of blood, but no one else could make that necessary trip to save the remaining passengers. Sharvarsh was so weak that he could not swim to the bottom of the lake without the assistance of a heavy rock to carry him down. He managed to reach the bottom and secured the crane's rope around the trolley.

When Sharvarsh finally collapsed with exhaustion on the shore, he was shivering all over. Because the lake was so polluted with sewage, Sharvarsh later suffered from blood poisoning. He also developed pneumonia.

Those who knew Sharvarsh were not surprised to hear about his heroic deed and the sacrifices he had made to save those people. Sharvarsh and his brothers had on many occasions volunteered their assistance to help anyone they could. When Sharvarsh was 15, he and his brother Kamo went to their grandfather's village for a summer holiday. They noticed that their grandfather's house was old and dilapidated and decided to build a new one. The brothers managed to finish the work in just two summers, never complaining that their peers were enjoying their school holidays by resting, swimming, and playing.

Sharvarsh's father always proudly displays the various athletic medals won by Sharvarsh and his two brothers. He presents them excitedly to all who will listen. "This one is Sharvarsh's. This medal is Anatoli's. This one is Kamo's . . ." and then the guest is shown the only medal that isn't for swimming. It is Sharvarsh's medal for rescuing the people in Erevan Lake. This is the last medal he ever received.

Sharvarsh returned to athletics after he recovered from the illness caused by the dramatic rescue. The intensity of his training was greater than ever before, and he won a place on the national team. At the European championship in Hungary, he was far in the lead in the 400-meter event where for many years he had no equal. However, 50 meters away from the finish line, a sudden, sharp pain in his side paralyzed his movements. Although he was able to overcome the pain as he had done on the bottom of Erevan Lake, he lost the race. The new champion helped him to get out of the pool.

Can the medal that Sharvarsh received for heroism be a substitute for championship titles that he didn't win and records he didn't break? He has never asked himself that question. It is true that his passion for swimming had consumed his life. He once raved about records and dreamed of victories, but he never considered that competition was his only purpose in life or that records were a way to satisfy his own pride. He firmly believed that all his training was preparation for

a trial and, when he faced that trial, he didn't falter. Sharvarsh was able to use his swimming excellence to perform a selfless deed exactly when it was needed the most.

Discussion Questions

1. How did Sharvarsh prepare for excellence as he grew up?
2. Can his medal for the rescue substitute for the championship title he didn't win and the records he did not break? Why or why not?
3. Perseverance is needed for excellence. Give examples of this from the story or from your own experience.

Story #14

Humility & Responsibility

S. T.

By Charlie W. Shedd and Martha Shedd

Accepting responsibility for our actions is the theme of this story. Two brothers choose different paths in meeting the challenge.

Once upon a time two brothers were convicted of stealing sheep. By the strange custom of that faraway land, they were branded on their foreheads with the two letters "S" and "T," meaning "Sheep Thief."

Reuben, unable to bear the shame of his crime, ran away. But wherever he fled, men asked about the two strange letters on his forehead, so he kept wandering. Restless, hopelessly miserable, and full of bitterness, he eventually took his own life.

Thomas, on the other hand, said to himself, "I can't run away from the fact that I stole sheep, so I'll face it. I will stay here and earn back my self-respect and hopefully the respect of others around me."

Years passed and, by his good deeds, Thomas built for himself a great reputation.

"Here," the people said, "is a man of integrity. He is a man to be honored. In fact, he is the finest man in many valleys."

Thomas lived to a ripe old age and the longer he lived, the more he dedicated his life to doing good deeds and blessing others. At last Thomas died and, so loved was he, that people came from miles around to the little church to pay their respects at his funeral.

If you had been there, people say you would have heard a strange exchange of words at his coffin. A newcomer to the village said to one of the men, "I haven't known Thomas long, but I have often wondered what those letters 'S. T.' mean on his forehead?"

"Aye," replied the man. "I have forgotten the particulars, but I believe they mean 'Saint Thomas.'"

Discussion Questions

1. Do you think most people are like Reuben or like Thomas?
2. How long do you think it took for people to trust Thomas again?
3. Why do you think it was impossible for Reuben to face his wrongdoing?
4. What does it mean, and what does it take, to accept responsibility for our mistakes? Give examples.

Story #15

Perseverance & Service

The Ambulance in the Valley

By Joseph Malins

Many people are willing to offer their services to help solve a problem, but this story illustrates the need to persevere and think through all possibilities before taking action.

'Twas a dangerous cliff, as they freely confessed,
Though to walk near its crest was so pleasant;
But over its terrible edge there had slipped
A duke, and full many a peasant.
The people said something would have to be done,
But their projects did not at all tally.
Some said, "Put a fence 'round the edge of the cliff,"
Some, "An ambulance down in the valley."

The lament of the crowd was profound and was loud,
As their tears overflowed with their pity;
But the cry for the ambulance carried the day
As it spread through the neighboring city.
A collection was made, to accumulate aid
And the dwellers in highway and alley
Gave dollars or cents—not to furnish a fence—
But an ambulance down in the valley.

"For the cliff is all right if you're careful," they said;
"And if folks ever slip and are dropping,
It isn't the slipping that hurts them so much
As the shock down below—when they're stopping."
So for years (we have heard), as these mishaps occurred
Quick forth would the rescuers sally,
To pick up the victims who fell from the cliff,
With the ambulance down in the valley.

Said one, to his pleas, "It's marvel to me
That you'd give so much greater attention
To repairing results than to curing the cause;
You had much better aim at prevention.

For the mischief, of course, should be stopped at its source;
Come, neighbors and friends, let us rally.
It is far better sense to rely on a fence
Than an ambulance down in the valley."

"He is wrong in his head," the majority said;
"He would end all our earnest endeavor.
He's a man who would shirk this responsible work,
But we will support it forever.
Aren't we picking up all, just as fast as they fall,
And giving them care liberally?
A superfluous fence is of no consequence,
If the ambulance works in the valley."

The story looks queer as we've written it here,
But things oft occur that are stranger
More humane, we assert, than to succour the hurt
Is the plan of removing the danger.
The best possible course is to safeguard the source
By attending to things rationally.
Yes, build up the fence and let us dispense
With the ambulance down in the valley.

Discussion Questions

1. Can you think of any modern-day examples of this story?
2. What does this story teach us about perseverance and peer pressure?
3. What was the attitude of those who were serving? Do you think they were more concerned about serving or about being right?

Story #16

Honesty & Patience

The Little Girl Who Waited

Retold by Deborah M. Garrick

A little girl is rewarded for her patience and reminded that good character traits don't go unnoticed.

A long time ago, a great famine overtook the land. For months, the fields yielded no crops. Food became scarce, and as the money ran out, the poor began to feel the pangs of starvation. Concerned for his village, one rich man invited the children of the town to his home. When they arrived, he pulled out a large basket full of bread and placed it before them.

"I know you and your families are hungry," he said. "In this basket I have a loaf of bread for each of you. Every day from now until the famine is over, there will be a loaf of bread for each of you here at my house. I will expect you to come each morning and take your loaf home to your family."

The children immediately lunged for the basket, each fighting for the largest loaf. The loaves were quickly gone, and the children disappeared down the street without so much as a thank you to the generous man who had provided the bread. Only one little girl, Gretchen, remained, cowering in the corner to avoid the mad rush of the older children. Timidly approaching what she feared was an empty basket, Gretchen broke into a wide grin when she saw one little loaf left in the bottom. Running to the man, she hugged him and thanked him for being so kind and then skipped home with her loaf tucked safely under her arm.

Day after day the children came to the rich man's house. Day after day Gretchen was left with the smallest of the loaves as she waited for the others rather than join the fight. And each day she thanked the man for his generosity.

One day, as Gretchen's mother cut the tiny loaf for their dinner, to their surprise, a handful of silver coins fell out onto the table. "Oh my!" her mother exclaimed. "There must be a mistake. Please take this money back to the gentleman right away and tell him that we did not mean to steal it."

Gretchen scooped up the coins and quickly ran back to the rich man's house. Knocking on the door, she worried that he would be angry with her. The rich man answered the door right away and smiled as if he were expecting her. Pulling the

coins out of her pocket, Gretchen attempted to put them into his hand. "No, no, my little Gretchen," the man said gently. "This was no mistake. I have watched you every day as you waited for the others to take their bread, knowing that you would be left with the smallest loaf. The coins are your reward for your patience. Always remember that the person who chooses to accept less rather than quarrel for more will find unexpected blessings that will be of far greater value in the end."

Discussion Questions

1. Why do you think Gretchen waited for the last loaf?
2. Has there been a time when you have been patient, but no one appreciated it? How did you feel? Why?
3. Would it have been dishonest for the girl to keep the money? Why or why not?

Story #17

Humility & Self-control

The Man, the Boy, and the Donkey

Retold by Deborah M. Garrick

A foolish man and his foolish son, in trying to please everybody, please no one and lose their donkey. This story has been told and retold for hundreds of years.

A man and his son were on their way to market to fetch supplies. Behind them followed their only donkey. Early in the journey they passed a neighboring farmer, who was amazed at their foolishness. "Why do you not ride your donkey?" he inquired. "Why else would you bring your donkey with you?"

Wanting to please his neighbor, the farmer very willingly placed his son on the back of the donkey and continued on their journey.

Not long after, the pair encountered a group of men eating lunch by the roadside. As they passed, the men yelled out at them, "Such a lazy son that he makes his father walk while he rides. This should not be!"

Disturbed by their words and wishing to please them as well, the father asked his son to dismount the donkey and he climbed up on the animal himself.

At a well along the road, several women noticed the trio passing by. "What is society coming to when a father would force his son to walk while he rides in ease? Such a thing should not be!"

Trying to find a solution that would be acceptable to both the men and the women, the father had the son mount the donkey behind him, and they completed their journey to town in this manner.

Upon their arrival, the townspeople began to gather on the street, pointing at them and shouting. "How can you be so cruel? Is not your donkey so small that the weight of both of you will cause his back to break? Do you not care for your animal?"

"What shall I do now?" the father cried. "If I please one group, the others are distraught. We must find a way to please them all." After a long time of consideration, they happened upon a plan they thought was perfect. The son was sent to find a strong pole and some rope. Then the father tied the donkey's feet to the pole. Next, after much effort, the two raised the pole over their shoulders and began to carry their donkey the rest of the way to the market.

Uncomfortable with this new solution, the donkey struggled against the bindings around his hoofs until at last, just as they were crossing the Market Bridge, he managed to get one hoof loose. The donkey's violent kicking took his owners by surprise, and much to their horror, the son lost his grip on the pole. With a crash, the donkey thudded onto the bridge and then plunged over the side into the river and was swept away by the current.

For a long while father and son stood on the bridge, staring down the river, trying to make sense of the day's events. Finally, after much thought, the father spoke up.

"It is too late for our donkey, but I think I finally understand."

"Understand what, Father?" the boy inquired.

"If you try to please everyone, you will please no one."

Discussion Questions

1. How did the father and son lack boundaries?
2. Where there any character traits missing in the lives of the father and son?
3. Can you think of practical examples of how people unwisely change their behavior to avoid the criticisms of others?
4. Why is approval so important to us? What does it take to be confident in our decisions, regardless of what others think?

Story #18

Fairness & Respect

The Man Who Would Not Drink Alone

Retold by Deborah M. Garrick

In his refusal to accept a special privilege, this king's soldiers witnessed a true leader's sense of fairness and respect for his men.

It had already been a long march home and there were still many miles to go. The emperor led his weary soldiers down the dusty road, knowing the distance they had already come without food or water. In the early afternoon, as the sun beat down upon the beleaguered band, they happened upon a farmer taking his wares to town. Instantly, recognizing the emperor, the farmer bowed low and then quickly offered what little water he had left for the emperor's refreshment. Taking the cup in hand, the proud ruler raised it in the air, looked intently out over his troops, and then slowly lowered the precious liquid without taking a drink.

"If I drink, my men will remain thirsty," he said, "for you do not have enough water for us all. My thirst would be quenched, but their spirits might also be quenched. I shall have none."

As the emperor placed the cup back in the grasp of the bewildered farmer, a wave of cheers arose from his men, hailing the emperor and demanding that he continue to lead them on their journey. This amazing leader was Alexander the Great.

Discussion Questions

1. Why did the men cheer?
2. To be fair, one must be aware of how others perceive a situation. How does one develop this awareness?
3. Besides fairness, what are other characteristics of true leaders? Would fairness be near the top of your list? Why or why not?

Story #19

Honesty & Responsibility

The Merchant and the Builder

Retold by Steven V. Cannizzaro

It is best to follow the Golden Rule, even when no one is looking.

A wealthy and generous merchant said to his friend, a builder, "I would like to build a house where I could live with my family and entertain my friends for the rest of my days. You are not only a builder of good reputation but also a long-standing friend whom I trust. Would you build it for me?"

"Certainly!" the builder replied, and immediately they began to make plans. The merchant asked the builder many questions about the house. "If it were your house, how would you design it? What materials would you use? How would you build it?" The builder answered these and many other questions about the house, and at every turn the merchant took the advice of his friend.

When the plans were complete and they agreed upon the builder's wage, the merchant said, "I must travel afar to take care of business, and I will be away for a lengthy time. I would like for you to build the house just as we planned. Use the finest materials. Spare no expense. In all things, I trust your judgment to do what is right and best." He embraced his friend and began his journey, calling over his shoulder, "Farewell! I look forward to seeing you and this house upon my return!"

The builder began to work immediately. He gathered the right tools, ordered the best materials, and carefully laid out his plans to build the house. Early in the morning he could be heard whistling as he worked. He followed the plans and paid great attention to every detail, often working late. People would stop to admire his work. It would be a magnificent house—perhaps the finest he had ever built!

One afternoon as the builder was working beneath the hot sun, three of his friends stopped by and called out to him. "We are going into the village to drink, play games, and be merry! Come join us!" When the builder replied that he could not, the first one asked, "Why are you using such expensive materials? These are far too costly. No one would notice if you used cheaper materials and made more money!" The second one asked, "Why are you following these plans? They will take far too long. You could easily take some shortcuts and finish this house much sooner! No one would notice, and then you could join us!" The third one asked, "Why are you working so hard and long, when the merchant is enjoying himself traveling afar?" With a smile and a wave of his hand, the builder dismissed his friends and continued to work. They went on their way laughing loudly.

He could not, however, as easily dismiss their comments. As he worked into the early evening, the same questions troubled him. "Why should I spend so much on the finest materials when cheaper materials will do? Why should I labor over these intricate plans when I could take some shortcuts and be finished with this house! Why should I bear the burden of building a place for the merchant to relax and enjoy the rest of his days while he is traveling afar and enjoying himself?" These questions entered the builder's thoughts and heart, and though he continued to work, he soon stopped whistling.

Betrayed by these thoughts, the builder looked for ways to build what appeared to be the same house but at less cost and in shorter time. He paid attention to the details one could easily observe, such as the paint, trim, and windows; but at every opportunity where no one would notice he used cheaper materials and took shortcuts. As he worked, the builder said to himself, "These little things really do not matter. I am actually being wise to look out for myself!" and though he started to whistle again, it was an empty and hollow tune.

Soon, the house was finished ahead of schedule, and it appeared just as it was planned. Its fresh paint shone. Its trim beamed. Its windows sparkled. And though the angles of the front door were not exactly square, its entrance was grand. The builder hastily cleaned and prepared for the merchant's arrival.

On the day the merchant arrived at the house to meet his friend, the builder, he exclaimed, "Oh! How I have looked forward to this day! I could hardly wait to see you and this house!" As he gazed in awe upon it, he said, "It is more magnificent than I imagined! You have done a wonderful job, just as I knew you would!" As the two stood admiring its beauty, the merchant handed the builder a silk purse full of money. "Thank you!" he said. "Here is the wage we agreed upon!"

"There is one more thing, my friend," said the merchant. Turning to look into the eyes of the builder, the merchant put his hand on his shoulder and said, "I asked for your advice on the design, material, and plans for this house not only because I trust you. I asked because I have long wanted to give you a gift to enjoy with your family forever. Here, my friend," he said as he handed the builder the deed to the house. "I asked you to build this house for yourself. It is now yours."

Discussion Questions

1. Why did the builder choose to use cheaper materials and take shortcuts on his plans to build the house? What was the result?
2. Who was truly the builder's friend: the friends on the way to the village or the merchant? To whom should he have listened?
3. Whom did the builder betray? What was the result? What could the builder have done to keep from making such a foolish mistake?
4. How does the story illustrate the Golden Rule and what does it teach us about character?

Story #20

The Oxpecker and the Giraffe

Gratitude & Responsibility

Retold by Steven V. Cannizzaro
Submitted by Angela Duthie (Capetown, South Africa)

This is a KhoiSan legend about the oxpecker, a bird that is found in South Africa. These birds appear to hitch rides on giraffes as they travel through the African bush. This is how a friendship began a very long time ago . . .

One summer afternoon the lions were lazily napping in the shade. The giraffes were grazing on tender treetops. The elephants and many, many others animals were refreshing themselves by the water hole. The monkeys pranced among them playfully.

They did not notice a storm gathering on the horizon. The swift, rain-swollen clouds were split by a sudden *crack!* of lightning and a deep drum roll of thunder. As the lightning struck a dead tree in the distance, the tree burst into flames, setting the surrounding dry grassland on fire. Fed by the rush of the storm's wind, the fire rose to an inferno and began to sweep across the peaceful African plain.

The animals fled in fear. Gathering the young and hurrying the old, the animals rushed to escape the fury of the fire.

High in an acacia tree a pair of oxpeckers, yellow-billed birds of the plain, protecting their newly hatched chicks, watched in horror as the fire approached. Fearful for the lives of their chicks, they called out to the animals rushing by to help them. "Wait! Please stop! Help us!" they cried, but they were not heard in midst of the noise and panic.

Among the animals running by was a giraffe whose long neck enabled him to see above the dust and smoke. He spotted the oxpeckers and heard their fearful cries. "What's the matter?!" he paused and asked breathlessly. "Why are you waiting? You must flee!"

The oxpeckers quickly explained their delay and begged the giraffe to help them. The giraffe felt the fire, sparks, and smoke enclosing them, and said, "Of course, I will help you!" Reaching up, up, up to the top of the tree with his long neck, he stretched out his tongue and plucked the chicks from their nest. On his long, lanky

legs, the giraffe speedily carried the young chicks to safety as their parents, the pair of oxpeckers, flew closely behind.

Once they were out of the fire's reach, the oxpeckers exclaimed to the giraffe, "Thank you! Thank you! We are so grateful for your help! How ever can we repay you for your kindness?"

Smiling at his new friends, he replied, "Well, if you would like to help me, I can think of two things. First, I am often bothered by these pesky insects and ticks I cannot reach on my coat. Would you be willing to pick them off for me?"

"Oh! Yes! Yes!" replied the oxpeckers. "That would be wonderful! Insects and ticks are delicious! What else can we do?"

"Well," replied the giraffe, "occasionally, I do not see or hear an enemy approach. If you were to see one, would you mind warning me?"

"Oh, no! Not at all," replied the oxpeckers.

From that day onward, the oxpeckers and giraffes became fast friends. Today, if you see giraffes lazily strolling across the savanna, they will often be accompanied by one or more of their friends, the oxpeckers, crawling over their necks, flanks, and ears picking off the tiny insects and ticks that bother them. And if the oxpeckers spot an approaching enemy? You will hear them cry out a warning to their friends, the giraffes.

Discussion Questions

1. The oxpecker responded to the giraffe's kindness in gratitude. How is this story an example for us in our relationships?
2. Who was the most responsible character in this story?
3. Why is it important for us to keep our promises?

Story #21

The Purse of Gold

Fairness & Gratitude

Anonymous

In this Jewish folktale, a wise judge teaches a greedy merchant a valuable lesson.

A beggar found a leather purse that someone had dropped in the marketplace. Opening it, he discovered that it contained 100 pieces of gold. Then he heard a merchant shout, "A reward! A reward to the one who finds my leather purse!"

Being an honest man, the beggar came forward and handed the purse to the merchant saying, "Here is your purse. May I have the reward now?"

"Reward?" scoffed the merchant, greedily counting his gold. "Why, the purse I dropped had 200 pieces of gold in it. You've already stolen more than the reward! Go away or I'll tell the police."

"I'm an honest man," said the beggar defiantly. "Let us take this matter to the court."

In court the judge patiently listened to both sides of the story and said, "I believe you both. Justice is possible! Merchant, you stated that the purse you lost contained 200 pieces of gold. Well, that's a considerable cost. But, the purse this beggar found had only 100 pieces of gold. Therefore, it couldn't be the one you lost."

And, with that, the judge gave the purse and all the gold to the beggar.

Discussion Questions

1. If you were the judge, what would you decide in this situation?
2. Why do you think the judge chose to give the purse to the beggar?
3. Did you agree or disagree with the judge's decision? Why or why not?

Story #22

Empathy & Service

The Two Gifts

Retold by Deborah M. Garrick

This tale reminds us that a mistake in judgment can be remedied, and that it is never too late to offer service to others.

Winter pressed in hard over the countryside, and an old woman sat by the side of the road begging for alms. She had not eaten that day, nor the day before, and was very hungry. As the sun began to set, a traveler appeared down the road, riding in a rough yet sturdy cart. As he neared the woman, the traveler's heart went out to her. However, he was in a hurry and decided that he must press on to his destination, so he passed by without stopping. That evening, however, was spent wrestling with his conscience. He knew he should have stopped to help the old woman even if it had meant a more difficult journey for himself.

Shortly after he passed, another traveler in a fine coach came by. Wrapped in thick fur, the man felt pity for the old woman braving the snow in her thin garments. Signaling his coachman to stop, he rolled down the carriage window and searched for a silver coin. The woman rose expectantly, thrilled at the thought of the food she could buy from such a man's generosity. The rich traveler, however, could find nothing but gold coins. Holding up one coin, he exclaimed, "This is far too much for such a woman" and sought to return the coin to his purse. Before he could do so, however, the wind whipped through the carriage and blew the coin out of his hand onto the fresh snow below. Unwilling to open the door and search for the coin in such foul weather, the traveler left it for the old woman and signaled his coachman to carry on. "She has no need for such gold," he thought smugly, "but I was indeed generous and expect that I will be well rewarded for it, no doubt."

As the coach disappeared from view, the old woman began frantically digging through the mounds of snow for the precious coin. Loathe to let such a prize slip away, she continued to search until her hands had no feeling left in them. Just as she was ready to give up, she heard a noise in the distance. She lifted her face into the driving wind and was shocked to see the old rugged cart of the first traveler emerging from the darkness.

The traveler guided his horse to the woman's side and beckoned her to climb up. Stunned, the woman obeyed and soon found herself seated before a sumptuous dinner at the traveler's inn, her frozen limbs regaining life from the warmth of the fire.

Were both travelers to be granted a peek into the heavenly book recording that night's events, the first traveler would have found his deed printed in large letters, reflecting his genuine gift of love to one less fortunate than himself. The second traveler, however, would have searched in vain for his name, just as the woman had searched in vain for his accidental offering to her on that wintry night. For only a gift given from pure motives is of any value in heaven's eyes.

Discussion Questions

1. Why do you think the two men were not inclined to help the woman?
2. What character traits did the rich man lack?
3. Have you ever passed up an opportunity to meet a need and then regretted your action? Describe the event and your feelings.
4. Have you ever been denied help that you truly needed? How did you feel?

Story #23

Responsibility & Self-control

Three Fish

Anonymous

This tale from India illustrates the value of making a responsible plan to deal with life's challenges.

Three fish lived in a pond. One was named Plan Ahead, another was Think Fast, and the third was named Wait and See. One day they heard a fisherman say that he was going to cast his net in their pond the next day.

Plan Ahead said, "I'm swimming down the river tonight!"

Think Fast said, "I'm sure I'll come up with a plan."

Wait and See lazily said, "I just can't think about it now!"

When the fisherman cast his net, Plan Ahead was long gone. But Think Fast and Wait and See were caught!

Think Fast quickly rolled his belly up and pretended to be dead.
"Oh, this fish is no good!" said the fisherman, and threw him safely back into the water. Wait and See, however, ended up in the fish market.

That is why they say, "In times of danger, when the net is cast, plan ahead or plan to think fast!"

Discussion Questions

1. How do these three fish exemplify the different ways people choose to handle their problems?
2. Which fish most describes how you handle challenges?
3. Which character qualities are illustrated, or lacking, in this story?

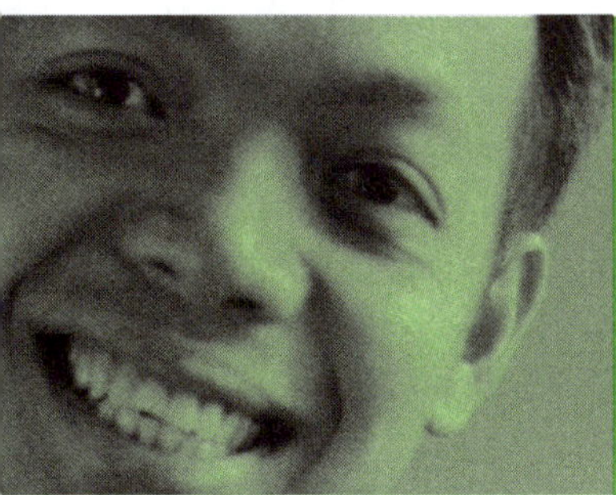

Teaching Through Storytelling – Activities

78. Character Card Banners	486
79. Story Connections	488
80. Literature Circles	492
81. Character Quilts	496
82. Venn Diagrams	498
83. Hot Seat Interviews	502
84. Character Trait Interviews	504

Activity #78 Character Card Banners

Variable Time

Character Connection
All Traits

Purpose To help participants capture the essential meaning of the 15 core character traits emphasized in the stories that are studied

Overview Each story in this section illustrates two character traits. Based on these stories, participants create a collection of illustrated character traits that can be attached to a ribbon or streamer and displayed in the room.

Life Skill Integrating all the character traits in one's life

Group Size Individual activity with any size group

Cultural and Age Considerations None

Materials For each participant: 16 index cards or small pieces of paper (these are handed out one at a time after each story); one strip of ribbon, streamers, or yarn approximately 1.75 meters (5½ feet) long (or simply tape the cards individually to a wall); pens, pencils, crayons, or marking pens

Preparation Cut the ribbons before class. In each story, identify the main character trait that participants should illustrate, so that each of the 15 core character traits is covered once.

Instructions

1. Give each participant two index cards. Explain that they will be illustrating each of the 15 core character traits and creating a banner on which to hang them in the room.
2. Allow participants a few minutes to write their name on a card and decorate it.
3. After each story is studied, ask participants to identify the main character trait that the story emphasizes and write it on their index card.
4. They can then create an illustration of the character trait or the part of the story that best captured the meaning of that specific character trait.

Character Card Banners

5. Instruct participants to gather in groups of three or four to share their illustrations with one another, and then collaborate on a definition for the character trait and write it on their index card (front or back).
6. Ask the small groups to share their definitions with the class.
7. Staple the card with each participant's name to the top of a ribbon.
8. Hang the ribbons from the ceiling, bulletin board, or wall so more character cards can be added as they are created.

Application and Insight

Understanding good character traits helps us build them into our lives.

Reviewing the definitions of character traits is an excellent reminder to practice those traits consistently.

Going Deeper

Revisit the character trait cards as they are discussed in related lessons.

Invite parents to meet with the group. Ask participants to share the meaning of each character trait.

Be more concerned of your character than your reputation, because your character is what you really are; your reputation is merely what others think you are. —John Wooden, author

It Takes Courage!

to consistently grow in character

Activity #79 Story Connections

15–30 Minutes

Character Connection
Varies with each story

Purpose To help participants imagine themselves in situations that require the same character quality demonstrated in the story

Overview This is a wrap-up activity for reviewing character traits learned through stories. Participants will personalize the lesson by illustrating what this situation might look like in their own lives and will apply the character trait to situations they may encounter.

Life Skill Applying life lessons through stories

Group Size Individual activity with any size group

Cultural and Age Considerations None

Materials Story, Story Connections Handout, pens or pencils

Preparation Make one copy of the Story Connections Handout for each participant.

Instructions

1. After the story has been read to the group, discuss the character trait being demonstrated. Give each participant a copy of the Story Connections Handout.

2. Ask participants to pretend to be in a situation that requires the same character trait as the one highlighted in the story. Have them describe the situation by answering the questions on the left side of the handout.
3. Give participants time to draw a picture that illustrates their own version of the story.
4. Ask volunteers to share their story with the group.

Story Connections

Application and Insight

Envisioning ourselves in a situation helps us understand how to apply that character trait to our own lives.

Hearing others' real-life stories about character is a great way to create trust and community.

Going Deeper

How can developing this character trait help you to manage situations that you may encounter in the future?

How would this character trait have helped you in the past?

How has this character trait emerged or developed through your experiences?

When the character of a person is not evident, look at his or her friends. —Unknown

It Takes Courage!

to honestly admit our character flaws

Story Connections

Story Title: ______________________________

Main Character: ______________________________

Character Trait Displayed: ______________________________

Pretend you are in a situation that requires the same character trait as the one demonstrated in this story. Write about your own story in the left-hand column. Draw a picture that illustrates your situation and your version of the story.

Tell about your story here:	***Illustrate your version of the story here:***

What challenge do you face in your story? ______________________________

____

How do you demonstrate this character trait in your story? ______________________________

____

What are some ways you can develop this character trait in your life? ______________________________

____

Notes

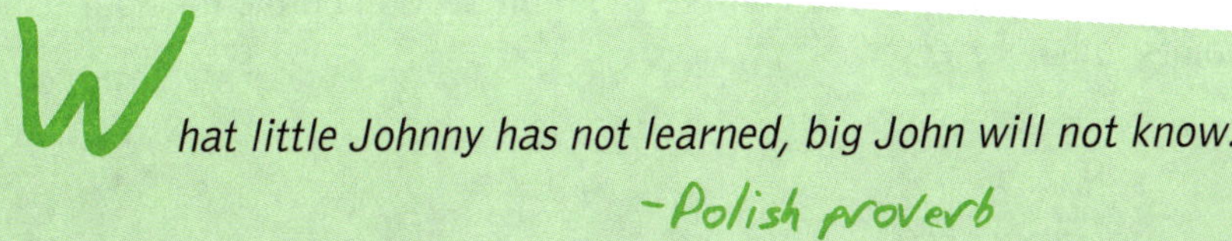
What little Johnny has not learned, big John will not know.
-Polish proverb

Activity #80 Literature Circles

30–45 Minutes

Character Connection
Varies with each story

Purpose To facilitate small-group discussions on stories the participants have read

Overview Literature circles provide an opportunity for participants to read stories with a specific focus in mind. After reading a story, participants will gather in small groups to discuss the story from the perspective of their assigned role as Discussion Leader, Artist, Analyzer, or Rewriter.

Life Skill Collaborating well in a group

Group Size Any

Cultural and Age Considerations None

Materials Story, Literature Circle Bookmarks (Activity Materials), Literature Circle Discussion Handout, pens or pencils

Preparation Make one copy of the Literature Circle Bookmarks (Activity Materials) for each group. Cut apart the bookmarks so there is one for each participant. Make one copy of the Literature Circle Discussion Handout for each participant.

Instructions

1. Divide participants into groups of four individuals.
2. Within each group, hand out the four bookmarks and assign a role to each person. Give each participant a copy of the Literature Circle Discussion Handout.
3. Each group of four should consist of a Discussion Leader, an Artist, an Analyzer, and a Rewriter. If any groups have more or fewer than four people, assign participants multiple roles or have them share a role.
4. Explain each role, asking participants to keep their role in mind as the story is read.
5. Each participant should prepare and present their assigned role during the literature circle time in their small group. Instruct them to use their section on the handout to write the main points to be presented.

Literature Circles

6. While participants are presenting their literature circle role, instruct the other group members to summarize on their copy of the handout the main points each person presented.
7. The next time literature circles are assigned, alternate the roles so that each participant has an opportunity to practice a different role.

Application and Insight

It is helpful to analyze components of a story and to see the relevance of developing one's personal character.

A person's understanding can be increased by viewing a situation from different perspectives.

Going Deeper

When you are in a challenging dilemma, do you think it would be helpful to

- analyze the situation?
- consider other ways the problem could end?
- draw a picture of how you feel and discuss it with others?

How did you feel about your assigned role in the group? Would you have enjoyed a different role more? Why or why not?

Adapted from Harvey Daniels, Literature Circles: Voice and Choice in the Student-Centered Classroom *(Portland, ME: Stenhouse Publishers, 1994).*

Kind words can be short and easy to speak but their echoes are truly endless. —Mother Teresa, Yugoslavian missionary to Calcutta, India

It Takes Courage!
to work together and trust others in the process

Literature Circle Bookmarks

Copy and cut out the bookmarks.

Discussion Leader

As you listen to the story, think of five questions you can ask your group members to help them think about the character trait that the main character displayed in this story. Try not to ask questions that require a simple yes, no, or one-word answer. Think of questions starting with phrases like, In what ways did . . . ," "What would have happened if . . . ," "How else could . . . ," and other open-ended questions to help people think more deeply.

Artist

As you listen to the story, think about some of the main benefits of developing this character trait. Create a poem, a song, or an illustration that tells about the main character, the character trait, or both, as well as the benefits associated with developing this character trait.

Analyzer

As you listen to the story, note how many of the 15 character traits are displayed. Begin your discussion by mentioning a character trait that the main character possessed. Ask your group members to identify how the main character displayed this trait. Add your example to the discussion. Continue with some of the other character traits that you identified in the story.

Rewriter

Rewrite the ending of the story by telling what might have happened if the main character had decided not to demonstrate good character when faced with a difficult situation. Create an ending to the story that shows an opposite trait, and then share about the ways this decision would have affected the main character and others around him or her.

Literature Circles Discussion

Summarize the most important points that each person presents in his or her assigned role. If you need help, ask the presenter to sum up the findings in a few sentences.

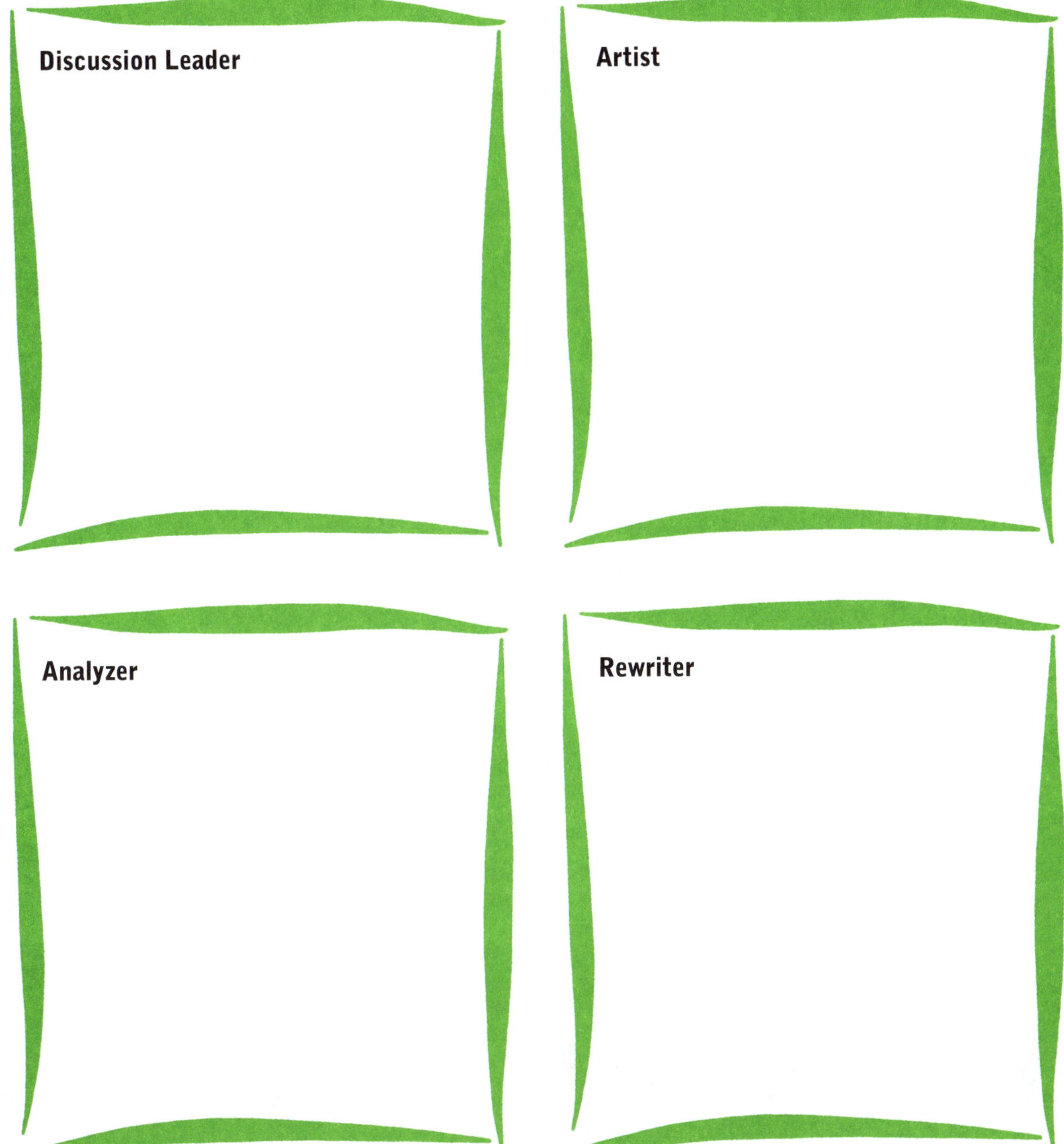

Activity #87 Character Quilts

15–30 Minutes

Character Connection
Varies with each story

Purpose To elaborate on the character trait emphasized in a story

Overview Participants collectively make a quilt by contributing one patch on which they have illustrated their favorite part of the story or the character trait discussed. The quilt, kept in a central location, serves as a decorative visual aid to reinforce the value of a special character quality.

Life Skill Valuing the contributions of others

Group Size Any

Cultural and Age Considerations None

Materials Story; one fabric or paper square for each participant; marking pens; choice of binding: tape, needle and thread, or hole punch and yarn

Preparation Cut out one paper or fabric square measuring 10 by 10 centimeters (4 by 4 inches) for each participant. These squares can be made larger or smaller depending on the size of the group.

Instructions

1. Read the story and discuss the highlighted character traits.
2. Give each participant one square. Ask participants to illustrate one of the highlighted character traits or their favorite part of the story.
3. Ask participants to gather in small groups and explain their squares to their group.
4. Bind the pieces together by using tape, by sewing with large stitches, or by punching holes in the squares and connecting them with yarn in stitch style or shoelace-type bows.
5. Place the quilt in a central location.

Character Quilts

Application and Insight

When thinking about various character qualities, it is helpful to have a good visual reminder of those traits.

A group working collaboratively can often make something much more creative and beautiful than someone working alone.

Going Deeper

How did others see the character trait differently from how you viewed it?

How does this quilt add to your understanding of this story or character trait?

Think of a title for your square. How can that new title be applied to your life?

No one knows what he is able to do until he tries. —Publilius Syrus, Greek philosopher (50 B.C.)

It Takes Courage!
to embrace the beauty of diversity

Activity #82 Venn Diagrams

30–45 Minutes

Character Connection
Varies with each story

Purpose To help participants gain a better understanding by comparing and contrasting the characters or character traits in stories

Overview After hearing two stories, participants will consider similarities and differences between the main characters. They will record these ideas using a Venn Diagram to help them analyze behavior and choices. For further self-analysis, participants will complete another Venn Diagram to describe their own character traits in relation to character traits in the stories.

Life Skill Analyzing similarities and differences

Group Size Individual activity with any size group

Cultural and Age Considerations None

Materials Two stories, two Venn Diagram Handouts, pens or pencils

Preparation Make one copy of each Venn Diagram Handout for each participant.

Instructions

1. After reading and discussing two stories, choose the two characters you would like to examine further.
2. Distribute the two Venn Diagram Handouts to each participant.
3. Ask participants to place the names of the characters at the top of Venn Diagram 1 and fill in the relevant story information.
4. Give participants time to identify qualities of each character and determine whether each quality was unique to one story character (write these on the differences side of the circle) or was one that both characters possessed (list these in the center where the two circles overlap).
5. Then discuss how the main characters were similar and different and how these qualities affected their behavior.

Venn Diagrams

6. Ask participants to complete the second Venn Diagram Handout by analyzing how their character traits compare to the character traits in the stories. Instruct them to write the differences between the characters and themselves on the outsides, and the traits they share in common in the inner portion of the circles.

Application and Insight

Developing good character takes time and commitment.

Each person is unique and special.

Looking at similarities and not just differences is good practice when relating to others.

Going Deeper

How are you similar to and different from these two characters?

With which of the two characters do you most relate?

In what areas do you need to grow to develop the character traits illustrated in these two stories?

Everyone thinks of changing the world, but no one thinks of changing himself. —Leo Tolstoy, Russian author (1828–1910)

It Takes Courage!

to see how many similarities we share with others

Venn Diagram 1

Story Title: ______________________________ Story Title: ______________________________

Main Character: ___________________________ Main Character: ___________________________

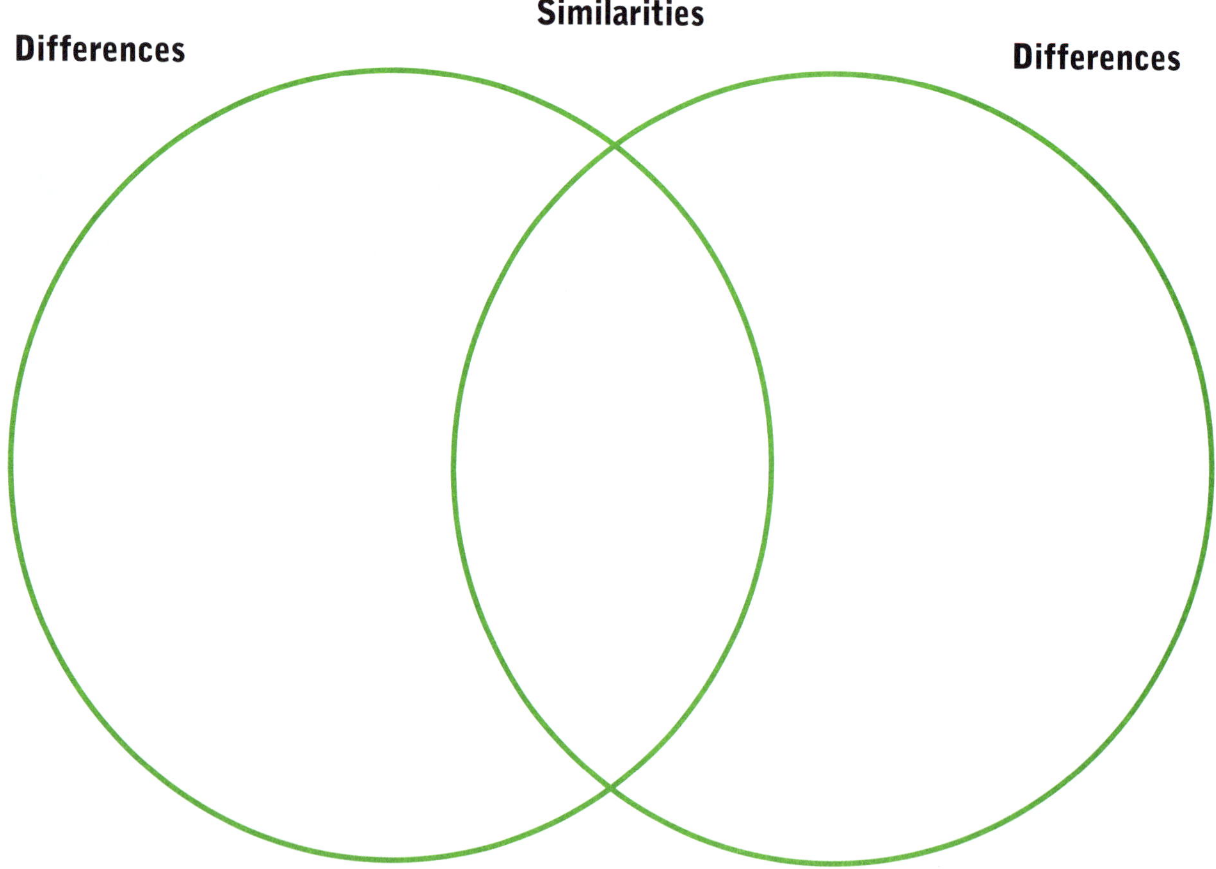

Venn Diagram 2

Story Title: ______________________ Story Title: ______________________

Main Character: ______________________ Main Character: ______________________

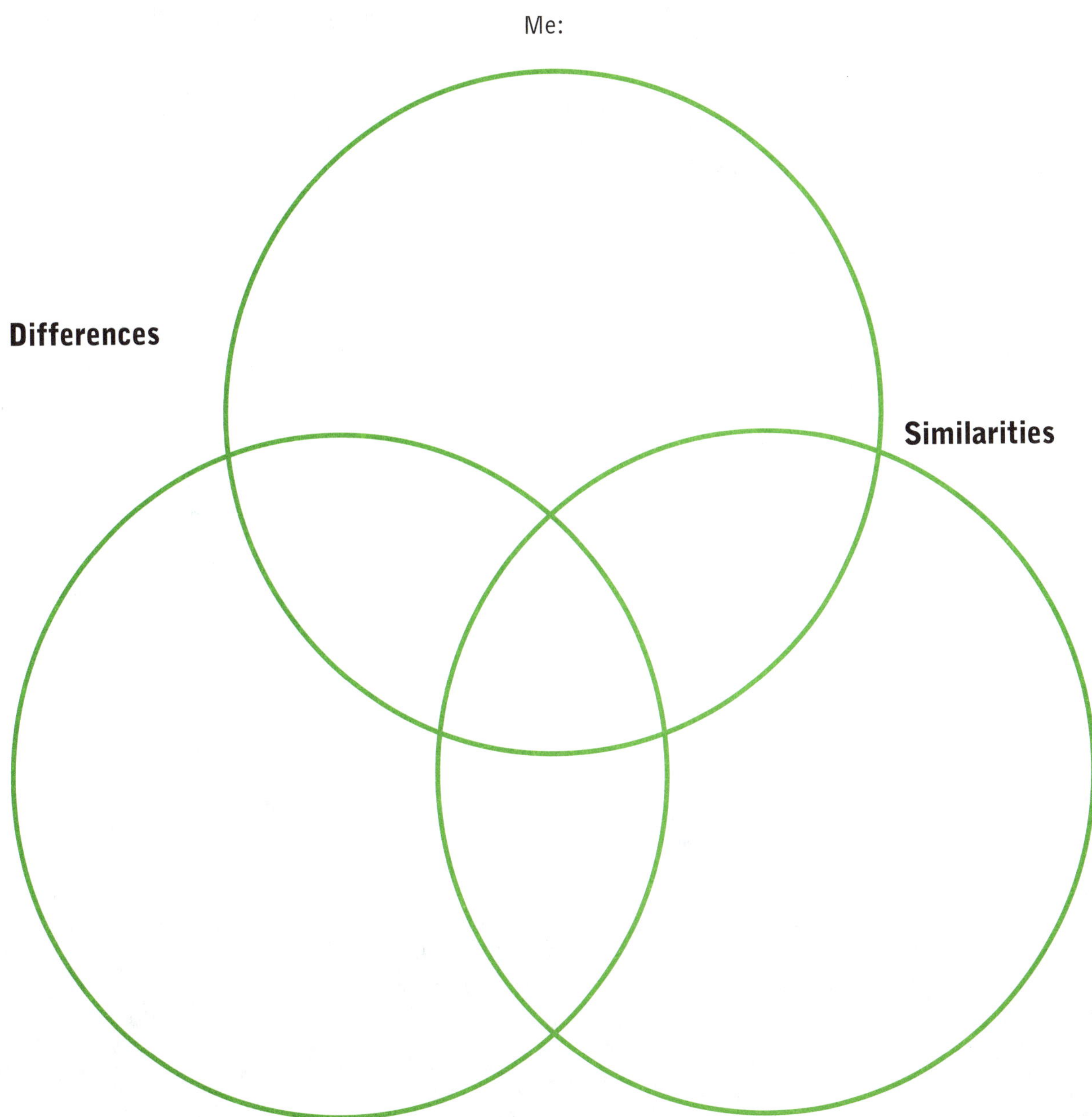

Activity #83 Hot Seat Interviews

30–45 Minutes

Character Connection
Varies with each story

Purpose To help participants better understand relationships and characters in a story, as well as recognize and discuss the importance of character traits demonstrated in the story

Overview Volunteers are selected to represent the characters in the story, while the rest of the group questions them about their situation, motives, thoughts, and feelings. The facilitator leads the group in discussion about how to apply the identified character traits.

Life Skill Viewing situations from someone else's perspective

Group Size Any

Cultural and Age Considerations None

Materials Story, chair

Preparation None

Instructions

1. Read the story to the group.
2. Place a chair in the front or middle of the room and explain that this is the "hot seat."
3. Choose participants to represent each character in the story.
4. Ask the volunteers one by one to sit in the "hot seat." Introduce each person as the particular character in the story; for example, "This is Lt. Blandford, and he will gladly answer your questions."
5. Instruct the rest of the group to ask the volunteers questions about their role in the story—their situation, motives, thoughts, and feelings.
6. Ask participants to identify the character traits of each character in the story.

Hot Seat Interviews

7. Discuss how hearing the characters' viewpoints helped participants better understand the situation.

Application and Insight

We learn to feel empathy for others when we put ourselves in their place.

It helps us to understand a situation when we view it from someone else's perspective.

Going Deeper

What are some situations in which you have you put yourself in another's place?

Did it help you to understand how the other person was feeling?

What are some of the major lessons we can learn from this story?

Don't judge a person until you've walked a mile in his moccasins.
—Native American proverb

It Takes Courage!
to "see" from another person's point of view

Activity #84 Character Trait Interviews

30–45 Minutes

Character Connection
Varies with each story

Purpose To provide participants with an opportunity to learn more about a specific character trait and how to develop that character trait

Overview After reading a story highlighting a given character trait, participants will interview someone who clearly models this character trait in his or her personal or professional life. They then analyze how this character trait is dependent on having personal courage.

Life Skill Learning from others

Group Size Individual activity with any size group

Cultural and Age Considerations None

Materials Story, Character Trait Interview Handout

Preparation Make one copy of the Character Trait Interview Handout for each participant.

Instructions

1. Read the story and identify the main character trait that is illustrated in the story.
2. Give each participant a copy of the Character Trait Interview Handout.
3. Ask participants to think of someone they know who clearly displays this character trait. Instruct them to record this character trait, as well as the person's name, on the handout.
4. Give participants a few moments to think of ways this person displays the character trait.
5. As homework, ask each participant to interview the person they chose using the questions on the handout.
6. Instruct them to bring the results of their interviews to the next session so they can report their findings to the group.

Character Trait Interviews

Application and Insight

Interviewing a person we respect can build a greater appreciation for the person and enhance the relationship.

Having positive role-models in our lives is vital for personal growth and development.

Building good character will take a lifetime of commitment to ourselves and to others.

Going Deeper

What did you learn about the development of this character trait in the life of the person you interviewed?

What was surprising or memorable about this interview?

How did courage influence the positive choices the person made?

How did positive choices result in good character development for the person you chose?

—Unknown

Character Trait Interview

Character trait to be studied: ____________________

Person to be interviewed: ____________________

Ways this person demonstrates this character trait: ____________________

____

____

Interview Questions

Write a summary of the responses in the space provided.

How did you develop this character trait?

Describe a time when you relied on this character trait to help you be a person of good character.

In what ways did your decisions in this situation require courage?

On the back of this paper, share something special you learned about this person.

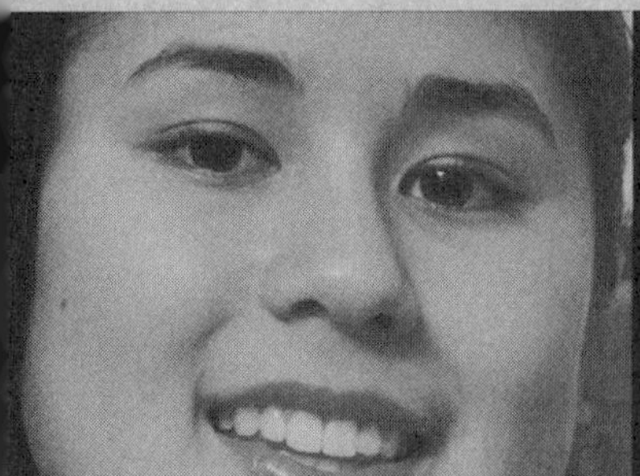

Resources

End Notes 509
Bibliography 513
About Kerus Global Education 517
About the Authors 519

End Notes

Front Matter

1. Ina J. Hughs, *A Prayer for Children* (William Morrow and Company, Inc., 1995).

Introduction

1. Haim Ginott, *Between Teacher and Child* (New York: Avon, 1976).
2. The Aspen Declaration on Character <www.charactercounts.org/aspen.htm>.
3. The Six Pillars of Character <www.charactercounts.org/defsix.htm>.
4. "Strengthening Mental Health Promotion," Fact Sheet No. 220. World Health Organization, 2001.
5. "New life skills-based education programme." UNICEF, 2004 <www.unicef.org/lifeskills/index_7308.html>.

Creating a Vision for Life

1. Os Guinness, *The Call: Finding and Fulfilling the Central Purpose of Your Life* (Nashville: W Publishing Group, A division of Thomas Nelson, Inc., 1998).
2. Rick Warren, *The Purpose-Driven Life* (Grand Rapids, MI: Zondervan, 2002).
3. Stephen Covey, *Growing Great Children.* In Michael S. Josephson and Wes Hanson (eds.), *The Power of Character: Prominent Americans Talk About Life, Family, Work, Values, and More* (San Francisco: Jossey-Bass, 1988), 102–104.
4. Thomas Lickona, Eric Schaps, and Catherine Lewis, *Eleven Principles of Character Education* (Alexandria, VA: The Character Education Partnership, 1997).
5. Rabbi Wayne Dosick, "Love Your Neighbor." In Josephson and Hanson, *The Power of Character*, 291.
6. Sean Covey, The Seven Habits of Highly Effective Teens (New York: Fireside, 1998), 90–91.

Communicating Effectively

1. Tony Alessandra and Phil Hunsaker, *Communicating at Work* (New York: Fireside, a division of Simon and Schuster, 1993).

Building Healthy Relationships

1. Tim Downs, *Finding Common Ground* (Chicago, IL: Moody Press, 1999).

2. Robert J. Sternberg, "The Triangular Theory of Love," *Psychological Review* (1986): 93,119–35.
3. Ron Herron and Kathleen Sorensen, *Unmasking Sexual Con Games: Helping Teens Identify Good and Bad Relationships* (Boys Town, NB: Boys Town Press, 1997), 29.
4. Val J. Peter and Tom Dowd, *Boundaries: A Guide for Teens* (Boys Town, NB: Boys Town Press, 2000), 22–25, 38, 44.
5. M. D. Resnick et al., "Protecting Adolescents from Harm—Findings from the National Longitudinal Study on Adolescent Health," *Journal of American Medical Association* (1997): 278(10), 823–32.

Making Wise Decisions

1. Interview with C. R. Snyder in *The New York Times*, Dec. 24, 1991. Quoted in Daniel Goleman, *Emotional Intelligence: Why It Can Matter More Than IQ* (New York: Bantam Books, 1995).
2. Michael Josephson, *You Don't Have to Be Sick to Get Better* (Marina del Rey, CA: Josephson Institute of Ethics, 2001), 28.

Preventing HIV/AIDS

1. Patricia Thickstun and Kate Hendricks (eds), *Evidence that Demands Action: Comparing Risk Avoidance and Risk Reduction Strategies for HIV Prevention* (Austin, TX: The Medical Institute for Sexual Health, 2004) <www.medinstitute.org/EvidenceMonograph.pdf>.
2. U.S. Department of Health and Human Services, Centers for Disease Control and Prevention, *Voluntary HIV Counseling and Testing: Facts, Issues, Answers*, January 1998.
3. B. Dillion. "Primary HIV Infections Associated with Oral Transmission," Poster Presentation at CDC's 7th Conference on Retroviruses & Opportunistic Infections; February 1, 2000; San Francisco, CA. Abstract 473.
4. "Mother-to-child transmission (MTCT) of HIV," UNAIDS Questions and Answers (August 1999) <www.unaids.org>.
5. USAID, "The 'ABCs' of HIV Prevention: Report of a USAID technical meeting on behavior change approaches to primary prevention of HIV/AIDS" (Washington, D.C.: Population, Health and Nutrition Information Project, 2003) <www.usaid.gov/our_work/global_health/aids/TechAreas/prevention/abc.pdf>.
6. The Medical Institute for Sexual Health, *Sex, Condoms and STDs: What We Know*, Monograph, 2003, Version 2.0.
7. "WHO Fact Sheets on HIV/AIDS for Nurses and Midwives," Fact Sheet 11 <www.who.int/health-services-delivery/hiv_aids/English/fact-sheet-11/index.html>.
8. U.S. Department of Health and Human Services, Centers for Disease Control and Prevention, *Caring for Someone with AIDS at Home*, February 2001 <www.cdc.gov/hiv/pubs/brochure/careathome.htm>.

9. "Living with AIDS" (brochure). U.S. Department of Health and Human Services, 2004 <www.cdc.gov/hiv/pubs/brochure/livingwithhiv.htm>

10. World Health Organization, International AIDS Society and UNAIDS, "Safe and Effective Use of Antiretroviral Treatments in Adults with Particular Reference to Resource Limited Settings," WHO/HSI/2000.04 (Geneva:WHO, 2000).

11. Philip Yancey, "Beethoven's Gift," *Helping the Hurting* (Sisters, OR: Multnomah Publishers, Inc., 1984).

Teaching Through Storytelling

We are grateful to the many publishers, authors, and organizations that have granted permission to reprint copyrighted material for this resource guide. Reasonable care has been taken to trace original sources and, when necessary, to obtain permission to reprint.

Permissions and Acknowledgments:

"Puppies for Sale." © Dan Clark. Reprinted by permission.

"A Father's Love." Taken from *What's So Amazing About Grace?* by Philip D. Yancey. Copyright © 1997 by Philip D. Yancey. Used by permission of The Zondervan Corporation.

"Are You Going to Help Me?" Taken from *Chicken Soup for the Soul: 101 Stories to Open the Heart and Rekindle the Spirit.* © 1993, Jack Canfield and Mark Victor Hansen. Used by permission of Health Communications, Inc.

"Appointment with Love." There are many versions of this story available today. The original story was published in a 1943 issue of *Collier's* magazine. This version appears in *The Art of Loving Well,* © 1993 Trustees of Boston University.

"S. T." Taken from *Tell Me a Story: Stories for Your Grandchildren and the Art of Telling Them.* © 1984 Charlie and Martha Shedd and the Abundance Foundation. Used by permission of Doubleday and Company, Inc., a division of Random House, Inc.

Bibliography

Bennett, William J. (ed.). *The Book of Virtues: A Treasury of Great Moral Stories.* New York: Simon & Schuster, 1993.

Bennett, William J. (ed.). *The Moral Compass: Stories for a Life's Journey.* New York: Simon & Schuster, 1995.

Brounstein, M. *Communicating Effectively for Dummies.* New York: Hungry Minds, Inc., 2001.

Booher, Dianna. *Communicate with Confidence! How to Say It Right the First Time and Every Time.* New York: McGraw-Hill, Inc., 1994.

Braude, Jacob M., revised by Glenn Van Ekeren. *Complete Speaker's and Toastmaster's Library,* 2nd edition. Paramus, NJ: Prentice-Hall, Inc., 1992.

Canfield, Jack and Mark Victor Hansen. *Chicken Soup for the Soul: 101 Stories to Open the Heart and Rekindle the Spirit.* Deerfield Beach, FL: Health Communications, Inc., 1993.

Canfield, Jack, Mark Victor Hansen, Hanoch McCarty, and Meladee McCarty. *A 4th Course of Chicken Soup for the Soul: 101 More Stories to Open the Heart and Rekindle the Spirit.* Deerfield Beach, FL: Health Communications, Inc., 1997.

Caroselli, Marlene. *The Big Book of Meeting Games.* New York: McGraw Hill, 2002.

Caroselli, Marlene. *Great Session Openers Closers and Energizers: Quick Activities for Warming Up Your Audience and Ending on a High Note.* New York: McGraw-Hill, 1998.

Cloud, Dr. Henry, and Dr. John Townsend. *How People Grow: What the Bible Reveals about Personal Growth.* Grand Rapids, MI: Zondervan, 2001.

Cook, John (comp.). *The Book of Positive Quotations.* Minneapolis, MN: Fairview Press, 1997.

Covey, Stephen R. *Principle-Centered Leadership.* New York: A Fireside Book, Published by Simon & Schuster, 1990.

Devine, Tony, Seuk, Joon Ho and Wilson, Andrew (eds.). *Cultivating Heart and Character: Educating for Life's Most Essential Goals.* Chapel Hill, NC: Character Development Publishing, 2000.

Dimitrius, Jo-Ellan, and Mark Mazzarella. *Reading People: How to Understand People and Predict Their Behavior—Anytime, Anyplace.* New York: The Ballentine Publishing Group, 1998.

Ehrlich, Eugene, and Marshall De Bruhl (comp.). *The International Thesaurus of Quotations, Revised and Updated.* New York: HarperCollins Publishers, Inc., 1996.

Evans, Sybil, and Sherry Suib Cohen. *Hot Buttons: How to Resolve Conflict and Cool Everyone Down.* New York: Cliff Street Books (an imprint of HarperCollins Publishers), 2000.

Fadiman, Clifton and Andre Bernard (eds.). *Bartlett's Book of Anecdotes, Revised Edition.* Boston: Little, Brown and Company, 2000.

Goleman, Daniel. *Emotional Intelligence: Why It Can Matter More than IQ.* New York: Bantam Books, 1995.

Gray, Alice. *Stories for the Heart: The Second Collection.* Sisters, OR: Multnomah Publishers, Inc., 1997.

Greathead, Erica, with Cathryn Devenish and Gillian Funnell (ed.). *Responsible Teenage Sexuality: A Manual for Teachers, Youth Leaders and Health Professionals.* Planned Parenthood Association of South Africa. Pretoria, South Africa: J. L. van Schaik Publishers, 1998.

Green, E. C. *Rethinking AIDS Prevention: Learning from Successes in Developing Countries.* Westport, CT: Praeger Publishers, 2003.

Guinness, Os. *Doing Well and Doing Good: Money, Giving, and Caring in a Free Society.* Colorado Springs, CO: NavPress, 2001.

Hall, Doug, with David Wecker. *Making the Courage Connection.* New York: A Fireside Book, Published by Simon & Schuster, 1997.

Herron, Ron, and Kathleen M. Sorensen. *Unmasking Sexual Con Games: Helping Teens Identify Good and Bad Relationships.* Boys Town, Nebraska: Boys Town Press, 1997.

Hogle, J. A. (ed.). *What Happened in Uganda? Declining HIV Prevalence, Behavior Change, and the National Response.* U.S. Agency for International Development, Sept. 2002.

International HIV/AIDS Alliance. *100 Ways to Energise Groups: Games to Use in Workshops, Meetings and the Community.* Brighton, UK: 2002.

Jacobs, Marjorie, Turk, Blossom, and Horn, Elizabeth. *Building A Positive Self-Concept: 113 Activities for Adolescents.* Portland, ME: J. Weston Walch, 1988.

Kravitz, S. Michael, and Susan D. Schubert. *Emotional Intelligence Works: Developing "People Smart" Strategies.* Menlo Park, CA: Crisp Publications, Inc., 2000.

Lickona, Thomas. *Character Matters: How to Help Our Children Develop Good Judgment, Integrity, and Other Essential Virtues.* New York: Simon & Schuster, 2004.

Lickona, Thomas. *Educating for Character: How Our Schools Can Teach Respect and Responsibility.* New York: Bantam Books, 1991.

Louw, Dr. Nelia, Darleen Edwards, and Joan Orr. *HIV/AIDS: Care and Support of Affected and Infected Learners: A Guide for Educators.* Pretoria, South Africa: HIV/AIDS and STD Directorate, Department of Health, 2001.

Low-Beer, Daniel and Rand Stoneburner. *Behaviour and Communication Change in Reducing HIV: Is Uganda Unique?* 2004. <www.cadre.org.za/publications.htm>

Maxwell, John C. *Developing the Leader Within You.* Nashville, TN: Thomas Nelson Publishers, 1993.

McGraw, Jay. *Life Strategies for Teens.* New York: A Fireside Book, Published by Simon & Schuster, 2000.

Meeker, Meg, M.D. *Epidemic: How Teen Sex is Killing Our Kids.* Lifeline Press, 2002.

Meeks, Linda and Philip Heit. *Sexuality and Character Education K-12: Abstinence Edition.* Chicago, IL: Meeks Heit Publishing Company and Everyday Learning Corporation, 2001.

Morgan, Robert J. *Nelson's Complete Book of Stories, Illustrations, & Quotes: The Ultimate Contemporary Resource for Speakers.* Nashville, TN: Thomas Nelson, Inc., 2000.

Resnick, et al. (1997). "Protecting Adolescents from Harm—Findings from the National Longitudinal Study on Adolescent Health." *Journal of American Medical Association* 278(10), 823–32.

Ryan, K., and K. E. Bohlin. *Building Character in Schools: Practical Ways to Bring Moral Instruction to Life.* San Francisco: Jossey-Bass, 2003.

Porro, Barbara. *Talk It Out: Conflict Resolution in the Elementary Classroom.* Alexandria, VA: Association for Supervision and Curriculum Development, 1996.

Scannell, Edward, and John Newstrom. *The Big Book of Presentation Games.* New York: McGraw Hill, 1998.

School Health Education to Prevent AIDS and STD: A Resource Package for Curriculum Planners, Teacher's Guide. Published by WHO and UNESCO, sponsored by the European Union, 1994.

"Sexual Health Update." Austin, TX: The Medical Institute. Fall 2003.

Stine, Gerald J. *AIDS Update 2001.* Upper Saddle River, NJ: Prentice-Hall, Inc. 2001.

The Art of Loving Well, A Character Education Curriculum for Today's Teenagers. Boston University, School of Ethics, 1993.

The Book of Wisdom. Sisters, OR: Multnomah Books, 1995.

The Heart of Training: A Manual of Approaches to Teaching About HIV/AIDS, a manual of the Health and Resources Administration (HRSA) Special Projects of National Significance (SPNS) Program.

The HIV/AIDS Emergency Guidelines for Educators. Pretoria, South Africa: Department of Education, 2000.

Thickstun, Patricia, and Kate Hendricks (eds). *Evidence that Demands Action: Comparing Risk Avoidance and Risk Reduction Strategies for HIV Prevention.* Austin, TX: The Medical Institute for Sexual Health, 2004 <www.medinstitute.org/EvidenceMonograph.pdf>

Thomas, Marlo and Friends (edited by Marlo Thomas). *The Right Words at the Right Time.* New York: Atria Books, 2002.

Understanding Your Sexuality and Your Choices. Community of Caring trademark, A Project of the Joseph P. Kennedy, Jr. Foundation, n.d.

Van Ekeren, Glenn. *Speaker's Sourcebook II: Quotes, Stories, and Anecdotes for Every Occasion.* New York: Prentice Hall Press, a member of Penguin Putnam Inc., 1994.

Warner, Mark J. *The Complete Idiot's Guide to Enhancing Self-Esteem.* New York: Alpha Books, a division of Macmillan General Reference, a Simon & Schuster Macmillian Company, 1999.

West, Edie. *201 Icebreakers, Group Mixers, Warm-Ups, Energizers, and Playful Activities.* New York: McGraw-Hill, 1997.

Wlodkowski, Raymond J. *Enhancing Adult Motivation to Learn: A Comprehensive Guide for Teaching All Adults.* San Francisco: Jossey-Bass Inc., Publishers, 1999.

About Kerus Global Education

The Greek word *Kerus* means "of the heart" or "to do something with passion." This word captures the organization's goal, which is to inspire and equip adults around the world to provide youth with core character traits, essential life skills, and the courage to live healthy, meaningful, and productive lives. Kerus Global Education empowers community leaders to promote healthy lifestyles by integrating the importance of character development with current health promotion efforts.

Kerus provides strategic consulting for both governmental and nongovernmental agencies, conducts professional training for educators and other health and human services professionals, and creates educational curricula for use in public schools and community outreach projects. Programs and services address prevention topics such as HIV/AIDS and other sexually transmitted infections; teen pregnancy; alcohol and other drug abuse; and youth violence. Kerus works with key professionals and community leaders to expand, adapt, and more effectively deliver youth development programs which include parents and faith communities in the educational process. To date, Kerus's efforts, in conjunction with other key organizations, have reached over 27,000 professionals and 1.5 million young people in 51 nations.

Kerus global education

1866-C East Market St. #300
Harrisonburg, VA 22801
www.kerusglobal.org

About the Authors

Dr. Cerullo and Dr. Ball are the founders of Kerus Global Education. They have been working worldwide in the fight against HIV/AIDS for over ten years. They provide strategic consulting and training for governmental and non-governmental health agencies, educational institutions, and faith communities throughout the world. Together, they have created and written curricula and training programs for key organizations interested in promoting the concepts of character-based sexuality education, consistent with the highly successful ABC Approach to HIV/AIDS prevention. Their work has been translated into 18 languages and is in use in 51 countries.

Their unique blend of art, science, and compassion has made them sought-after speakers and trainers for organizations and communities desiring to find common ground and to mobilize caring adults to reach out to adolescents and their parents with positive health messages.

Marcia L. Ball, Ed.D.

Prior to cofounding Kerus, Dr. Ball was a tenured Associate Professor in the Department of Health Sciences at James Madison University in Harrisonburg, Virginia, where she coordinated the Office of Substance Abuse Prevention Education and the International Health Concentration. She taught a variety of health education courses and developed academic service-learning health courses taught in Honduras and Haiti. Dr. Ball has 11 years of experience in higher education and has written and directed numerous state and federal grant projects related to the prevention of youth risk behavior.

Jennie A. Cerullo, Ph.D.

Dr. Cerullo holds academic degrees in education, human resource leadership, and cross-cultural education. She has taught in private and public schools in the U.S and served as a principal in a United Nations High Commissioner for Refugees camp in Hong Kong. Dr. Cerullo was also an administrator for the Covina Valley Unified School District English Language Development program. Additionally, she served for eight years as a faculty member in the Department of Education and Behavioral Studies at Azusa Pacific University in Azusa, California.

For information about the authors and the services of Kerus Global Education, visit www.kerusglobal.org.